D1569342

## DATE DUE

# WAR AND STATE TERRORISM

# War and Peace Library
Series Editor: Mark Selden

# WAR AND STATE TERRORISM
The United States, Japan, and the Asia-Pacific
in the Long Twentieth Century

Edited by
Mark Selden
and
Alvin Y. So

ROWMAN & LITTLEFIELD PUBLISHERS, INC.
*Lanham · Boulder · New York · Toronto · Oxford*

ROWMAN & LITTLEFIELD PUBLISHERS, INC.

Published in the United States of America
by Rowman & Littlefield Publishers, Inc.
A wholly owned subsidary of the Rowman & Littlefield Publishing Group, Inc.
4501 Forbes Boulevard, Suite 200, Lanham, Maryland 20706
www.rowmanlittlefield.com

P.O. Box 317, Oxford, OX2 9RU, UK

British Library Cataloguing in Publication Information Available

**Library of Congress Cataloging-in-Publication Data**

War and state terrorism : the United States, Japan, and the Asia-Pacific in the long
twentieth century / edited by Mark Selden and Alvin Y. So.
        p. cm. — (War and peace library)
Includes index.
    ISBN 0-7425-2390-X (cloth : alk. paper) — ISBN 0-7425-2391-8 (pbk. : alk. paper)
    1. Asia—History, Military—20th century. 2. State-sponsored
terrorism—Asia—History—20th century. 3. Asia—History—20th century.
4. United States—History, Military—20th century. 5. Japan—History,
Military—20th century. I. Selden, Mark. II. So, Alvin Y., 1953– III. Series

    DS354.W37 2004
    950.4'1—dc21

                                                                    2003011864

Printed in the United States of America

⊗™ The paper used in this publication meets the minimum requirements of American
National Standard for Information Sciences—Permanence of Paper for Printed Library
Materials, ANSI/NISO Z39.48-1992.

# Contents

# Acknowledgments

THIS VOLUME GREW OUT of a workshop on "Asia and the U.S. at War: The Twentieth Century Experience" at the Hong Kong University of Science and Technology on June 27–28, 2001. We are indebted to Professor Ting Pang-hsin, dean of the School of Humanities and Social Science, for his generous support, and to the Hong Kong University of Science and Technology for an Emerging High Impact Areas grant to support the workshop.

We thank colleagues who participated in the workshop as chairs and discussants, especially Greg Felker, Ravi Palat, Toshiyuki Tanaka, and David Zweig. We are grateful for the support of the superb staff at the Division of Social Science—Peggy Chan, Vicky Lai, Dora Lee, Wendy Tsang, and especially Josephine Wong—who efficiently organized the workshop and cheerfully lent a hand in preparation of the manuscript for publication.

Perhaps it was the fact that our work proceeded as the twin towers went up in flames on September 11 and the bombs fell in American wars in Afghanistan and Iraq, but we are grateful for the unusual willingness of the contributors to heed our requests for several rounds of revisions in moving the volume to completion.

# 1

# Introduction: War and State Terrorism

## Mark Selden and Alvin Y. So

### Asia's Long Century of War

IF THE TWENTIETH CENTURY will be remembered as a century of war, Asia is surely central to that story. In Asia, the first half of that century, from 1895 to 1945, may be glossed over as the mounting conflict between two rising imperial powers and those they sought to conquer, on the one hand, and their eventual clash in the Pacific War, on the other. Together, the two sets of wars were arguably the most costly in human lives of any in the twentieth century, the heaviest toll coming in Japan's abortive fifteen-year war of conquest in China.

With Japan's swift victory in the China–Japan War of 1894–95, the Japanese empire was launched on a career of conquests that would eventually, for a brief moment, allow it to create a vast Asian empire that spanned most of East, Northeast, and Southeast Asia and parts of Central and South Asia and to expel the European and American powers. The United States began its Asian conquests with the Spanish–American War of 1898 and the Philippine–American War of 1898–1902, which led to conquest and control of the Philippines and Hawaii for another latecomer to the imperialist club.

In the Pacific War of 1941–45, the clash between the two rising colonial powers marked the culmination of more than a decade of mounting conflicts that led to the U.S. embargo against Japan in the trade of oil and scrap iron, the immediate cause of the Pearl Harbor attack. Like all the major wars fought in Asia in the twentieth century, this one, too, was fought in the lands of the colonial and peripheral areas, leaving the homelands and their peoples intact—until, that is, the final and most savage months of the U.S.–Japan conflict.

Then, beginning in June 1945, in the fiercest combat of the Pacific War, U.S. forces attacked Japan's 32nd Army, which had entrenched itself in Okinawa prefecture, an area that Japan had colonized in 1879. In that battle, the Japanese military, its navy and air force by this time a virtual shadow of a force, was decimated. Barely noted in U.S. and Japanese military histories of the battle is the fact that some 150,000 Okinawans, one-third to one-fourth of the population, died and that the land and cities of Okinawa were destroyed.

Among the distinctive features of the present volume is the attention that its authors pay to civilian casualties of war, notably colonial and semicolonial peoples resisting conquest or striving for independence, and the civilian populations in all the wars reviewed here. In particular, authors pay close attention to the range and variety of crimes of war and crimes against humanity committed by a wide range of powers, the toll in lives that these exacted, and efforts to control such crimes throughout the twentieth century.

The final six months of the U.S.–Japan war carried to new heights the application of airpower to destroy cities and their populations. This story, which has been memorably inscribed in the history of World War II in Europe in such landmark names as Guernica, Rotterdam, and Dresden, was carried to its extremes in Asia, notably in the U.S. bombing, and finally nuclear bombing, of Japan in the final six months of World War II.

The Asian wars of the second half of the century were conducted within two interrelated frameworks: struggles for national independence against the former colonial powers, and above all the United States, and the U.S.–Soviet conflict. The influence of the latter was framed and limited by the arc of military bases that the United States constructed throughout the key areas of Europe and East Asia, which shaped power relations between 1945 and the collapse of the Soviet Union in 1990. Although the United States was the historic colonial power in either Korea or Indochina, ultimately it took the lead in both brutal and lengthy wars, continuing the pattern of fighting all major land wars in the peripheral regions of the former colonized nations and carrying to new levels the destructiveness of technology, above all airpower, directed against civilian populations. At the same time, the framework of U.S.–Soviet confrontation acted as a check both on the use of nuclear weapons and on the spread of war into Europe or into direct Soviet–American warfare. With the final years of the long twentieth century, following the collapse of the Soviet Union and, later, the terrorist attacks of September 11, 2001, the United States would extend its power in the form both of new military bases and a succession of wars in the farthest reaches of Central Asia and the Middle East, areas in which its military presence had previously been muted.

In examining Asian wars of the twentieth century, this volume pays particular attention to issues of war, state terror and the civilian, in the context both of understanding the changing face of international law and grasping the praxis of twentieth-century warfare. If the chapters pay particular attention to the nature of Japanese and American wars, they examine, too, important instances of warfare conducted by other nations, including China, Cambodia, and Indonesia. They also address issues of antinuclear and antiwar movements and their effects on twentieth-century warfare and the quest for peace.

## State Terrorism: Conceptions and Definitions

No word in the contemporary American and international political lexicon is more frequently invoked or more emotionally charged than "terrorist."[1] But what is terrorism? Who are the "terrorists?" Why do they commit terrorism? What is the relationship between states, wars, and terrorism? And does "state terrorism" differ from the "terrorism" evoked by the mass media?

Although it is widely believed that the U.S. preoccupation with terrorism began with 9/11, this is not the case. Facing a growing number of terrorist attacks on U.S. citizens abroad in the 1980s, the Reagan administration raised the specter and profile of terrorism, singling out what it described as terrorist organizations as targets of U.S. policy. In 1984, the administration shifted the brunt of its attack from terrorist organizations to *state-sponsored* terrorism. "States that support and sponsor terrorist actions have managed in recent years to co-opt and manipulate the phenomenon in pursuit of their own strategic goals," Secretary of State George Shultz charged.

The following year, anticipating the "axis of evil" speech of George W. Bush, President Reagan named Cuba, Iran, Libya, Nicaragua, and North Korea as leading members of "a confederation of terrorist states." These "outlaw states" were deemed responsible for training and financing terrorist actions that targeted U.S. citizens. In the course of the 1980s, the profile of outlaw or rogue states was extended to states said to be seeking weapons of mass destruction (WMD), hence posing a direct threat to U.S. interests and to the stability of the international system.[2] From the Reagan and the Bush administrations' viewpoints, these rogue-state rulers frequently manipulate nationalist sentiment to justify in the name of national security their own direct or sponsored terrorist activities both in the course of wars with other nations and to suppress or control others within their own nations.

Social science literature and the mass media, however, have rarely followed this line of thinking to its logical conclusion, that is, that terrorism, far from being committed exclusively by rogue states, may also be committed by pillars of the international community, including democratic states. Rather, adhering to Max Weber's classical definition that "a state is a human community that (successfully) claims the monopoly of the legitimate use of physical force within a given territory,"[3] mainstream social scientists have failed to recognize the possibility that states—including the United States—can and do carry out acts of terrorism.

States are in fact uniquely imbued with the capacity to commit not only acts of war but also acts of terrorism as they go about seeking to monopolize violence for their own purposes. A textbook example of myopia with respect to state terrorism is *The Terrorism Reader*. Following a lengthy discussion of definitions, editor David Whittaker offers his own definition, which concludes with the fact that terrorism "is perpetrated by a sub-national group or non-state entity."[4]

In fact, an abundant literature points to the connection between states and terrorism, even while American politicians and most social scientists definitionally exclude actions and policies of the United States and its allies.

The following discussion of violence seeks to examine the factors that differentiate war from various forms of terrorism and other violent activities by looking into questions of agency and object in light of international law and morality. Following major developments of international law in the long twentieth century, and consistent with official U.S. definitions of terror, we pay particular attention to violence against civilians and noncombatants as central to the understanding of terror in general and state terror in particular. Stripping the categories to essentials, even ideal types, we advance the following definitions:

- In *war,* a state directs means of violence against one or more other states, targeting military objectives.
- In *state terrorism,* a state systematically directs violence against the civilian population of its own or another state.
- In *oppositional terrorism,* nonstate actors direct violence against a state, including its military, its officials, and its functions.
- In *violent crime,* one segment of a civilian population acts against groups, individuals, or a society (see tab. 1.1).

In practice, of course, each of the above-mentioned activities spills out of these definitional boundaries. Throughout human history, while heroic discourse has focused on combat between warriors, wars have invariably wrought destruction on civilian and noncombatant populations, not only on opposing armies. Among the achievements of twentieth-century international law has been the creation of internationally ratified frameworks to define conditions under which war may legitimately be waged, to limit the scope of legitimate violence, and particularly to protect civilians from in-

**TABLE 1.1**
**War, Terrorism, Crime**

| Targets of Violence | Agents of Violence | |
| --- | --- | --- |
| | *The State* | *Nonstate Actors* |
| The state/military | WAR | OPPOSITIONAL TERRORISM |
| Civilians or nonstate actors | STATE TERRORISM | VIOLENT CRIME[1] |

[1] Of course, the boundary between "oppositional terrorism" and "violent crime" can be fuzzy. For example, "oppositional terrorism" may also involve violence against civilians, while violent crime may also be committed against the state machinery. However, even when "oppositional terrorism" targets civilians, the main target of attack is the state machinery, and violence against civilians is merely a by-product of the attack against state machinery. Similarly, even when a violent crime is directed against the state and its personnel, the main target of attack is usually civilians. For example, an off-duty policeman is robbed and stabbed. In such a case, he is the victim of a crime that targeted a civilian and is not killed as a representative of the state machinery.

jury and death in time of war, as well as to convene tribunals to prosecute violations of these norms. Among its greatest failures, however, has been the inability effectively to constrain military powers from inflicting death on civilians in the course of a century in which civilian deaths in war have exceeded those in all earlier epochs. The authors in this volume consider both sides of the equation in the course of documenting major instances of state terror in twentieth-century Asian wars and assessing efforts by international organizations and peace movements to halt the march of state terror.

The 1949 Geneva Convention Relative to the Protection of Civilian Persons in Time of War is perhaps the single most authoritative document establishing the principles of protecting civilians from the ravages of war. It stipulates that:

Persons taking no active part in the hostilities, including members of armed forces who have laid down their arms and those placed *hors de combat* by sickness, wounds, detention, or any other cause, shall in all circumstances be treated humanely, without any adverse distinction founded on race, color, religion or faith, sex, birth or wealth, or any other similar criteria.

To this end, the following acts are and shall remain prohibited at any time and in any place whatsoever with respect to the above-mentioned persons:

(a) violence to life and person, in particular murder of all kinds, mutilation, cruel treatment and torture.

But the Geneva Convention was hardly alone in seeking to place such limits on the ravages of war. The U.S. Federal Bureau of Investigation defines terrorism as "The unlawful use of force or violence against persons or property to intimidate or coerce a government, the civilian population, or any segment thereof, in furtherance of political or social objectives." The U.S.

State Department defines terrorism as "Premeditated, politically motivated violence perpetrated against noncombatant targets by sub-national groups or clandestine agents, usually intended to influence an audience."[5] U.S. official documents and those of many other nations, as well as numerous international accords, including those of the International Criminal Court, have sought to distinguish war from terrorism in an effort to safeguard civilians and noncombatants. By the early twenty-first century, moreover, a substantial body of international court judgments made it a crime to intimidate, coerce, or kill civilians both in war and in peace.

Drawing on these and other legal precedents discussed below, we define state terrorism as *systematic state violence against civilians in violation of international agreements, state edicts, and precedents established by international courts designed to protect the rights of civilians.* As the chapters of this volume show in painstaking detail, terrorism is not, nor has it ever been, the monopoly of individuals and shadowy groups or networks. Examples of state terror are scrutinized in wars waged by multiple nations in the course of the great Asian wars of the twentieth century. We focus our attention on those acts of war that systematically target civilian and noncombatant populations for dislocation, injury, and death, that is, acts of state terrorism.

While certain acts of violence perpetrated by individuals and groups against the state or its citizens are often labeled as terrorism, violent acts committed by the state against a civilian population have rarely been conceived in these terms, despite the clarity of international law in defining such acts as terrorist. Too often, state violence, including acts directed against civilians, is portrayed as right and just, even noble. Cumings, Falk, Kiernan, Lary, Victoria, Scott, and Selden in this volume provide abundant examples of state terrorism committed by diverse governments in the course of twentieth-century wars, including some that merit classification as genocide. Some of these, notably those carried out by Japan in the fifteen-year war and the Asia-Pacific War, would subsequently be excoriated by the victorious allies in war crimes tribunals; most others have remained free of serious scrutiny. Moreover, nationalist leaders, including Japanese and Americans, would subsequently speak of these acts with pride. As Richard Falk observes in this volume, "anti-state violence is demonized, while the greater state violence is virtually immunized from criticism."

In short, while war, crime, and oppositional terrorism have all been intensively studied and theorized, state terrorism remains understudied and virtually untheorized. In addition, war and state terrorism have rarely been systematically studied within a single framework or comparatively. It is in these spheres that this book hopes to break new ground.

## Critical Issues in the Study of War and State Terrorism

This book seeks to overcome the conceptual barrier imposed by Weber's definition and, especially, by the obfuscation of states whose primary definitions of terrorism routinely exclude their own behavior. Drawing upon studies of the major wars fought in Asia and the Pacific in the long twentieth century, we seek to understand the following:

- The nature, frequency, and most important examples of state terrorism in Asia.
- How state terrorism has been justified during an epoch simultaneously characterized by rising human rights consciousness and the emergence of international laws designed to protect civilians.
- The results of previous efforts and future prospects for resistance to state terrorism.

## State Terrorism in Asia in the Long Twentieth Century

This volume pays particular attention to examples of Japanese and American state terrorism in the major Asian wars of the twentieth century. While these two nations account for the most important examples of state terrorism in Asia, we note that Japan's involvement in such acts terminated with that nation's defeat in World War II in 1945, while those of the United States have grown in number and intensity in the postwar era down to the present.

Important dimensions of wartime killing of civilians examined here include those inflicted in Japan's fifteen-year war in China, World War II in the Pacific, the Korean War, the Indochina wars, and Indonesia's invasion of East Timor. They reveal multiple ways in which the military machines not only of Japan but also of the United States and Nationalist China in World War II; the United States in the Korean, Indochina, Gulf, and Afghanistan wars; the Cambodian forces of Pol Pot; and Indonesian forces in East Timor all carried out large-scale, and in most cases systematic, slaughter of civilians (see the Victoria, Cumings, Falk, Kiernan, Lary, Scott, and Selden chapters).[6] These findings suggest the necessity to broaden the understanding of crimes against humanity in twentieth-century wars and to closely reexamine the heroic narratives of victors.

In a century in which nationalism and racism contributed to the ferocity of war and the extension of violence to target civilians directly, it is notable that in certain times and places the military did take pains to limit its attacks to military targets. Bruce Cumings makes an observation that would surely astonish most Americans. It is that Japan's devastating attack on Pearl Harbor, which largely destroyed the U.S. Pacific fleet and much of its airpower, resulted in the killing of 2,335 naval, army, and marine personnel, while only sixty-eight civilians were killed. This thirty-four-to-one soldier-to-civilian kill ratio demonstrates that the Pearl Harbor attack was an act of war in the sense that it rigorously targeted the military. The Japanese military was not always so punctilious, as Victoria, Utsumi, and Selden point out in examining a range of Japanese crimes against humanity. Japan carried out systematic torture and slaughter of Asian civilians in myriad ways in the course of the fifteen-year war against China and, from 1942, against Asia and the Allied forces.

For their part, leading U.S. Air Force generals long resisted what Winston Churchill forthrightly called the terror bombing of Germany. However, first at Dresden and then against Japan, the United States breached the taboo against civilian bombings with a vengeance. In March 1945, U.S. bombers burnt Tokyo to the ground, leaving an estimated 100,000 and possibly many more dead and many times that number injured, and creating more than one million refugees. This was quickly followed by the firebombing of sixty-one other cities, which paved the way for the atomic bombings of Hiroshima and Nagasaki. While Japan launched the opening attack at Pearl Harbor with scrupulous avoidance of civilian casualties, the United States brought the war to a close with the two atomic attacks whose twin goals were the complete destruction of the cities and their civilian populations and the creation of a sense of the utter futility of war that would force surrender. From this time forward, civilian bombing would figure centrally, and without serious moral scruple, in all future U.S. wars, and if this became the staple of U.S. war making, other technologically advanced powers followed suit.

New forms of state terrorism would emerge in the Korean and Vietnam Wars. For example, the U.S. military employed tactics ranging from the use of indiscriminate airpower to search-and-destroy and strategic-hamlet missions that drew no distinction between military and civilian targets and inflicted large-scale civilian deaths (see the Falk and Cumings chapters). One innovation was the extension of bombing in these wars from the cities and their inhabitants to the countryside, where the use of Agent Orange as a defoliant was combined with the cluster bombs that wrought havoc throughout rural areas. Bombing campaigns well exemplify the contemporary face of state terrorism in war, as illustrated by both the Soviet and the American wars in Afghanistan, the 1991 Gulf War, and the Bosnia war involving West European nations as well as the United States.

Everywhere, state terror, particularly the use of airpower, inflicted a heavy toll on civilians, yet it proved no guarantee of victory, as the United States learned in Korea and Indochina, and as the Soviet Union learned in Afghanistan. U.S. strategists drew lessons from their costly defeat in Indochina that would intensify the application of technologies of terror. Subsequent U.S. military doctrine emphasized approaches to war making that assured swift victories and minimized *U.S.* casualties, a formula to be met above all by the application of ever more advanced weapons of mass destruction.

In documenting the frequent linkages between war and state terrorism, this book challenges the argument of "terrorist exceptionalism" that holds that state terrorism is the product of deranged generals and individual soldiers. Particular attention is paid to acts of state terrorism that are inherent in the fundamental structure of everyday war making, notably those acts undertaken by major powers in efforts to pacify nations far less endowed with weapons of mass destruction.

Although war and state terrorism have been intertwined throughout human history, certain features of the long twentieth century have given new shape to the phenomenon and increased its deadly impact. Three important elements stand out:

1. *Nationalism and War.* We can trace linkages between nationalism and war at least back to the French Revolution, but with the weakening of colonialism, the rise of national independence movements, and the birth of new nations, nationalism became central to virtually all wars. Nationalist movements persisted in Korea, Vietnam, East Timor, Cambodia, and China, among others, in the face of technologically superior invaders and despite, some would suggest precisely *because,* of sustaining massive casualties. Nationalism also arguably eased the consciences of military planners who possessed weapons of mass destruction associated with air and sea power, including nuclear, chemical, and biological weapons, and who saw themselves as protecting national interests in the face of enemy others frequently labeled as terrorists (see the Cumings, Falk, Kiernan, Victoria, Scott, and Selden chapters).

2. *Total War.* The twentieth century marked a shift from wars primarily pitting professional armies against one another to wars that mobilized entire populations and subjected entire economies and societies to attack. This is not an entirely new phenomenon: colonial wars in particular frequently targeted the local population in the effort to break resistance, a pattern evident as well in American efforts to drive Indians from their land. Nevertheless, we note that the Chinese and Vietnamese Communist movements pioneered forms of guerrilla warfare that rested on broad popular mobilization, while Japanese and American forces in turn obliterated all distinction between soldier and civilian in launching attacks that sought to annihilate entire communities in an effort to break resistance. Bruce Cumings points out that the U.S. Air Force ROTC

manual of Vietnam War vintage defines a "military target" as "Any person, thing, idea, entity, or location selected for destruction, inactivation, or rendering non-usable with weapons which will reduce or destroy the will or ability of the enemy to resist." Perhaps it is the contrast of the high-flown pronouncements of international law with the frequent barbarity of the conduct of war that is most startling here.

3. *Technological "Progress."* In addition to air and sea power, development of nuclear, chemical, and biological weapons, missiles, submarines, radar, and computer technology all increased the destructive capability of weaponry that would frequently target civilians. The atomic bombings of Hiroshima and Nagasaki were, of course, landmark events in the breakdown of the distinction between military and civilian targets, events that sped efforts to create an international legal structure to protect citizen rights.

Nuclear weapons quintessentially do not distinguish civilian from military targets. As Falk notes, the atomic bombs that leveled Hiroshima and Nagasaki aimed to "terrorize the population through mass slaughter and to confront its leaders with the prospect of national annihilation." The debate over the use of nuclear weapons as a means to "save lives," a claim that President Truman would make with respect both to Americans and Japanese, has reverberated ever since. Nuclear issues, including the attempts to prevent nuclear war, are addressed from several angles here in chapters by Falk, Cumings, and Wittner.

## Dynamics of War and Terrorism

We examine some of the ways in which wars repeatedly spill over into state terrorism. The chapters of this book assess a range of strategies implemented by Japan, the United States, and China in the fifteen-year war and World War II from the perspective of terrorism. These include Japan's Nanjing Massacre, the sexual slave labor of the military comfort women, the murderous experiments of biowar Unit 731, and the denial of prisoner-of-war status to Asian captives. By refining techniques such as search-and-destroy missions and forced relocation of populations, Japan repeatedly turned the weapons of war against civilians in China and throughout Asia. A substantial literature exists on each of these events, but ours is the first to study them from the perspective of state terrorism.

Among the costliest examples of state policies resulting in the deaths of hundreds of thousands of civilians was the Chinese Nationalist government's decision to breach the dikes of the Yellow River in 1938 in an abortive effort to slow the advance of Japanese forces. In this instance, however, the intentionality of state terrorism was lacking. As Diana Lary shows, "there was no deliberate intent in the Chinese high command to kill vast numbers of civilians, just 'huge miscalculations' that led to the death of large numbers of civilians." Was this state terrorism, and if not, how is it to be classified?

No nation has a monopoly on the resort to state terror in the course of war. Other important examples of state terror include U.S. attacks on the dikes in North Korea and the U.S. use of Agent Orange to defoliate Vietnamese forests. As Cumings observes, in the 1953 bombing of North Korean dikes, the U.S. Air Force boasted, "The subsequent flash flood scooped clean 27 miles of valley below, and the plunging flood waters wiped out [supply routes, etc.]. . . . The Westerner can little conceive the awesome meaning which the loss of [rice] has for the Asian—starvation and slow death." The United States threatened the use of nuclear weapons repeatedly in both the Korean and Vietnam Wars; it also threatened to bomb Vietnam's Red River dikes. In these latter attempts to terrorize the Vietnamese, it did not follow through on its threats, perhaps primarily with an eye to Soviet retaliation.

A state may be particularly prone to use terrorism if it faces no harmful consequences as a result of using it. The United States has long enjoyed a double immunity in its use of state terrorism. One element of this was its historical immunity to attack on its home soil by other powers, in part a fortuitous accident of location far from the major centers of power of military rivals. For the United States, ever since its independence war more than two centuries ago, war has almost invariably meant the destruction of other lands and peoples, while the American mainland has remained impregnable. The second was impunity from liability, and especially prosecution, for war crimes and human rights violations, that is, the impunity enjoyed since World War II by the hegemonic power that played a decisive role in establishing the international norms that defined terror and the laws of war. Since it is the United States that for the most part sets the terms and designates the targets of prosecution, it invariably excludes itself from responsibility for terror and human rights violations.

At what point does state terror cross the line of genocide? Ben Kiernan examines this issue with respect to the Khmer Rouge slaughter of the Cham and Vietnamese and the annihilation of more than 1.7 million Cambodian villagers, comparing these acts with a case that has rarely been viewed through the lens of genocide. This is the Indonesian slaughter in the course of a twenty-five-year invasion of approximately 150,000 out of an East Timorese population of 650,000. Both are examined in light of the 1948 United Nations Genocide Convention, which defines genocide as the attempted destruction "in whole or in part" of "a national, ethnical, racial or religious group, as such." Kiernan also assesses U.S. responsibility for genocide, particularly in

Cambodia. He concludes that both the Khmer Rouge and Indonesia, with U.S. diplomatic support, committed genocide in Cambodia and East Timor, respectively, in the years 1975–79. If this is true, should the charge of genocide also be applied to other wars such as Japan's China War and U.S. wars in Korea and Vietnam?

## Justifications for State Terrorism

If state terrorism has been rampant in twentieth-century wars, how has it been explained and justified in light of the rising discourse on human rights and the proliferation of international rights conventions? To be sure, the acts of violence against civilians that we have identified as state terrorism, and in some instances genocide, are never explicitly justified as terrorism. Rather, such acts are either concealed, reported straightforwardly as legitimate war actions, or rationalized on grounds of a higher humanitarianism, for example, to assure the defeat of a despotic regime (e.g., U.S. bombing in Afghanistan), to turn back aggression (the U.S. invasion of Vietnam, in this case premised on a claim of North Vietnamese aggression against South Vietnam), or to liberate a people from a brutal colonialism (e.g., Japan in Asia).

Charges of terrorism may also be rationalized by dehumanizing the enemy. From the use of the term "gooks" for Filipinos in the Philippine–American War of 1898–1902 on through its use for Koreans and Vietnamese in subsequent U.S. wars, dehumanization has paved the way for terrorist acts. Falk suggests that U.S. saturation bombings of Japanese cities at the end of World War II embodied "vengeful and racist elements, . . . an acceptance of the image of the Asian as the incomprehensible other whose supposed absolute devotion to a political cause is treated as a form of barbarism." Utsumi Aiko highlights racist factors in Japanese decisions to differentiate Asian and American prisoners and grant only the latter the rights of prisoners of war, while depriving the former of those rights and subjecting them to far harsher treatment.

Finally, religion may provide a vehicle for sanctioning state terrorism. Brian Victoria observes, "Religion has again and again served to demonize (and dehumanize) the enemy and to sacralize the act of killing as part of a just struggle against evil." Tracing the roots of Japanese state terror to values inculcated through Zen Buddhist teachings, he draws powerful analogies to Protestant teachings in both Germany and the United States. For example, *kamikaze* pilots were regularly sent for periods of intense meditation at Zen temples before being dispatched on suicide missions. The analysis has powerful contemporary resonance.

Victoria observes, "Although in Islam the term *jihad* properly refers to the struggle against evil *both within oneself* and *in the external world* rather than holy war per se, it is nevertheless an integral part of the Islamic faith embraced by the terrorists." For his part, President George W. Bush repeatedly invokes religious imagery, as in "the axis of evil" and the role of a divine power in assuring U.S. victory. For example, in February 2003 the president said of the September 11, 2001, terrorist attacks: "We're being challenged. We're meeting those challenges because of our faith. . . . We carried our grief to the Lord Almighty in prayer."[7]

## Hegemonic versus Nonhegemonic State Terrorism

Arno Mayer observes that, since 1947,

America has been the chief perpetrator of "preemptive" state terror. . . . Besides the unexceptional subversion and overthrow of governments in competition with the Soviet Union during the Cold War, Washington has resorted to political assassinations, surrogate death squads, and unseemly freedom fighters (e.g., bin Laden). It masterminded the killing of Lumumba and Allende; and it unsuccessfully tried to put to death Castro, Khadafi, and Saddam Hussein. These "rogue" actions worsened local political and economic conditions and were of a piece with equally unscrupulous blockades, embargoes, military interventions, punitive air (missile) strikes, and kidnappings, always in the name of democracy, liberty, and justice.

The record of Asian wars suggests that the range, scope, and frequency of U.S. state terrorist actions have had no rival since World War II.[8]

Peter Dale Scott locates important dimensions of the succession of U.S. wars in what he calls the parapolitics of drugs and oil. He argues, "Parapolitics, the exercise of power by covert means, tends to metastasize into *deep politics,* an interplay of unacknowledged forces over which the original parapolitical agent no longer has control." An example of this phenomenon not addressed in this chapter is that of Osama bin Laden, a primary agent of U.S. intelligence as a "freedom fighter" for the liberation of Afghanistan from Soviet rule, following the permanent stationing of U.S. forces in Saudi Arabia after the defeat of Iraq in the Gulf War, that is, in the Islamic Mecca. Bin Laden then turned his rage against the United States, initiating a course that may have led to the terrorist attacks of September 11.

Scott examines the convergence of U.S. intelligence interests with illicit drugs and oil interests in major U.S. wars in Asia over the past half century: the Indochina wars, the Gulf War, and the Afghanistan War. Noting the growing U.S. dependence on oil imports and the geostrategic value of controlling oil to dominate rival powers, he points to the danger of U.S. wars in Central Asia and the Middle East that are waged with an eye to dominate the world's proven oil reserves and, through that, the powers that depend on Middle East oil to fuel their economies.

The studies in this volume suggest that the dividing lines between war and state terrorism, and between state terrorism and genocide, have long been obscure. They also demonstrate that state terrorism has been practiced by a wide range of nations. Great, and particularly hegemonic, powers, moreover, uniquely enjoy impunity for their actions, even as they set and maintain global standards that define terrorism, invariably in ways that conceal or condone their own actions. While the United States was the driving force behind war crimes tribunals at Nuremberg and Tokyo after World War II, and in the Rwanda and Bosnia cases subsequently, not only would it face no significant international tribunal to assess its conduct in such conflicts as the Korean War, the Indochina wars, and the Gulf War, but with few exceptions, the victims of U.S. state terrorism have been unable to build sustained movements for apology and redress. This is as true of the victims of nuclear attacks on Hiroshima and Nagasaki as it has been of the Korean victims of massacres at Nogun ri and Vietnamese victims of the My Lai massacre.

The collapse of the Soviet Union in 1990 marked a sea change in the character of state terrorism. Soviet–American rivalry had failed to check the repeated eruption of wars in Asia and elsewhere, although it may have restrained the United States from using nuclear weapons in the Korean and Indochina wars and contributed to the unprecedented long peace in Europe. In the era of a single superpower, however, with U.S. military spending soaring to $400 billion in 2003, far outstripping not only all competitors but virtually all combinations of competitors, and with unchallenged U.S. military supremacy, such restraints, including the alienation of allies and other powers, no longer exist. Whatever the long-term costs incurred, in the short run the ability to engage in preemptive war, to scrap international agreements, and to impose state terrorism on other countries with the acquiescence of the international community has increased.

At the same time, the nationally proclaimed "war on terrorism" marked a new stage in American war making, one in which, almost by definition, there could be no victory that would allow national leaders to bring the war to an end, given the elusiveness of an enemy that could "nestle anywhere, settle anywhere" and that was unconstrained by state boundaries. Walter LaFeber has underlined the processes of fragmentation that are central to the post–Cold War situation and that produce a situation in which enemies and potential enemies proliferate. He finds fragmentation in the proliferation of new states (as in the new states following the collapse of the Soviet Union) and in the growing challenges to state power inherent in the increasing mobility of people across borders and the proliferation of NGOs of every description with their increasing capacity to vie with states to shape national and global policy. The new technologies that are the very foundation of U.S. power also provide means that can be used by challengers to state power, whether Al Qaeda, the Japanese sect Aum Shinrikyo, or China's Falungong, each of which have shown a facility for using new technologies for communication purposes, financing their global operations, preventing state crackdown on their activities, and in some instances attacking state and society. When fragmentation is combined with mounting inequality, as is evident both in the United States and on a world scale, the potential for challenge to the status quo, including terrorist challenges, grows exponentially. Ironically, a Bush administration, which took office determined to dismantle big government, has become the agent of the centralization of state, and particularly presidential, power in the name of crushing terrorism, on a scale without precedent in U.S. history. Thus the Bush administration would move immediately from a swift war that ended Taliban rule in Afghanistan to a U.S.–British invasion in an allegedly preventive war using the justifications of destroying weapons of mass destruction and bringing "democracy" to Iraq. In this way, state terrorism and the attempt to crush terrorism move to the center of the U.S. and the global agenda.[9]

## Resistance to State Terrorism

Are there mechanisms through which state terrorism, particularly that inflicted by the most powerful nations, might be constrained? This volume has pointed to a number of arenas in which such efforts have been made, including the framing of international human rights laws, the actions of the United Nations and of individual states, the convening of war crimes tribunals, and diverse antiwar and other social movements.

In defining and proscribing many forms of state terrorism, such as the deliberate killing of civilians and noncombatants, international law has created a language, a set of principles and practices such as international tribunals, and an authority that contributes to an awareness of crimes against humanity and encourages international treaties and groups of citizens to curb state terrorism. U.S. official concern with the issues is suggested by a Pentagon proposal soberly reported in the *New York Times* of March 1, 2003, providing a list of twenty-four war crimes that the United States would prosecute in military courts in waging war on terrorism, and that would apply in future wars as well.[10] The crimes listed included "the willful killing of protected persons; attacking civilians, civilian objects or protected property; pillaging; taking hostages; and employing poison or similar weapons." Needless to say, there was no hint that U.S. commanders or forces would be punishable for war crimes that precisely fit this official U.S. definition of state terrorism, or that the United States has repeatedly acted in violation of such proscriptions.

Herein lies the central problem of the international law regime. With a few notable exceptions, such as early restraints on airpower and on chemical and biological weapons, powerful nations have scarcely been restrained by legal norms from deploying new technologies in the service of national power. The international system has yet to seriously address, let alone overcome, problems associated with the impunity of the great powers. The record of the long twentieth century leaves little reason for optimism that an international legal order that is itself the product of agreement among the powers can enforce the laws of war when confronted by challenges from great, and particularly hegemonic, powers. Yet the legal order, in contributing to consciousness of state terror, legitimizes efforts to control it. In this sense, it is intimately related to the social movements that have repeatedly challenged its workings.

Lawrence Wittner points out that "If the deliberate murder of noncombatants is a form of terror, then two of the largest and most effective antiterrorist organizations of the postwar era have been the Japanese and American anti-nuclear movements." Those movements, as part of a global antiwar movement, have achieved success in setting limits on nuclear terror by helping to stigmatize nuclear weapons, curb the nuclear arms race, and prevent nuclear war. That is, while state terrorism in wartime continued in the course of the nuclear era, in part as a result of antinuclear struggles, the nuclear powers, and particularly the United States, refrained from using nuclear weapons after 1945. There is an important caveat, however. This is that depleted uranium weapons introduced by the United States in the Gulf War of 1991 and used again in the Afghanistan War of 2001 and the Iraq War of 2003 have weakened the distinction between nuclear and nonnuclear weapons. And the United States has continued to develop powerful new weapons that erode the conventional/nuclear weapons distinction.

Focusing on antiwar movements, Marilyn Young points to the impact of various antiwar acts during the Indochina wars. She underlines the cumulative significance of

> [d]raft counseling; draft card burning; sit-ins at draft centers; draft resistance, through flight to Canada or surrendering oneself to arrest; nonviolent demonstrations (local, regional, national); demonstrations with violence against property; teach-ins; movements to remove ROTC and war research from university campuses; barring or removing from campuses recruiters for the CIA, Dow Chemical, and other companies involved in war-related industries; sanctuary and support for military deserters at home and abroad; antiwar coffee houses and underground newspapers near army bases; support for the movement against the war inside the military; and so on. (see chapter 10)

The diverse American and international antiwar movements, by challenging the dominant ideology of war and by generating social chaos, raised the economic and political costs of waging war and may have helped to restrict and eventually bring to an end the war. In the end, the Indochina antiwar movement may have exercised greater influence than any other antiwar movement to date, an effectiveness that hinged in part on the length of the war and the fact that it was fought by an army of draftees. The Indochina antiwar movement leaves open the question of whether antiwar movements can prevent powers, particularly hegemonic powers, from embarking on adventurous wars that will bring to new heights the uses of state terrorism.

## Notes

1. Lon Troyer, "The Calling of Counter-terrorism" *Theory and Event* 5, no. 4 (2001), at muse.jhu.edu/journals/theory_&_event/.

2. George Shultz, "Terrorism: The Challenge to the Democracies," June 24, 1984, *Current Policy,* no. 589 (U.S. Department of State); Ronald Reagan speech to the American Bar Association, Washington, D.C., July 8, 1985, *Current Policy,* no. 721 (U.S. Department of State). This analysis draws on Michael Klare, *Rogue States and Nuclear Outlaws: American's Search for a New Foreign Policy* (New York: Hill and Wang, 1995), 26–28. Saddam Hussein's Iraq, then a key U.S. ally in the U.S. conflict with Iran, was not among those targeted at the time by the United States.

3. Max Weber, *From Max Weber: Essays in Sociology,* ed. H. Gerth and C. W. Mills (New York: Galaxy, 1958).

4. David J. Whittaker, in *The Terrorism Reader,* 2d ed. (London: Routledge, 2003), 9.

5. These are among several definitions provided by David J. Whittaker in *The Terrorism Reader,* 2d ed. (London: Routledge, 2003), 3–4.

6. The authors of this volume focus primarily, although not exclusively, on acts of state terrorism committed by major powers, particularly Japan and the United States, because the label has rarely been applied to such actions. It is not our intention to suggest that colonial, great, or hegemonic powers exercise a monopoly on state terrorism, and indeed other examples addressed in this volume, including acts of the Nationalist Chinese government, the Indonesian government, and the Cambodian government, reveal other faces of state terrorism. Many other examples could be selected to reveal dimensions of the problem.

7. Dana Milbank, "Bush Delivers Religious Address: President Tackles Foreign, Domestic and Economic Issues in Spiritual Terms," *Washington Post,* February 10, 2003. This perspective has not gone unchallenged among church leaders. Reverend Fritz Ritsch, a Bethesda, Maryland, pastor, responded to the president's call for preemptive war with Iraq by noting that "The president confidently (dare I say 'religiously'?) asserts a worldview that most Christian denominations reject outright as heresy: the myth of redemptive violence, which posits a war between good and evil, with God on

the side of good and Satan on the side of evil and the battle lines pretty clearly drawn. War is essential in this line of thinking. For God to win, evil needs to be defined and destroyed by God's faithful followers, thus proving their faithfulness. Christians have held this view to be heretical since at least the third century. It is the bread-and-butter theology of fundamentalists, whether Muslim, Jewish or Christian." "Of God, and Man, in the Oval Office," *Washington Post,* March 2, 2003.

8. Arno Mayer, "Untimely Reflections upon the State of the World," *Daily Princetonian,* October 5, 2001, at www.dailyprincetonian.com/archives/2001/10/05/opinion/3509.shtml (accessed March 3, 2003).

9. Walter LaFeber, "The Post September 11 Debate over Empire, Globalization, and Fragmentation," in *September 11, Terrorist Attacks, and US Foreign Policy,* ed. Demetrios James Carley (New York: Academy of Political Science, 2002).

10. "The Pentagon Releases a Proposed List of War Crimes to Be Judged by Tribunals," *New York Times,* March 1, 2003.

# 2

# The United States and Japan in Twentieth-Century Asian Wars

## Mark Selden

THE UNITED STATES AND JAPAN have been at the center of virtually every major war and many smaller wars fought in Asia and the Pacific throughout the long twentieth century. Indeed, their battlefield conflicts constitute a virtual history of war and destruction in the region that arguably has been plagued by more, and more devastating, wars than any other.

Asian and Pacific wars of the long twentieth century pose troubling questions not only about the nature of modern warfare, colonial and postcolonial wars, and core–periphery conflict, but also about state terror and human rights. Using American and Japanese wars in the Asia–Pacific region as a social laboratory for reflecting on a century of war and the contemporary post-9/11 world, I examine a paradox: On the one hand, the twentieth century was the epoch in which far-reaching efforts were made to create a regime of international law ostensibly designed to protect civilians from the ravages of war. At the same time, civilians and noncombatants became targets of war on an unprecedented scale in what Eric Hobsbawm describes as "this rising curve of barbarism after 1914."[1] This chapter examines the record of war with respect to its impact on civilians, locating the discussion in questions of international law and terror.

### War, International Law, and the Rights of Civilians

Throughout the twentieth century, efforts to define the limits of war and expand the scope of human rights repeatedly collided with, and were repeatedly

overwhelmed by, new technologies and inhumane strategic and political calculations that rationalized their use. Beginning with the Hague Peace Conferences of 1899 and 1907, the major European powers as well as the United
States, Japan, and others signed treaties designed to protect the rights of civilian prisoners of war and noncombatants.[2] Many other efforts would follow, of
which the 1925 Geneva Agreement banning the use of poison gas, the 1928
Kellogg–Briand Pact outlawing aggressive war, the Nuremberg and Tokyo
Principles of 1945, and the Geneva Convention of 1949 are landmark events.

The 1949 Geneva Convention Relative to the Protection of Civilian Persons
in Time of War[3] stipulates that:

> Persons taking no active part in the hostilities, including members of armed
> forces who have laid down their arms and those placed *hors de combat* by sick-
> ness, wounds, detention, or any other cause, shall in all circumstances be treated
> humanely, without any adverse distinction founded on race, colour, religion or
> faith, sex, birth or wealth, or any other similar criteria.
>
> To this end, the following acts are and shall remain prohibited at any time and
> in any place whatsoever with respect to the above-mentioned persons:
> (a) violence to life and person, in particular murder of all kinds, mutilation,
> cruel treatment and torture.

Provisions guaranteeing the rights of civilians and prisoners of war (POWs)
are not confined to international law. In the United States Code, the official
U.S. statement on terror, a document carried into battle by every soldier, offers a more detailed definition that is both consistent with the Geneva Convention and rooted in U.S. law:

> [An] act of terrorism means any activity that (A) involves a violent act or an act
> dangerous to human life that is a violation of the criminal laws of the United
> States or any State, or that would be a criminal violation if committed within the
> jurisdiction of the United States or of any State; and (B) appears to be intended
> (i) to intimidate or coerce a civilian population; (ii) to influence the policy of a
> government by intimidation or coercion; or (iii) to affect the conduct of a gov-
> ernment by assassination or kidnapping.[4]

By the final decades of the twentieth century, a substantial body of international legal agreements and international court judgments, as well as laws and
edicts of many nations, made it a crime to intimidate, coerce, or kill civilians
both in war and peace.

Among the most important such efforts were those that culminated in the
establishment of the International Criminal Court in 1999. Article 8(2)(b)I
defines as a war crime "intentionally directing attacks against the civilian population as such or against individual civilians not taking direct part in hostil-

ities." The statute also addresses unintentional or "collateral damage," specifying that "intentionally launching an attack in the knowledge that such an attack will cause incidental loss of life or injury to civilians or damage to civilian objects or widespread, long-term and severe damage to the natural environment which would be clearly excessive in relation to the concrete and direct overall military advantage anticipated" is a criminal act (iv).[5]

Terrorism has never been exclusively the acts of individual criminals or groups of criminals in defiance of states; quite the contrary, states and their military forces have been responsible for the overwhelming majority of terrorist crimes resulting in injury and death of civilians. I define state terrorism as *systematic state violence against civilians in violation of international norms, state edicts, and precedents established by international courts designed to protect the rights of civilians.* This chapter reviews the wartime record of the United States and Japan within the framework of the laws of war, with particular attention to the killing of civilians and other war atrocities. It inquires whether certain acts, both those sanctioned at the highest levels of power and those carried out by state agents more or less exercising a degree of autonomy, should be classified as state terrorism. Indeed, it examines whether the very fabric of their approaches to war embodied premises of state terrorism.

Evolving strategic conceptions and technologies of total war in the course of the long twentieth century increased the vulnerability of civilians to acts of war. The result was a sharp growth in civilian casualties. For example, the numbers and percentages of civilians killed in World War II soared compared with World War I.[6] Mary Kaldor calculates that whereas the ratio of military to civilian deaths was eight to one at the dawn of the twentieth century, by the 1990s it had reversed to approximately one to eight.[7] At the same time, throughout the century, states, international organizations, and nongovernmental organizations all articulated a human rights discourse that sought to define and protect the rights of civilians and noncombatants and to prevent wartime violations of human rights perpetrated by states and their militaries. As Paul Lauren observed, "In contrast with earlier 'laws of war' that focused primarily on the use of objects such as weapons or ships, this new form of law focused on people." Moreover, in many instances, "positive law in the form of international treaties established certain rights for the protection of individual victims of war."[8] Our task is to gauge the interplay between the articulation of humanitarian principles seeking to narrow the scope of killing in war and the reality on the ground, on the battlefield, and in society.

World War I produced an international consensus that economic and social justice and peace were inextricably linked, a consensus articulated, for example, by both Wilson and Lenin. The International Labor Organization was created to define and protect labor rights, and a series of agreements known collectively as the Minorities Treaties guaranteed minorities in signatory states "protection of life and liberty" "without distinction of birth, nationality, language, race, or religion." However, the global empires of the victors—Britain, France, the United States, and Japan—remained intact. While critics quickly noted that the principled declarations were largely reserved in practice for protection of the rights of white males in the defeated nations of Europe, notice was nevertheless served that the days of empire were numbered, a message that colonial peoples were quick to heed as anticolonial movements surged throughout Asia and Africa.

World War II likewise spurred high aspirations for national independence, human rights, and the curbing of a pattern of war run amok. Landmark events included international war crimes tribunals at Nuremberg, Tokyo, and elsewhere that established the principle of personal responsibility for human rights violations of both soldiers in the field and government and military leaders. The formation of the United Nations was quickly followed by the Universal Declaration of Human Rights and other key documents that defined the laws of war, and by the establishment of a UN Commission on Human Rights. Yet, as Chris Jochnik and Roger Normand note in their critical review of the history of international human rights law, "despite noble rhetoric to the contrary, the laws of war have been formulated deliberately to privilege military necessity at the cost of humanitarian values. As a result, the laws of war have facilitated rather than restrained wartime violence. Through law, violence has been legitimated."[9] Specifically, they find that with each new set of restrictions on weaponry, not only do the major powers reserve the right to pursue war as an instrument of state power, but they also refuse to proscribe most of the major weapons that they monopolize, such as advanced airpower and bombs. Reviewing half a century of efforts to restrict the use of nuclear weapons, we note that agreements invariably preserved the nuclear monopoly of the powers who possessed nuclear weapons, left largely intact their nuclear stockpiles, and protected their right to use nuclear weapons while seeking to prevent nonnuclear powers from entering the nuclear club.

With the ink on post–World War II documents barely dry, major wars were in the making, above all in Asia and the Pacific, where the effects of the war, including dismantling of Japan's colonial empire and challenges to European empires, continued to reverberate. These wars would severely test the new international human rights regime, notably from the perspective of protecting the rights of civilians. In the great national independence struggles, as in Vietnam and the Philippines, in civil wars as in Korea and China, and in internationalized conflicts such as the U.S. military interventions in China, Korea, and Vietnam, the civilian toll was many times heavier than that exacted on the military. The sharp death toll imbalance would characterize subsequent Asian wars such as those waged by the Soviet Union in Afghanistan and by the United States in the Gulf War and Afghanistan.

The dominant discourse on terror in the post–9/11 world, emanating from the George W. Bush White House but extending to world leaders and cross-cutting historical Cold War and North–South divisions, decries ruthless fanatics who target innocent people. While initially focused on Al Qaeda and other nonstate actors, it was soon extended to any state bent on gaining access to "weapons of mass destruction" (chemical, biological, and atomic weapons) that purportedly posed a threat to the United States, the ultimate wielder and merchant of WMD and a nation whose military supremacy is perhaps without parallel since the Mongol empire. Thus the official branding of Iraq, Iran, and North Korea—three nations with no common bond—as an "axis of evil" and hence candidates for "regime change" through preemptive U.S. attack, with many other nations placed on warning that they might be next.[10]

This terrorism discourse is central to defining a new hegemonic world order subsequent to Soviet collapse and the demise of world communism. The new discourse has been used to justify military strikes anywhere in a world in which the historic U.S. enemies, the Soviet Union and world communism, have disintegrated yet disorder and the threat of attack appear to have multiplied, despite the lack of any credible military threat by another power or combination of powers. Major examples of twentieth-century state terror in Asian wars provide a useful perspective for gauging this contemporary discourse and praxis. Examining the consequences of twentieth-century Asian wars from the perspective of the civilian, this chapter reflects on the prospects of achieving and enforcing an equitable human rights regime that places strictures not only on the losers in international conflicts but on dominant and even hegemonic powers.

## War in the Asia–Pacific: Japanese and American Experiences

Beginning with the Sino–Japanese War of 1894–95 and the Russo–Japanese War of 1905, Japan obtained Taiwan, the Pescadores, Southern Sakhalin, and the Liaodong peninsula as well as control over South Manchuria and Korea. In 1910, Japan annexed Korea. It then fought in World War I on the side of its British ally, for which it secured Micronesia and displaced Germany to control China's Shandong Province. In 1931, Japan embarked on the fifteen-year China War (1931–45). Following the attack on Pearl Harbor, Japan fought the United States and its allies while trying to displace the Western powers and consolidate its power over a far-flung Asian empire of conquest.

The United States announced its arrival as a Pacific power at approximately the same time as Japan with the seizure of the Philippines and Hawaii and the Philippine–American War of 1898–1902. Japan's defeat in the Pacific War, ending half a century of territorial conquests, brought an end to that nation's military adventures. After 1945, the United States replaced Japan as the protagonist in the major wars fought in a region that has remained the world's most contested. These included interventions in the Chinese revolution and civil war of 1945–49, the Korean and Vietnam wars, the Gulf War of 1991, and the Afghanistan War of 2001–02.

Each of these great war epochs—Japan in Asia and the Pacific (1895–1945) and the United States in Asia and the Pacific (1898–2003)—left an indelible legacy not only on the lands and peoples of the region, but also on the praxis of total war, with profound implications for civilians and noncombatants. All of them were fought outside the homelands of the United States and Japan, with the exception of the Battle of Okinawa, the bloodiest and last great battle of the Pacific War, and U.S. bombing of Japan in the spring and summer of 1945. And in all cases the casualties suffered by the United States and Japan were a tiny fraction of those suffered by their Asian adversaries. Moreover, the U.S. homeland was secure from attack for a period that extended from the War of 1812 until the September 11, 2001, bombings of the World Trade Center and the Pentagon.[11]

## Total War, State Terror, and the Civilian

Civilians have been victims of war throughout human history. A number of factors, however, were critical in obliterating the fragile distinction between soldier and civilian that is the hallmark both of total war and of state terror in modern warfare. First was the perfection of technologies of mass destruction, above all those associated with airpower and bombing, notably the firebombing and atomic bombing of cities during World War II, but also the development of chemical, biological, electronic, and radioactive technologies. From the breach of constraints on civilian bombing in World War II, the scale and scope of these weapons would expand from cities to the countryside with the application of new technologies such as napalm in World War II, Agent Orange in Vietnam, and depleted uranium ordinance in the Gulf War.[12] Second was the increase in the number, intensity, and persistence of wars driven by nationalism and by racist or religious ideologies. This proved conducive to depriving the enemy "other" of all vestiges of humanity, paving the way for ethnic cleansing or exterminist logics frequently applied across racial, ethnic, linguistic, religious, or cultural lines.

To be sure, total war was not the exclusive prerogative of the technologically advanced, who faced new forms of guerrilla warfare and other mobilizational strategies of resistance. If the twentieth century brought the destructive power associated with state terror to new heights, anticolonial and revolutionary forces sometimes stalemated or defeated their rich and powerful adversaries, albeit at immense human and material cost. The Chinese, Korean, and Vietnamese wars and revolutions best exemplify this phenomenon of nationalist mobilizations.

Japan, in the period 1895–1945, and the United States, throughout the century and particularly since 1941, stood in the forefront of nations that pressed outward the limits of the conduct of war in Asia and globally, with particularly devastating consequences for civilian populations. Discussion will focus on instances in which their actions directly violated the growing corpus of international laws and norms seeking to define and limit the scope of war in general, and to protect the rights of civilians in particular. Especially noteworthy are the contradictions between the emancipatory claims each power made for its external or overseas military activities and the ruthlessness with which it attacked civilians in the name of liberation.

## At War with Asia: Japan, State Terror, and the Civilian

I discuss Japanese wars in Asia from two interrelated perspectives relevant to the theme of state terrorism. The first concerns such high-profile human rights violations as the Nanjing Massacre that were the unique product of a particular wartime conjuncture. The second, which views such subjects as the military comfort women, the human experiments conducted by biowarfare Unit 731, and the treatment of forced or slave labor, examines structural elements of Japanese war making, that is, institutionalized patterns of the war machine, with particular attention to their impact on civilians, POWs, and other noncombatants. Each of the issues has been the source both of protracted international political campaigns, lawsuits, and citizens tribunals and of fierce debate within Japan, throughout Asia, and globally.[13]

### The Nanjing Massacre

The Nanjing Massacre refers to the wave of murders and rapes of captured troops and civilians carried out by Japanese forces between November 1937 and January 1938 in the course of capturing and pacifying Nanjing, the Nationalist Chinese capital. With the Japanese military on a rampage that was sanctioned and sustained on the orders of local commanders, including

Prince Asaka Yasuhiko, the uncle of Emperor Hirohito, thousands of prisoners, notably former Guomindang soldiers who had surrendered or were captured after laying down their arms, as well as numerous civilians, were summarily executed while uncontrolled mass rapes targeted thousands of women
and girls. Widely publicized estimates of the numbers of unarmed people
killed remain contentious and include a low estimate of 40,000, estimates of
more than 100,000 and of 300,000, and recently, one as high as 430,000, the
low figures provided by Japanese researchers who come close to denying the
massacre, the high figures by Chinese researchers and authorities.[14] What is
certain is that the Japanese military rounded up and summarily executed large
numbers of demobilized Chinese forces and civilians, surely more than
100,000, though how many more remains elusive. The Nanjing Massacre may
have been the single largest massacre of civilians and noncombatants of the
Pacific War, but the disregard for civilian rights takes on deeper meaning in
the context of systemic forms of state terror that continued throughout the
war years.

## The "Comfort Women"

Among the major lessons that the Japanese military absorbed from the
Nanjing Massacre was the necessity to strengthen discipline in the ranks. One
result was the institutionalization of the military comfort woman system,
which resulted in the sexual enslavement of an estimated 80,000 to 200,000
women by the Japanese military between 1937 and 1945.

The Japanese military organized and controlled the comfort woman system of brothels that serviced the military throughout the empire. The largest
number of comfort women were Koreans and Chinese, but their numbers included women and girls from Taiwan, Indonesia, the Philippines, Burma,
Vietnam, Thailand, East Timor, and Hong Kong among other places, that is
from all the colonial, occupied, and dependent areas of the empire, as well as
Dutch and Australian women who were captured in Indonesia. The few surviving Japanese military and government documents that escaped destruction make clear that recruitment, transportation, and organization of the system was directed by the Japanese military, including the highest levels of
command, and that comfort women followed the Japanese military everywhere throughout Asia. In the final years of the war, comfort women served
on the front lines, where many died, were abandoned, or were killed to prevent their surrender or capture.

The comfort woman system directly violated three international covenants
against the international trafficking in women and girls ratified by Japan in
1925: the International Convention for the Suppression of the Traffic in

Women and Children of 1921–1922, the International Agreement for the Suppression of the White Slave Traffic of 1904, and the International Convention for the Suppression of the White Slave Traffic of 1910.[15]

The comfort woman system was a distinctive Japanese form of state terror in its enslavement of large numbers of women and girls in the colonies and occupied areas. The British, French, German, and American military forces, and many others, also maintained large-scale prostitution systems. The special features that distinguished the Japanese comfort woman system from World War II and later systems of military prostitution elsewhere were the direct role that the Japanese military played in organizing and promoting the kidnapping, the entrapment and overseas shipment of large numbers of women and girls, and particularly, their sexual enslavement including multiple rape, forced detention within comfort stations, and the fact that many women were never paid for their services.

## Unit 731 and Chemical and Biological Warfare

Unit 731 was the Japanese military's top chemical and biological weapons experimental and production unit. With headquarters outside Harbin in Manchuria, it conducted experiments on human victims styled as *maruta* (logs), most of them Chinese captives, but some of them Russians, Koreans, and Mongols. For three thousand subjects, the experiments ended in torture and agonizing death. Unit 731's chief, General Ishii Shiro, commanded a staff of twenty thousand at the unit's peak. The experiments, conducted between 1932 and 1945, not only share much in common with better-known Nazi genocidal vivisection and scientific murder, but also invite comparison with U.S. and British Cold War–era radioactive experiments on civilians who were never told that they had received radioactive doses of plutonium.[16]

Japan, Germany, and the United States among others conducted chemical and biological warfare research and produced weapons during World War II. But others appear to have exercised restraint with respect to the introduction of chemical and biological weapons, perhaps primarily because of the difficulty in turning the volatile weapons to effective military use, particularly the problem of avoiding having the agents blow back on their own troops and assuring that death would be inflicted on hostile rather than friendly forces. The best-documented Japanese uses include the introduction of typhoid pathogens into rivers on the Mongolian–Manchurian border during the 1939 Battle of Nomonhan with the Russians, and the introduction of typhoid, cholera, plague, and dysentery in Zhejiang Province and other parts of China in 1942.[17]

## Forced and Slave Labor and the
## Treatment of Prisoners of War

While the treatment of POWs, as in the Bataan Death March and atrocities committed during the building of the Thai–Burma Railway, has long provoked severe criticisms of Japanese handling of Western POWs and engraved on Western consciousness an indelible image of Japanese savagery, new issues of a more systemic character came to the fore in the late 1990s. One is the question of the extensive use of slave labor. In Japan, as well as in China and in Japan's colonies, tens of thousands of Koreans, Chinese, Southeast Asians, and others, including several thousand American and Asian POWs and kidnapped civilians, were subjected to forced labor for protracted periods in mines, mills, construction companies, factories, and other units. Some of these enterprises and units were run by the military or the government, others by private companies including Mitsui, Mitsubishi, Japan Steel, and other corporate giants. International law did not prohibit labor by POWs. However, both POW and forced civilian laborers, mainly Koreans and Chinese, were physically abused, particularly in periods of resistance, and many died as a result of malnutrition or physical maltreatment.[18] Since the 1990s, a series of lawsuits have been filed against both the Japanese government and corporations by former POWs and forced laborers, including Chinese, Korean, and American POWs. In 2001–2002, some victims won negotiated settlements with Japanese enterprises, and in April 2002 a Japanese court ordered Mitsui to pay reparations to forced Chinese laborers.[19]

While each of the cases described above pertains to major human rights violations, the striking fact is that the most widespread quotidian abuses of Asian civilians, the core of Japanese state terror, are rarely mentioned in the litany of protest against war crimes. I refer to the systematic ravaging of the Chinese countryside in search-and-destroy, or three all *(sanko sakusen)* missions, campaigns that targeted people and property in resistance or contested areas throughout the fifteen-year China War (1931–45). Japan was a pioneer in counter–guerrilla warfare, including the indiscriminate murder of civilians in hostile and contested areas, and its program subsequently became an important model for the United States in Vietnam and elsewhere.[20] Japanese missions turned large areas of the countryside into free-fire zones; they also pioneered strategic hamlet approaches that drove villagers from their communities into areas where they could be tightly controlled. As captured documentation in the Bureau of Investigation on Taiwan makes plain, and as the testimony of Chinese witnesses graphically substantiates, these systematic atrocities carried out against Chinese villagers by Japanese forces in the course of a fifteen-year war included forced resettlement, rape, and rounding up of entire villages followed by the torture and murder of suspects and at times entire communities.

In China, where resistance continued over fifteen years, the Japanese military obliterated all distinction between combatant and noncombatant, between military and civilian. Japanese forces neither accepted constraints on their power nor operated in ways consistent with the evolving statutes and norms of the era pertaining to international law or human rights of civilians.[21] For example, captured Chinese and other Asians, in contrast to Europeans and Americans, did not receive POW status, as Utsumi Aiko documents in this volume. They were simply shot, were relocated, or became forced laborers: in short, they enjoyed none of the rights defined by international law.

Behind the widening gap between international legal norms to protect the rights of civilians engulfed in war and repeated violation of those rights lies perhaps the fundamental flaw of the international regime of human rights throughout the long twentieth century. Created for the most part by the great powers, it leaves intact the fundamental assumptions of the legitimacy of rule by the strong and places few checks on wars fought to impose that rule. These laws and international norms, in short, fail to problematize, still less reject, the most basic elements of the inequality of power. Specifically, the international legal order, despite articulating broad principles for the protection of civilians and noncombatants, fails to defend as a basic right the autonomy of invaded or colonized peoples and has proven incapable of curbing abuses of power by the most powerful nations.

## The United States and Japan at War: Airpower, the Civilian, and the Fragility of Human Rights

A second landmark set of cases involves the war between Japan and the United States in the years 1941–45. In contrast to Japanese atrocities, some of which captured world attention at the time and continue to reverberate six decades later, United States conduct during what Americans remember as "the Good War" has rarely been framed in terms of atrocities, still less as examples of state terror.

I focus on a single important issue in gauging the legacy of state terror in the U.S.–Japan war. From the perspective of the history of warfare, and the question of civilians and human rights, World War II shaped all subsequent wars with respect to the use of airpower. In the course of World War II, each of the major powers abandoned earlier compunctions about strategic bombing of cities, that is, the large-scale massacre of civilians.

In the course of World War II, the major airpowers—Germany, Japan, Britain, and the United States—all moved from sporadic, selective, and tactical bombing to systematic area destruction, that is, they shifted from attempts to destroy verifiable military and military-industrial objectives, such as army bases and munitions factories, to the use of airpower primarily to destroy cities and to terrorize and kill civilians. Landmark attacks included Japanese incendiary raids on Chongqing, the Nationalist Chinese capital, in May 1939, which took an estimated 5,400 lives, and German destruction of central Rotterdam in May 1940, which exacted 40,000 lives.[22]

From 1941, with the development of radar-guided night bombing, whatever the official claims, most British and German raids targeted not "military targets" but cities and their populations. For its part, throughout 1943–44, the United States held back, hewing to tactical bombing, striking by day at critical military targets while resisting the temptation to attempt to destroy German cities. However, at Dresden in February 1945, with Britain taking the lead, U.S. bombers joined in night raids that took the lives of more than 35,000 people. "Along with the Nazi extermination camps, the killing of Soviet and American prisoners, and other enemy atrocities," Ronald Schaffer observes, "Dresden became one of the moral causes célèbres of World War II."[23] Following Dresden, the constraints on the area bombing of cities were permanently eliminated for the United States. Thereafter, the slaughter of civilians in area bombing of cities became the hallmark of American warfare. Over the next half century, the United States would destroy with impunity cities and urban and rural populations throughout Asia, beginning in Japan and continuing in North Korea, Indochina, Iraq, and Afghanistan, to mention only the most heavily bombed nations and people among scores of wars and military actions conducted by the United States.

## The U.S. Military, Terror, and Asian Wars, 1945 to the Twenty-First Century: Responsibility and Impunity

Between March and August 1945, the U.S. air war in Japan—the firebombing and napalming of sixty-two cities and the nuclear bombing of two others took the lives of hundreds of thousands and made refugees of millions—reached an intensity that arguably remains unrivaled in the magnitude of technological slaughter directed against a nation's cities and its people.[24] That moment was a product of the combination of technological breakthroughs together with the erosion of moral and political restraints on the killing of civilians. Awareness of the importance of this routinization of slaughter by technologically superior powers would be hidden by the event that has mesmerized the world ever since, and marked an additional cruel step in erasing the combatant/noncombatant distinction: the atomic bombings of Hiroshima and Nagasaki.[25]

For all its importance, from the perspective of overcoming the taboo on mass destruction of civilians, the atomic bombing, the hallmark of the nuclear age in which we live, appears as virtually a footnote to the firebombing of cities that took place in the European theatre and Japan in the final months of the war and to the pattern of war making since. (The Falk and Cumings chapters offer further perspective on nuclear bombing.) If nuclear weapons defined important elements of the global balance of terror centered on U.S.–Soviet conflict, "conventional" bomb attacks defined the trajectory of the subsequent half century of warfare.

If the final months of World War II permanently breached the taboo on targeting civilians through the use of airpower, subsequent U.S. wars would extend the scope of strategic air attack and bombing, first by targeting civilian populations in rural areas and then extending the targets to nature and the environment, with the use of Agent Orange and various other chemical defoliants in Vietnam as the classic example.

In Vietnam from 1963 to 1975, the United States fought a war that made use of most of the techniques pioneered while pacifying the American West and the Philippines, and in Japan's fifteen-year war in China, but with a combination of airpower and targeted assassination that ratcheted up the civilian death toll to levels far higher than those of previous campaigns. For example, death and destruction in the Vietnamese countryside was the other side of the coin of a forced urbanization strategy that utilized napalm, chemical defoliants, and cluster bombs to destroy forests and crops, and to kill and maim hundreds of thousands of civilians and force millions of others to migrate to cities, where they could be better controlled. Building on the concept of "free-fire zones," a term articulated by Brigadier General Rollen Anthis in 1962 and that came to designate all contested areas, under U.S. policy "anything that moved, anything at all, was a fair target. By 1964–65 the zones had multiplied to encompass ever larger sections of the countryside, including those most heavily populated. . . . In addition to napalm . . . white phosphorous and cluster bombs were added to the arsenal."[26] These were the strategic bases for American state terrorism in Vietnam.

While the most important violations of the human rights of civilians were the product of the systematic uses of airpower, the issues that attracted press, public attention, and international outrage were primarily those that occurred on the ground, where the faces and bodies of victims could be seen in the first war to be carried out live on prime-time television. These included the use of "tiger cages" to retain and torture prisoners by the U.S.–supported government of South Vietnam and, above all, the My Lai massacre.[27] The March 1968 My Lai massacre was a routine search-and-destroy mission that resulted in the torching of a village and killing of virtually its entire population of more than five hundred people after the raping of many of the women. Lt. William Calley, and he alone, would eventually be judged responsible for these combat murders and convicted and sentenced to life imprisonment at hard labor after the army's cover-up was exposed. (Two years later, President Nixon released him from prison and placed him under house arrest; subsequently his conviction was overturned in court.) General William Westmoreland, the U.S. commander in Vietnam, and President Richard Nixon, the commander in chief of U.S. forces, remained insulated from any onus for these and other "abuses," just as they enforced impunity from prosecution for the systematic war crimes inherent in the use of airpower and weapons against civilians. As novelist and Vietnam veteran Tim O'Brien observed of My Lai's province, Quang Ngai, "Back in 1969, . . . brutality was S.O.P. Scalded children, pistol-whipped women, burning hootches, free-fire zones, body counts, indiscriminate bombing and harassment fire, villagers in ash, M-60 machine guns hosing down dark green tree lines and any human life behind them."[28] As Robert Lifton observed, "My Lai illuminates, as nothing else has, the essential nature of America's war in Vietnam."[29]

Over the half century since World War II, U.S. reliance on airpower and bombing would grow even as it experienced constraints on the unleashing of nuclear power within a framework of U.S.–Soviet nuclear stalemate. This turn to airpower would be accentuated by the U.S. defeat in Vietnam and major political lessons drawn from that war by U.S. military leaders. The conclusion that large-scale U.S. casualties were politically unacceptable led to an increased premium on airpower and other weapons of mass destruction that would inflict heavy death tolls on civilian populations while destroying the capacity of an enemy military to fight. In September 2002, in discussing plans for a second invasion of Iraq, for example, the United States proclaimed that its strategy would begin with a massive air assault. As reported in the *Washington Post,* "Air Force officials say an attack on Iraq likely would begin with hundreds of bombers, cruise missiles and fighter aircraft executing a series of air strikes with a barrage of firepower only hinted at in other recent U.S. air campaigns. Their warheads would rain down on antiaircraft systems and missiles and aircraft that could deliver chemical or biological weapons. Then the campaign would concentrate on 'regime targets'—presidential palaces, Hussein's bodyguards, military communications systems, secret police facilities, and the bases of the elite Republican Guard and other diehard supporters."[30] The entire record of terror bombing, beginning in the final years of World War II and down to the Afghanistan War and the second war with Iraq demonstrates that air assault, notably assault on cities, exacts the heaviest toll on civilians.

In both the Bush administration's preparation for and combat in the second Gulf War, the consequences of the war for the Iraqi people were elided from official discourse. However, for the people of Iraq, the first war never ended, with U.S.–British bombing continuing for more than a decade and U.S.-led efforts to bring the Iraq economy and the most basic social services to their knees. This pattern of warfare cum state terror shares much in common with Japanese war crimes against civilians detailed earlier in this chapter. A major difference, however, is that the immediacy of many Japanese atrocities, including rape and the use of bayonet and sword to kill civilians and POWs, were replaced for the most part by technologies of death that distanced assailant from victim and mass-produced the dispatch of far larger numbers of civilians through the deployment of weapons of mass destruction.

Dr. David Hilfiker wrote at the end of a December 2002 humanitarian mission to Iraq of evidence of one million excess deaths of Iraqi citizens as a result of the invisible war waged by the United States and Britain since 1991:

I've visited pediatric cancer wards in both south and north, where an incidence of certain cancers (especially leukemia) some three to four times higher than before the war is certainly due to some combination of depleted uranium, vastly increased pollution in the country (for a variety of sanction-related causes), poor nutrition, waterborne contaminants, general ill-health, and lack of effective treatment options . . . all due to the war and the sanctions. . . .

We've visited a number of water treatment plants that are falling apart across the country because of the effects of the war and the sanctions. Without purified drinking water, the children are dying, an under-five mortality rate 2½ times higher than before the war. How can we possibly explain to ourselves not allowing parts for water treatment, money to pay for installation of new plants, and so on, when the water and sanitation disaster is the primary cause of the increased child mortality that now takes 13% of all young children?[31]

The United States has long been an active player in the military politics of the Gulf, yet the establishment of a permanent military presence all across Central Asia and the Gulf following 9/11 is breathtaking. As William D. Hartung, Frida Berrigan, and Michelle Ciarrocca point out:

Since September 2001 US forces have built, upgraded or expanded military facilities in Bahrain, Qatar, Kuwait, Saudi Arabia, Oman, Turkey, Bulgaria, Pakistan, Afghanistan, Uzbekistan and Kyrgyzstan; authorized extended training missions or open-ended troop deployments in Djibouti, the Philippines and the former Soviet republic of Georgia; negotiated access to airfields in Kazakhstan; and engaged in major military exercises, involving thousands of US personnel, in Jordan, Kuwait and India. Thousands of tons of military equipment have been added to stockpiles already pre-positioned in Middle Eastern and Persian Gulf states, including Israel, Jordan, Kuwait and Qatar.[32]

## Immunity, Impunity, Responsibility

In the course of six decades of war since World War II, the United States would enjoy a double immunity. One part of this was the United States' historical immunity to attack on its home soil by other powers. For Americans, wars meant the destruction of other lands and people. The second was immunity, or more appropriately impunity, from liability and especially prosecution for human rights violations, that is, the impunity enjoyed by the superpower that played a decisive role in establishing those norms. As at the Nuremberg and Tokyo trials of 1945 and in the prosecution of Slobodan Milošević and others beginning in 2001–2002, the United States would set the terms and designate the targets of prosecution, invariably, of course, excluding itself and such privileged allies as Israel from responsibility for terror and human rights violations. As in the case of Japan's wars against China and other Asian nations, we have shown that it is the fundamental structure of everyday war making, not the exceptional or idiosyncratic violations of human rights, that merits closest attention, for the latter was invariably a product of the former, faithful to its inherent logic. The examples linking the individual atrocities and the structure of war making dictated from on high apply equally to the Korean, Vietnam, Gulf, and Afghanistan wars in their violations of the rights of civilians and noncombatants. To be sure, specifics differ as new technologies produce new atrocities for new conditions such as the use of napalm in the bombing of Japanese cities, Agent Orange in the defoliation of Vietnam, and depleted uranium weapons in the Gulf War.

In light of our analysis of the structural aspects of everyday abuses of human rights and the systematic targeting of civilians for military attack, points common to both Japan's military aggression throughout Asia and American wars in Korea, Vietnam, the Gulf, Afghanistan, and Iraq two points require emphasis with respect to international human rights theory and praxis. The first is the necessity for the international human rights community to frame legally enforceable structures that work to inhibit wars of aggression and are not restricted to prosecuting the war crimes of the defeated. Such a task is as formidable as it is urgent, given the array of justifications for intervention provided by the great powers and the fact that the United States, which for decades has had no rival in the commission of war atrocities, dominates the international order and the framing of human rights laws. This is, of course, made more difficult by the ability of the U.S. administration following the attacks of September 11 to shape international political and strategic discourse around definitions of terrorism, definitions that exculpate itself from legitimate charges of the systematic exercise of state terrorism, and the administration's insistence that U.S. forces and all U.S. citizens be explicitly exempted from punishment by the International Court of Justice, regardless of what crimes they may commit.

The second is the necessity to reaffirm the principle of individual responsibility for human rights violations and to recognize the need to trace responsibility from the individual perpetrator to the highest levels of authority that structured the crime in question, on up to generals and heads of state. Eloquently framed at Nuremberg more than half a century ago, the principle has been enforced to date only in the most selective ways, generally with respect to defeated nations and never to the major powers. To apply this principle universally would be to challenge in fundamental ways the present international law regime and to make possible the beginnings of a serious effort to place international law in the service of victims of terror in ways that facilitate reconciliation, reparation, and reconstruction.

## Conclusion

Throughout the second half of the twentieth century, the United States was a protagonist in many Asian wars and it alone established a permanent global network of Asian bases, one that has been dramatically expanded throughout Central Asia, the Middle East, and Africa since September 11, 2001. By contrast, a semisovereign Japan, with the no war clause in its U.S.–imposed constitution and U.S. troops permanently based on its soil, has been at "peace" for nearly six decades, albeit a peace in which it provided critical economic, technological, diplomatic, and other support for every U.S. war in the region. In this half century, East Asia took on an importance in U.S. international policy in strategic, political, and economic terms rivaling that of Europe. In contrast to Europe, however, where a balance of terror and U.S.–Soviet divisions acted to constrain war for nearly half a century, throughout the postwar era, Asia was and remains the site of the world's major protracted wars, conflagrations that would contribute to redefinition of the laws of war and human rights practice as well as transform power relations.

Over the past six decades, the United States has pioneered the routine targeting of civilians from the air as the centerpiece of a war strategy predicated on U.S. technological supremacy and designed to minimize U.S. military casualties and maximize casualties among opposing military forces and civilians. We have traced this pattern from the firebombing, napalming, and atomic bombing of Japanese cities to the use of antipersonnel bombs and Agent Orange intertwined with search-and-destroy and strategic hamlet approaches to pacification in Vietnam and of depleted uranium weapons in the Gulf War, Afghanistan, and Iraq—cumulative strategies that assured the heavy toll of civilians, including the dispossession and destruction of life and society in successive nations that dared defy U.S. fiat. In the wake of September 11, Washington has extended its reach and claimed the right to invade and attack anywhere in the name of counterterrorism, with no limits on the right of intervention and no limits on the use of weaponry. The national security strategy of the United States proclaimed by the Bush administration in 2002 articulates a doctrine of unilateral intervention, the right to initiate regime change anywhere, and impunity from international human rights norms.[33] At the same time that the United States has exerted leadership in the prosecution of war crimes by international tribunals targeting its enemies, its global power has effectively shielded it from serious criticism, not to speak of prosecution for its own crimes of war and violation of human rights in war after war against technologically and materially weaker nations. Recognition and rectification of this situation is among the most urgent issues that challenge the development of an equitable approach to war, peace, and human rights in an era militarily dominated by a single ruthless superpower.

# Notes

I thank Steve Shalom for wise comments and suggestions on earlier drafts of this chapter.

1. Eric Hobsbawm, *The Age of Extremes: A History of the World, 1914–1991* (New York: Vintage, 1996), 49.

2. A number of the basic texts as well as discussion can be found in Richard A. Falk, Gabriel Kolko, and Robert Jay Lifton, eds., *Crimes of War: A Legal, Political–Documentary, and Psychological Inquiry into the Responsibility of Leaders, Citizens, and Soldiers for Criminal Acts in Wars* (New York: Vintage, 1971), and Burns H. Weston, Richard A. Falk, and Anthony A. D'Amato, eds., *Basic Documents in International Law and World Order* (St. Paul, Minn.: West, 1980).

3. "Convention for the Amelioration of the Condition of the Wounded and Sick in Armed Forces in the Field," and "Convention Relative to the Protection of Civilian Persons in Time of War," done at Geneva August 12, 1949 (entered into force for the United States on February 2, 1956), in Weston, Falk, and D'Amato, eds., *Basic Documents*, 98–105, 112–16.

4. *United States Code Congressional and Administrative News,* 98th Congress, 2d Sess., 1984, October 19, vol. 2, par. 3077, 98 STAT.2707 (St. Paul, Minn.: West, 1984). For a discussion of the U.S. Code, in particular a critique of the U.S. position that the label of terrorist acts should be limited to those committed by others against the United States and its allies, see Noam Chomsky, *9-11* (New York: Seven Stories, 2001), 16–17.

5. Rome Statute of the International Criminal Court (ICC) as corrected July 12, 1999, at www.un.org/law/icc/statute/99_corr/2.htm (accessed February 1, 2003). It is precisely such provisions that have led the United States to refuse to accept the authority of the ICC over its military actions.

6. For thoughtful attempts to gauge and assess civilian and military casualties in the two world wars, see Hobsbawm, *Age of Extremes*, 24–26, 43–44, 49–52, 434–35, and John W. Dower, *War without Mercy: Race and Power in the Pacific War* (New York: Pantheon, 1986), 294–300. As Dower observes, the widely used figure of 55 million deaths in World War II greatly underestimates Asian deaths. With the gross underestimate of civilian and Asian deaths in the available sources (above all in China, where figures of ten to twenty million deaths in the course of the fifteen-year war are plausible and twenty to thirty million are possible, but also throughout Southeast Asia, for which no figures are given in most sources) and with the addition of millions of fatalities in subsequent wars, notably those in Korea, Vietnam, and the Iran–Iraq War, a total in the range of 100 million war dead, the great majority being civilians, is plausible for twentieth-century wars.

7. Mary Kaldor, *New & Old Wars: Organized Violence in a Global Era* (Stanford, Calif.: Stanford University Press, 1999), 8; Dan Smith, *The State of War and Peace Atlas* (London: Penguin, 1997). The numbers are elusive and subject to large swings depending both on definitions (whether deaths due to illness and starvation are included, for example) and the fact that data on mortality outside the military, such as deaths due to starvation and diseases, are often crude at best. The trend nevertheless seems all too plausible.

8. Paul Gordon Lauren, *The Evolution of International Human Rights: Visions Seen* (Philadelphia: University of Pennsylvania Press, 1998), 61–62. The following paragraphs draw on Lauren, especially 92–98, 297–303.

9. Chris Jochnik and Roger Normand, "The Legitimation of Violence: A Critical History of the Laws of War," *Harvard International Law Journal* 35, no. 1 (Winter 1994): 387–416.

10. George W. Bush, state of the union address, January 2001, at www.whitehouse.gov/news/releases/2002/01/20020129-11.html (accessed April 2, 2003). Undersecretary of State John Bolton subsequently explicitly expanded the list to include Cuba, Libya, and Syria. BBC News, May 6, 2002.

11. Japan's attack on Pearl Harbor was directed against a U.S. territorial possession, not the U.S. homeland.

12. For discussion of contemporary U.S. state-of-the-art technology, see William M. Arkin, "'Sci-Fi' Weapons Going to War," *Los Angeles Times*, December 7, 2002. See also, Marc Herold's website devoted to depleted uranium weapons and their consequences at globalalternatives.org/911.html (accessed December 1, 2002); James Sterngold, "Resurgence for Nuclear Labor, Designing Weapons for Terror War, 'Planning Underground Tests,'" *San Francisco Chronicle*, October 22, 2002; Julian Borger, "US Weapons Secrets Exposed," *Guardian*, October 29, 2002.

13. On the persistence and ever growing strength of criticism of Japanese atrocities nearly six decades after the end of the Pacific War, see Laura Hein and Mark Selden, eds., *Censoring History: Citizenship and Memory in Japan, Germany and the United*

*States* (Armonk, N.Y.: M. E. Sharpe, 2000), and Hein and Selden, eds., *Islands of Discontent: Okinawa, Japan and the United States* (Lanham, Md.: Rowman & Littlefield, 2003).

14. The estimate of more than 100,000 is Honda Katsuichi's. For discussion of the debate over the numbers of victims and over the military and civilian components of the toll, as well as detailed discussion of the atrocities committed, see Honda Katsuichi, *The Nanjing Massacre: A Japanese Journalist Confronts Japan's National Shame* (Armonk, N.Y.: M. E. Sharpe, 1999), especially vii–xiii; Mark Eykholt, "Aggression, Victimization, and Chinese Historiography of the Nanjing Massacre," and Takashi Yoshida, "A Battle over History: The Nanjing Massacre in Japan," in *The Nanjing Massacre in History and Historiography,* ed. Joshua Fogel, 11–69, 70–132 (Berkeley: University of California, 2000); Iris Chang, *The Rape of Nanking: The Forgotten Holocaust of World War II* (New York: Penguin, 1997); Timothy Brook, ed., *Documents on the Rape of Nanking* (Ann Arbor: University of Michigan Press, 1999). Matsuoka Tamaki, ed., *Nankin Sen. Toza sareta kioku o tazunete* (The Nanjing battle) (Tokyo: Shakai Hyôronsha, 2002), presents the oral testimony of 102 Japanese soldiers who fought at Nanjing. Brian Victoria, *Zen War Stories* (London: RoutledgeCurzon, 2002), presents the deathbed testimony of Commanding General Matsui Iwane, which suggests that primary responsibility for the massacre lay with Prince Asaka, who was in command during Matsui's absence from Nanjing, when he was undergoing treatment for tuberculosis. Earlier and publicly, Matsui had placed responsibility for the massacre on lower-ranking officers.

15. For discussion both of the comfort woman system and of relevant international law provisions, see Yoshimi Yoshiaki, *Comfort Women: Sexual Slavery in the Japanese Military during World War II* (New York: Columbia University Press, 2000); Yuki Tanaka, *Japan's Comfort Women: Sexual Slavery and Prostitution during World War II and the US Occupation* (London: Routledge, 2002); Yoshimi Yoshiaki and Hayashi Hirofumi, eds., *Nihongun Ianfu* (Japanese military comfort women) (Tokyo: Otsuki Shôten, 1995); Laura Hein, "Claiming Humanity and Legal Standing: Contemporary Demands for Redress from Japan for Its World War II Policies," in *Politics and the Past: On Repairing Historical Injustices,* ed. John Torpey (Lanham, Md.: Rowman & Littlefield, 2003); and Cynthia Enloe, *Maneuvers: The International Politics of Militarizing Women's Lives* (Berkeley: University of California, 2000), 79–123. The 80,000 figure for the number of comfort women is Yoshimi's. Tanaka estimates there were 80,000–100,000 comfort women (p. 31). Other informed estimates range upward to approximately 200,000, including that of Hayashi Hirofumi, who points to the large number of Chinese women pressed into service (personal communication, August 2001). See also Hayashi, "The Japanese Movement to Protest Wartime Sexual Violence: A Survey of Japanese and International Literature," *Critical Asian Studies* 33, no. 4 (December 2001): 572–80.

16. Yuki Tanaka discusses the Japanese, German, and U.S. comparisons in *Hidden Horrors: Japanese War Crimes in World War II* (Boulder, Colo.: Westview, 1996), especially on pp. 135–45 and 160–65. See also Sheldon Harris, *Factories of Death: Japanese Biological Warfare 1932–45* (London: Routledge, 1994); William Winkenwerder Jr., "Briefing on Cold War Era Chemical and Biological Warfare Tests," *Defense Link* (Washington, D.C.: U.S. Department of Defense, October 9, 2002).

17. Tanaka, *Hidden Horrors*, 137–39. See Kei-ichi Tsuneishi, "Japan's Unit 731: Biological Warfare and the Responsibility of the Scientist" (Lanham, Md.: Rowman & Littlefield, forthcoming).

18. "NKK Pays 4.1 Million Yen to Wartime Laborer," *Japan Times*, April 7, 1999.

19. Mark Magnier, "Japanese Firm Must Pay War Laborers in Asia," *Los Angeles Times*, April 27, 2002; Kinue Tokudome, "POW Forced Labor Suits against Japanese Companies," JPRI Working Paper 82 (November 2001); Linda Goetz Holmes, *Unjust Enrichment: How Japan's Companies Built Postwar Fortunes Using American POWs* (Mechanicsburg, Pa.: Stackpole, 2001).

20. Chong-sik Lee, *Counterinsurgency in Manchuria: The Japanese Experience, 1931–1940*, Rand Corporation Memorandum RM-5012-ARPA (Santa Monica, Calif.: Rand Corporation, 1967).

21. See Yuki Tanaka, *Hidden Horrors: Japanese War Crimes in World War II* (Boulder, Colo.: Westview, 1995); Chalmers Johnson, *Peasant Nationalism and Communist Power: The Rise of Revolutionary China* (Stanford, Calif.: Stanford University Press, 1992); Mark Selden, *China in Revolution: The Yenan Way Revisited* (Armonk, N.Y.: M. E. Sharpe, 1995); Yung-fa Chen, *Making Revolution: The Communist Movement in Eastern and Central China* (Berkeley: University of California Press, 1986); and Diana Lary and Stephen MacKinnon, eds., *Scars of War: The Impact of Warfare on Modern China* (Vancouver: University of British Columbia Press, 2001).

22. Mark Selden, "The Logic of Mass Destruction," in *Hiroshima's Shadow: Writings on the Denial of History and the Smithsonian Controversy*, ed. Kai Bird and Lawrence Lifschultz (Stony Creek, Conn.: Pamphleteer's, 1998); W. G. Sebald, "A Natural History of Destruction: Why Germans Forgot the Ruin of Their Cities," *New Yorker*, November 4, 2002, 66–77.

23. Ronald Schaffer, *Wings of Judgment: American Bombing in World War II* (New York: Oxford University Press, 1985), 20-30, 108–109.

24. Michael Sherry, *The Rise of American Air Power: The Creation of Armageddon* (New Haven, Conn.: Yale University Press, 1987), 253, emphasizes the importance of U.S. bombing of Japanese cities for the subsequent history of air war. The onslaught against North Korea after 1950 invites comparison. But given the far smaller urban population there, the scale of that destruction, and that of North Vietnamese cities, was far smaller.

25. I have addressed ethical issues associated with the atomic bombing as well as issues of historical memory in Kyoko Selden and Mark Selden, eds., *The Atomic Bomb: Voices from Hiroshima and Nagasaki* (Armonk, N.Y.: M. E. Sharpe, 1989), and Laura Hein and Mark Selden, eds., *Living with the Bomb: American and Japanese Cultural Conflicts in the Nuclear Age* (Armonk, N.Y.: M. E. Sharpe, 1997).

26. Marilyn B. Young, *The Vietnam Wars* (New York, HarperCollins, 1991), 129, 86.

27. "Statement on Con Son Prison by the Honorable Augustus F. Hawkins, July 1970," in *Crimes of War: A Legal, Political–Documentary, and Psychological Inquiry into the Responsibility of Leaders, Citizens, and Soldiers for Criminal Acts in Wars*, ed. Richard A. Falk, Gabriel Kolko, and Robert Jay Lifton (New York: Vintage, 1971), 258–60. See also "Statement on Con Son Prison," 377–79, and Seymour Hersh, *My Lai 4* (New York: Random House, 1970).

28. H. Bruce Franklin, *Vietnam and Other American Fantasies* (Amherst: University of Massachusetts Press, 2000), 34–43 (quote on p. 39). See also William H. Miller, "Letter to His Parents," reporting on the many My Lai-type operations in which he, too, had participated and denouncing the scapegoating of Calley for policies that were honed and ordered from on high. Miller, "Letter to His Parents," *Bridgeport Post*, February 17, 1970, in *Crimes of War: A Legal, Political–Documentary, and Psychological Inquiry into the Responsibility of Leaders, Citizens, and Soldiers for Criminal Acts in Wars*, ed. Richard A. Falk, Gabriel Kolko, and Robert Jay Lifton (New York: Vintage, 1971), 395–96.

29. Falk, Kolko, and Lifton, *Crimes of War*, 23.

30. Thomas Ricks, "War Planes Target Hussein Power Base," *Washington Post*, September 21, 2002.

31. "Letter from David Hilfiker," weblog of the Nation Institute, at www.tomdispatch.com (accessed December 22, 2002); see also Joy Gordon, "Cool War," *Harper's* (November 2002), on the deadly U.S. use of sanctions to punish Iraqi civilians.

32. "Operation Endless Deployment," *Nation*, October 21, 2002.

33. See for example, Center for Defense Information, "The Bush National Security Strategy: A First Step," September 26, 2002, at www.cdi.org/national-security-strategy/washington.cfm and www.whitehouse.gov/nsc/nss.html. (accessed September 27, 2002).

# 3

# State Terror versus Humanitarian Law

*Richard Falk*

## Continuities in the American
## Approach to War and Peace

ESPECIALLY SINCE SEPTEMBER 11, 2001, but also throughout their history, the great majority of Americans have imagined themselves the victims of unlawful aggression and terrorism and regarded their country as essentially innocent, associated in its international behavior exclusively with defensive and essentially just uses of force. We can trace the origins of an American conception of normative (moral, legal, religious) self-justification to the long period of colonial existence under British dominion. This self-created myth is often identified as "moral exceptionalism," and expressed in religious language by reference to America as "the new Jerusalem" or "the city on the hill." Whatever the ugly and bloody realities of postindependence American expansionism and Western Hemisphere interventionary diplomacy, no amount of contradictory behavior, even that exhibited with respect to Indians and slaves over several centuries, would tarnish this national sense of moral superiority over other countries. During the Cold War era, American establishment figures with apparent sincerity claimed in various ways that America was "a Lockean nation in a Hobbesian world," that is, it was concerned with the protection of natural rights rather than seeking to maximize its power at the expense of other sovereign states.

In the aftermath of September 11, these self-serving claims have been given an imperialist twist. In the course of projecting American power to carry on the war against Al Qaeda and global terrorism, the U.S. government also affirms its resolve to use its influence to spread American civic culture and political values. President Bush has declared this intention in several major speeches, suggesting that the American way of life embodies universally valid values that are equally applicable elsewhere.

Such influential realist diplomats as George Kennan and Henry Kissinger repeatedly issued admonitions that America's moralism and legalism impaired the country's capacity to pursue its national interests by an appropriate focus on strategic concerns rather than by a grandiose insistence on acting to project and defend American values globally.[1] Although these realists commanded the heights of governmental power in the United States from the 1940s, they could never orient the American citizenry to an acceptance of their view that states are much better off when they eschew moralism and legalism, pragmatically and selfishly pursue their interests internationally, and act and think as a *normal* state. Of course, American politicians fostered this highly suspect nationalistic view that America was morally superior to other countries, thereby giving themselves a free rein to mobilize the country for war and intervention by invoking a posture of righteous indignation. And so realist intellectuals and diplomats, often against their better judgment, felt obliged in public pronouncements to conceal their policy recommendations beneath a legitimating cloak of moral fervor. In so doing, it was possible for them to hide the crasser sides of American material and imperial interests at stake in a foreign policy debate and confuse the public as to the real motivations of American foreign policy, while at the same time producing an impression abroad that claims of American exceptionalism were mainly designed to hide American imperialism.

American diplomats can discuss ideological "interests" associated with defending foreign countries against such threats as "communism" and opposing such developments as the acquisition of nuclear weapons by so-called rogue states, a group of states distinguished less by their erratic behavior than by their unwillingness to submit to U.S. geopolitical discipline. What is not allowed, especially since 1945, is the acknowledgment that foreign policy in a given instance may be driven by economic and financial interests. For example, the dirty words "oil" and "military bases" are never mentioned in official American explanations of Iraqi wrongdoing, or in relation to the alleged threat posed by the Baghdad regime that made the goals of "regime change" and "disarmament" so important as to justify recourse to aggressive war unconvincingly rationalized by a claim of preemptive rights against supposed terrorist threats in the aftermath of the September 11 attacks. This Bush doctrine of preemption undermines the historic efforts of the UN Charter and of international law since 1945 to prohibit recourse to international force except in instances of self-defense against a *prior* armed attack.

Despite this dubious record of American statecraft, it would be a mistake to write off entirely this normative posturing as nothing more than American cynicism, hypocrisy, and a mask for economic imperialism. An alternative American world narrative is one in which its role, especially in the twentieth century, and particularly in relation to world politics in the North, may validly be depicted in terms of a defense of liberal democratic values in contrast to the colonialism of Europe and against the totalitarian assaults of fascism and Stalinist communism. The two leaders who most fully articulated a vision of a more humane world order in the past century were both Americans: Woodrow Wilson with his championship of collective security and self-determination and Franklin Roosevelt with his advocacy of the Four Freedoms within the framework of collective security under United Nations auspices. It was America that pushed hardest after 1945 to incorporate human rights within international law, including in its role as principal sponsor of the Universal Declaration of Human Rights adopted by the General Assembly in 1948. And it was certainly a consequence of U.S. diplomacy that the defeated leaders of Germany and Japan were prosecuted at Nuremberg and Tokyo as war criminals after World War II within a constitutional framework rather than being subjected to summary battlefield justice, as was the preference of Stalin and Churchill. It was the United States that was seen around the world as the only appropriate site for the United Nations, which was partly an acknowledgment of its hegemonic stature and ambitions, but also a recognition of its role in articulating human rights norms and goals that included its pioneering insistence on prosecuting German and Japanese war criminals, as well as an expression of the hope that it would be America that would facilitate the transition from colonialism to independence in Asia and Africa.

And for all its ambivalence, and even periodic hostility, it was the U.S. government that provided the symbolic and substantive setting that has allowed the UN to persist for more than five decades as the first truly universal organization of states. In this respect, it is worth contrasting the UN experience with that of its precursor, the League of Nations, set up after World War I. The League never gained the membership of such important states as the United States and was further weakened by the withdrawal of other major states and by the League's acceptance of a colonial world order as legitimate. Of course, the UN also proved useful to Washington, lending legitimating support to the geopolitical designs that American leaders pursued in the period immediately after 1945. These designs were often associated in the minds of American policy makers with the fulfillment of the UN Charter, especially as directed against supposed Soviet expansionism. Such an identification of American interests with the legal framework of the United Nations was most prominently illustrated in relation to the scope of this chapter, with respect to validating recourse to an American-led war against North Korea in 1950, a response to an attack on South Korea.

Even in the midst of the Cold War, it was John F. Kennedy and then Jimmy Carter who most effectively captured the imagination of the world as leaders who projected a vision of a humane future for the peoples of the world that could not be altogether explained away as a pleasing disguise for the hegemonic ambitions of the strongest state. Earlier, it had been the U.S. government that had accepted the main financial burdens of European economic recovery in 1945 (via the Marshall Plan), of supporting the UN, of lending qualified and inconsistent, but periodically important, support for the right of self-determination and the national independence of colonized peoples, of providing the main initiative to establish arms control arrangements, and of promoting modest levels of foreign economic assistance to Third World countries. In this regard, the belief in American exceptionalism is to some significant extent shared by many non-Americans who continue to this day to view the United States as a land of opportunity and the best hope of peoples everywhere for global peace and justice in the future. Whether this positive image, always no more than a part of the story, can survive at all in the face of the U.S. war-making praxis taking shape since the end of the Cold War seems doubtful. These positive aspects of the American global role have been placed under dramatic additional strain due to the American global response to September 11.

The pathological dualism of America's global role persists, creating a confusingly symbiotic link between self-righteous protective claims based on confusing admixtures of defensive necessity, idealistic endorsements of democracy and freedom, and a greedy geopolitics that seeks to sustain military, economic, and cultural dominance into the indefinite future.[2] Such an undertaking of global empire confronts the entire world with the horrifying choice of devastating violence or humiliating submission, while marking a transition for Americans from a dominant political tradition based on republicanism to one premised on empire.[3] Of course, virtually from the beginning the United States exhibited imperial tendencies by way of territorial expansionism in North America, which throughout the eighteenth and nineteenth centuries involved the bloody dispossession of Native Americans in the westward push as well as seizure of Mexican land through aggressive warfare in 1846–48. Later, American interventionary diplomacy throughout the Western Hemisphere was designed to keep in power dictatorial leaders receptive to American foreign investments and business concessions. The Spanish–American War of 1898 involved the United States in the business of formal empire, as it incorporated under its control the Philippines, Puerto Rico, and Hawaii, while claiming interventionary prerogatives in Cuba.

What has occurred in recent years is far more extensive in scope and ambition, as well as seeming to negate that part of the American tradition based on republicanism. This twenty-first-century transition to global imperial state has been highlighted by an embrace of unilateralism in American foreign policy during the Bush presidency, which was made evident prior to September 11 in the rejection of widely ratified multilateral treaties on such matters as climate change, the control of international arms trade, the prohibition of anti–ballistic missile systems, and the establishment of an international criminal court. Such a pattern was dangerously weakening the emergent framework of global cooperative arrangements that had been accepted by all other states as a necessary and desirable adjustment of sovereign rights in response to the multidimensional challenge of economic globalization. American unilateralism has also seriously eroded the fragile framework of international law that had been developing through the decades in the global order to regulate recourse to international force.

In the aftermath of September 11, it becomes more important than ever to disentangle this dual American legacy that is blind to its own faults and acts so mercilessly toward its enemies of the moment, while continuing to claim a unique idealistic mission on the global stage. Although it is important to be aware of this dual global identity associated with American diplomacy, pointing toward liberal internationalism in one direction and toward xenophobic imperialism in the other, this chapter devoted to explicating the realities of state terrorism will stress the dark side of the picture. This pattern of state terrorism is particularly notable in the Asian wars fought by the United States during the last sixty years of the twentieth century. During these wars, the United States made the fullest possible use of its technological prowess to inflict extreme harm on the exceedingly vulnerable civilian populations of its adversaries as a deliberate tactic of warfare under circumstances in which the American population did not face comparable threats.[4] These realities, earlier obscured and even sanitized by the language of "total war" or "military necessity," can only be properly understood as instances of state terror.[5] It is especially relevant at this historic juncture, given the identification of terrorist forms of antistate violence as unconditional evil, to situate this past state violence within the domain of terrorism. Only by so doing is it possible to recover a degree of moral and political perspective in responding to the new forms of international terrorism that now challenge both the imagination and the capabilities of the United States.[6]

Undoubtedly, the most extreme and permanently traumatizing instance of state terrorism, perhaps in the history of warfare, involved the use of atomic bombs against the cities of Hiroshima and Nagasaki in military settings in which the explicit function of the attacks was to terrorize the population

through mass slaughter and to confront its leaders with the prospect of national annihilation. (There were, in addition, the secondary geopolitical goals
of avoiding sharing the fruits of an American victory in the Pacific with the
Soviet Union and intimidating Moscow in relation to the future.) The public
justification for the attacks given by the U.S. government then and now was
mainly to save lives that might otherwise have been lost in a military campaign to conquer and occupy the Japanese home islands, which was alleged as
necessary to attain the wartime goal of unconditional surrender.[7] The policy
was applauded by most Americans at the time, and has been since, despite the
horrors inflicted, as leading to a shortening of the war.

But even accepting the rationale for the atomic attacks at face value, which
means discounting both the geopolitical motivations and the pressures to
show that the immense investment of the Manhattan Project had struck pay
dirt, and disregarding the Japanese diplomatic efforts to arrange their surrender prior to the attacks, the idea that massive death can be deliberately inflicted on a helpless civilian population as a tactic of war certainly qualifies as
state terror of unprecedented magnitude, particularly as the United States
stood on the edge of victory, which might well have been consummated by
diplomacy. As Michael Walzer puts it, the United States in 1945 owed the
Japanese people "an experiment in negotiation," but even if such an initiative
had failed there was no foundation in law or morality for atomic attacks on
civilian targets.[8]

Recourse to such tactics in World War II should not be viewed as novel or
without historical background, aside from the specific connection with the
apocalyptic technology of strategic airpower and atomic weaponry.[9] With the
advent of American technological superiority, which made its weight felt in
the course of World War II, especially in the war against Japan, this logic of
state terror assumed more lethal forms of mass violence, disrupting reciprocity as an essential moderating element in military conflict.[10] It has been this
technological one-sidedness that has made America's Pacific wars of the past
sixty years such blatant instances of state terror in its most extreme forms.
Perhaps this extremity also embodies vengeful and racist elements, a payback
for Pearl Harbor and an acceptance of the image of the Asian as the incomprehensible other whose supposed absolute devotion to a political cause is
treated as a form of barbarism.[11] However understood, these Pacific wars
(World War II, the Korean War, and the Vietnam, or Indochina, War) are each
characterized by a massive and unacknowledged American reliance on state
terror as the central modality of belligerency.[12]

As suggested above, the pursuit of strategic goals during wartime has in the
course of history subordinated moral and legal guidelines identifying the limits of acceptable behavior *for all states*. From this perspective, war represents a

fundamental breakdown of rule-governed relationships among states (despite the efforts in modern times to develop a legal code governing the conduct of warfare). The resultant pattern of lawlessness should not be associated exclusively with the United States. The absence of restraint in war, including the refusal to respect civilian innocence, applies across the board to the behavior of virtually every state in wartime situations, although to significantly varied extents depending on circumstances, technological capacity, and the stakes of the conflict. After all, no lesser champion of international law than Sir Hersch Lauterpacht asserted that "[i]f international law is, in some ways, at the vanishing-point of law, the law of war is, perhaps even more conspicuously, at the vanishing-point of international law."[13]

At the same time, the struggle to place limits on the barbarism of war by adherence to the laws of warfare has probably saved many thousands of lives and has represented a continuous effort by international lawyers and diplomats, at least since the seventeenth century, when the Dutch founder of modern international law, Hugo Grotius, powerfully advocated the establishment and observance of the law of war as the essential features of an emergent modernity. What success these efforts have had are matters of debate and conjecture, but seem to have depended partly on pragmatic considerations of reciprocity (for instance, in the treatment of prisoners of war) and the avoidance of gratuitous suffering (that is, avoidance of destructive behavior beyond what is deemed to be military necessity). For this reason, where the conduct of war is one-sided, the structure of reciprocity breaks down, and with it the sense of the sort of restraint that is embodied in the law of war, which to some extent, while problematic at best, nevertheless moderates the behavior of most belligerents. One might have expected that America's moral pretensions of humanitarianism and exceptionalism would have led it to be more scrupulous in its behavior during wartime and at least to refrain from the deliberate targeting of civilians crowded together in large urban centers. But clearly, America's moral pretensions have not led it to more scrupulous wartime behavior, such as restraint in targeting civilians.

What is striking about American conduct in the Asian and Pacific wars of the last half of the twentieth century is the absence of reciprocity. American technological superiority, especially with respect to strategic air and naval power, allowed the United States to inflict death and destruction on Asian peoples while keeping its own homeland secure from attack. Such was the case in the wars against Japan, Korea, and Vietnam and, indeed, in all subsequent U.S. wars. This absence of American restraint is further accentuated by the one-sidedness of attempts to hold political and military leaders of Asian countries accountable for violations of the laws of war, while refusing accountability for U.S. conduct. It is only the dominant international position of the United States that has shielded its conduct in these wars from the dynamics of formal condemnation and criminalization. Among the many examples of military conduct in flagrant violation of the laws of war as generally understood are the strategic bombing of Japanese cities aggravated by the use of atomic bombs that spread radioactive contamination and inflicted severe genetic damage; the deliberate bombing of dikes and dams during the Korean War with the evident intention of flooding villages in a manner that caused large numbers of civilian casualties; the widespread dissemination of Agent Orange in rural areas of Vietnam, causing immediate and long-range health problems there; and the adoption of civilian assassination (the Phoenix Program), free-fire zones, and a variety of other tactics that victimized the civilian population of Vietnam. When assessed by inquiries under the independent auspices of civil society, the United States was repeatedly found to have relied on practices tainted with international criminality.[14]

The main conclusion is that American reliance on state terror has been greatly facilitated by technological innovations in weaponry that have deprived adversaries of reciprocal means to strike back. Further, the American conduct of warfare in the Pacific region over the course of the past century has been shielded from critical scrutiny due to the geopolitical status of the United States, its leverage over the formal procedures assessing legal accountability that operate in international society, its influence on the media, and its refusal to impose international legal accountability on its own leadership.[15] As a result, American wartime practices involving the deliberate targeting of civilians have been shielded from authoritative scrutiny and the United States has been spared official condemnation of its tactics as tantamount to state terrorism. Such a shielding appears particularly blatant as the United States has taken on the mantle of leading a worldwide antiterrorist crusade, the scope of which is defined in such a way as to conceive of terrorism as confined to antistate violence. This distorting control of language and of media presentations of terrorism has a profoundly misleading effect, obscuring the primary reality of terrorism, namely, that states rather than antistate actors are responsible for the great majority of civilian deaths over the course of the past several decades, as well as throughout modern history. As a consequence, the lesser antistate violence is demonized, while the greater state violence is virtually immunized from criticism. This chapter views both forms of political violence directed at civilians as terroristic, deserving condemnation from the perspectives of law and morality.[16]

## 2003 Reflections on the Atomic Attacks in World War II

State terrorism has managed to avoid condemnation, and even identification, because leading governments exert control over political discourse relating to national security and the mainstream media is acquiescent even in democratic societies. Reinforcing these distorted perceptions relating to impermissible forms of political violence attributable to states are the extremes of moral pretension that have frequently put major *victims* of state terrorism in the dock of criminal accountability. It is not that these "victims" are not themselves guilty of criminality, as was certainly the case with respect to German and Japanese civilian and military leaders in relation to World War II, but by isolating and punishing only these individuals, the tactics of the victorious states tended to be whitewashed. In this respect, the one-sidedness of criminal accountability has increasingly reinforced the one-sidedness of military capabilities and tactics, compounding the confusions about respect for the restraints of international law and morality in relation to war and violent struggle among states. Focusing on the wrongdoing of the losers while according impunity to the victors has generated a misleading set of impressions that persist to this day.[17] It is true that in American academic circles there was some criticism of "victors' justice," especially in the setting of the Tokyo War Crimes Tribunal, but only rarely and peripherally was this coupled with a real critique of the state terror relied upon by the United States in the pursuit of its war aims against Japan.[18]

The volatility of the issue has recently resurfaced in relation to the establishment of an International Criminal Court (ICC) that is vested with authority to prosecute individuals charged with such serious offenses as genocide, crimes against humanity, and crimes of war. Geopolitically ambitious state actors such as the United States and China are defiant in their refusal to submit their leaders to such standards of accountability, which is less an expression of distrust toward the ICC as a judicial institution than of the belief that the behavior of these nations should not be restricted or subject to procedures of accountability under international law.

The evaluation of the struggle to establish international procedures to impose criminal accountability often adopts a narrowly provincial tone in the United States. For instance, Gary Jonathan Bass contends that the phrase "victors' justice" is "largely uninformative," as it does not focus on "the nature of the conquering state," which he seems to understand as meaning that if the victor is a liberal state with a concern for individual rights, then the accused is likely to receive a fair trial, but that if it is illiberal then the judicial process would likely be a show trial.[19] With this argument, Bass manages to sidestep the main complaints about victors' justice by suggesting that reliance on a bona fide war crimes approach should be primarily understood as a preferable alternative to vengeful impulses, and that since the imposition of criminal accountability has invariably been a project of liberal democracies, the legal process tends to be procedurally fair. This assessment is insightful as far as it concerns the issue of the fairness of the adjudication (and the appropriate contrast with show trials in totalitarian countries). At the same time, it avoids the larger substantive and procedural questions as to whether legal norms of criminal accountability should not be applied to liberal victors in war as much as to illiberal losers. To say the least! It also fails to address the arguments of the Pal dissent at Tokyo about the dubious status of the antiaggression norm, given the character of world order based on making the security of sovereign states an absolute priority.[20]

While our focus is on state terrorism as a feature of American warfare in Asia and the Pacific, other issues complicate analysis and assessment. For instance, as earlier discussed, the American global role has had two contrasting faces: that of presiding over escalations in the logic of destruction in wartime and that of bringing to bear law and more orderly methods in dealing with defeated enemies. Despite the bitterness of World War II combat and propaganda, after its victory the United States projected an image, and substantially achieved its reality, of itself as a benign occupier.[21] Rather than being summarily shot, Japanese accused of war crimes were prosecuted before courts of law presided over by distinguished jurists, and were given differential punishments depending on the severity of their crimes, and in some instances were acquitted or not prosecuted. Japan was permitted to retain the emperor, despite the evidence that the emperor system had encouraged Japanese militarism. And the military occupation aimed by 1947 at restoring full Japanese sovereignty and facilitating economic recovery. The result was one of the great successes of the post-1945 period, a genuine reconciliation between the victorious and defeated societies. This dynamic was greatly facilitated by the Cold War pressures on Washington to enlist Japan as an ally in the struggle against the Soviet Union and by Japan's ready acceptance of an American security umbrella giving free-rider protection against such potentially menacing neighbors as China, the Soviet Union, and North Korea. Both sides had ample incentive to downplay the degree to which state terror had been relied upon by both the victors and the vanquished in World War II, the Japanese because of their preoccupation with recovery and security, the Americans for strategic reasons (see the discussion in chapter 2).

What is most relevant to an inquiry into American state terrorism in World War II is not only the *practice* alluded to above, but also the hypocrisy involved in shifting the entire burden of criminality in the Pacific phases of the war to the Japanese side. There is no doubt that Japanese military and political leaders engaged in practices that were inhumane and in flagrant violation of international law, but by turning the Japanese defeat into an occasion for such a one-sided process of legal inquiry, America's own state terrorist operations were exempted from any serious scrutiny and indeed were assimilated into a self-congratulatory historic judgment that Asia was rescued from Japanese imperialism and Japan was itself redeemed as a result of the American occupation, which conferred gifts of constitutional democracy and economic prosperity. Despite the horrors inflicted on Hiroshima and Nagasaki, following on the heels of the leveling of sixty-two Japanese cities by "conventional" bombs and napalm, America emerged from World War II with virtually no taint of self-doubt about the appropriateness of future reliance on nuclear weaponry, although it seemed at first to favor moves toward nuclear disarmament in the immediate aftermath of the war.

In World War I, aside from submarine warfare, the fighting and dying occurred on the battlefield, with military forces bearing the main burden. Attitudes toward the bombing of civilians shifted with perceptions of military advantage and weapons innovations, as well as doctrinal ideas about how to achieve "victory"; in large-scale warfare between industrialized adversaries in World War II, the decisive shift occurred in relation to Germany, where the struggles on the front lines were increasingly complemented by Allied attacks on the civilian infrastructure, but this strategy was then applied to Japan with strategic bombing of cities, culminating in the atomic attacks. The atomic bombs were more terrifying instances of the sorts of attacks earlier carried out by conventional means against such cities as Dresden, Hamburg, and Tokyo.[22]

In the wake of World War II, the United States proposed a series of nuclear disarmament initiatives. It became increasingly clear as the years passed, however, that the United States and other leading states were unwilling to negotiate away their nuclear weapons option.[23] The Cold War provided the pretext of mutual deterrence for continuing with the development of this weaponry, especially crossing the threshold that augmented greatly the destructive impact by the decision to test and produce hydrogen bombs. To accommodate nuclearism in these ways involved incorporating "state terrorism" into the strategic doctrine of the United States at the highest level, and with an acceptance of its potentially catastrophic results for the entire planet.[24] The disingenuousness of claiming that only deterrence justified the retention and deployment of nuclear weaponry became clear as soon as the Soviet Union collapsed and its successor, Russia, aligned itself with the West. At such a historic moment it would have seemed plausible to explore the prospects for phased disarmament agreements among the nuclear weapons states. The failure to do so was notable, as it also put the United States (and other nuclear weapons states) in material breach of the Non-Proliferation Treaty (NPT), which pledged nuclear weapons states to seek nuclear disarmament in good faith, an understanding of legal duty reinforced a few years ago by the unanimous finding of the International Court of Justice in its historic 1996 Advisory Opinion.[25]

Indeed, the situation is even more disturbing. The U.S. government seems to be exploring an enhanced role for nuclear weapons, given the reduced threat that it could be drawn into a nuclear war. The use of depleted uranium to enhance the penetration of artillery shells and missiles beginning in the Gulf War and continuing in Afghanistan dangerously blurs the firewall between conventional and nuclear weapons, and at its worst can be interpreted as a major step by the U.S. government toward the routinization of nuclear war. Toward the end of 2001, a leaked Pentagon document on the role of nuclear weapons indicated an upgrading of their military relevance that conceived of their use against an adversary that introduced chemical or biological weapons or to reach targets buried underground that could not be destroyed by conventional weaponry. The unifying consensual element in American nuclear weapons policy seems to be perceived military risks and advantages associated with reliance on the weapons. When weaponry that produces state terrorism is available against an enemy, and is seen as likely to be effective, then it will be used without serious moral and legal inhibitions. When such weaponry seems unnecessary, and where the adversary is not a strategic rival, then some measure of restraint may be exercised. The willingness of the Bush administration to move toward normalizing this ultimate form of state terrorism is frightening, and to do this with a seeming disregard for the dangers and opportunities of the global political setting adds further to a perception of irresponsibility.

The accidents of history play a big role in the designation of certain practices as "crimes" and others as "acts of war." It is a virtual certainty that if either Germany or Japan had developed and used an atomic weapon against an Allied city, and then gone on to lose the war, their action would have been treated as a momentous war crime and such weaponry would then have been definitively criminalized, and possibly the world would have been spared the specter of nuclear war. Such speculation is not meant to invalidate the idea of holding officials responsible for crimes of state, but to suggest that the historical outcome of World War II did not allow for an assessment of the most extreme form of state terror associated with American wartime behavior. Furthermore, this scenario is meant to show that, despite the moral pretensions of the victors in that war, no dynamic of self-doubt took hold of the American political imagination with respect to state terrorism, an experience that might have prompted some doubts and even voluntary renunciation of such tactics in the future. Of course, if Germany and Japan had prevailed, there would have been no impulse by their leaders to question their tactics or weaponry, as their embrace of militarism was unchallengeable from within their totalizing structures. The victorious powers, in not holding Germans and Japanese accountable in the war crime trials for bombing civilians, thus implicitly endorsed the principle that the practices of the victors cannot be prosecuted as crimes when they are undertaken by the losers. From the perspective of state terrorism, however, this elemental fairness to individual defendants had the effect of exempting the most serious form of state terrorism from any legal scrutiny in the war crimes process. It was without doubt a jurisprudential dilemma presenting the choice between such an exemption and imposing an extreme variant of victors' justice, that is, a double standard, with respect to this behavior.

Consistent with earlier analysis in this chapter, victors' justice is not primarily a matter of fairness to those accused or even the selective imposition of double standards that erode the authority of the legal process, but a matter of the pedagogy of law with respect to war and peace, which includes retribution for criminality and a hope for reconciliation. Thus to achieve true justice both winners and losers must be treated equally. Victors' justice, in contrast, places the legally dubious practices of the victor in a war beyond the reach of a condemnatory judgment, almost surely ensuring their repetition in future wars, indeed assuring the likelihood of their repetition in even more objectionable forms due to technological advances and more aggressive doctrinal thinking. Such was the case most dramatically with respect to the status of atomic weapons as permissible options in wartime. Although such weapons have not been used subsequently, their development has persisted and their use was threatened when conventional warfare seemed stalemated in the Cold War years. Such threats were made during the Korean and Vietnam wars and in several other settings, including in relation to Cold War tensions periodically arising in the Taiwan Straits.

## The Vietnam War

The Korean War disclosed the difficulty of relying on high-technology weaponry against a Third World country whose people are mobilized for resistance and have the backing of such powerful states as China and the Soviet Union. Massive casualties and unlimited destruction can be inflicted on such an adversary without necessarily achieving victory.[26] State terrorism reached a dead end in Korea. This difficulty of translating military superiority, as measured by modern weaponry, financial resources, and diplomatic leverage into political outcomes became an agonizing challenge in the main Cold War encounters, especially in Asia.[27] It was especially agonizing because of American lives lost in a cause that seemed to lead nowhere, and in the end seemed unnecessary, even given an acceptance of prevailing assumptions about containment of Soviet expansion.

The Vietnam War deepened this experience of geopolitical frustration as unprecedented strategic bombing and naval artillery shelling, tactics of state terrorism, failed to produce victory. As Gabriel Kolko expressed this ugly reality, "the necessary logic of American strategy in Vietnam is to wage war against the entire Vietnamese people, men, women, and children alike, wherever they may be found."

In Vietnam, the American military machine with its firepower edge of between 250:1 and 500:1, quickly ran out of military targets, although heavy B-52 carpet bombing continued to disrupt North Vietnamese logistical supply lines along "the Ho Chi Minh Trail." The "enemy" was everywhere and nowhere, anticipating in important respects, but at a safe distance from the American homeland, the security dilemmas faced by the U.S. government in the aftermath of September 11. New tactics were devised to respond to this challenge being mounted by a Third World nationalist movement in a highly decentralized society, but these invariably were indiscriminate in relation to the civilian population and converted the war into an instance of state terror. Millions of Vietnamese were forcibly relocated to strategic hamlets or to cities in order to deprive the enemy of support in its struggle. The entire war being conducted from Washington was a gigantic effort to break the will of Vietnamese nationalist resistance, and this included the extension of the air war to North Vietnam, where it bombed repeatedly a countryside of villages and small towns that had few large structures other than hospitals, temples, and churches. These tactics and others maintained for more than a decade involved flagrant violations of the laws of war and as a cumulative reality certainly warrant the label "state terrorism." The degree of awareness by government officials in Washington had been documented by the Pentagon late in the war and this was then made available to the public by the unauthorized release of the Pentagon Papers.

In the end, American forms of technological superiority proved no match for Vietnamese resolve, perseverance, and ingenuity. To be sure, the Vietnamese losses were colossal, in the millions, greatly outweighing those sustained by the United States, but it was also evident that "acceptable" levels of state terrorism, given the relatively low stakes of the conflict and the risks of escalation, were not effective against such a determined and capable opponent. At the same time, the United States could find no other way to engage an adversary that enjoyed broad nationalist support, benefited from geographical familiarity and came to realize that the way to fight against a powerful, high-tech, distant enemy was to avoid conventional battlefield situations under almost all circumstances and rely on ambushes, surprise small-unit attacks on isolated outposts, and occasional daring strikes such as the Tet Offensive. (This event finally convinced a significant portion of the American mainstream policy community that the war was being lost, and certainly could not be won at a tolerable cost.)

Of course, it is important to take note of Vietnam's geopolitical assets without which the outcome might have been very different. These assets included the support given to North Vietnam by China and the Soviet Union, which was relevant to the Vietnamese success in several ways: first, the Americans were reluctant to use nuclear weapons or to attack Hanoi and the other main cities in the North because of fears of escalation involving the Soviet Union and China and because the action would be precedent-setting; second, critical military and economic assistance allowed North Vietnam to bear the burdens of war and enabled it to inflict significant damage on the Americans, especially through antiaircraft fire that raised the risks for Americans of attacking heavily defended areas; and third, Soviet and Chinese aid created an important source of countervailing diplomatic power and international public opinion that challenged the American version of the war. At the same time, it was the presumed affinity of North Vietnam for China and the Soviet Union that provided the main American rationale for its intervention in what was essentially a civil war to determine Vietnam's future. The intervention was costly beyond every initial expectation, eventually costing more than 58,000 American lives and billions of dollars, as well as deeply dividing American society. In other words, without the ideological and geopolitical background of the Cold War, it would have been inconceivable that the United States would have intervened in the unresolved colonial war waged by Vietnamese nationalist forces against the French. It was only Cold War factors that led the United States to seek to convert the French defeat in a struggle for the whole of Vietnam into the defense of South Vietnam as a sovereign state that deserved to be defended. Such a defense was linked in the foreign policy mind-set that prevailed in Washington in such abstractions as "falling dominoes" and "extended containment."

To this day, some American defenders of the war complain that the United States did not unleash its full military power: it never bombed Hanoi or tried extensively to destroy the dikes that prevented flooding in the Red River Delta, it never used nuclear weapons and it did not invade North Vietnam with ground forces. Each of these escalations was at one time or another influentially advocated in policy-making circles, but none was accepted by the leadership, either because of doubts about its effectiveness or cost, worries about a domestic or international backlash, concerns about escalations in relation to China and the Soviet Union, or inhibitions relating to tactics that might produce civilian casualties in the hundreds of thousands, if not millions, in a context in which the United States was not directly at risk. In retrospect, it certainly seems likely that limits on the scale and intensity of state terrorism were

influenced by a global structure that was bipolar, that is, associated with the
existence of two superpowers, although of unequal power and influence. Such
a reality contrasts with the current global structure, which rests on a single
imperial superpower, one that has invoked visionary goals to justify war to defeat the evil of terrorism. Of course, the United States during the Cold War invoked visionary goals to validate war against the evil of communism, but it
also qualified such propaganda with a realist recognition that it needed to accept the Soviet Union and China as facts of life. Hence, periodic summits between leaders, arms control agreements, and even periods of reduced tensions
that produced the rhetoric of détente. Such pragmatic accommodation of
America's current adversaries seems strategically unnecessary and diplomati-
cally impossible, and so the strategic thinking associated with post–September
11 warfare can be usefully described as "postrealist."

The Vietnam War exemplified the pattern of reliance on state terror by the
United States in the conduct of warfare during the Cold War era against a
Third World adversary capable of relying on the indigenous population for
support and intelligent enough to avoid military encounters that allowed
high-tech weaponry to inflict decisive damage. Whether military innovations
associated with accurate targeting, night vision, smart munitions, and missiles
would have changed the course of such a war is difficult to assess.

## Conclusion

America's Pacific wars in the twentieth century exhibited in different ways a
reliance on state terrorism. This reliance was generally unappreciated by the
American people, as the message of the leadership was always couched in
terms of an American commitment to a just cause (a standard self-serving
claim of powerful countries), whether the defeat of Japanese imperialism, the
defense of South Korea against North Korean aggression, or the defense of
freedom in South Vietnam, as well as the defense of South Vietnam against aggression from the North. In each of these settings, the United States had dirty
hands due to an involvement with provocative action that set the stage for the
"aggression."[28]

At the same time, it is worth concentrating on the distinctiveness of American aggressive behavior. Of course, all expansionist powers make self-serving
claims about the benefits of their domination. Japanese expansionists claimed
that they were liberating Asian countries from Western imperialism, but their
domination proved to be purely self-serving strategically, economically, and
psychologically. In contrast, America's role simultaneously as an occupier and a
global leader is more complicated and contradictory. The reliance on state

terrorism is unquestionable, but so are the advocacy and promotion of international human rights and constitutional democracy, the contributions to a tradition of international criminal accountability, and the American role in contributing to the economic well-being of countries over which it wields its influence. It is also important that a lively civic tradition of self-criticism has existed within American society that, while subordinate to the self-congratulatory mainstream, still gives rise to a certain critical tension that at times exerts some positive influence on American behavior in wartime situations. The extent of this influence is hard to calculate, but it leads leaders to present their wartime tactics as justifiable from a moral perspective, and this inhibits some policies that might otherwise be implemented (for example, bombing the dikes in the Red River Delta in North Vietnam). To grasp properly the American role in the Pacific wars of the past century, we need to perceive both of these major dimensions, resisting the temptation to present the American impact as either fully destructive or completely positive.

The dark side of state terrorism needs to be comprehended, theorized, and challenged, including its moralizing war myth that was coupled with the dehumanization of the enemy, an emphasis on the atrocities of only the other side, and a propagandistic insistence that responsibility for terror tactics should be attributed to the enemy. While the United States never achieved victory in wars in Korea and Vietnam, its policies were never held to account as were those of the Japanese after World War II. Thus the practices that we have designated state terrorism in these wars, whether strategic bombing, the atomic attacks, or the high-technology ravaging of a low-technology countryside, were never formally challenged or even seriously debated in the United States or internationally. Due to America's hegemonic status and its role in the Cold War as guarantor of Western European security, there was a widespread tendency throughout the noncommunist world to turn a blind eye toward the criminal nature of America's military tactics. Peace militants did convene a variety of people's tribunals and engage in civil disobedience, and thus the story of state terrorism was narrated at the margins of American society and became generally known outside of the United States, although it was rarely described, as it is here, as state terrorism. In the war on terror under way since 9/11, America is again in a situation in which it engages in warfare without accepting the restraining relevance of international law and is thus engaging in practices that need to be understood as state terrorism. The pseudorecourse to the United Nations during the Iraq crisis for the alleged purpose of fulfilling Security Council obligations seems to have been cynically motivated by the hope of building domestic and international support for an American recourse to war that had already been decided upon by the Bush leadership, and that was motivated by other strategic considerations. The analysis offered here suggests that the Bush administration's approach is likely to intensify reliance on state terrorism beneath the banner of antiterrorism, while at the same time the administration renounces the traditional American role as the champion of the rule of law and of international institutions as the means to improve the quality of life for all peoples. It is not an encouraging prospect.

## Notes

I wish to acknowledge with gratitude the exceptional editorial efforts of Mark Selden, which while demanding, definitely made the end result better.

1. See Kennan lectures on foreign policy in George F. Kennan, *American Diplomacy 1900–1950* (Chicago: University of Chicago Press, 1951); also see Henry Kissinger, *Diplomacy* (New York: Simon & Schuster, 1994).

2. For an authoritative presentation of the U.S. government outlook, see *The National Security Strategy of the United States of America* (Washington, D.C.: Office of the President, September 2002).

3. Precisely this option is discussed in Michael Ignatieff, "The Burden," *New York Times Magazine*, January 5, 2003, 22–27, 50–54.

4. Arguably, the Afghanistan War is an exception, with care being taken to minimize civilian casualties and to spare cities from destruction, although not sufficient care to satisfy either critics or the rules of warfare embodied in international law.

5. For a series of essays on U.S. reliance on state terrorism in the setting of the Cold War, see Alexander George, ed., *Western State Terrorism* (London: Routledge, 1991).

6. For a definition of state terrorism, see chapter 1; also see Falk, *Revolutionaries and Functionaries: The Dual Face of Terrorism* (New York: Dutton, 1988), especially 1–10; also see Charles W. Kegley Jr., ed., *The New Global Terrorism: Characteristics, Causes, Controls* (Upper Saddle River, N.J.: Prentice-Hall, 2003).

7. Such an argument is still seriously, although ambiguously, supported by some historians. For instance, Cimbala notes that the U.S. Strategic Bombing Survey conducted after World War II concluded that the Japanese government would probably have surrendered prior to the atomic attacks if offered the terms that were finally imposed, which permitted the emperor to remain in power and not face criminal charges for his role in the war. But Cimbala suggests that such hindsight should not be confused with the perceptions of American leadership during wartime, which supposedly believed that the Japanese would under no circumstances accede to the demand for unconditional surrender. See Stephen J. Cimbala, *The Politics of Warfare: The Great Powers in the Twentieth Century* (University Park: Pennsylvania State University Press, 1997), 38–39.

8. Michael Walzer, *Just and Unjust Wars: A Moral Argument with Historical Illustrations*, 3d ed. (New York: Basic, 2000), 268; Walzer goes on to write in the same passage that "to use the atomic bomb, to kill and terrorize civilians, was a double crime." There were, of course, earlier serious American "crimes of war," most notably the firebomb-

ing of Tokyo that caused an estimated 100,000 deaths, that also adopted the military logic of state terror. Military historians have noted the irony that the German Luft-waffe, despite its capabilities, pursued more restrained strategic bombing patterns than did its British and American counterparts, although it could have probably gained possibly decisive military advantages from an unrestrained bombing of British cities early in World War II. See Ward Thomas, *The Ethics of Destruction: Norms and Force in International Relations* (Ithaca, N.Y.: Cornell University Press, 2001), 144–46. See also Mark Selden, "The Logic of Mass Destruction," in *Hiroshima's Shadow: Writings on the Denial of History and the Smithsonian Controversy,* ed. Kai Bird and Lawrence Lifschultz (Stony Creek, Conn.: Pamphleteer's, 1998).

9. Even in the course of the American Civil War, Abraham Lincoln, the most widely admired of American wartime presidents, assented in 1864 to state terror by endorsing the war plans of the Union generals that called for deliberately attacking Confederate farms, homes, and factories. The justification, never absent in circumstances of warfare, was this: war is Hell, and thus the quickest possible way to peace should be sought. For references, see Robert D. Kaplan, "The Faceless Enemy," *New York Times Book Review,* October 14, 2001. See also Kaplan's *Warrior Politics: Why Leadership Demands a Pagan Ethos* (New York: Random House, 2002).

10. Of course, the earlier colonial experiences of conquest throughout the non-Western world, as well as the violent dispossession of Native Americans in the Indian wars, were notable for the lack of restraint and the absence of reciprocity with respect to war-fighting capabilities. Columbus records in his diary that a single Spanish soldier was the equivalent of one thousand indigenous fighters encountered in the West Indies.

11. This one-sidedness has reached its temporary climax in the American wars of the 1990s, especially the Kosovo war, in which a large-scale air war was sustained for seventy-eight days without the NATO side suffering a single combat death. It was also evident in the almost total absence of American casualties during the main combat phases of the Afghanistan War.

12. This type of technological capability to cause massive casualties has undoubt-edly grown with the passage of time, although primitive methods can produce large-scale slaughters. Such a capacity has been illustrated also in low-technology contexts as in the 1994 massacres in Rwanda of as many as 800,000 people in a matter of a few weeks. It is also true that the spread of advanced weaponry, including nuclear weapons, accentuates the overall danger of catastrophic loss of life in countries throughout the world.

13. As quoted in Geoffrey Best, *War and Law Since 1945* (Oxford: Oxford University Press, 1994), xv. Lauterpacht's statement was made in a 1952 article appearing in the *British Yearbook of International Law.*

14. A compilation of practices deemed in direct violation of the laws of war, as reported in the media, that was endorsed as descriptively reliable by a distinguished panel of American religious leaders. See "Clergy and Laymen Concerned about Vietnam," in *In The Name of America* (Annandale, Va.: Turnpike, 1968). Perhaps, the most notable of such efforts to assess the alleged criminality of American warfare in Vietnam was organized by the British philosopher Bertrand Russell. For the proceedings, see

John Duffett, ed., *Against the Crime of Silence: Proceedings of the Russell International War Crimes Tribunal* (Flanders, N.J.: O'Hare, 1968). Such initiatives make a contribution by documenting some of the legally dubious behavior of the United States and thereby to some slight extent offsetting the one-sidedness of formal statist procedures, including those under the authority of the United Nations. At the same time, these initiatives are themselves vulnerable to countercharges of their own one-sidedness by looking only at the crimes of the United States.

15. It did prosecute and convict some low-ranking military officers for the My Lai massacre, but shielded higher ranking of civilian and military officials from legal accountability. See the series of articles and statements reprinted in Richard A. Falk, Gabriel Kolko, and Robert Jay Lifton, eds., *Crimes of War: A Legal, Political–Documentary, and Psychological Inquiry into the Responsibility of Leaders, Citizens, and Soldiers for Criminal Acts in Wars* (New York: Random House, 1971), 220–55.

16. There are further moral complications arising from assessments of motivation. For instance, resistance to Nazi occupation of European countries was uncritically acclaimed as heroic, even when violence was directed at civilians, and there was never even a whisper of implication that such tactics should be viewed as constituting terrorism. For a sympathetic account of recourse to violent resistance by inhabitants and sects in Judea and Samaria to oppressive Roman rule during the period of Jesus's birth, see Richard A. Horsley, *Jesus and Empire: The Kingdom of God and the New World Disorder* (Minneapolis: Fortress, 2003), especially 40–45.

17. The furor caused by a proposed exhibition at the Smithsonian Institution to commemorate the fiftieth anniversary of the atomic attacks was indicative of the persisting refusal by the American mainstream to accept responsibility for long past state terrorism or even to allow public exposure to the massive and severe human suffering caused. See Edward T. Linenthal and Tom Englehardt, eds., *History Wars: The Enola Gay and Other Battles for the American Past* (New York: Metropolitan, 1996); Robert Jay Lifton and Greg Mitchell, *Hiroshima in America: Fifty Years of Denial* (New York: Putnam, 1995). See also Laura Hein and Mark Selden, eds., *Living with the Bomb: Japanese and American Cultural Conflicts in the Nuclear Age* (Armonk, N.Y.: M. E. Sharpe, 1997).

18. For example, see the important book by Richard H. Minear, *Victors' Justice: The Tokyo War Crimes Tribunal* (Princeton, N.J.: Princeton University Press, 1971).

19. Gary Jonathan Bass, *Stay the Hand of Vengeance: The Politics of War Crimes Tribunals* (Princeton, N.J.: Princeton University Press, 2000), 8–16.

20. Radhabinod Pal, *International Military Tribunal for the Far East: Dissentient Judgement* (Calcutta: Sanyal, 1953). For an insightful analysis of victors' justice from a Japanese perspective, see Yasuaki Onuma, "The Tokyo War Crimes Trial, War Responsibility, and Postwar Responsibility," in *Nanking 1937: Memory and Healing,* ed. Fei Fei Li, Robert Sabella, and David Liu (Armonk, N.Y.: M. E. Sharpe, 2002), 205–235.

21. Compare the approach to the responsibilities of occupation in relation to Afghanistan and Iraq after the Gulf War.

22. See Raymond Aron, *The Century of Total* War (Garden City, N.Y.: Doubleday, 1954). Such a role for strategic bombing then shifted with the advent of the Cold War, and especially as a result of the Soviet acquisition of a nuclear deterrent. In the Asian

wars during the Cold War, the United States, although using its military superiority to devastating effect, refrained from destroying the main enemy cities, and gradually a partial taboo on bombing the civilian population reemerged. Such a taboo was least evident in the conduct of the Korean War, which included heavy bombardment of most North Korean cities. In the Vietnam War, Hanoi was spared from destruction, as was Haiphong to some extent. The impact of the taboo was notable in that in the Gulf War, the Kosovo war, and the Afghanistan War a stress was placed on "smart" bombs and missiles that could focus on military targets, and the U.S. government claimed to be making a special effort to avoid civilian casualties. There is considerable debate about the reasons for this, but what seems clear is that, unlike in World War II, major cities were spared from destruction when the military capabilities to destroy existed and there was no prospect of retaliation.

23. Richard J. Barnet, *Who Wants Disarmament?* (Boston: Beacon, 1960).

24. See Jonathan Schell, *The Fate of the Earth* (New York: Knopf, 1982); Robert Jay Lifton and Richard Falk, *Indefensible Weapons: The Political and Psychological Case against Nuclearism*, rev. ed. (New York: Basic, 1991). See also E. P. Thompson, "Notes on Exterminism: The Last Stage of Civilisation," in *Beyond the Cold War: A New Approach to the Arms Race and Nuclear Annihilation*, ed. E. P. Thompson, 41–79 (New York: Pantheon, 1982).

25. Article VI of the NPT clearly spells out the obligation of nuclear weapons states to seek in good faith to achieve nuclear disarmament by way of international negotiations. In effect, it is impermissible to be a party to the NPT regime and oppose nuclear disarmament, but that is what the U.S. government has done for many years. Other nuclear weapons states are also guilty of this flagrant violation of their treaty obligations. See Richard Falk, "Nuclear Weapons, International Law, and the World Court: A Historic Encounter," *American Journal of International Law* 91, no. 1 (1977): 64–75.

26. See chapter 4 for elaboration on U.S. military tactics in the Korean War.

27. There is some ambiguity surrounding the phrase "military superiority" in these settings. Low-technology societies with the will and capacity to endure devastating losses while inflicting casualties may in the end achieve a stalemate or victory. One characteristic of such wars is their unequal stakes: abstract and contested geopolitical goals on one side, territorial integrity and political independence on the other.

28. For the Korean instance, see chapter 4. As for World War II, the American economic policy of squeezing Japan out of world trade is well established; and in Vietnam, the U.S. role in frustrating the arrangements negotiated with France at the end of First Indochina War in 1954 have been abundantly documented.

# 4

# American Airpower and Nuclear Strategy in Northeast Asia since 1945

## Bruce Cumings

THE CRISES OVER the North Korean nuclear program in 1993–94 and 2002–2003 have served to show just how volatile the Korean peninsula and the Northeast Asian region continue to be, and to underline how little most Americans, from the person in the street to the national commentators, still know about Korea. Another Korean War nearly occurred in June 1994, and another war may still come in the new century as leaders in Washington and Pyongyang contemplate a new state of affairs and new doctrines of national security in the aftermath of the terrorist attacks on September 11, 2001. Almost always, media discussion assumes that Washington is in a position of original innocence and North Korea is assiduously trying to obtain and then to use "weapons of mass destruction"—the ubiquitous media trope for the arsenals of American enemies. Yet the American record in Northeast Asia since the 1940s is one of consistent use of, combined with threats to use, those same weapons. The United States is the only power ever to have used nuclear weapons in anger, at Hiroshima and Nagasaki, and for decades it has consistently based its deterrence on threats to use them again, as in Korea and Vietnam.

The Korean War, which raged from 1950 to 1953, is often called "The Forgotten War" in the United States, but it might better be called the *unknown* war. From the viewpoint of a historian of that war, what is indelible in its history is the extraordinary destructiveness of the American air campaigns against North Korea, ranging from the widespread and continuous use of firebombing, to threats to use nuclear and chemical weapons, and finally to the destruction of huge North Korean dams in the final stages of the war. Yet this history is almost unknown even to most historians, let alone to the average citizen, and it has virtually never been cited in press analysis of the North Korean nuclear problem in the past decade. Instead, almost everyone has assumed that the only nuclear threat involving Korea came from Pyongyang. Korea is also assumed to have been a limited war, but its prosecution bore a strong resemblance to the air war against Imperial Japan in World War II, which was directed by many of the same American military leaders.

In this chapter, I will examine U.S. nuclear and conventional bombing strategy in three periods: the last phase of the Pacific War; the Korean War, 1950–53; and the period 1957–1991, when the United States positioned nuclear weapons in South Korea and drew up plans to use them very early in any new war on the peninsula. If the atomic attacks against Hiroshima and Nagasaki have been examined from many different perspectives, incendiary air attacks against Japanese and Korean cities have received much less attention. Meanwhile, America's post-Korean War airpower and nuclear strategy in Northeast Asia are even less well understood, yet these strategies have dramatically shaped North Korean (and to a lesser extent Chinese) strategic choices, and remain a key factor shaping regional national security strategies today. I will end this chapter by ruminating on morality in warfare, and on American responsibility for the prevalent exterminism of our age.

## An Unjust Ending to a Just War

On the morning of December 7, 1941, with the opening shot at 7:57 A.M., two waves of Japanese bombers, 250 planes in all, destroyed large portions of the American Pacific Fleet at Pearl Harbor (conveniently huddled together to "prevent sabotage") and hit nine airfields elsewhere in the American territory called Hawaii. Nine hours later, more Japanese aircraft hit Clark Field in the Philippines, where MacArthur and his staff inexplicably still had various aircraft gathered together (again to "prevent sabotage"), including two squadrons of valuable B-17D bombers. Total American casualties in the Pearl Harbor raid were 2,335 naval, army, and marine personnel dead and 1,143 wounded. The Americans lost eight battleships, three light cruisers, three destroyers, and four auxiliary craft. Total civilians killed: sixty-eight.[1] The stunning (if Pyrrhic) success of Japan's strategic operation is frequently noted, but few note the precision with which the attack separated soldier and civilian. A counterforce attack directed exclusively at military targets, it had a soldier-to-civilian kill ratio of about thirty-four to one.

Still, in the Clausewitzian sense Pearl Harbor was mere garden-variety aggression, differing little from numerous other military adventures, and therefore does not qualify as a special sort of war crime. Nor was it a bolt from the blue, but the culmination of sharp and intensifying conflict between the United States and Japan. Given the precise targeting and the conduct of the attack, it was certainly not atrocious. The most important corollary is this: Pearl Harbor did not provide sufficient justification for any act of revenge that went beyond compelling the aggressor to surrender.

The U.S.–Japan war was short: as most historians now understand, the die for Japan's defeat was cast in the Pacific at Midway (July 1942) and on land at Guadalcanal (December 1942). *How* the war would end (if not when) was visible within six months to a year of Pearl Harbor: Japan was going to lose. From that quick denouement, we arrive at an important juncture: the war would end soon enough with an American victory, and so the point of moral leadership would be not to use every element of power at hand to bring about surrender. This aspect of the U.S.–Japan war—after Guadalcanal, a contest of unequals—poses another element of justice in warfare. As Friedrich Nietzsche, a great student of power, said "Equality before the enemy: the first presupposition of an *honest* duel. Where one feels contempt, one *cannot* wage war; where one commands, where one sees something beneath oneself, one has no business waging war."[2]

Jean Bethke Elshtain finds in Nietzsche's teaching a "refusal to bring all one's power to bear," and thus an argument against revenge. As Hannah Arendt understood, this was also Christ's radical teaching—"freedom from vengeance, which encloses both doer and sufferer in the relentless automatism of the action process."[3] The renunciation of power, of course, is a principle also enshrined in Japan's *bushido* tradition;[4] but here we are talking about American responsibility for *jus in bello* (justice in warfare), for the *conduct* of a Good War. As Michael Walzer argues over and over, "war is always judged twice," first by its ends and second by its means. Good wars can be fought unjustly and bad wars can be fought justly.[5] Being a victim of aggression does not absolve the victim of responsibilities for civilized warfare.

## Hurricanes of Fire

Baptisms come by fire and water, but according to time-honored mythology humans are tried and judged only by fire. Los Angeles has always had too much of the capricious elements, fire and wind, and not enough of the propitiating other: water. And so it sits poised on catastrophe, violating the Confucian middle way, the composed balance that regulates life. In the months after Pearl Harbor, there were rumors and alarms about Japanese air raids on West Coast cities. Let us imagine Los Angeles in the midst of a prolonged heat wave, no rain for weeks, the lawns and the hillsides parched and dead, the dense and ubiquitous chaparral fire plants at their most combustible, and the red wind howling through the mountain passes from the desert. Suddenly, 334 bombers appear in the distance, their motors droning in unison, their bellies full of bombs, the bombs full of jellied gasoline, phosphorous, magnesium, and napalm. The bombers come in low, at six thousand feet, conscious of the prevailing winds and the turbulence of the Los Angeles basin. Suddenly the entire city is put to the torch; the atmospheric conditions are such that the two thousand tons of incendiaries create wild firestorms, fire hurricanes, that course back and forth across the city:

> The wind had whipped hundreds of small fires into great walls of flame, which began leaping streets, firebreaks, and canals at dizzying speed.[6]

> Under the wind and the gigantic breath of fire, immense incandescent vortices rose in a number of places, swirling, flattening, sucking whole blocks of houses into their maelstrom of fire.[7]

> [T]he conflagration . . . was rapaciously expansive, a pillar of fire that was pushed over by the surface winds to touch the ground and gain new fury from the oxygen and combustibles it seized.[8]

Wind- and fire-driven temperatures as high as 1,800 degrees Fahrenheit send Angelenos running toward the river basins, but they are dry. So they then flock to the coast for relief, but the Pacific is salt to their wounds:

> A woman spent the night knee-deep in the bay, holding onto a piling with her three-year-old son clinging to her back; by morning several of the people around her were dead of burns, shock, fatigue and hypothermia. Thousands submerged themselves in stagnant, foul-smelling canals with their mouths just above the surface, but many died from smoke inhalation, anoxia, or carbon monoxide poisoning, or were boiled to death with the fire storm heated water.[9]

It was of course Tokyo, not Los Angeles, that experienced the *akakaze* or "red winds" on March 9–10, 1945; sixty-five more cities would be razed before the war ended, but none with the hurricane and tornado force of air force commander Curtis LeMay's pyromania on that night. Napalm might have been made just for the wooden houses that are all densely packed throughout the city. Sixteen square miles of a densely populated, modern city burned, leaving at least 100,000 dead and a like or greater number injured—often cruelly and horribly so.[10] More than one million people were forced to flee the city when their homes were destroyed.

In a recent book, *On the Natural History of Destruction,* W. G. Sebald writes of a clinical autopsy report on the mummified victims of intense firebombing in Hamburg: "Depending on the dryness of the joints, heads and extremities could frequently be broken off without difficulty. . . . [However] organs which were in an advanced state of autolysis or had been completely hardened by the effects of the heat were usually difficult to cut with the knife; decomposing, cheesy, claylike, buttery, or charred-crumbly masses of tissue or organ residues were broken, torn, crumbled or plucked apart."[11]

What would the American people have felt then—or today—if Tokyo or Hamburg had been Los Angeles? Would they be forgiving? Would they offer to a Japanese counterpart of LeMay the American equivalent of the Japanese medal LeMay received in Tokyo on December 6, 1964, the First Class of the Rising Sun?[12] Would they call this man-made inferno a war crime? With his dull wit, utter absence of reflective mind, crude racism,[13] and mindless devotion to the use of every weapon put at his disposal, LeMay was a classic representative of Clausewitz's "blind instinct" and Hannah Arendt's "banality of evil." To put it simply, LeMay's *akakaze* was an atrocity, a war crime.

At 8:15 A.M. on August 6, 1945, the American B-29 Superfortress *Enola Gay* swooped down over Hiroshima and released a uranium 235 bomb weighing eight thousand pounds that burst over the city at a height of 580 meters. Within one millionth of a second the billowing fireball reached several million degrees centigrade:

> Thereafter, with the movement of the shock front, or wave, a tremendous pressure rapidly builds up, and the fireball now consists of two concentric regions—an inner hot region and an outer region of somewhat lower temperature. For some time the fireball continues to expand, but the shock spreads more rapidly. With the spread of the shock front, the temperature of the air surrounding the fireball rises and becomes luminous.

Whereas LeMay had to concentrate large numbers of incendiaries to create a firestorm, the atomic bomb caused an immense volume of hyperhot air to spiral upward, a cataclysmic "black wind" funneling the evaporated human and material substance of Hiroshima into a terrible void at the center, hurling it skyward while bringing cold air flushing in from all directions behind and below it. This fresh oxygen fueled the firestorm, which blew for hours in the city, with velocities of eighteen meters per second. The fireball of a conventional incendiary bomb would burn or blow away wooden houses within forty meters of the epicenter. The Hiroshima bomb, deploying a force equivalent to 12.5 kilotons of TNT, did the same thing at a radius of two kilometers, destroying a total of about thirteen square kilometers. Starting from about

11 A.M., a violent whirlwind blew northward through the city from the epi-center that calmed down only by the late afternoon.

Meanwhile, amid the firestorms, about an hour after the blast an ominous, highly radioactive "black rain" began to fall on the northern and western neighborhoods of Hiroshima that was composed of minute particles of the evaporated city—carbonized wood, flesh, and bone. The dreadful drops fell for another five hours, leading not a few to assume that the heavens wept for the dead of Hiroshima. Those who were far enough away to survive the blast now witnessed a march of the walking dead, as silent people with no faces filed by, trying to escape to the hills (there might be another bomb) or find water. "Great sheets of skin had peeled away from their tissues to hang down like rags on a scarecrow."[14] This single uranium 235 bomb killed 80,000 people initially, followed by another 100,000 who died in succeeding months and years. It also left scores of thousands to live with the ravages and fears of ra-dioactivity and heavy burns and wounds that they would bear throughout their lives.

Three days later, at 11:00 A.M. on August 9, the B-29 nicknamed *Bock's Car* appeared over Nagasaki, with a bombardier named Kermit Beahan sitting in the Plexiglas nose of the plane. It was his twenty-seventh birthday. He released a plutonium 239 bomb called "the Fat Man," weighing nine thousand pounds, over the city. The bomb took forty seconds to fall one and a half miles under a parachute to its point of detonation, five hundred meters above a Catholic cathedral. This bomb nearly doubled the force of the first atomic bomb at an equivalent to twenty-two kilotons of TNT. But it created a smaller firestorm, because the blast direction carried it through the north of the Nagasaki valley, where there was a lower density of population and housing. About twenty minutes after the explosion, more black rain fell, now on the Nishiyama neighborhood east of the Nagasaki epicenter.[15]

At the Junshin School that morning, a nun led the girls in chanting psalms, honoring twenty-six Catholic martyrs who had died centuries earlier. They all perished in the Nagasaki firestorm, leading Nagai Takashi to write,

Virgins like lilies white
Disappeared burning red
In the flames of the holocaust
Chanting psalms
To the Lord.[16]

About 30,000 people died in the first minutes after the blast, and 44,000 more perished later of wounds, burns, or radiation poisoning.

It has now become commonplace to argue for a kind of mindless reflex in the use of atomic bombs against Hiroshima and Nagasaki: the automaticity of an unthinking, inexorable follow-on to the strategic bombing begun by Hitler's Luftwaffe over London, then adopted by London and Washington to punish German cities and culminating in the firestorms of Dresden and Tokyo.[17] To most people and to many historians, the burden of a historian is first and foremost to be a custodian of "the facts," and once they are "found," to let the facts "speak for themselves." That this is an epistemologically naïve notion does not stop people—including historians—from believing it.[18] Knowing what we know now, Hiroshima and perhaps especially Nagasaki cannot be looked at from the innocent perspective of the facts, because the facts they find keep reporting back that, whatever one may say about "automaticity," these devilish bombs were not necessary to get a quick Japanese surrender. Or they tell us that hundreds of thousands of innocent civilians perished to save tens of thousands of invading combatants, something that does not find a justification in just war (or good war) doctrine.

Of course there is still much controversy among the historians over these decisions,[19] but the consensus, as given by a moderate and mainstream historian (J. Samuel Walker), is that the official story of Truman's decision to use the atomic bomb—that it was done to save American lives, an argument presented to the public in the first instance by none other than Henry Stimson in a famous *Harper's* article in 1947—is wrong. "The United States did not drop the bomb to save hundreds of thousands of American lives," Walker writes. The number of lives that might be lost in an invasion of Japan set to commence with the island of Kyushu in November, according to military estimates from the time, was around 25,000—not the half million to one million that Stimson and Truman later claimed. Nor did the bombs end the war: "The scholarly consensus holds that the war would have ended within a relatively short time without the atomic attacks and that an invasion of the Japanese islands was an unlikely possibility."[20]

The consensus also extends to the second bomb, the plutonium device detonated over Nagasaki. Martin Sherwin's 1975 book contains evidence that the Nagasaki bomb made a gratuitous contribution to the end of the war at best, and was genocidal at worst. Although Nagasaki does not draw the attention that Hiroshima does, it is fair to say that most historians now agree with Sherwin.[21] There is a doubly and triply unsettling element about Nagasaki, however, and that is the city's location and history. This is the port city through which "Dutch learning" first came, thus it is the site of the beginning of Japan's modernization and Westernization. A diverse trading city situated at the nexus of Japan's connection to the world during the Tokugawa isolation of 1600 to 1868, it was home to various heterodoxies less tolerated in other places in Japan; it was home also to many Christians, the one shining success for Christian missionaries in a nation otherwise impervious to proselytism. To imagine all this going up in the swirling black wind of August 9, from a bomb gratuitous to the war effort or any other clear purpose, exploded above the red domes of the Catholic cathedral at Urakami, long claimed to be the most splendid church in East Asia, is really too much to contemplate.

## Korea, "The Limited War"

Five years after Hiroshima and Nagasaki, a major war again raged in Northeast Asia. And it is now clear that from the first days of the Korean War, Washington contemplated the use of atomic weapons in what historians like to call this "limited" war. Moreover, this civil war, prepared long before the ostensible "start" in June 1950 and continuing today, became the predicate for one of the few cases of extended nuclear deterrence against nonnuclear powers: that is, U.S. actions directed against China, until it developed its own atomic bombs in the mid-1960s, and North Korea, which in the 1990s may or may not have developed an atomic capability.

On July 9, 1950—a mere two weeks into the war, it is worth remembering—the United Nations commander, General Douglas MacArthur, sent General Matthew Ridgway a "hot message" that prompted the Joint Chiefs of Staff (JCS) "to consider whether or not A-bombs should be made available to MacArthur." General Charles Bolte, chief of operations, was asked to talk to MacArthur about using atomic bombs "in direct support [of] ground combat"; some ten to twenty bombs could be spared for the Korean theater, Bolte thought, without "unduly" jeopardizing American global war capabilities. Bolte got back from MacArthur an early suggestion for the tactical use of atomic weapons and an indication of MacArthur's extraordinary ambitions for the war, which included occupying the North and handling potential Chinese—or Soviet—intervention as follows: "I would cut them off in North Korea. In Korea I visualize a cul-de-sac. The only passages leading from Manchuria and Vladivostok have many tunnels and bridges. I see here a unique use for the atomic bomb—to strike a blocking blow—which would require a six months repair job. Sweeten up my B-29 force." At this point in the war, however, the JCS rejected use of the bomb because targets sufficiently large to require atomic weapons were lacking, because of concerns about world opinion five years after Hiroshima, and because the JCS expected the tide of battle to be reversed by conventional military means.[22] Of course, some also worried about Soviet or Chinese reactions and the moral dimensions of the United States again using atomic weapons against Asian peoples. That calculus changed, however, when large numbers of Chinese troops entered the war in October and November of 1950.

At a famous news conference on November 30, President Truman implicitly threatened use of the atomic bomb, saying the United States might use any weapon in its arsenal;[23] it was a threat based on contingency planning to use the bomb, rather than the faux pas so many assumed it to be. On this same day, air force general Edward Stratemeyer sent an order to General Hoyt Vandenberg that the Strategic Air Command should be put on warning, "to be prepared to dispatch without delay medium bomb groups to the Far East. . . . [T]his augmentation should include atomic capabilities." Air force general Curtis LeMay remembered correctly that the JCS had earlier concluded that atomic weapons would probably not be useful in Korea, except as part of "an overall atomic campaign against Red China." But, if these orders were now being changed because of the entry of Chinese forces into the war, LeMay wanted the job: he told Stratemeyer that his headquarters was the only one with the experience, technical training, and "intimate knowledge" of delivery methods. The man who directed the firebombing of Tokyo in March 1945 was again ready to proceed to the Far East to direct the attacks.[24]

British prime minister Clement Atlee sensed that Truman was serious about using the bomb, and amid "grave perturbation" in London he left immediately for Washington. He knew that the United States had a strong advantage in atomic weaponry over the Soviets at this time, possessing at least 450 weapons to the Soviets 25. There was general disagreement between the British and American representatives in several days of meetings. According to British Foreign Office records, the Americans pushed for a "limited war" against China, including air attacks, a blockade of the coast, and covert introduction of anticommunist forces in southern China; General George Marshall, however, expressed doubts about the "efficacy and success" of such a program. Atlee sought a written promise that the bomb would not be used in Korea, but Truman would only give him oral assurances that it would not. Atlee told the French prime minister that he thought American threats to use the bomb would suggest that "Europeans and Americans have a low regard for the value of Asiatic lives," and that such weapons should be reserved only for times when "desperate measures" were warranted—"certainly not [in] a conflict in which the U.S. were confronted with a Power like Korea."[25]

A short while later (on December 9), MacArthur said that he wanted commander's discretion to use atomic weapons in the Korean theater, and on December 24 he submitted "a list of retardation targets" for which he said that he required twenty-six atomic bombs. He also wanted four to drop on the "invasion forces" and four more for "critical concentrations of enemy air power." In interviews published posthumously, MacArthur said he had a plan that would have won the war in ten days: "I would have dropped between 30 and 50 atomic bombs . . . strung across the neck of Manchuria"; then he would have introduced half a million Chinese Nationalist troops at the Yalu, and then, "spread behind us—from the Sea of Japan to the Yellow Sea—a belt of radioactive cobalt, . . . [which] has an active life of between 60 and 120 years. For at least 60 years there could have been no land invasion of Korea from the North." He expressed certainty that the Russians would have done nothing about this extreme strategy: "my plan was a cinch."[26]

Cobalt 60 has 320 times the radioactivity of radium. One four-hundred-ton cobalt H-bomb, historian Carroll Quigley wrote, could wipe out all animal life on earth. MacArthur sounds like a warmongering lunatic in these interviews, but if so he was not alone. Before the Sino–Korean offensive, a committee of the JCS had said that atomic bombs might be the "decisive factor" in cutting off a Chinese advance into Korea; initially they could be useful in "a 'cordon sanitaire' [that] might be established by the U.N. in a strip in Manchuria immediately north of the Manchurian border." A few months later, Congressman Albert Gore complained that "Korea has become a meat grinder of American manhood," and suggested "something cataclysmic" to end the war: a radiation belt dividing the Korean peninsula. Although General Ridgway said nothing about a cobalt bomb, after replacing MacArthur as the U.S. commander in Korea in May 1951 he renewed MacArthur's request of December 24, this time for thirty-eight atomic bombs.[27] The request was not approved.

The United States came closest to using atomic weapons in early April 1951, precisely at the time when Truman removed MacArthur. Although much related to this episode is still highly classified, it is now clear that Truman did not remove MacArthur simply because of his repeated insubordination, but because he wanted a reliable commander on the scene should Washington decide to use nuclear weapons: that is, Truman traded MacArthur for his atomic policies. On March 10, 1951, MacArthur asked for a "'D' Day atomic capability" to retain air superiority in the Korean theater, after the Chinese massed huge new forces near the Korean border and after the Soviets moved thirteen air divisions to the vicinity of Korea and put two hundred Soviet bombers into air bases in Manchuria (from which they could strike not just Korea but also American bases in Japan). On April 5, the JCS ordered immediate atomic retaliation against Manchurian bases if large numbers of new troops came into the fighting or, it appears, if bombers were launched against American assets from there. On that same day Gordon Dean, chairman of the Atomic Energy Commission, began arrangements for transferring nine Mark IV nuclear capsules to the air force's 9th Bomb Group, the designated carrier for atomic weapons.

The main atomic capsule or core[28] available to the United States in early 1951 was the Mark IV. The Mark IV could be fitted with one of three nuclear cores, yielding a blast range equivalent to twenty to forty kilotons of TNT, depending on which core was used. In other words, the Mark IV in its smallest version was the equivalent of the Hiroshima bomb.[29]

General Omar Bradley (the JCS chairman) got Truman's approval to transfer the Mark IVs "from AEC to military custody" on April 6, and the president signed an order to use them against Chinese and North Korean targets. The 9th Air Force Group deployed out to Guam. "In the confusion attendant upon General MacArthur's removal," however, Truman's order was never sent. Why was Truman's order never implemented? The reasons were two: Truman had used this extraordinary crisis to get the JCS to approve MacArthur's removal (something Truman announced on April 11) and the Chinese did not dramatically escalate the war. So the bombs were not used.[30]

The Joint Chiefs again considered the use of nuclear weapons in Korea in June 1951, this time in tactical battlefield circumstances,[31] and there were many more such suggestions as the war continued to 1953. Robert Oppenheimer, former director of the Manhattan Project, went to Korea as part of Project Vista, which was designed to gauge the feasibility of the tactical use of atomic weapons.[32] Perhaps the most daunting and terrible nuclear project that the United States ran in Korea was Operation Hudson Harbor. This appears to have been part of a larger project involving "overt exploitation in Korea by the Department of Defense and covert exploitation by the Central Intelligence Agency of the possible use of novel weapons." Operation Hudson Harbor sought to establish the capability to use atomic weapons on the battlefield, and in pursuit of this goal lone B-29 bombers were lifted from Okinawa in September and October 1951 (while being controlled from an American air base in Japan) and sent over North Korea on simulated atomic bombing runs, dropping "dummy" A-bombs or heavy TNT bombs. The project called for "actual functioning of all activities which would be involved in an atomic strike, including weapons assembly and testing, leading, ground control of bomb aiming," and the like. The results indicated that the bombs were probably not useful, for purely technical reasons: "timely identification of large masses of enemy troops was extremely rare."[33] But one may imagine the steel nerves required of leaders in Pyongyang, observing a lone B-29 simulating the attack lines that had resulted in the devastation of Hiroshima and Nagasaki just five years earlier, each time unsure of whether the bomb was real or a dummy.

The declassified record also shows that American commanders considered the massive use of chemical weapons against Sino–North Korean forces. In penciled diary notes written on December 16, 1950, Ridgway referred cryptically to a subcommittee on "clandestine introduction [of] wea[pon]s of mass destruction and unconventional warfare"; I know nothing more about this item, but it may refer to Ridgway's request to MacArthur that chemical weapons be used in Korea. Ridgway's original telegram is unavailable, but MacArthur's reply on January 7, 1951, read as follows: "I do not believe there is any chance of using chemicals on the enemy in case [American] evacuation is ordered. As you know, U.S. inhibitions on such use are complete and drastic." In the transcript of a conference held the next day with General Almond and others, Ridgway is recorded as saying, "If we use gas we will lay ourselves open to retaliation. This question has been taken up with General MacArthur for decision. We have requested sufficient quantities to be shipped immediately in the event use of gas is approved."[34]

Without the use of "novel weapons"—although napalm was very new at the time, having been introduced just at the end of World War II, and although unprecedentedly big conventional bombs were dropped during the war—the air war nonetheless leveled North Korea and killed millions of civilians before the war ended. Before the Chinese entry into the war, the best evidence of the destructiveness of this air campaign is to be found in personal observations of the war. Reginald Thomson, a British journalist, provided an unforgettable account of the nature of this war in his much-neglected eyewitness account, *Cry Korea.*

Thomson was sickened by the carnage of the American air war, with the latest machined military might used against "an almost unarmed enemy, unable to challenge the aircraft in the skies." In September 1950, he wrote, "handfuls of peasants defied the immense weight of modern arms with a few rifles and carbines and a hopeless courage . . . and brought down upon themselves and all the inhabitants the appalling horror of jellied petrol bombs." Every enemy shot, he said, "released a deluge of destruction. Every village and township in the path of war was blotted out." In such warfare, "the slayer needs merely touch a button, and death is on the wing, blindly blotting out the remote, the unknown people, holocausts of death, veritable mass productions of death, spreading an abysmal desolation over whole communities."

The Chinese entry into the war caused an immediate escalation of the air campaign. From early November 1950 onward, MacArthur ordered that a wasteland be created between the fighting front and the Chinese border, destroying from the air every "installation, factory, city, and village" over thousands of square miles of North Korean territory. On November 8, seventy B-29s dropped 550 tons of incendiary bombs on the Sino–Korean border city of Sinûiju, "removing [it] from off the map"; a week later Hoeryông was hit with napalm "to burn out the place." By November 25, "a large part of [the] North West area between Yalu River and southwards to enemy lines . . . [was] more or less burning." Soon the area would be a "wilderness of scorched earth."[35]

This was all before the major Sino–Korean offensive that cleared northern Korea of UN forces. When that began, the air force on December 14–15 hit Pyongyang with seven hundred five-hundred-pound bombs—napalm dropped from Mustang fighters—and 175 tons of delayed-fuse demolition bombs, which landed with a thud and then blew up at odd moments, when people were trying to rescue the dead from the napalm fires. At the beginning of January, Ridgway again ordered the air force to hit the capital, Pyongyang, "with the goal of burning the city to the ground with incendiary bombs" (in two strikes that occurred on January 3 and 5). At about the same time, American B-29s dropped "tarzon" bombs on the town of Kanggye, where the Kim Il Sung leadership was bunkered; the tarzon was an enormous new twelve-thousand-pound bomb that had never been used before. As Americans retreated below the parallel, the scorched-earth policy of "torching" continued, burning Ŭijŏngbu, Wŏnju, and other small cities in the South as the enemy drew near them.[36] Even Winston Churchill, late in the war, was moved to tell Washington that when napalm was invented in the latter stages of World War II no one contemplated that it would be "splashed" all over a civilian population.[37]

By 1952, just about everything in northern and central Korea was completely leveled. What was left of the population survived in caves, the North Koreans creating an entire life underground, in complexes of dwellings, schools, hospitals, and factories. In spite of World War II, bombing studies showing that such attacks against civilian populations only stiffened enemy resistance, American officials sought to use aerial bombing as a type of psychological and social warfare. As Robert Lovett later put it, "If we keep on tearing the place apart, we can make it a most unpopular affair for the North Koreans. We ought to go right ahead."[38] The Americans did go right ahead and, in the final act of this barbaric air war, hit huge irrigation dams that provided water for 75 percent of the North's food production.

On June 20, 1953, the *New York Times* announced the execution of alleged Soviet spies Julius and Ethel Rosenberg at Sing Sing Prison. In the fine print of daily war coverage in the *Times,* the U.S. Air Force reported that its planes had bombed dams at Kusŏng and Tŏksan in North Korea—and in even finer print the North Korean radio acknowledged "great damage" to these large reservoirs. By this time, agriculture was the only major element of the Korean economy that was still functioning; the attacks came just after the backbreaking work of rice transplantation had been done in the spring of 1953. The air force was proud of the destruction it wrought: "The subsequent flash flood scooped clean 27 miles of valley below, and the plunging flood waters wiped out [supply routes, etc.]. . . . The Westerner can little conceive the awesome meaning which the loss of [rice] has for the Asian—starvation and slow death." Many villages were inundated, "washed downstream," and even Pyongyang, some twenty-seven miles south of one dam, was badly flooded. According to the official air force history, when the high containing wall of the Tôksan Reservoir collapsed, the onrushing flood destroyed six miles of railway, five bridges, two miles of highway, and five square miles of rice paddies. After the war it took 200,000 man-days of labor to reconstruct the reservoir. The Pujôn River dam was also hit. It had been built in 1932 and was designed to hold 670 million meters of water; the dam station generated 200,000 kilowatts of electrical capacity from the collected water, which then flowed down into rice paddies for irrigation.[39]

There is no record of how many peasants perished in the assault on this and several other dams, but they were assumed to be "loyal" to the enemy, providing "direct support to the Communist armed forces" (that is, they were feeding the northern population). The "lessons" adduced from this experience "gave the enemy a sample of the totality of war . . . embracing the whole of a nation's economy and people."[40] In fact this was a war crime, recognized as such by international law; in the latter stages of World War II, American leaders had declined to bomb agriculture dams and dikes in Holland, precisely because they knew it to be a war crime.

Hungarian Tibor Meray had been a correspondent in North Korea during the war when he left Budapest for Paris after his participation in the 1956 rebellion against communism. When a London television team interviewed him in 1986, he said that however brutal Koreans on either side might have been in this war, "I saw destruction and horrible things committed by the American forces: "Everything which moved in North Korea was a military target, peasants in the fields often were machine gunned by pilots who I, this was my impression, amused themselves to shoot the targets which moved." Meray had crossed the Yalu in August 1951 and witnessed "a complete devastation between the Yalu River and the capital," Pyongyang. There were simply "no more cities in North Korea." The incessant, indiscriminate bombing forced his party always to drive by night: "We travelled in moonlight, so my impression was that I am travelling on the moon, because there was only devastation. . . . [E]very city was a collection of chimneys. I don't know why houses collapsed and chimneys did not, but I went through a city of 200,000 inhabitants and I saw thousands of chimneys and that—that was all."[41] This was Korea, "the limited war." We may leave as an epitaph for this unrestrained air war the views of its architect, General Curtis LeMay. After the war started, he said:

We slipped a note kind of under the door into the Pentagon and said, "Look, let us go up there . . . and burn down five of the biggest towns in North Korea—and they're not very big—and that ought to stop it." Well, the answer to that was four or five screams—"You'll kill a lot of non-combatants," and "It's too horrible." Yet over a period of three years or so . . . we burned down *every* [sic] town in North Korea and South Korea, too.

## Atomic Diplomacy in Korea, 1957 to the Present

Unfortunately, Korea's nuclear history did not stop with the war's termination. Four years after the fighting ended, the United States introduced nuclear weapons into South Korea, in violation of the 1953 armistice agreement that prohibited the introduction of qualitatively new weaponry. It maintained a variety of atomic weapons in South Korea until 1991, and thereafter continued to plan for the use of nuclear weapons in any new war on the peninsula.

The United States took this drastic step primarily to stabilize the volatile civil war. In 1953, the president of South Korea (or Republic of Korea, ROK), Syngman Rhee, had opposed any armistice settlement, refused to sign the agreement when it was made, and frequently threatened to reopen the war. In November 1953, Vice President Richard Nixon visited Korea "and sought to extract written assurances from President Rhee 'that he is not going to start the war up again on the gamble that he can get us involved in his effort to unite Korea by force.'" Nixon got no such written assurance, but in the absence of it the American commander was directed, in a highly secret annex circulated to only a few American leaders, to secure "prompt warning of any decision by Rhee to order an attack" and to prevent its issuance or receipt by ROK Army (ROKA) field commanders.[42] (The implication, of course, was that American intelligence would monitor activity in the presidential mansion and intercept new orders for war.)

In spite of being hamstrung in this way, Rhee well knew that there were Americans who supported his provocative behavior—critically placed people who advocated the use of nuclear weapons—should the war be reignited and the act clearly laid at the communist door. Among them was Chairman of the JCS Admiral Radford, who at a conference between the State and Defense departments in September 1956 had "bluntly stated the military intention to introduce atomic warheads into Korea."

On January 14, 1957, the National Security Council (NSC) Planning Board, at the instruction of President Eisenhower, "prepared an evaluation of four alternative military programs for Korea." A key question was "the kinds of nuclear-capable weapons to be introduced, and the question of storage of nuclear warheads in Korea." In the ensuing six months of discussions, Secretary of State John Foster Dulles agreed with the Joint Chiefs of Staff that such weapons should be sent to Korea. There were two problems, however: the armistice agreement and Syngman Rhee.

A subparagraph in the agreement (section 13d) restricted both sides from introducing new types of weapons into the Korean theater. Radford simply wanted unilaterally to suspend 13d, since in his view it could not be "interpreted" to allow nuclear weapons. Dulles, however, conditioned his support of the JCS proposal on the provision of "publishable evidence confirming Communist violations of the armistice sufficient to justify such action to our Allies and before the UN." The problem was that the "publishable evidence" was not satisfactory, because the communist side had not seriously violated section 13d. It had introduced new jet aircraft, but so had the United States, and neither innovation was considered a radical upgrading of capabilities. Nuclear weapons were quite a different matter. This bothered the British, but the United States went ahead in spite of its worries and in June 1957 relieved itself of its 13d obligations.[43]

But there remained the problem of Syngman Rhee. Unverified intelligence reports in February 1955 "spoke of meetings in which Rhee told Korean military and civilian leaders to prepare for military actions against North Korea." In October came reports that he had ordered plans for the retaking of Kaesông and the Ongjin Peninsula, firmly in North Korean territory since the armistice, and in 1956 came more alarms and diversions. Meanwhile, unbeknownst to Rhee, the Eisenhower administration in August 1957 had approved NSC 5702/2, a major revision of Korea policy that approved the stationing of nuclear weapons in Korea and, in what one official called "a small change," allowed for the possibility of "U.S. support for a unilateral ROK military initiative in response to a mass uprising, Hungarian style, in North Korea."[44] This is an amazing statement. It may have been a response to rumors at the time that a North Korean general had tried to defect across the demilitarized zone (DMZ) with his whole division in tow, or it may merely have been a harbinger of the thinking that subsequently led to the Bay of Pigs fiasco in Cuba (i.e., a small provocation might touch off a general uprising against communism). It was, however, exactly what Rhee and his allies were looking for; who knows if they got wind of it, but John Foster Dulles certainly did.

Dulles was the man, it will be remembered, who famously eyeballed Kim Il Sung across the 38th parallel a week before the war started. He appears to have spent the rest of his life with unsettling whispers from that sudden Sunday, as if Banquo's ghost were shaking his gory locks. At an NSC meeting in 1954, he worried that the North might start the war up again—and in a rather creative fashion: "[Dulles] thought it quite possible that the Communists would launch their attack by infiltrating ROK units and staging an attack on the Communist lines in order to make it appear as though hostilities had been started on ROK initiative."[45] At several other high-level meetings, Dulles worried aloud that, if a war started in Korea, the United States would not be able to determine who had started it, and that Rhee might be the one to do so. At the 168th meeting of the NSC in October 1953, Dulles had warned that "all our efforts" must be to forestall a resumption of war by Rhee. In 1957, at the 332nd meeting, he still worried that Rhee might "start a war"; two weeks later, it was clear that "If war were to start in Korea . . . it was going to be very hard indeed to determine which side had begun the war."[46]

It is in this context that Dulles lent his agreement to the JCS desire to place nuclear weapons in Korea. Pursuing the civil war deterrent that Dean Acheson had applied to Korea before the war, he wanted to restrain both sides. Hotheads such as Rhee and Kim Il Sung would think twice before starting a war that would rain nuclear destruction on the peninsula. Rhee had not shrunk from advocating the use of the H-bomb to have his way; he shocked even his Republican supporters by calling for its use in an address to a joint session of Congress in 1954. But Dulles's nukes would be kept under exclusive American control and would be used only in the event of a massive and uncontainable North Korean invasion.

In January 1958, the United States positioned 280 mm nuclear cannons and Honest John nuclear-tipped missiles in South Korea, and a year later the air force "permanently stationed a squadron of nuclear-tipped Matador cruise missiles in Korea." With a range of 1,100 kilometers, the Matadors were aimed at China and the USSR as well as North Korea.[47] By the mid-1960s, Korean defense strategy was pinned on routine plans to use nuclear weapons very early in any new war. As a 1967 Pentagon war game script put it, "The twelve ROKA and two U.S. divisions in South Korea had . . . keyed their defense plans almost entirely to the early use of nuclear weapons." In January 1968, the North Koreans seized the U.S. spy ship *Pueblo,* capturing the crew and keeping it in prison for eleven months. "[T]he initial reaction of American decisionmakers was to drop a nuclear weapon on Pyongyang. . . . [T]he fact that all the U.S. F-4 fighter planes held on constant alert on Korean airfields were loaded only with nuclear weapons did not help the leaders to think clearly."[48]

U.S. atomic demolition mines (ADM) were also deployed in South Korea, and were designed "to contaminate an advance area and to stop an armored attack," as one ADM engineer put it. ADMs weighed only sixty pounds and yet had a twenty kiloton explosive force: "you could get two weeks worth of contamination out of it so that an area was impassable."[49] The ADMs were moved around in jeeps and placed by special teams who carried them in backpacks; meanwhile U.S. helicopters, as the *Washington Post* pointed out in 1974, routinely flew nuclear weapons near the DMZ. That one of them might stray across the DMZ during a training exercise (as a small reconnaissance helicopter did in December 1994) and give Pyongyang an atomic bomb was a constant possibility.

In 1991, I heard a high-level, retired general and former commander of U.S. forces in Korea give an off-the-record presentation of U.S. strategy as it had developed by the 1980s:

1. The United States planned to use tactical nuclear weapons in the very early stages of a new Korean conflict, at "H + 1," or within one hour of the

outbreak of war, if large masses of North Korean troops were attacking south of the DMZ. This he contrasted with the established strategy in Europe, which was to delay an invasion with conventional weapons and then use nuclear weapons only if necessary to stop the assault. The logic was that, because the other side had nuclear weapons, we dare not use them in Europe except in the greatest extremity, but that we could use them in Korea because the other side did not have them there. South Korean commanders, he said, had gotten used to the idea that the United States would use nuclear weapons at an early point in a war with North Korea.

2. The "AirLand Battle" strategy developed in the mid-1970s called for early, quick, deep strikes into enemy territory, again with the likely use of nuclear weapons, especially against hardened underground facilities (of which there are many in North Korea). In other words the strategy itself implies rollback rather than simple containment of a North Korean invasion.

3. Neutron bombs—or "enhanced radiation" weapons—might well be used if North Korean forces occupied Seoul, that is, to kill the enemy but save the buildings. (The neutron bomb was invented by Samuel Cohen, who first conceived of such a bomb while watching the battle to retake Seoul in 1951, and in the early 1980s news accounts spoke of its possible deployment to Korea).[50]

4. North Korean forces both expanded and redeployed in the late 1970s as a response to the AirLand Battle doctrine. The redeployment led to the stationing of nearly 80 percent of their ground forces near the DMZ. American and South Korean sources routinely cite this expansion and redeployment as evidence of North Korean aggressive intent; in fact, it was done so that as many soldiers as possible could get into the South (regardless of how a war started), to mingle with ROK Army forces and civilians before nuclear weapons could be used, thus making their use less likely.[51]

This harrowing scenario became standard operating procedure in the 1980s, the kind written into military field manuals; the annual Team Spirit military exercises, begun in the late 1970s and last held in 1993, played out AirLand Battle games.[52] These implied an initial containment of a North Korean attack, followed by thrusts into the North, ultimately to seize and hold Pyongyang and topple the regime. Such war games were also conducted in Korea, because in the early 1980s NATO governments and strong peace movements would not allow similar exercises in Europe.

The Gulf War, however (again according to this former general), caused a reevaluation of the role of nuclear weapons. With "smart" bombs that reliably reach their targets, high-yield conventional weapons are more useful than nuclear warheads, the effects of which were messy and uncontrollable. The army, the general said, wanted out of battlefield nuclear weapons as soon as possible. Thus American policy reached a point at which its own interests dictated withdrawal of obsolescent nuclear weapons from Korea in the fall of 1991. (The weapons removed from South Korea included forty 203 mm and thirty 155 mm nuclear artillery shells, plus large numbers of ADMs.) The perceived success in deploying large masses of troops halfway around the world for the Gulf War also would make it much easier, the general thought, to respond to pressures (mainly from cost-cutting Congressmen) to withdraw American ground forces from Korea. But of course, thirty-eight thousand American troops remain in Korea today.

From the Korean War onward, North Korea responded to this nuclear blackmail by building enormous facilities underground or in mountain redoubts, from troop and materiel depots to munitions factories, and even including subterranean warplane hangars. American control of the air in that war illustrated a deterrence principle supposedly developed only with "smart" weapons, namely that "what can be seen is already lost."[53] The North Koreans have long known this, and have acted upon the principle.

In the mid-1970s Pyongyang faced more threats as the Park Chung Hee government sought to develop nuclear capabilities. The ROK went ahead with its clandestine program to develop an "indigenous ability to build ballistic missiles" capable of carrying nuclear warheads, ceasing the activity only under enormous American pressure, while retaining formidable potentialities. Also, South Korea garnered a reputation as a "renegade" arms supplier to pariah countries such as South Africa, and to Iran and Iraq during their war.[54] This South Korean activity puts Pyongyang's activity into perspective: much of it was in response to U.S. pressure and ROK initiatives.

In late 1998 the Pentagon leaked a new war plan that would take advantage of prevalent North Korean infirmities to wipe out the entire regime should the North attack across the DMZ: to "abolish North Korea as a state and . . . 're-organize' it under South Korean control." "We will kill them all," a Pentagon insider told veteran East Asia correspondent Richard Halloran.[55] These leaks made clear that nuclear weapons would still be quickly resorted to in a war initiated by the North. Documents recently obtained by Hans M. Kristensen of the *Bulletin of the Atomic Scientists* also show that in June 1998 the Pentagon staged simulated long-range nuclear attack drills on North Korea out of the Seymour Johnson Air Base in North Carolina. F-15E fighter-bombers of the 4th Fighter Wing dropped dummy BDU-38 nuclear bombs on concrete emplacements arrayed like the hundreds that protect Korean underground facilities. Such "stand-off" nuclear attacks replaced previous plans to utilize nukes in the South. Kristensen emphasized that this new strategy, of targeting hardened underground facilities, was to be used preemptively "as early in a crisis as possible."[56]

In September 2002, the National Security Council released the new "Bush doctrine," which moved beyond the Cold War staples of containment and deterrence, toward preemptive attacks against adversaries that might possess weapons of mass destruction. In the Korean case, this new doctrine conflates existing plans for nuclear preemption in a crisis initiated by North Korea, plans that as I have shown have been standard operating procedure for the U.S. military in Korea for decades, with the apparent determination to attack states such as North Korea simply because they have or would like to have nuclear weapons, and indeed, quite rudimentary ones compared to those that the United States still amasses by the thousands. National Security Council director Condoleezza Rice later explained to reporters that preemption could be understood as "anticipatory self-defense," that is, "the right of the United States to attack a country that *it thinks* could attack it first" (emphasis added).[57] The document itself reads that other nations "should [not] use preemption as a pretext for aggression."[58] In the Korean theater, however, a new war could erupt over something like the recent "June crab wars" that have frequently occurred as North and South Korean fishermen compete for lucrative catches in the Yellow Sea, and a vicious cycle of preemption and counterpreemption could immediately plunge the Northeast Asian region into general war.

Adding to the danger is a new threat to the existing deterrent structure on the peninsula: according to a retired U.S. Army general with much experience in Korea,[59] American advances in precision-guided munitions now make it feasible to take out the ten thousand artillery tubes that the North has imbedded in mountains north of Seoul, which were heretofore impregnable and constituted the North's basic guarantee against an attack from the South. To the extent that this is true, in the absence of credible security guarantees any general sitting in Pyongyang would now move to a more reliable deterrent.

## Morality in Warfare

I hope that I have provided enough evidence to convince the independent observer that since 1950 the main threat of nuclear war on the Korean peninsula has come from the United States, the only power ever to use nuclear weapons. In the case of Korea, the object of these nuclear strategies, namely North Korea, possesses neither atomic weapons nor a fraction of the firepower of the United States and has been the target of nuclear threats for half a century.

Since Harry Truman made the ultimate decision to drop atomic bombs on Hiroshima and Nagasaki and also took the United States into the Korean War, a consideration of morality in warfare may begin with him.

On August 9, 1945, Samuel McCrea Cavert, head of the Federal Council of the Church of Christ, wrote to Truman and condemned the "indiscriminate" killing at Hiroshima. Two days later, Truman responded,

> Nobody is more disturbed over the use of the Atomic bombs than I am but I was greatly disturbed over the unwarranted attack by the Japanese on Pearl Harbor and their murder of our prisoners of war. The only language they seem to understand is the one we have been using to bombard them. When you have to deal with a beast you have to treat him as a beast. It is most regrettable but nevertheless true.[60]

This would seem to be Truman's reasoning: Japanese naval and air units attacked our naval and air outposts, and some of their soldiers killed captured U.S. soldiers. Therefore, the Japanese are beasts. To deal with beasts you must become a beast, however regrettable that may be. Such thinking makes it painfully apparent that President Truman could not rise above the racism inherent in American attitudes toward Imperial Japan, which made no distinction between leadership by fanatical militarists and the Japanese people, or between combatants and innocent civilians. Barton Bernstein comments cogently, "which group—American leaders or ordinary citizens—was more willing to kill the Japanese in vast numbers, including non-combatants? Is not the process of trying to reach an answer, as well as the answer itself, profoundly troubling?"

For Michael Walzer, the test of morality in wartime is the *intent* to kill innocents, when the proper course for the soldier ought to be the intent to *save* civilian lives, even at the risk of soldiers' lives.[61] Some argue that the killing of noncombatants in warfare is "merely foreseen and [therefore] not intended."[62] Innocents will be killed in wars, just as they will in automobile crashes on interstate highways.

By not exercising his moral faculty and instead yielding to the passions of war, Truman is morally culpable. We have said that war is judged twice; most will say that Truman's ends were noble in bringing a quick end to a just war, but his means were ignoble. Walzer, however, finds American leaders guilty of "a double crime"; arguing that the war could have been concluded before Hiroshima, he writes: "To press the war further . . . is to re-commit the crime of aggression. In the summer of 1945, the victorious Americans owed the Japanese people an experiment in negotiation. To use the atomic bomb, to kill and terrorize civilians, without even attempting such an experiment, was a double crime."[63] Many will disagree, but few can justify Truman's methods as *jus in bello;* instead they have prejudiced the course of modern history ever since. Joseph Schumpeter, the great Austrian economist who had visited Japan in the early 1930s, provided the best epitaph for Hiroshima and Nagasaki when he wrote in his diary shortly after the bombs were dropped, "It is a stupid bestiality or a bestial stupidity."[64]

Hiroshima and Nagasaki inaugurated a unique new type of warfare, and ever since nuclear weapons have carried with them "a dimension of totality, a sense of ultimate annihilation—of cities, nations, the world."[65] That is, this was the dawn of what we now call exterminism. In a recent book on war and morality, Robert L. Holmes examines Augustinian just war theory and argues that no modern war can be just because innocents will always be sacrificed, given the horrible destructiveness of modern technology.[66] In somewhat similar fashion, Anatole Rapoport suggested that Clausewitz's concept of "total war" must be different than total war concepts of mid-twentieth-century strategists. If the first concept involves the mobilization of all national capacities, the second conjures up exterminism and therefore all discussion of "just war" becomes moot.

Rapoport showed how the exterminism acquiesced to by all the powers in World War II became the reigning doctrine during the long years of the Soviet–American "balance of terror":

> It is doubtful whether Clausewitz ever envisaged "civilized war" as a slaughter of civilian populations. Even in his "absolute war" he saw slaughter confined to the battlefield. . . . The modern advocates of "total war," e.g. the Nazis and some partisans of "total victory" in the United States, explicitly included (and now include) civilian populations as military targets. For example, the U.S. Air Force ROTC manual, *Fundamentals of Aerospace Weapons Systems,* defines a "military target," as follows: "Any person, thing, idea, entity, or location selected for destruction, inactivation, or rendering non-usable with weapons which will reduce or destroy the will or ability of the enemy to resist."[67]

How should we think about the use of incendiary weapons in the Korean War, and the nuclear threat ever since? What is meant by the use of terms such as "genocide" and "holocaust" in the context of air warfare? Historian John Dower has argued that Hiroshima and Nagasaki constituted "nuclear genocide," while Richard Minear, in a fascinating and provocative recent essay, likens these acts to the destruction of European Jewry—that is, a holocaust.[68] Genocide clearly refers to violence "intended to destroy, in whole or in part, a national, ethnical, racial or religious group, as such," as the 1948 convention put it.[69] But genocide can also occur in the absence of rudimentary concern about taking innocent lives in large numbers. Hiroshima, I would argue, was not genocide. It was an atrocity on a large scale and therefore a war crime. It was comparable to the rape of Nanjing in scale, but not in intent. Why? Because American leaders did in fact conceive of Hiroshima as a means toward ending suffering rather than prolonging it—that is the best that can be said for their intent, and it does not override the atrocious nature of the act. Nagasaki, however, was different: if it was gratuitous at best (atomic annihilation as an afterthought), it was therefore genocidal at worst, because it served no clear war purpose and failed the test of "rudimentary concern." The large scale of the attack and its lack of rudimentary concern for innocent life places it alongside the firebombing of March 1945: both were genocidal.

By the same reasoning, American military strategy in Korea was also genocidal, precisely in the absence of "rudimentary concern for innocent life." Perhaps the official American logic for the past several decades has been this: North Koreans invaded South Korea in June 1950. The United States responded to this, terming it an outrageous breach of the peace (even though it was a case of Koreans invading their own country). And ever since 1950, this act of aggression, as the United States defined that term, has justified whatever weapon the United States may wish to use in Korea, and however much the United States may wish to terrorize North Korea. Just war doctrines have always emphasized rules of proportionality, however: if militarist Japan was a clear threat to world peace, a North Korea that wanted to unify the Korean peninsula in 1950 was at best a threat to regional stability. The proper response to the North's aggression, most analysts within the just war tradition believe, was to reestablish the 38th parallel. Instead, the United States decided to carry the war to the North, whereupon China entered the battle and the world stood at the brink of general war. If extreme measures and threats may have been justified in the dark winter of 1950–51, they were not justified after the battle stabilized in the spring of 1951. Yet for the next two years, the United States rained destruction on North Korea.

Often the rationale was to use American high-technology firepower to save the lives of American soldiers. The clear result was a massive destruction of civilian lives, apart from considerations of justice in warfare *(jus in bello)*. People who have not thought about crucial just war questions of proportionality, and the difference between the soldier's solemn oath and the innocence of the woman or child, have no right to tell us that saving combatant lives by killing thousands or hundreds of thousands of civilians is justified. Korea was therefore a clear case of genocide, made worse by American protestations of limited war-making intent legally bound by the United Nations, by the incommensurability of the North Korean enemy in the sense discussed above, and by the seemingly endless threat to use atomic weapons ever since.

Assessment of American strategy toward North Korea since the hot war concluded does not pivot on whether North Korea has been governed by people we like or respect, or by people who are better than American leaders. The question instead is the same question as with militarist Japan, namely, that morality in warfare always requires the separation of the perceived evil of enemy leadership from the innocence of the people whom they lead— whether in the 1950s or today, when twenty-two million human beings live in North Korea.

I know of no better statement on the immorality of nuclear war and its inevitable exterminism than the *Pastoral Letter on War and Peace* produced by the American Catholic bishops in 1983.[70] Because the nuclear era raises the possibility of annihilating all human life, the bishops wrote, "we read the book of Genesis with a new awareness; the moral issue at stake in nuclear war involves the meaning of sin in its most graphic dimensions. Every sinful act is a confrontation of the creature and the Creator." Richard Minear writes that "the words of the bishops allow us to see Hiroshima in a new light. Hiroshima was *the* first use of atomic weapons in war; that we always knew. But Hiroshima was also *a* first use, on a predominantly civilian target, against an enemy already demonstrably in the throes of defeat: it was 'a deliberate initiation of nuclear warfare'" (emphasis in original).[71] Nothing in the history of American strategy in Northeast Asia since that determining beginning on August 6, 1945, suggests that any lessons have been learned or that anything would be different when the next war breaks out.

## Notes

1. Gordon Prange, *At Dawn We Slept: The Untold Story of Pearl Harbor* (New York: Penguin, 1981), 539.

2. Friedrich Nietzsche, *Ecce Homo,* trans. Walter Kaufmann (New York: Vintage, 1969), 232.

3. Jean Bethke Elshtain, "Reflections on War and Political Discourse," in *Just War Theory,* ed. Jean Bethke Elshtain (New York: New York University Press, 1992), 275–77; Hannah Arendt, *The Human Condition* (Chicago: University of Chicago Press, 1958), 238–42, cited in Elshtain, *Just War Theory,* 332 n.

4. Or as Admiral Yamamoto Isoroku put it, "It is the custom of *bushido* to select an equal or stronger opponent." Quoted in Prange, *At Dawn We Slept,* 344.

5. Michael Walzer, *Just and Unjust Wars: A Moral Argument with Historical Illustrations* (New York: Basic, 1977), 21.

6. Journalist Kato Masuo, quoted in Michael Sherry, *The Rise of American Airpower: The Creation of Armageddon* (New York: Yale University Press, 1987), 276.

7. Tokyo police cameraman Ishikawa Koyo, cited in Thomas Havens, *Valley of Darkness: The Japanese People and World War Two* (New York: University Press of America, 1986), which is cited in Mark Selden's excellent essay, "The 'Good War' and

the Logic of Exterminism." I am indebted to him for allowing me to cite his forth-coming essay.

8. Sherry, *Rise of American Airpower*, 276.

9. Ronald Schaffer, *Wings of Judgement: American Bombing in World War II* (New York: Oxford University Press, 1985), 134.

10. Sherry, *Rise of American Airpower*, 277, 406; Selden, "Good War," has figures from various sources that range from 87,000 to 97,000 dead and upwards of 125,000 wounded.

11. W. G. Sebald, *On the Natural History of Destruction*, trans. Anthea Bell (New York: Random House, 2003), 59–60.

12. Curtis E. LeMay, with MacKinlay Kantor, *Mission with Lemay: My Story* (Garden City, N.Y.: Doubleday, 1965), 466–67.

13. See, for example, *Mission with LeMay*, 460–62, where (in 1965) LeMay tells crude jokes about "Japs" and "Chinamen" and writes that "human attrition means nothing to such people." In this passage, LeMay is talking about the Korean War and no doubt such racist beliefs emboldened him to call for burning North Korea to a crisp as a means of ending the war overnight, something that in 1965 he still thought would have been right (464).

14. Hachiya Michihiko, *Hiroshima Diary: The Journal of a Japanese Physician, August 6–September 30, 1945*, trans. Warner Wells (Chapel Hill: University of North Carolina Press, 1955), 14.

15. All information is from the Committee for the Compilation of Materials on Damage Caused by the Atomic Bombs in Hiroshima and Nagasaki, *Hiroshima and Nagasaki: The Physical, Medical and Social Effects of the Bombings,* trans. Eisei Ishikawa and David L. Swain (New York: Basic, 1981), 21–56.

16. It is fitting that the first effective writing about Nagasaki after the easing of censorship in 1948 was by Nagai Takashi, a devout Catholic who also happened to be a medical specialist on radiology, and who later died of radiation poisoning in 1951. John Dower, "The Bombed: Hiroshimas and Nagasakis in Japanese Memory," *Diplomatic History* 19, no. 2 (Spring 1995): 285. For the English version of his 1951 book, see Takashi Nagai, *We of Nagasaki: The Story of Survivors in an Atomic Wasteland,* trans. Ichiro Shirato and Herbert B. L. Silverman (New York: 1951). The poem is from Nagai, *The Bells of Nagasaki,* trans. William Johnston (New York: Kodansha International, 1984), xviii.

17. An early argument along these lines was made by G. E. M. Anscombe in an essay entitled "Mr. Truman's Degree," which she wrote in protest of the honorary doctorate Oxford University bestowed on President Truman in 1957. See Thomas Nagle, "War and Massacre," in *War and Moral Responsibility,* ed. Marshall Cohen, Thomas Nagel, and Thomas Scanlon (Princeton: Princeton University Press, 1974), 7. The change that occurred during World War II is easily visible in the protests that various governments, and especially the Roosevelt administration, directed at Japanese bombing of Chinese cities and Franco's bombing of Spanish cities (especially Guernica) in 1937–39, before the global war began. Here is what the Department of State said about Japanese aerial bombing in 1937: "any general bombing of an extensive area wherein resides a large population engaged in peaceful pursuits is unwarranted and contrary to principles of law and humanity."

18. The best account of how historians have thought about this problem (and about their calling) is Peter Novick, *That Noble Dream: The "Objectivity Question" and the American Historical Profession* (New York: Cambridge University Press, 1988).

19. See, for example, the spring 1995 issue of *Diplomatic History.*

20. J. Samuel Walker, "The Decision to Use the Bomb," *Diplomatic History* 19, no. 2 (Spring 1995): 321. Walker is the chief historian of the U.S. Nuclear Regulatory Commission.

21. Hans Bethe drew the conclusion that Nagasaki "was . . . unnecessary" in his foreword to Martin Sherwin's *A World Destroyed: The Atomic Bomb and the Grand Alliance* (New York: Knopf, 1975), xiv. For Sherwin's analysis of Nagasaki, see pp. 233–34. Other historians agree; for example, Barton Bernstein argues that without the Nagasaki bombing "Japan would have surrendered—very probably on the 10th" of August. See Bernstein, "Understanding the Atomic Bomb," *Diplomatic History* 19, no. 2 (Spring 1995): 255, and Herbert Bix, "Japan's Delayed Surrender," *Diplomatic History,* 19, no. 2 (Spring 1995): 218 n. But Bix has a different stance from Sherwin on the question of surrender.

22. For a fuller account with documentation in formerly classified archives, see Bruce Cumings, *The Origins of the Korean War, vol. II: The Roaring of the Cataract, 1947–1950* (Princeton, N.J.: Princeton University Press, 1990), 747–53.

23. *New York Times,* November 30 and December 1, 1950.

24. Stratemeyer to Vandenberg, November 30, 1950; LeMay to Vandenberg, December 2, 1950, Hoyt Vandenberg Papers, box 86. Also see Richard Rhodes, *Dark Sun: The Making of the Hydrogen Bomb* (New York: Simon & Schuster, 1995), 444–46.

25. Cumings, *Origins of the Korean War,* 749.

26. Cumings, *Origins of the Korean War,* 750; interviews by Bob Considine and Jim Lucas in 1954, printed in *New York Times,* April 9, 1964, in Charles Willoughby Papers, box 8.

27. Carroll Quigley, *Tragedy and Hope: A History of the World in Our Time* (New York: MacMillan, 1966), 875. Quigley was President Bill Clinton's favorite teacher at Georgetown University. See also Cumings, *Origins of the Korean War,* 750.

28. Referred to variously as the "capsule," "core," or "softball," this is the fissionable center around which the rest of an atomic bomb is built.

29. Thomas B. Cochran, William M. Arkin, Robert S. Norris, and Milton M. Hoenig, *Nuclear Weapons Databook,* Vol. 1: *Nuclear Forces and Capabilities* (Cambridge, Mass.: Ballinger, 1987), 26, and Vol. 2: *United States Nuclear Warhead Production,* 10. See also Charles Hansen, *United States Nuclear Weapons: The Secret History* (Arlington, Tex.: Aerofax, 1988), 125–33.

30. Cumings, *Origins of the Korean War,* 750–51; Rhodes, *Dark Sun,* 448–51.

31. This does not mean the use of so-called tactical nuclear weapons, which were not available in 1951, but of the eleven-thousand-pound Mark IVs in battlefield tactical strategy, much as heavy conventional bombs dropped by B-29 bombers had been used in battlefield fighting since late August 1950.

32. On Oppenheimer and Project Vista, see Cumings, *Origins of the Korean War,* 751–52. Also see David C. Elliot, "Project Vista and Nuclear Weapons in Europe," *International Security* 2, no. 1 (Summer 1986): 163–83.

33. Cumings, *Origins of the Korean War,* 752.

34. MacArthur to Ridgway, January 7, 1951, Matthew Ridgway Papers, box 20; memo of Ridgway's conference with Almond and others, January 8, 1951.

35. Cumings, *Origins of the Korean War,* 749.

36. Cumings, *Origins of the Korean War,* 753–54; *New York Times,* December 13 1950, January 3, 1951.

37. Jon Halliday and Bruce Cumings, *Korea: The Unknown War* (New York: Pantheon, 1988), 166.

38. Matthew Connelly Papers, "Notes on Cabinet Meetings," September 12, 1952. I am indebted to Barton Bernstein for calling this reference to my attention.

39. Hermann Lautensach, *Korea: A Geography Based on the Author's Travels and Literature,* trans. Katherine Dege and Eckart Dege (1945; Berlin: Springer-Verlag, 1988), 202.

40. "The Attack on the Irrigation Dams in North Korea," *Air University Quarterly* 6, no. 4 (Winter 1953–54): 40–51.

41. Thames Television, transcript from the fifth seminar for the documentary *Korea: The Unknown War* (November 1986); Thames interview with Tibor Meray (also 1986).

42. Donald Stone Macdonald, *U.S.–Korean Relations from Liberation to Self-Reliance: The Twenty-Year Record: An Interpretive Summary of the Archives of the U.S. Department of State for the Period 1945 to 1965* (Boulder, Colo.: Westview, 1992), 18–20.

43. Macdonald, *U.S.–Korean Relations,* 23, 78–79.

44. Macdonald, *U.S.–Korean Relations,* 23–24, 80.

45. Eisenhower Library, Anne Whitman file, NSC, 179th Mtg., box 5, January 8, 1954.

46. Eisenhower Library, Anne Whitman file, NSC, 179th Mtg., boxes 4 and 9.

47. Peter Hayes, *Pacific Powderkeg: American Nuclear Dilemmas in Korea* (Lexington, Mass.: Lexington, 1991), 35.

48. Hayes, *Pacific Powderkeg,* 47–48.

49. Quoted in Hayes, *Pacific Powderkeg,* 49.

50. Samuel Cohen was a childhood friend of Herman Kahn. See Fred Kaplan, *The Wizards of Armageddon* (New York: Simon & Schuster, 1983), 220.

51. Peter Hayes also makes this point in *Pacific Powderkeg,* 148–49.

52. Hayes, *Pacific Powderkeg,* 91.

53. See President Bill Clinton's defense secretary William Perry quoted to this effect in Paul Virilio, *War and Cinema: The Logistics of Perception,* trans. Patrick Camiller (New York: Verso, 1989).

54. Jeanne E. Nolan, *Trappings of Power: Ballistic Missiles in the Third World* (Washington, D.C.: Brookings Institution, 1991), 48–52.

55. Richard Halloran, *Far Eastern Economic Review,* December 3, 1998. The second quote by Halloran appeared in his November 14, 1998, story, "New Warplan Calls for Invasion of North Korea," *Global Beat,* at www.nyu.edu/globalbeat/asia/Halloran111498.html.

56. Hans M. Kristensen, "Preemptive Posturing," *Bulletin of the Atomic Scientists* 58, no. 5 (September–October 2002): 54–59.

57. The *New York Times* on September 20, 2002, quoted this phrase from "a senior administration official," but David Sanger later attributed these remarks directly to Rice. See *New York Times,* September 20, 2002, A-17.

58. *New York Times,* September 20, 2002, 12.

59. A retired general who ran army intelligence in Korea told me this on a not-for-attribution basis, at a conference in Chicago on December 5, 2002.

60. Quoted in Bernstein, "Understanding the Atomic Bomb," 268.

61. Walzer, *Just and Unjust Wars,* 155–56.

62. Robert L. Holmes, *On War and Morality* (Princeton, N.J.: Princeton University Press, 195. Holmes goes on to the say that the argument about the intentions of war makers (which is central to Christian just war doctrine) cannot be carried out consistently (196–97). But that is a different point than mine.

63. Walzer, *Just and Unjust Wars,* 268.

64. Quoted in Richard Swedberg, *Schumpeter: A Biography* (Princeton, N.J.: Princeton University Press, 1991), 276 n.

65. Robert Lifton, *Death in Life: Survivors of Hiroshima* (New York, 1967), 14.

66. Holmes, *On War and Morality,* 117–32, 260–94.

67. Rapoport, "Editor's Introduction," in Carl von Clausewitz, *On War* (New York: Penguin Books, 1968), 62–63. This is not the only point at which Rapoport adduces a similarity between Nazi and American exterminist doctrine (see also 411–12).

68. John Dower, "The Bombed: Hiroshimas and Nagasakis in Japanese Memory," *Diplomatic History,* 19, no. 2 (Spring 1995): 275; Richard H. Minear, "Atomic Holocaust, Nazi Holocaust," *Diplomatic History,* 19, no. 2 (Spring 1995): 347–66.

69. "Convention on the Prevention and Punishment of the Crime of Genocide," December 9, 1948, in *The Laws of War,* ed. Michael Reisman and Chris T. Antoniou (New York: Vintage, 1994), 84–86.

70. For an excerpted version, see Elshtain, *Just War Theory,* 77–168.

71. Minear, "Atomic Holocaust, Nazi Holocaust," 362.

# 5

# When God(s) and Buddhas Go to War

*Brian Daizen Victoria*

A S A RESULT OF THE TERRORIST attacks of September 11, 2001, the words "holy war" have seared themselves into the collective consciousness of the West, if not the world. The question is often asked, with a mixture of disbelief and outrage, how the terrorist hijackers could have convinced themselves that their barbaric acts were in any way "holy"?

In a June 2002 interview broadcast on al-Jazeera Television, Khalid Sheikh Mohammed, head of the Al Qaeda military committee, referred to the attacks of September 11 as their "Holy Tuesday operation." He claimed that similar operations would continue "as long as we are in *jihad* against the infidels and the Zionists," linking the attacks to the wider canvas of the Israel–Palestine conflict.[1]

Although in Islam the term *jihad* properly refers to the struggle against evil rather than holy war per se, it is nevertheless an integral part of the Islamic faith embraced by the terrorists. This has led numerous Western commentators to describe Islamic fundamentalism, if not Islam as a whole, as a violence-prone religion inciting its followers to subjugate if not kill non-Muslims in pursuit of its ultimate goal of bringing the entire world under Islamic rule.

In the Qur'an, the prophet Muhammad does in fact call on the faithful to kill Islam's adversaries. *Sura 2*, for example, states:

> Slay [unbelievers] wherever you find them, and drive them out of the places they drove you from. Idolatry is worse than war. . . . If they mend their ways, know that God is forgiving and merciful. Fight them until idolatry is no more, and God's religion is supreme.[2]

Small wonder, then, that the Taliban targeted for destruction the "idolatrous" Great Buddha at Bamiyan.

But what of Christianity? True, Church leaders did once exhort the faithful to take up the sword in the blood-soaked Crusades of the eleventh through the thirteenth centuries, but that was ages ago and, thanks especially to the Protestant Reformation, the West long ago renounced such acts as "un-Christian."

Yet, if the Protestant Reformation contributed to a rekindling of a loving Christian spirit, how does one account for the following passage in Martin Luther's 1523 treatise, *Secular Authority?*

> If your opponent is your equal, your inferior, or of a foreign government, you should first offer him justice and peace, as Moses taught the children of Israel. If he is unwilling, then use your best strategy and defend yourself by force against force. . . . And in such a war *it is a Christian act and an act of love confidently to kill, rob, and pillage the enemy,* and to do everything that can injure him until one has conquered him according to the methods of war. . . . *Such happenings must be considered as sent of God,* that He may now and then cleanse the land and drive out the knaves.[3] (emphasis added)

Luther was, of course, not the first to endorse warfare as God's instrument. Thanks to the earlier teachings of Saints Augustine and Thomas Aquinas, the Roman Catholic Church had long embraced the belief that a "just war" was in accord with God's will. As the above passage graphically illustrates, the belief in just war made its way unchanged from Catholic into mainstream Protestant Christianity. If anything, in calling the faithful to "rob and pillage" the enemy, not just kill them, Luther went beyond the teachings of Augustine and Aquinas. Thus the holy war of the Crusades did not disappear in the West but was only transmuted into support for a so-called just war.

What is striking about the words of Muhammad and Luther quoted above is how similar they are in spirit, even though they represent the thinking of two leaders who are of disparate religions and separated by nearly a thousand years of history. What then of religion and religious wars today? It was this *universal* religious sanctioning of violence, continuing even to the present, that led Martin Marty of the University of Chicago to comment in 1996:

> One must note the feature of religion that keeps it on the front page and on prime time: it kills. Or, if, as the gun lobbies say of weapons—that they do not kill; people do—one must say of religion that if it does not kill, many of its forms and expressions motivate people to kill. Experts on what motivates the scores of wars or, as some would have it, "tribal conflicts," today know that not only do many belligerent partisans wear names like "Protestant" and "Catholic," "Shi'ite"

and "Sunni," "Jewish" and "Sikh," but leaders and followers alike fire on the demonized Other, the enemy, in the name of God or the gods.[4]

At the heart of the intimate relationship between religion and violence is the historically close relationship between institutional religion and the state. As early as 1932, theologian Reinhold Niebuhr noted: "The nation is always endowed with an aura of the sacred, which is one reason why religions, which claim universality, are so easily captured and tamed by national sentiment, religion and patriotism merging in the process."[5]

Sociologist Peter Berger pointed to another cause for this close relationship—the reality of death on the battlefield. Berger wrote:

> Whenever a society must motivate its members to kill or to risk their lives, thus consenting to being placed in extreme marginal situations, religious legitimations become important. . . . Killing under the auspices of the legitimate authorities has, for this reason, been accompanied from ancient times to today by religious paraphernalia and ritualism. Men go to war and men are put to death amid prayers, blessings, and incantations.[6]

Military chaplains do more than simply minister to the religious needs of individual soldiers. They also validate, even sacralize, the act of killing. In 1995, Major Gary Perry, a Protestant chaplain at Yokota Air Force Base in Tokyo, asked about the relationship between the Christian teaching prohibiting killing and the U.S. military, replied: "I interpret killing as a willful taking of life for personal gain, or because of hate or convenience. I view the military as an institution that when going to war, takes life to save people. . . . I believe it's sometimes necessary to kill in order to preserve life."[7]

Rebutting Perry, peace activist and Jesuit Daniel Berrigan argues:

> Everybody has always killed the bad guys. Nobody kills the good guys. The Church is tainted in this way as well. The Church plays the same cards; it likes the taste of imperial power too. This is the most profound kind of betrayal I can think of. Terrible! Jews and Christians and Buddhists and all kinds of people who come from a good place, who come from revolutionary beginnings and are descended from heroes and saints. . . . Religion becomes another resource for the same old death-game.[8]

The historical truth of Berrigan's comments is demonstrated by the Crusades of the Middle Ages. As church historian Paul Johnson notes: "The effect of the Crusades was to undermine the intellectual content of Islam, to destroy the chances of peaceful adjustment to Christianity, and to make the Muslims far less tolerant: crusading fossilized Islam into a fanatic posture."[9] The Crusades, in Johnson's view, were "wars of conquest and primitive experiments in colonization; and the only specific Christian institutions they produced, the three knightly orders, were military."[10]

Turning to the wars fought in Asia in the twentieth century, we find that the role of religion in these conflicts was substantial. In fact, with the advent of "total war" in the twentieth century, it can be argued that, if anything, the close relationship between religion and warfare deepened and intensified. Given the high numbers of civilian casualties and deprivation brought about by modern weaponry, concern directed solely to the morale of one's soldiers was no longer sufficient. Instead, total war required that the fighting spirit of *all* citizens, not just those directly engaged in combat, be enhanced.

Religion, therefore, has been repeatedly called upon to legitimize the nation's cause to all its citizens. In so doing, religion has again and again served to demonize (and dehumanize) the enemy and to sacralize the act of killing as part of a just struggle against evil, what Martin Luther described as God's plan to periodically "cleanse the land and drive out the knaves." Finally, should those engaged in this holy cause, be they military or civilian, die in the process, they are promised "eternal life" as their just reward.

If this is true, why has religion's role in international affairs, most especially warfare, been so little recognized, let alone seriously studied? Addressing this question in a major 1998 essay entitled "Religion in Diplomatic History," Walter McDougall notes that many in the West falsely believe that as a result of the bloody wars accompanying the Protestant Reformation in the Middle Ages, Western nations now practice diplomacy solely on the secular principle of national self-interest, having purged their conflicts of religious passions. In particular, McDougall concludes: "Americans have been especially prone to justify their behavior abroad in Protestant Christian terms. . . . The fact that most American churches were on board for the Spanish–American War and acquisition of colonies goes far to explain the United States' abrupt shift into self-confident overseas expansion in 1898."[11]

Indeed, President William McKinley personally acted to ensure that church leaders supported his decision to colonize the Philippines. In 1898, McKinley appealed to a group of leading clergymen invited to the White House as follows:

I walked the floor of the White House night after night until midnight, and I am not ashamed to tell you, gentlemen, that I went down on my knees and prayed to Almighty God for light and guidance more than one night. And one night late it came to me this way—I don't know how it was, but it came . . . that there was nothing left for us to do but to take them all, and to educate the Filipinos, and *uplift them and civilize and Christianize them, and by God's grace do the very best we could by them, as our fellow-men for whom Christ also died.* And then I went to bed, and went to sleep, and slept soundly, and the next morning I sent for the chief engineer of the War Department (our map-maker), and I told him to put the Philippines on the map of the United States, and there they are, and there they will stay while I am President![12] (emphasis added)

## Toward a New Zion

The U.S. was not, of course, the first Western power to justify its takeover of the Philippines (let alone other colonies) in the name of "civilizing and Christianizing" its inhabitants. Ever since Magellan's arrival in 1521, Spain had done likewise, initially employing Catholic friars to burn and destroy the artifacts of precolonial culture as the handiwork of the devil. Then, in classic feudal fashion, Spain created a union of church and state with friars responsible for such things as collecting taxes, running parochial schools, certifying the correctness of residence certificates, and selecting municipal officials. In short, Filipinos were under control of the church from birth until death.

Given this, it is clear that what McKinley, a Methodist, really meant by Christianizing the Filipinos was converting them from Catholicism to the Protestant faith. Historically, this call was rooted in the Puritan belief dating from the seventeenth century that they, as inheritors of the true religion of the Reformation, had been chosen by God to bring forth a New Zion, a "city on the hill" on the North American continent. This belief was subsequently recast in the nineteenth century as the doctrine of "Manifest Destiny," which justified the expansion of the United States from coast to coast as a reflection of God's will and in accord with His divine plan.

By 1885, a crude form of social Darwinism had been inserted into the debate. Josiah Strong, general secretary of the Evangelical Alliance, envisaged

the final competition of races, for which the Anglo-Saxon is being schooled . . . this race of unequalled energy with all the majesty of numbers and the might of wealth behind it—the representative, let us hope, of the largest liberty, the purest Christianity, the highest civilization—having developed *peculiarly aggressive traits* calculated to impress its institutions upon mankind, will spread itself over the earth. And can any one doubt that the result of this competition of the races will be the survival of the fittest?[13] (emphasis added)

Only a few years later, these sentiments were echoed in the political debate. As President McKinley addressed clergymen in the White House, U.S. Senator Albert J. Beveridge of Indiana confidently informed the Senate:

God has not been preparing the English-speaking and Teutonic peoples for a thousand years for nothing but vain and idle self-admiration. No! He has made us the master organizers of the world to establish a system where chaos reigns. . . .

He has made us adepts in government that we may administer government among savages and senile peoples.[14]

The problem, of course, was what to do when "savages and senile peoples" rejected the divinely appointed Protestant Christian civilization proffered them? The Puritans once again provided the solution to this problem, for they knew that the real reason for the resistance of savage heathens was quite straightforward—they were trapped in the "snare of the Divell."[15] Thus, as Satan's agents, the rebellious heathens were evil incarnate and death their just dessert. And herein lies the religious justification for the sometimes-genocidal practices first directed against "bloodthirsty" Native Americans and subsequently employed in a succession of Asian wars that spanned the twentieth century and continue into the twenty-first.

The use of religion to justify national expansion was not limited to Christianity alone. Buddhism, especially in colonial and wartime Japan, played a similar role. This chapter offers a comparative perspective on the uses of religion in the service of the nation-state in twentieth-century wars in Asia, with particular reference to Japanese Buddhism and American Protestantism.

## The Filipino–American War

When Filipinos declared independence, the United States poured in more than 125,000 troops to insure compliance with the Treaty of Paris signed on December 10, 1898, between the United States and Spain without so much as consulting the Filipinos, the provisions of which allowed the United States to purchase the Philippines from Spain for the sum of $20 million. On April 27, 1898, Senator Beveridge explained the rationale behind the U.S. expansion into Asia (and beyond):

We will establish trading posts throughout the world as distributing posts for American products. We will cover the ocean with our merchant marine. We will build a navy to the measure of our greatness. *Great colonies*, governing themselves, flying our flag and trading with us, will grow about our posts of trade. Our institutions will follow our trade on the wings of our commerce. And American law, American order, American civilization, and the American flag will plant themselves on shores hitherto bloody and benighted, *by those agencies of God henceforth made beautiful and bright*.[16]

Geographically, the colonization of the Philippines, contested in the Filipino–American War of 1899–1902, marked a shift in the exercise of American power from the "New World," including Latin America and the

Caribbean, to Asia. In religious terms, however, it was no more than an extension of America's long-standing Protestant triumphalism, for many Americans shared McKinley's view that they were but doing God's work, that is, extending an invincible and preordained Protestant Christian civilization throughout the world. That they prospered financially in the process signified God's blessing on His chosen people.

At the same time, it was entirely just that those who rebelled against God's divine plan should be punished, for the Bible teaches that "the wages of sin are death" and those trapped in the "snare of the Divell" must, with God's assistance, be defeated at all costs and by any means. Thus, U.S. troops, many of whom were veterans of the recently ended Great Plains Indian wars, found no difficulty in framing their task in identical terms. For example, U.S. Army colonel Frederick Funston explained the forced relocation of potential peasant insurgents into *reconcentrados* (concentration camps) as follows: "The boys go for the enemy as if they were chasing jack-rabbits. I, for one, hope that Uncle Sam will apply the chastening rod, good, hard, and plenty, and lay it on until the [Filipinos] come into the reservation and promise to be good 'injuns.'"[17]

Fresh from participation in the Wounded Knee massacre of the Sioux in 1890, Brigadier General Jacob "Howling Jake" Smith told the marines sent to invade the island of Samar:

> I want no prisoners, I wish you to kill and burn, the more you kill and burn the better it will please me. I want all persons killed who are capable of bearing arms [ten years of age and above] in actual hostilities against the United States. . . . The interior of Samar must be made a howling wilderness.[18]

The end result of actions like these was the loss of 250,000 to one million or more Filipino lives. Most of the dead were noncombatants who died either from famine and disease or from other war-related causes. The United States, for its part, lost slightly more than five thousand soldiers from all causes.[19]

For our purposes, the central point is that, as Paul Johnson noted, the Protestant churches, notably their missionary wings, strongly supported America's expansion into the Philippines based on their belief that they were part of "a God-determined process by which 'Romish superstition' was being replaced by 'Christian civilization.'"[20] Stuart Miller pointed out that "to the missionaries Dewey's victory was nothing other than 'God's vengeance.' . . . Almost in unison, religious editors across the nation immediately following the news of Manila asked what God intended 'by laying these naked foundlings at our door.' Clearly, to them, 'the American Republic' was 'on the way to a larger ministry in world affairs.'"[21]

## The Birth of Japanese Imperialism

Compared with European powers, the United States was a latecomer to the imperialist game in Asia. Its advance into Asia coincided roughly with the birth of an imperialist state native to the region, the Empire of Japan. In 1895, Japan's defeat of China brought it control of Taiwan and the Pescadores and paved the way for the Japanese advance on Korea.

The role of religion in rationalizing and sanctifying wars, so central to American war making, had an equally important place in Japan, where both Buddhism and State Shinto served as its main avatars. For example, the noted Meiji Buddhist scholar–priest Inoue Enryo portrayed the Russo–Japanese War of 1904–1905 as a holy undertaking even prior to the outbreak of hostilities:

> Buddhism is a teaching of compassion, a teaching for living human beings. Therefore, fighting on behalf of living human beings is in accord with the spirit of compassion. In the event hostilities break out between Japan and Russia, it is only natural that Buddhists should fight willingly, for what is this if not repaying the debt of gratitude we owe the Buddha?
>
> It goes without saying that this is a war to protect the state and sustain our fellow countrymen. Beyond that, however, it is the conduct of a Bodhisattva seeking to save untold millions of living souls throughout China and Korea from the jaws of death. . . .
>
> *If theirs is the army of God, then ours is the army of the Buddha. . . .*
>
> Buddhism would not exist [in Japan] without the devotion of the Imperial family. When looked at from this viewpoint, it is only natural for Buddhists to fight to the death in order to repay the debt of gratitude they owe to the Buddha and the emperor.[22] (emphasis added)

The Russo–Japanese War of 1905 also marked a new awareness within the Imperial Japanese military itself of the importance of religion, especially Buddhism. On the one hand, this awareness came out of the personal experiences of that war's most famous generals, Nogi Maresuke and Kodama Gentaro, both of whom had trained for many years under the guidance of Rinzai Zen Master Nantembô.

Nantembô recalled that Kodama had once asked him how a military man should handle Zen. In reply, Nantembô asked the general how he would handle three thousand soldiers if they were in front of him right at that moment. When Kodama protested that he did not have any soldiers in front of him, Nantembô attacked him, saying, "This should be obvious to you. . . . You fake soldier!" "How would *you* do it then?" Kodama asked in exasperation. Nantembô thereupon hurled Kodama to the ground, jumped on his back, and, slapping his buttocks with a stick, shouted: "Troops, forward march!"[23]

Many officers in the field were impressed by the Buddhist faith of Japan's ordinary soldiers, especially adherents of the Shin (True Pure Land) sect. Though lying mortally wounded on the battlefield, these soldiers did not cry out for help but died silently, without complaint. The Shin sect scholar–priest Osuga Shudo explained: "Reciting the name of Amida Buddha makes it possible to march onto the battlefield firm in the belief that death will bring rebirth in paradise."[24]

A combination of these experiences led to the creation within the military of a formal program of "spiritual education" *(seishin kyōiku)* designed to enhance the fighting spirit of soldiers. A cornerstone of this program was the belief that "faith is power," which asserted that a sufficiently strong will could overcome all material obstacles, including the lack of modern weaponry. It was the responsibility of every company commander to indoctrinate his subordinates in the basic tenets of this program, which also included absolute loyalty to the emperor, unquestioning obedience to superiors, and a readiness to sacrifice one's life. As Mark Peattie observed, "With the possible exception of the pre–World War I French army, no other army articulated such an extreme code of sacrifice in the attack."[25] While the program was not overtly associated with any particular religion or sect, it did claim its roots lay in the Zen-inspired Bushido code and the Buddhist/Shinto "Spirit of Japan."

## Japanese Buddhism and the Asia–Pacific War

From 1895 forward, Japan was more or less continuously on the road to war, annexing Taiwan in 1895 and Korea in 1910, seizing Manchuria in 1931 and North China in 1935, and launching a full-scale invasion of China in July 1937. On July 28, 1937, the leaders of Japan's major sects issued the following statement of war support through a pan-Buddhist organization known as the Myowa-kai:

> In order to establish eternal peace in East Asia, arousing the great benevolence and compassion of Buddhism, we . . . now have no choice but to exercise the benevolent forcefulness of "killing one in order that many may live." . . .
> We believe it is time to effect a major change in the course of human history, which has been centered on Caucasians and inequality among humanity.[26]

The fact that their nation was now fighting fellow Buddhists presented a special challenge for Japan's Buddhist proponents of war. For how could the claim be substantiated that by invading China Japan was, in Inoue Enryo's words, "seeking to save untold millions of living souls throughout China . . . from the jaws of death"?

The answer was not long in coming, for in a book published later that year, two Buddhist scholars, Hayashiya Tomojiro and Shimakage Chikai of Komazawa University, asserted that unlike the Japanese, the Chinese were not really Buddhists. According to these scholars, it was Chinese "defilements" *(bonnô)* that had caused the war.[27]

If sentiments like these represented overall Buddhist thinking, it was still particularly hard for Japan's Zen Buddhists to endorse aggression against the very country in which their school of Buddhism had first emerged. By 1939, however, Rinzai Zen scholar–priest Fukuba Hoshu came up with the solution in a sectarian journal article entitled "What Is Japanese, What Is Chinese." Once again it was in Japan alone that "Zen's true nature had been made manifest." According to Fukuba, the Chinese Zen patriarchs' understanding of Zen had been limited by the cultural flaws in Chinese society. Specifically, where loyalty to one's sovereign came into conflict with filial piety owed one's parents, the Chinese patriarchs had given precedence to filial piety.[28]

Between 10 million and 30 million Chinese, as well as 3 million Japanese, would die before the Japanese government was forced to abandon its benevolent and compassionate efforts to create "true friendship between Japan and China," cleanse the Chinese of their "defilements," and "repay the benevolence of the Chinese patriarchs."

If Japan's Buddhist leaders supported their country's advance into China, many reacted almost ecstatically to the Pearl Harbor attack, which took place on the very day Shakyamuni Buddha is said to have realized enlightenment. Suzuki Nikkyo, head of the Orthodox branch of the Nichiren sect (Nichiren Shoshu), put it this way:

> Today we are truly carried away in everlasting emotion and stand awestruck at the glittering Imperial Edict declaring war on the United States and Britain that has been so graciously bestowed upon us. . . . We are fortunate in having an army and navy that are incomparably loyal and brave under the August Virtue of His Majesty, the Emperor. . . .
>
> Adherents of this sect must, in obedience to the Holy Mind [of the Emperor] and in accordance with the parting instructions of the Buddha and Patriarchs, brandish the religious faith acquired through years of training, surmount all difficulties with untiring perseverance, and do their duty to the utmost, confident of certain victory in this great war of unprecedented proportions.[29]

Nichiren leaders were hardly alone in their fervent endorsement of the war. Reflecting on Pearl Harbor in December 1942, Zen Master Hata Esho, head of Eiheiji, one of the Soto sect's two main monasteries, wrote:

> On 8 December Shakyamuni Buddha looked at the morning star and realized perfect enlightenment while seated under the *bodhi* tree. One year ago, on this

very day, through the proclamation of the imperial edict to annihilate America and England, our country started afresh toward a new East Asia, a great East Asia. This signifies nothing less than the enlightenment of East Asia. . . . In terms of developing the spiritual power of the people, there is a way for us, incompetent though we be, to do our public duty. I believe that we should do everything in our power to go in this direction.[30]

Zen priests did in fact excel in "developing the spiritual power of the people." Among other things, they conducted religious ceremonies for the avowed purpose of ensuring "certain victory"; held intensive meditation sessions for both military personnel and their civilian "industrial warrior" *(sangyô senshi)* counterparts; served as military chaplains; and valorized the deaths of those who fell on the battlefield, designated "heroic spirits" *(eirei),* by conducting their funerals. Zen was not alone. All of Japan's other Buddhist sects acted similarly.

Of all these activities, the most important to the Japanese military was the practice of Zen. Sôtô Zen priest Ishihara Shummyo, president of the influential pan-Buddhist magazine, *Daihôrin,* explained the military importance of Zen practice in preparing Japanese soldiers to face death with equanimity: "I believe that if one is called upon to die, one should not be the least bit agitated. On the contrary, one should be in a realm where something called 'oneself' does not intrude even slightly. Such a realm is no different from that derived from the practice of Zen."[31]

Through the practice of Zen meditation, that is, *zazen,* a soldier was empowered to selflessly lay down his life on the battlefield with equanimity as a loyal subject of the emperor. The military high command regularly sent *kamikaze* pilots for periods of intense meditation at Zen temples before dispatching them on their suicide missions. One of wartime Japan's most lauded military heroes, Lieutenant Colonel Sugimoro Goro, wrote: "Through my practice of Zen I am able to get rid of my ego. In facilitating the accomplishment of this, Zen becomes, as it is, the true spirit of the Imperial military."[32]

Western military writers would later comment on the willingness, even eagerness, of Japanese soldiers to die on the battlefield. For example, Thomas Allen and Norman Polmar observed that a "dark, unfathomable acceptance of death drove the Japanese fighting man."[33]

The Zen doctrine of "no self" allowed Zen to claim that since the self did not really exist there was no difference between life and death, the two states being one and indivisible. This doctrine expressed within the Zen tradition as the "identity of life and death" *(shôji ichinyo),* Japanese soldiers were indoctrinated to go into battle believing, in effect, that they were already dead. Thus the only question of importance was not whether they would die but whether they would die honorably so as not to bring shame on their family.

Nothing better epitomized the willingness of Japanese soldiers to die on the battlefield than the *kamikaze* pilots who hurled themselves at Allied ships and planes. Nevertheless, not all Japanese soldiers went willingly to their deaths, especially toward war's end. Despite great pressure, even some *kamikaze* pilots tried to flee and many more Japanese soldiers attempted to surrender, if not always successfully.

Still, large numbers of Japanese troops did choose death over surrender. After fighting the Japanese at Guadalcanal in August 1942, Marine major general Alexander Archer Vandegrift wrote: "I have never heard or read of this kind of fighting. These people refuse to surrender. The wounded wait until men come up to examine them . . . and blow themselves and the other fellow to pieces with a hand grenade."[34] Vandegrift's observation is given added weight by the 98.8 percent Japanese fatality rate at Attu in the Aleutians, the 99.7 percent fatality rate at Tarawa in the Gilbert Islands, and the 98.5 percent fatality rate at Roi-Namur in the Marshalls. In 1944, 97 percent of the 30,000 Japanese troops on Saipan fought to the death, while the following year 92,000 regular and militia troops, out of a total of a little more than 100,000, died defending Okinawa.[35]

These deaths, coupled with the widespread devastation visited on the peoples of Asia and the reflection made possible by Japan's defeat, led many Japanese to regret Japan's military adventures in Asia and adopt broadly pacifist sentiments. Eventually, a handful of Buddhist sects in postwar Japan publicly acknowledged and repented their complicity in Japanese aggression. For example, in 1992 the Sôtô Zen sect issued a "Statement of Repentance" *(Sanshabun)*. Although nearly a half century in the coming, the sect finally admitted that it had "both supported and eagerly sought to cooperate with a war of aggression against other peoples of Asia, calling it a holy war."[36] Nevertheless, there was no suggestion of reparations for the victims of the aggression it had supported.

Most postwar Buddhist leaders, however, continued to provide religious justification for the war and support the claims of veterans. Thus Yamada Mumon, head of the Myoshinji, the Rinzai Zen sect's largest branch, helped found the Association to Repay the Heroic Spirits (i.e, of dead soldiers; *Eirei ni Kotaeru-kai*) in 1976. The purpose of this organization was to lobby the Japanese Diet for reinstatement of state funding for Yasukuni Shrine, the Shinto shrine in Tokyo dedicated to the veneration of the "heroic spirits" of Japan's war dead. Yamada addressed the association's inaugural meeting as follows:

Japan destroyed itself in order to grandly give the countries of Asia their independence. I think this is truly an accomplishment worthy of the name "holy war." All of this is the result of the meritorious deeds of two million five hundred thousand heroic spirits in our country who were loyal, brave, and without rival. I think the various peoples of Asia who achieved their independence will ceaselessly praise their accomplishments for all eternity.[37]

Zen masters, moreover, have been directly involved in boosting the morale of soldiers in Japan's postwar military, the Self-Defense Forces *(Jieitai)*, and military leaders still regularly call on Zen masters to instruct their troops.

While "hot" holy war had ended, the alleged "unity of Zen and the sword" could still be called on when needed.

## The U.S. and European Churches and War

U.S. Christian triumphalism reached its zenith in World War I after the United States joined the Allied effort in 1917. The Reverend Randolph H. McKim of Washington typified the thinking of that era when he opined: "This conflict is indeed a crusade. The greatest in history. The holiest. It is in the profoundest and truest sense a Holy War. . . . Yes, it is Christ, the king of righteousness, who calls us up to grapple in deadly strife with this unholy and blasphemous power."[38] Newell Dwight Hillis, minister of the Brooklyn Plymouth church, went further, proposing a plan for "exterminating the German people, . . . the sterilization of 10 million German soldiers and the segregation of the women."[39] Not to be outdone, Henry B. Wright, evangelical YMCA (Young Men's Christian Association) director and former professor of divinity at Yale, told soldiers who felt qualms about killing that he could "see Jesus himself sighting down a gun-barrel and running a bayonet through an enemy's body."[40]

Nevertheless, the fact that Germany had, prior to World War I, been regarded as a Christian nation—indeed, it was the ancestral home of Martin Luther—presented church leaders with something of a dilemma. Yet this dilemma was readily overcome by men such as the Reverend Courtland Meyers, who preached in Boston, "If the Kaiser is a Christian, the devil in Hell is a Christian, and I am an atheist."[41] In Australia, the Anglican Synod confidently declared in 1916, "This synod is convinced that the forces of the Allies are being used of God to vindicate the rights of the weak and to maintain the moral order of the world."[42]

The Roman Catholic Church, seeing the war as an opportunity to promote the submission of all Christians to Rome, suspended the provision in canon law forbidding priests to bear arms or shed blood. This allowed the mobilization of seventy-nine thousand priests and nuns, forty-five thousand of whom came from France alone. Of the latter, more than five thousand were killed in action.[43]

The end of "the war to end all wars," however, was followed by near universal revulsion among both victor and vanquished against the mass carnage. In the United States, this revulsion, intertwined with isolationist attitudes, led to a determination, shared by many church leaders, to never again be drawn into solving Europe's problems with American blood. The result was that pacifism and the determination to avoid military entanglement enjoyed greater support in the United States in the 1920s and 1930s than at anytime before or since. In 1929, the Federal Council of Churches passed a resolution that "the churches should condemn resort to the war-system as sin and should henceforth refuse ... to sanction it or to be used as agencies of its support."[44] In May 1940, the Methodist Church, the country's largest Protestant denomination, proclaimed that it would never "officially support, endorse or participate in war."[45]

Yet, there was another force at work in the church in the 1920s and 1930s— its growing fear of the spread of "godless" communism, both at home and abroad. This would lead to calls for yet another Christian crusade, this time against communism. Significantly, a number of U.S. church leaders initially saw fascism as the best hope of fighting the communist menace abroad and preserving "law and order" at home in the midst of the ongoing social unrest caused by the Great Depression. Thus many initially viewed Hitler and Mussolini, as well as Spain's Franco, as the new champions of Christian civilization.

On the Protestant side, the Reverend Gerald B. Winrod and his Defenders of the Christian Faith were active across the Bible Belt of the American Midwest. Claiming to speak on the basis of Divine Inspiration, Winrod stated that "the Hitler revolution has saved Germany and perhaps all Europe from an invasion of Jewish Communism directed from Moscow."[46] Further, in 1935 his paper, the *Defender,* compared Hitler with Martin Luther and said, "Germany stands alone. Of all the countries of Europe, Germany is the only one that has had the courage to defy Jewish Masonic Occultism, Jewish Communism and the international Jewish money power."[47]

For its part, the Roman Catholic Church had its "Radio priest," Father Charles E. Coughlin. With an estimated audience of up to fifteen million listeners, Coughlin created an organization known as the Christian Front to unite Christians in the fight against communism and the money power of the Jews. "Germany's war is a battle for Christianity," Coughlin claimed on July 7, 1941.[48] Three weeks later, on July 30, 1941, Pope Pius XII stated, "Hitler's war is a noble enterprise in the defense of European culture."[49]

In the United States, the support that some, though by no means all, church leaders had given to fascism came to an abrupt end with Japan's attack on

Pearl Harbor on December 7, 1941. Catholic archbishop Francis Spellman captured the spirit of the moment when he wrote, "With fire and brimstone came December 7, America's throat was clutched, her back was stabbed, her brain was stunned; but her great heart still throbbed."[50]

Those Methodist bishops who had earlier taken a pacifist stance quickly declared, "The Methodists of America will loyally support our President and our nation." The Northern Baptist Convention reported, "Baptist ministers are 'all out' to win," and the Synagogue Council of America called on its congregations "to offer prayer for a speedy victory." The administrative board of the National Catholic Welfare Conference sent a letter to President Roosevelt pledging "our institutions and their consecrated personnel" to the war effort.[51]

Nevertheless, by comparison with World War I, few American ministers endorsed America's efforts as a "holy war." *Time* magazine noted that while most religious leaders endorsed the war, "not one of them directly answered *Time*'s question as to whether most ministers feel America is fighting for the cause of righteousness."[52] The Federal Council of Churches found that all parties involved "share in responsibility for the present evils. There is none who does not need forgiveness. A mood of genuine penitence is therefore demanded of us—individuals and nations alike."[53]

This somewhat muted church support for the war helps explain why, on the whole, American religious leaders did not indulge in the frenzy of "Jap-bashing" that followed in the aftermath of Pearl Harbor. Initially, it was Americans of Japanese descent who became the targets of racist hysteria, contributing to their forced evacuation from the West Coast to "relocation camps." When it was suggested that Idaho accept some of the evacuees, the governor expressed his opposition, stating: "A good solution to the Jap problem would be to send them all back to Japan, then sink the island. They live like rats, breed like rats and act like rats."[54]

This reference to Japanese, *all* Japanese, as either "rats" or "monkeys" was normative throughout the war years. *Time* magazine, for example, entitled its article on the Battle of Iwo Jima "Rodent Exterminators" and went on to state: "The ordinary unreasoning Jap is ignorant. Perhaps he is human. Nothing . . . indicates it."[55] Admiral William F. "Bull" Halsey remarked, "We are drowning and burning the bestial apes all over the Pacific, and it is just as much pleasure to burn them as to drown them."[56]

To their credit, some church leaders opposed this blatant racism. One of the most prominent of these was the liberal and pacifist-oriented Reverend Harry Emerson Fosdick. In a wartime sermon entitled "A Time to Stress Unity," Fosdick noted the growth of what he called "certain Nazi elements in America," by which he meant racial prejudice directed against not only Japanese but American blacks as well. Criticizing this tendency, Fosdick said,

"In any situation at any time, no matter what the emotional provocation is, to lump a whole race or nation in an inclusive prejudice and hatred is as ignorant as it is unchristian."[57]

Nevertheless, there was one aspect of Protestant triumphalism that even Fosdick was unable to abandon—the belief that the day was fast approaching when, like America herself, Asia's destiny would rest in Christian hands. For Fosdick, Generalissimo and Madame Chiang Kai-shek, both Methodists, represented the great hope for China's future. In a second wartime sermon entitled "Starting with Trouble and Ending with Hope," Fosdick opined: "Who can be grateful enough for such characters as Generalissimo and Madame Chiang Kai-shek? Yet only a few years ago the idea that the destiny of China would thus rest in Christian hands would have been a mad dream."[58]

## China and Civil War

Fosdick was only one of many Americans enamored with the generalissimo and his American-educated wife, Madame Chiang. In January 1938, *Time* magazine named the couple "International Man and Wife of the Year." *Time* labeled Chiang "China's Christian Warrior" and, quoting Chiang, explained the rationale behind his conversion to the Christian faith as follows: "To my mind, the reason we should believe in Jesus is that He was the leader of a national revolution."[59]

Chiang, needless to say, perceived himself as the leader of yet another national revolution. However, far from being Christlike, Chiang suffered from a plethora of leadership deficiencies. As Lloyd Eastman notes, "There is . . . cause to suspect that Chiang used his periodic crack-downs on corruption less as a means to eliminate it than as a device to control his subordinates."[60]

As early as August 1932, Chiang revealed his enthusiasm for fascism. One of his Nazi military advisers wrote "His Excellency Chiang Kai-shek has shown great interest in the development of the national-socialist movement. . . . One point is especially important to him: how our party leadership succeeds to maintain such strict discipline among its followers and to take harsh measures against dissidents or opponents, and does all this with such success."[61] By 1935, Chiang told his followers that "Fascism is a stimulant for a declining society. . . . Can fascism save China? We answer: yes. Fascism is what China now most needs. . . . At the present stage of China's critical situation, fascism is a wonderful medicine exactly suited to China, and the *only* spirit that can save it"[62] (emphasis added).

And fascist rule, with himself as supreme leader, is exactly what Chiang had in mind. In this he was aided by the "Blue Shirts," a secret organization formed in early 1932 similar to the "Brown Shirts," that is, Storm Troopers, in the Nazi Party. Composed of younger military officers, the Blue Shirts swore absolute loyalty to Chiang. Their program stated, "Chiang Kai-shek is the Guomindang's only supreme leader and also China's only great leader; therefore, members must resolutely support him, follow his orders only, and make his will their own."[63] Democracy with its endless debates and recognition of individual rights (as opposed to duties) was anathema to the Blue Shirts, whose goal was "the totalitarian one of the unqualified submission of the individual to the nation."[64] To achieve this goal, they were ever willing to employ violence, typically by assassinating those who stood in their way.

It should be noted that Chiang's embrace of fascism came *after* his 1927 conversion to Protestant Christianity. Chiang sought to marry into the financially powerful Soong family, that is, to marry Soong Mei-ling (Madame Chiang). The Soong family, however, would only approve of the marriage on the condition that Chiang agree to adopt the family faith—Methodism—and rid himself of his concubines.

As far as the American press and public were concerned, having an English-speaking, Wellesley-educated, Protestant wife was one more reason for supporting Chiang in his valiant struggle against Japanese aggression. In addition, as Lloyd Eastman notes, when it suited his purposes, Chiang was quite "capable of beguiling foreign missionaries with his protestations of his Christian belief."[65]

For this reason, Chiang placed a number of missionaries in leadership positions within his "New Life Movement," the public face of the Blue Shirts. Nevertheless, while the New Life Movement maintained a façade of Christian and Confucian values, George Shepherd, a Protestant missionary and one of the movement's directors, complained in 1936 of the dominant role played by military officers. More telling, in the same year, some of the secretaries of the YMCA expressed their concern that the New Life Movement was "really a blue-shirt movement, looking forward to the regimentation of the country under a sort of Fascist regime."[66]

As will be shown below, in both the Korean and Vietnamese wars that followed, Americans would again look to Christian leaders, no matter how corrupt or autocratic, to save their predominantly non-Christian countries.

## The Korean War

The Christian hope in Korea was vested in Dr. Syngman Rhee, president of South Korea from 1948 until his overthrow in 1960. It was his Protestant faith and Christian credentials, coupled with his fanatical anticommunism, that assured him of American support.

Rhee first came into contact with Christianity when, having completed a traditional Confucian education, he began to study English at an American Methodist mission school. He became a Christian after being sentenced to six years in prison for having encouraged fellow students to oppose the corrupt Yi government prior to Japan's takeover. Thus Rhee's religious faith and his political activism, closely linked early in his career, would become the defining characteristics of his life.

American Protestant missionaries had been active in Korea since 1882, preaching what historian Frank Baldwin describes as a "stiff, conservative brand of Christianity."[67] While only a relatively small number of missionaries remained behind after Korea was annexed by Japan in 1910, they continued to attract many young people to the church. Like Rhee, many early converts became Korea's future leaders.

Of a group of thirty-three Korean patriots who secretly gathered in Seoul in March 1919 to sign a declaration of independence, sixteen were Christians and only two were Buddhists. Publication of the declaration sparked the March First Movement, resulting in demonstrations throughout the country demanding independence.

Under the leadership of Syngman Rhee and Philip Jaisohn, hundreds of representatives of Korean organizations in the United States gathered in Philadelphia in April 1919 to issue a call for Korea's independence from Japan. Their "Appeal to America" proclaimed: "Our cause is a just one before the laws of God and Man. Our aim is freedom from militaristic autocracy; our objective is democracy for Asia; our hope is universal Christianity."[68] Rhee returned to Korea in 1910, having completed a Princeton doctorate in international law, as a Methodist missionary assigned to teach at the Seoul YMCA. Two years later, he fled the country to avoid arrest by the Japanese. In 1912, he became headmaster of the Korean Christian Institute, a Methodist school in Honolulu where he founded the *Korean Pacific Magazine* in 1913 as a forum for his efforts to free his native land from Japanese control.

In yet another outgrowth of the March First Movement, the Korean Provisional Government (KPG) was established in the French Concession of Shanghai in April 1919. Rhee was chosen the KPG's first president in absentia and he traveled to Shanghai in December 1920 to assume his new position. However, in 1925 he was charged with embezzlement and expelled from the KPG, and he returned to Hawaii in disgrace.

In Hawaii, Rhee continued his activity in the Korean exile movement. In 1943, he was again charged with embezzling money earmarked for independence activities, this time by the Korean National Association in the United States. By then, U.S. State Department officials had written him off as "an old man out of touch and representing no one but himself in Korea."[69]

Thus when in October 1945 Generals MacArthur and Hodges, together with former Office of Strategic Services deputy director Goodfellow, plucked Rhee from relative obscurity, they did so in opposition to established State Department policy. The reasoning behind their decision was contained in a series of political reports written in September and October 1945 by H. Merrell Benninghoff, State Department political adviser to General John Reed Hodge, commander of U.S. armed forces in Korea. Benninghoff noted: "The most encouraging single factor in the political situation is the presence in Seoul of several hundred conservatives among the older and better educated Koreans. Although many of them have served with the Japanese, that stigma ought eventually to disappear."

Two weeks later, Benninghoff observed that many of the conservative group's members were "professional and educated leaders who were educated in the U.S. or in American missionary institutions in Korea. . . . [T]hey demonstrate a desire to follow the western democracies, and they almost unanimously desire the early return of Dr. Syngman Rhee."[70]

Whatever his other failings, Rhee could not be charged with having been a Japanese collaborator, unlike those the United States was already working with to build a new anticommunist government in the south. The Central Intelligence Agency (CIA) candidly acknowledged the liabilities of leadership provided by Rhee and his group in a report dated March 10, 1948:

> The Korean leadership is provided by [a] numerically small class which virtually monopolizes the native wealth and education of the country. . . . Since this class could not have acquired and maintained its favored position under Japanese rule without a certain minimum of collaboration, it has experienced difficulty in finding acceptable candidates for political office and has been forced to support imported expatriate politicians such as Syngman Rhee and Kim Ku. These, while they have no pro-Japanese taint, are *essentially demagogues bent on autocratic rule.*[71] (emphasis added)

Rhee quickly went to work with the collaborators. As Bruce Cumings observes:

> Rhee provided, in return for their contributions, protection for a class of people who might well have been dispossessed for their collaboration, by either a communist or nationalist Korean regime. . . . Rhee was the one who could provide patriotic legitimacy. . . . All in all, Rhee's performance was worthy of, and rather similar to, Chiang Kai-shek's marriage of convenience with Shanghai bankers in 1927.[72]

With U.S. backing for his anticommunist group in 1948, Rhee became the first "democratically elected" president of the newly founded South Korean republic.

In April 1960, however, in the face of massive student-led demonstrations, a DC-4 belonging to Civil Air Transport (operated by the CIA) spirited him out of the country. In addition to anger directed at his many years of demagogic and corrupt rule, Rhee was accused of embezzlement for a third time—amounting to some $20 million in government funds.

Like China's "Christian Warrior" Chiang Kai-shek, Rhee was ultimately rejected by his own people despite massive American support. Unlike Chiang, however, Rhee fled to the United States.

## The Vietnam War

In Vietnam, the United States supported a Christian political leader in a land where 80 percent of the people were Buddhists, while only approximately 8 percent were Christian, nearly all Roman Catholic. The U.S. acolyte was Ngo Dinh Diem, a Catholic who became the first president of American-backed South Vietnam. Unlike Syngman Rhee, who owed his rise to power to the good offices of American generals, Diem was heavily indebted to the Catholic archbishop of New York, Cardinal Frances Spellman.

Diem's mandarin ancestors had converted to Christianity in the seventeenth century under the Portuguese and served at the imperial court in Hue until 1907, when Emperor Thanh Thai was deposed by the French. After an education in French Catholic schools in Vietnam, Diem served the French-controlled Emperor Bao Dai as minister of interior. Diem, however, demanded that the French invest real power in a Vietnamese legislature, and when they refused he resigned after only three months in office. This event marked the beginning of Diem's opposition to the French and earned him his nationalist credentials.

Diem was equally opposed to the growing Communist movement in Vietnam led by Ho Chi Minh. Apart from his Catholic faith, there was the fact that the Communist-led Vietminh had killed his brother Khoi and Khoi's son. In 1950, he fled the country, initially to the Vatican and then to the United States.

In the United States, Diem was brought to Spellman's attention by Ngo Dinh Thuc, Diem's brother and a Catholic bishop. Spellman arranged a meeting between Diem and the head of the Asia desk at the State Department, Dean Rusk. From there, Diem's circle spread to include some of America's most prominent Catholics, including Joseph Kennedy and his son John, the senator from Massachusetts, as well as publisher Henry Luce, husband of Claire Booth Luce, a Catholic convert. All these figures saw in Diem the possibility for a "third way" in Vietnam, one that eschewed both direct colonial control by France and Communism while, at the same time, securing U.S. influence.

In the wake of the French defeat by Communist forces at Dien Bien Phu in May 1954, Emperor Bao Dai appointed Diem prime minister. At the same time, Thuc was appointed archbishop of Hue.

With Diem in power, in August 1954 Cardinal Spellman told the American Legion convention in Washington that were Diem's regime to fail it would be "taps for the buried hopes of freedom in Southeast Asia, . . . bartering our liberties for lunacies, betraying the sacred trust of our forefathers, becoming serfs and slaves to the Red rulers' godless goons."[73]

In 1956, Senator John F. Kennedy added his voice to the growing chorus of support, stating: "Vietnam represents the cornerstone of the Free World in Southeast Asia. It is our offspring. We cannot abandon it, we cannot ignore its needs."[74] While formerly French Vietnam was far from being America's "offspring," there could be no doubt that Diem himself was. And the church benefited from this arrangement as well, since millions of dollars in U.S. aid monies were funneled through the Catholic Relief Service for distribution in Vietnam.

Diem's influential patrons provided ample support through such lobbying groups as the American Friends of Vietnam, but he was yet another deeply flawed leader, not least because of his intolerance of other faiths. American author, and former Catholic priest, James Carroll describes Diem's brand of Catholicism:

> He had the Catholic faith of the Inquisition, and he sought to impose it especially on rural peasants, who unlike city dwellers were not beneficiaries of lavish American aid. Diem was the Vietminh's dream, driving more and more of the populace into its arms. Americans expected him to be a democrat, but he was a true medieval Catholic . . . [who] believed that *he ruled by the will of God.*[75] (emphasis added)

Nowhere was Diem and his family's medieval Catholicism more apparent than in his relations with Vietnam's Buddhists. Buddhism, which commanded the loyalty of the great majority of Vietnamese, had long suffered repression at the hands of the French. On May 8, 1963, when the Buddhists gathered in Hue to celebrate the Buddha's birthday, they were prohibited from flying their multicolored flag. This occurred only a week after Hue's Catholics had triumphantly flown blue-and-white papal banners as they celebrated the twenty-fifth anniversary of Archbishop Thuc's entrance into the priesthood.

When several thousand Buddhists gathered peacefully in front of a local radio station to protest, the government forces opened fire, killing one woman and eight children. Buddhist unrest spread throughout the country, climaxing in the self-immolation of sixty-six-year-old monk Thich Quang Duc at a busy Saigon intersection on June 11, 1963.

Quang Duc chose the ultimate form of Buddhist protest, sacrificing himself in support of his faith rather than inflict harm on his oppressors. Madame Nhu, Diem's sister-in-law, designated this and self-immolations that followed as a "barbecue," adding, "Let them burn, and we shall clap our hands."[76] As for those Buddhists who continued to demonstrate against the government, they were, in her eyes, nothing more than "hooligans in robes."[77]

As these events dramatically illustrate, while Diem would reap important political allies from the ranks of the one million Catholics who fled the North for the South after 1954, he never won support from the Buddhist majority.[78] Nevertheless, in May 1957 U.S. president Dwight Eisenhower called Diem the "miracle man" of Asia. During a 1961 visit to Saigon, then–Vice President Lyndon Johnson described Diem as "the Churchill of the decade . . . in the vanguard of those leaders who stand for freedom."[79] With Diem at the helm, the United States steadfastly refused to deal with, let alone support, Buddhist-affiliated religious or political figures.

Defense Secretary Robert McNamara later characterized the U.S. experience with Diem as follows: "That he had studied at a Catholic seminary in New Jersey in the early 1950s seemed evidence that he shared Western values. As we got closer and closer to the situation, however, we came to learn otherwise. . . . We totally misjudged that."[80]

In 1963, with Diem's government on the brink of collapse, the United States endorsed a coup d'etat led by dissident Vietnamese generals. The coup began on the afternoon of November 1 and by the evening both Diem and his brother Nhu had fled the Presidential Palace disguised as Catholic priests, but they were eventually caught and shot.

Diem's overthrow not only marked the end of a Christian reign but also ushered in an era in which one general after another took charge of the country. By mid-1965, there had been no fewer than thirteen changes in government, each promising victory over the Communists only to disappear almost as quickly as it appeared. In sanctioning the elimination of its failed Christian avatar, the United States had sown the wind and would reap the whirlwind during its remaining years in Vietnam. As for Cardinal Spellman, Diem's demise did nothing to diminish his support for the American cause. As James Carroll notes, Spellman "became [SAC Commander] Curtis LeMay in a red soutane."[81]

Spellman, however, was not the only Christian to address the war. On November 2, 1965, a Quaker by the name of Norman Morrison, in opposition to the war, immolated himself in the parking lot just beneath Robert McNamara's office window at the Pentagon. This was followed a week later by Roger Laporte's self-immolation at the United Nations in New York. "I am a Catholic Worker," Laporte said before dying, "I am anti-war, all wars. I did this as a religious act."[82] At a funeral mass for Laporte conducted at the Catholic Worker house, Jesuit priest, poet, and antiwar activist Daniel Berrigan stated that Laporte's "death was offered so that others may live."[83]

Not only was Berrigan rebuked for his remarks by Catholic monastic Thomas Merton, but he was also ordered out of New York by Cardinal Spellman, who arranged for him to be sent on a tour of mission outposts in Latin America. Eventually, after months of protests and petitions, Spellman was forced to bring Berrigan back, but not before another Catholic Worker, David Miller, immolated not himself but his draft card in what Daniel Berrigan's brother (and fellow Jesuit) Philip called "the highest expression of loyalty" to his country.[84]

In the months and years that followed, the Catholic protest movement devised dramatic tactics to convey its antiwar message. In October 1967, Philip Berrigan and others illegally poured blood on draft files in Baltimore while on the twenty-first of that same month 100,000 religious and secular protesters marched on Washington. Then, on November 30, 1967, Senator Eugene McCarthy, a devout Catholic and former seminarian, declared his candidacy against President Johnston on an antiwar platform.

Roman Catholics were not, of course, the only religious figures to protest the war. Protestant leaders such as Yale chaplain and former CIA man William Sloane Coffin also spoke out. Dr. Martin Luther King, a recent recipient of the Nobel Peace Prize, added his voice to the chorus on April 4, 1967, in a speech delivered at Riverside Church in New York City. King noted "the cruel irony of watching Negro and white boys on TV screens as they kill and die together for a nation that has been unable to seat them together in the same schools. So we watch them in brutal solidarity burning the huts of a poor village, but we realize that they would never live on the same block in Detroit."[85]

"Surely," King continued, "this is the first time in our nation's history that a significant number of its religious leaders have chosen to move beyond the prophesying of smooth patriotism to the high grounds of a firm dissent based on the mandates of conscience and the reading of history."[86]

While some might criticize King for ignoring the role of the historic "peace churches," such as the Quakers and Mennonites, in their steadfast opposition to all wars, King correctly noted that the Vietnam War marked the first time large numbers of mainstream clergy actively opposed a war *already under way*. Note, for example, how quickly pacifist sentiment faded after Pearl Harbor.

Equally significant, King realized that the Vietnam War was not a momentary aberration in American foreign policy but an outgrowth of longstanding policy assumptions. These included the assumption that, like other backward and uncivilized peoples, "the Vietnamese people were not 'ready' for independence," based on "the deadly Western arrogance that has poisoned the international atmosphere for so long." And he added, almost prophetically, "A nation that continues year after year to spend more money on military defense than on programs of social uplift is approaching spiritual death."[87]

The mass media, including the *New York Times*, pilloried King, most especially for his recommendation that America's churches and synagogues join together in encouraging "all those who find the American course in Vietnam a dishonorable and unjust one" to apply for conscientious objector status. Nevertheless, in what would be the last year of his life, King continued to speak out against the war, even noting that it was the United States that had "cooperated in the crushing of [Vietnam's] only non-communist revolutionary political force—the unified Buddhist church."[88]

## Conclusion

This chapter has traced the expansion of U.S. power into Asia, from the colonization of the Philippines at the dawn of the twentieth century through World War II, the Korean War, and the Vietnam War. In all of these instances, Christianity was the handmaiden of the state in providing moral and spiritual support and an ethical rationalization for U.S. wars. We have also noted certain important religious-inspired countercurrents, most notably in the antiwar movement that surged in the course of the Indochina wars. In each of these Asian wars, the U.S. encountered other religions, from various animist faiths to Buddhism, but also, in the case of the Philippines and Vietnam, Catholicism.

This chapter has confirmed Martin Marty's words: "One must note the feature of religion that keeps it on the front page and on prime time: it kills." In numerous situations in twentieth-century Asia, this has applied to Christianity, Buddhism, Shinto, Islam, and Hinduism, among others, wherever religions stoked the flames of intolerance. While religion is not invariably the wellspring for hatreds, it has repeatedly been used to sharpen and rationalize conflicts and hatreds that are rooted in economic, political, social, and strategic differences.

This chapter has also described another face of religion: its capacity to articulate visions of peace and brotherhood and to provide the moral foundations for speaking ethical truth to those in power and providing inspiration for creative approaches to peace, for example, in the eloquent words and actions of some American Christians and Vietnamese Buddhists during the Vietnam War. But such precious examples have been set off against far more numerous instances of religious support for the most illegitimate uses of state power, including aggression, repression, mass murder of noncombatants, and even genocide.

Whether or not religion is a primary cause of modern wars between nations or within them, we have attempted to establish that *at a minimum* religion has repeatedly played the role of "force multiplier" in twentieth-century wars fought throughout Asia by enhancing commitment and self-sacrifice on the part of combatants.

Given this, one of the chief challenges of the twenty-first century is for religious and nonreligious alike to compete not so much in saving souls as putting in place systems, creeds, and practices that will no longer serve to foster "the same old death-game." Failure to collectively take up this challenge cannot but doom future generations to continue killing, maiming, and destroying others in the name of God(s) and Buddhas.

## Notes

1. Quoted in the *Australian,* September 9, 2002, 8.

2. Quoted in Robert Payne, *The History of Islam* (New York: Dorset, 1959), 84.

3. Martin Luther, *Martin Luther: Selections from His Writings,* ed. John Dillenberger (Garden City, N.Y.: Doubleday, 1961), 398–99.

4. Martin E. Marty, "An Exuberant Adventure: The Academic Study and Teaching of Religion," *Academe* 82, no. 6 (1996): 14.

5. Reinhold Niebuhr, *Moral Man and Immoral Society* (New York: Scribner's, 1932), 96.

6. Peter L. Berger, *The Social Reality of Religion* (Middlesex, England: Penguin University Books, 1973), 53.

7. Quoted in *Fuji Flyer,* August 18, 1995, 4.

8. Daniel Berrigan and Thich Nhat Hanh, *The Raft Is Not the Shore* (Boston: Beacon, 1975), 34.

9. Paul Johnson, *A History of Christianity* (New York: Atheneum, 1979), 246.

10. Johnson, *History of Christianity,* 241.

11. Walter A. McDougall, "Religion in Diplomatic History," at www.unc.edu/depts/diplomat/articles/mcdougall_religion/mcdougall_religion.html (accessed May 26, 2003), adapted from an essay published in *Orbis* (Spring 1998).

12. Quoted in Margaret Leech, *In the Days of McKinley* (New York: Harper & Brothers, 1959), 345.

13. Quoted in Johnson, *History of Christianity,* 456.

14. Quoted in Michael T. Lubragge, "The Components of Manifest Destiny," in *The American Revolution—An .HTML Project,* at odur.let.rug.nl/~usa/E/manifest/manif2.htm (accessed on February 1, 2002).

15. Quoted in Robert Berkhofer Jr., *The White Man's Indian* (New York: Vintage, 1979), 83.

16. Quoted in Felix Greene, *The Enemy* (New York: Vintage, 1971), 105.

17. Quoted in Victor Nebrida, "The Balanigiga Massacre: Getting Even," in *Philippine Centennial Series,* ed. Hector Santos, June 15, 1997, at www.bibingka.com/phg/balangiga/ (accessed on November 3, 2002).

18. Nebrida, "Balanigiga Massacre."

19. There are conflicting views concerning the numbers of Filipino dead. In its 1998 study, the Philippine–American War Centennial Initiative (PAWCI) arrived at a total figure of 510,000 civilian casualties. For further details, see the PAWCI's report entitled "Parallels to the Vietnam War," at www.phil-am-war.org/vietpar.

20. Johnson, *History of Christianity,* 456.

21. Stuart Creighton Miller, *Benevolent Assimilation: The American Conquest of the Philippines, 1899–1903* (New Haven, Conn.: Yale University Press, 1984), 17–19, 117–18, 138–40, offers a detailed discussion of religious support for and opposition to the Philippines War and U.S. imperialism.

22. Quoted in Brian Victoria, *Zen at War* (New York: Weatherhill, 1997), 29–30.

23. Quoted in Victoria, *Zen at War,* 36.

24. Quoted in Victoria, *Zen at War,* 31.

25. Mark Peattie, *Ishiwara Kanji, and Japan's Confrontation with the West* (Princeton, N.J.: Princeton University Press, 1975), 5.

26. Quoted in Victoria, *Zen at War,* 87.

27. Victoria, *Zen at War,* 90.

28. Victoria, *Zen at War,* 135.

29. Suzuki Nikkyo, "Kun'yu Dai Nijû-go" (Exhortation, number twenty-nine) *Dai-Nichiren* (January 1942): 1.

30. Quoted in Victoria, *Zen at War,* 131.

31. Quoted in Victoria, *Zen at War,* 102–103.

32. Quoted in Victoria, *Zen at War,* 124.

33. Thomas B. Allen and Norman Polmar, *Code-Name Downfall* (New York: Simon & Schuster, 1995), 165.

34. Quoted in Richard B. Frank, *Downfall: The End of the Imperial Japanese Empire* (New York: Random House, 1999), 28.

35. For further details on these and other casualty figures, see Frank, *Downfall,* 28–29, 71–72.

36. Quoted in Victoria, *Zen at War,* 156.

37. Quoted in Victoria, *Zen at War,* 162.

38. Johnson, *History of Christianity,* 478.

39. Quoted in Johnson, *History of Christianity,* 478.

40. Quoted in Johnson, *History of Christianity,* 478.

41. Quoted in Johnson, *History of Christianity,* 478.

42. Quoted in Tony Stephens, "Holy War," *Sydney Morning Herald,* at www.smh.com.au/news/specials/natl/anzac2001/ (accessed February 1, 2002).

43. Johnson, *History of Christianity,* 477.

44. Quoted in Lawrence Wittner, *Rebels against War* (New York: Columbia University Press, 1969), 5.

45. Quoted in Wittner, *Rebels against War,* 37.

46. Quoted in Mark Mason, *The Christian Holocaust* (Hong Kong: Markwell, 1981), 300.

47. Quoted in Mason, *Christian Holocaust*, 301.

48. Quoted in Mason, *Christian Holocaust*, 343.

49. Quoted in Mason, *Christian Holocaust*, 350.

50. Quoted in Wittner, *Rebels against War*, 36.

51. Quoted in Wittner, *Rebels against War*, 37.

52. Quoted in Wittner, *Rebels against War*, 43.

53. Quoted in Wittner, *Rebels against War*, 43.

54. Quoted in John Dower, *War without Mercy* (New York: Pantheon, 1986), 92.

55. Quoted in Wittner, *Rebels against War*, 105.

56. Quoted in Wittner, *Rebels against War*, 105.

57. Harry Emerson Fosdick, *A Great Time to Be Alive* (New York: Harper & Bros., 1944), 147.

58. Fosdick, *Great Time*, 123.

59. Quoted in Lori Reese, "China's Christian Warrior," *Time*, August 23–30, 1999, at www.time.com/time/asia/asia/magazine/1999/990823/cks.html (accessed September 2002).

60. Lloyd Eastman, *The Abortive Revolution—China under Nationalist Rule, 1927–1937* (Cambridge, Mass.: Harvard University Press, 1974), 20.

61. Quoted in Eastman, *Abortive Revolution*, 40.

62. Quoted in Eastman, *Abortive Revolution*, 40.

63. Eastman, *Abortive Revolution*, 42.

64. Eastman, *Abortive Revolution*, 41.

65. Eastman, *Abortive Revolution*, 83.

66. Eastman, *Abortive Revolution*, 69.

67. Frank Baldwin, ed., *Without Parallel—The American–Korean Relationship since 1945* (New York: Pantheon, 1974), 5.

68. Andrew Nahm, *Korea: Tradition and Transformation* (Elizabeth, N.J.: Hollym, 1988), 310.

69. Quoted in Lee Wha Rang, "Who Was Rhee Syngman?" February 22, 2000, 1, at www.ku.edu/~ibetext/korean-war-l/2000/04/msg00031.html (accessed May 26, 2003).

70. Bruce Cumings, "American Policy and Korean Liberation," in *Without Parallel: The American–Korean Relationship since 1945*, ed. Frank Baldwin (New York: Pantheon, 1974), 60–61.

71. Quoted in Lee Wha Rang, "Who Was Rhee Syngman?"

72. Bruce Cumings, *The Origins of the Korean War, Vol. II: The Roaring of the Cataract, 1947–1950* (Princeton, N.J.: Princeton University Press, 1990), 208.

73. Quoted in James Carroll, *An American Requiem: God, My Father, and the War That Came between Us* (New York: Houghton Mifflin, 1996), 165.

74. Quoted in Carroll, *An American Requiem*, 166.

75. Carroll, *An American Requiem*, 167.

76. Quoted in Stanley Karnow, *Vietnam: A History* (New York: Viking Press, 1983), 281.

77. Quoted in Karnow, *Vietnam*, 296.

78. Marilyn Young, *The Vietnam Wars 1945–1990* (New York: HarperPerennial, 1991), 45.

79. Quoted in Young, *Vietnam Wars*, 213.

80. Quoted in Carroll, *American Requiem*, 167.

81. Carroll, *American Requiem*, 168.

82. Quoted in Carroll, *American Requiem*, 171.

83. Carroll, *American Requiem*, 172.

84. Quoted in Carroll, *American Requiem*, 173.

85. Martin Luther King, "Beyond Vietnam: A Time to Break Silence" (speech delivered at Riverside Church in New York City at a meeting of Clergy and Laity Concerned), at, www.hartford-hwp.com/archives/45a/058.html (accessed September 1, 2002).

86. See also Young, *Vietnam Wars*, 198–200.

87. Young, *Vietnam Wars*.

88. Young, *Vietnam Wars*.

# 6

# Japanese Racism, War, and the POW Experience

## Utsumi Aiko

IN THE COURSE OF THE FIFTEEN-YEAR WAR in China (1931–45) and the Pacific War (1941–45), Japan developed a two-tier policy concerning the classification and treatment of prisoners of war: one policy for dealing with the Allied powers ("whites" for the most part), whose prisoners were treated with cognizance of international law on the rights of POWs, and quite a different policy for Asian captives, who were not classified as POWs and who had no rights under international law. Chinese POWs, for example, were treated as laborers called "Romusha." This chapter examines the reasons for the differences in treatment between "white" and Asian POWs and the consequences of those differences in light both of human rights issues and Japan's acute wartime labor shortage and its attempts to use POWs to build morale. It also shows that as the Japanese military position deteriorated and resources of all kinds fell into short supply, the treatment of "white POWs" too often fell far short of international norms, as all prisoners, and indeed Japan's own soldiers, faced life-threatening conditions.

### The Representation of POWs as Racial Stereotypes

#### Happy "Hakujin" Workers

Postwar occupation is commonly imagined to be the first time when the Japanese public saw a large number of *hakujin* or "white people." This is not entirely correct. Indeed, there were more than thirty thousand "white POWs" in Japan at the end of the Pacific War in 1945. The Japanese army had been transporting POWs, both "white" and Asian, to Japan since 1942, putting them to work in various factories, ports, and mines. The sight of these "white POWs" working under Japanese command was part of the everyday wartime landscape for many Japanese. Although it was strictly forbidden to talk to them, many Japanese worked alongside these POWs and the media regularly featured them.

The novelist Yamada Futaro recorded in his diary on November 26, 1942, the sight of trucks filled with POWs seen on his way to work in the Shibaura district of Tokyo:

> They were wearing khaki coats and rimless khaki hats, which shielded red faces that seemed much warmer than those of the Japanese workers on the street, who cast a curious gaze upon them as they drove by.
>
> We passersby, too, did not feel much hatred toward these enemy soldiers. We are a scrawny people. Yet we have captured these men of impressive physical endowment and hold their lives in our hands. Their superior physical appearance actually heightened our feeling of satisfaction and delight.[1]

Yamada often saw trucks of POWs hurrying toward the Tokyo port. While studying to become a doctor, he also read widely in European philosophy, history, and literature. On one occasion, Yamada declared that the works of Basho and Saikaku were mere childish gimmicks compared to the monuments of Western art. Despite, or perhaps because of, his sense of Western superiority, Yamada drew great satisfaction from Japanese control over these towering prisoners.

"White POWs" were frequently depicted in wartime cartoons. On November 25, 1942, *Asahi gurafu* published a cartoon entitled "A Field Day for POWs" depicting an athletic competition between Japanese soldiers and white POWs. A tall POW with a well-defined nose and big eyes pleads: "May I please exchange these for red flags? I don't want to wave white flags anymore." With Japan still on the offensive, the cartoon radiates confidence.

The POW Management Office in the Ministry of the Army directed the media to cover the subject of "white POWs" on a regular basis. Newspapers and magazines regularly featured photographs of them at work. For example, the Tokyo edition of the *Asahi Shinbun* of November 8, 1942, headlined:

American and British POWs contribute to Japan at war
Blue-eyed laborers carry bales of rice:
happily engaged in physical labor with a sense of gratitude.

The phrase "blue-eyed" conveyed to readers an archetypal image of "*haku-jin*" (whites). A photograph showed white POWs carrying bales of rice at a train station. A front-page story the previous day had reported the Ministry of Foreign Affairs' protest against the persecution of Japanese in the United States. A few months later, on January 7, 1943, the *Asahi* published an article entitled "Red-haired laborers work with dirt: the hand that once held a gun against Japan now carries a hoe." An accompanying photograph showed POWs working at a landfill in the Shinagawa district of Tokyo. Illustrated magazines such as *Asahi gurafu, Domei gurafu,* and *Shashin shuho,* a weekly published by the Cabinet Public Information Bureau, all carried articles in a similar vein. For example, *Asahi gurafu* on November 25, 1942, headlined a feature story: "American and British POWs Sweat." Several photographs showed POWs, including shots of them lining up for morning call, unloading bales of rice, working with a hammer or machines, and returning to their internment camp at the end of the day. The article began with this description:

> British POWs, about six feet tall and with their navy caps turned sideways, unload bales of rice that have just arrived at the dock. American soldiers unload large items with that optimistic smile of theirs. Their bodies show tattoos bearing their girlfriend's name or a picture of a woman's face. Such are the snapshots of the American and British POWs at work in the Port of Tokyo, the gateway to the Imperial capital.

The image of American and British POWs working diligently under Japanese supervision heightened Japanese will to fight.

## Grateful Asian POWs

The intended effect of the sight of "white POWs" was to strengthen belief in the invincibility of the Imperial Army among the Japanese public. Another prominent image featured Filipino and Burmese former prisoners of war enjoying their newly liberated status. In contrast to European and American POWs who labored in internment camps throughout the war, most Asian prisoners remained in their country and were quickly released. The photographs carried the message of "Asian liberation." *Asahi gurafu* on July 29, 1942, published the following headline: "The joyful day of parole: Filipino soldiers reunite with their families and cry with gratitude." An accompanying photograph showed a smiling Filipino soldier and his wife basking in the warmth of the Japanese army. In March 1943, newspapers reported the parole of three thousand Filipino soldiers who "swore an oath of absolute loyalty [to Japan] and firm resolve to work to build the new Philippines."[2] What was demanded of these Asian parolees was gratitude and warmth toward their Japanese liberators.

Obedient white workers and gratefully liberated Asians together projected gratitude for "Imperial grace" in this serendipitous picture transmitted to the Japanese public. Covering subjects that would complicate this image, such as the forced labor of East Asian prisoners, was forbidden. In fact, the largest numbers of prisoner labor and forced labor in Japan were Koreans and Chinese. Between 1939 and 1945, 808,965 Korean forced laborers *(kyosei renko)* were brought to Japan, many of them to work in the mines. By 1945, 2,098 Chinese and 4,931 Koreans worked in Mitsui's Miike mine alone (see tab. 6.1).[3]

Hybridity presented the Japanese with problems. The POW Management Office in the Ministry of the Army specified that "white" POWs whose appearance was more "Asian" than "European," such as Dutch soldiers captured in Indonesia who were of mixed racial background, should not be sent to East Asia. The POWs interned in Japan, Korea, and Taiwan had to measure up to the image of *"hakujin"* exemplified by "red hair" and "blue eyes." Their appearance alone, emblematic of the strength of the Imperial Army, would increase the will of the Japanese public to fight.

The presence of white POWs was also intended to dispel Japanese "worship" of Europeans. The so-called "how pitiful" *(okawaisoni)* affair illuminates the Japanese army's attempt to solve this problem. On December 5, 1942, the *Asahi shinbun* headlined a story entitled "Defeat 'the United States' within: what do you mean by saying 'how pitiful' to American POWs?" The subject was an NHK radio program in which a well-to-do Japanese woman had sighed and said "how pitiful" at the sight of American POWs. Lieutenant colonel and press attaché Akiyama Kunio reproached the woman for expressing such sentimentality toward enemy POWs. The message was that one must defeat the United States that resides within oneself.

TABLE 6.1
Number of Workers at the Miike Mine of the Mitsui Mining Company

|  | 1941 | 1942 | 1943 | 1944 | 1945 (May) |
|---|---|---|---|---|---|
| Registered workers (A) | 19,751 | 21,096 | 19,464 | 24,919 | 25,477 |
| Regular employees (B) | 17,305 | 14,626 | 11,606 | 12,205 | 12,378 |
| B/A | 88% | 69% | 60% | 49% | 49% |
| Temporary workers | – | 2,828 | 1,494 | 1,775 | 1,329 |
| Women | 1,746 | 1,677 | 2,377 | 3,070 | 3,271 |
| Chinese | – | – | – | 1,719 | 2,098 |
| POW | – | – | 498 | 1,321 | 1,470 |
| Koreans | 700 | 1,965 | 3,489 | 4,829 | 4,931 |

Source: *Renrakubo* (Monthly report), no. 39, February 15, 2002, published by a former staff member at the Mitsui Miike mine.

## Japanese Treatment of POWs and International Law

### Basic Policies of the Japanese Government

International law relating to the treatment of prisoners of war includes the Hague Treaty on the Rules of Land Warfare, ratified by Japan in 1911, and the 1929 Geneva Treaty on the Treatment of Prisoners of War.

Following the outbreak of World War II, on December 27, 1941, the United States proposed to Japan through the Swiss Embassy in Tokyo that the treaties concerning POWs be "mutually applied." The following January, the Argentine Embassy, acting as the representative of the English, Canadian, Australian, and New Zealand governments, presented a similar proposal to Japan.

In response, on January 21, 1942, Japan's Foreign Ministry gathered representatives from the army's Military Affairs Bureau, the Home Affairs Police Department, and the Overseas Development Ministry to discuss the issue. The Foreign Ministry recommended that "Every effort be made to apply the provisions of the Treaties regarding prisoners of enemy countries that fall under the authority of Japan, including issues such as food, clothing, and treatment of prisoners in accordance with internationally recognized standards of human rights."

Other documents make clear that the army took this to mean, in the words of General Tojo Hideki, minister of war, that "necessary revisions of the principles of the Treaties could be made in accordance with the demands of the immediate situation, and in accordance with Japan's domestic law."[4] According to the head of the Treaty Bureau in the Foreign Ministry, Matsumoto Shunichi, the decision to restrict Japan's application of the Geneva Treaty to "corresponding" application of its principles is explicable in light of government recognition that it might face enormous difficulties in applying the treaty principles to the letter. This did not, he argued, detract from Japan's intention "to apply the principles of the Geneva Treaty wherever appropriate, except in situations where there were insurmountable difficulties involved."[5]

In late April 1942, the Ministry of the Army took up the subject of the Allied soldiers who had been captured in Singapore, the Philippines, and Java. On May 5, the following basic policies regarding the treatment of POWs in the so-called Southern Region were promulgated:[6]

- Intern white POWs in locations such as Korea, Taiwan, Manchuria, and China, and use them as menial labor in order to increase the productivity of Japanese industry and military construction;
- Make nonwhite [Asian] POWs swear an oath and promptly release them so that their labor can be used locally.

To implement these polices, the army proposed to:

- Intern some white POWs from Singapore in Korea and Taiwan;
- Intern skilled workers and high-ranking officers (colonels and up) in Taiwan;
- Construct camps for local internment of the remaining POWs;
- Form special units consisting of Koreans and Taiwanese to patrol and guard the camps.

The fundamental policy of the Japanese army was to use white POWs to increase domestic production and military construction, and to use Asian prisoners as local labor or "liberate" them.[7]

These policies were hastily arranged and many points remained unclear. References to the internment in the Japanese "homeland" *(naichi)* were, moreover, omitted from the document after a member of the General Staff Headquarters protested against "transporting a group of people such as the POWs into the sacred domain of the homeland."[8]

The POW Information Bureau conducted a statistical survey in which POWs were divided into "white" and "nonwhite" categories, although it never clearly defined these categories. When the basic policies were instituted in May 1942, the number of white POWs was 94,347, and by September the number had increased to 125,309.[9]

## "He Who Does Not Work, Neither Shall He Eat"

In May 1942, Japan's Army Ministry approved a new set of "Regulations for the Treatment of Prisoners of War." It was at this time that the strategy of

TABLE 6.2
Number of "White" POWs, May 1942

| Nationality | Officers | Noncommissioned officers and other soldiers | Total |
|---|---|---|---|
| Great Britain | 4,809 | 41,518 | 46,327 |
| United States | 456 | 5,184 | 5,640[1] |
| Canada | 73 | 1,611 | 1,684 |
| Australia | 987 | 15,814 | 16,801 |
| Netherlands | 2,357 | 21,211 | 23,568 |
| Others | 44 | 283 | 327 |
| TOTAL | 8,726 | 85,621 | 94,347 |

[1] This number does not include the 10,633 soldiers captured in the Philippines. The majority of these 5,640 soldiers (4,240) were captured in Java.
*Source:* POW Information Bureau, *Furyo geppo,* no. 3 (May 1942), appendix 5.

using *hakujin horyo*, or white POWs, to replenish a dwindling labor supply was approved and the decision made to transfer white POWs from Southeast Asia to Japan, Taiwan, and Korea.

After inspecting the Zentsuji Division near Osaka on May 30, 1942, Minister of War Tojo Hideki issued the following injunction: "The current state of our nation does not permit those who sit idly to eat along with those who toil. The same rule applies to POWs. I hope you will make them work to their full potential and make them live up to this principle." Tojo thus unambiguously directed that POWs be used as labor. In May 1942, the head of the POW Management Office, Lieutenant Uemura Mikio, invoked Tojo's instructions, informing his troops that "In keeping with the current situation in our own country, where nobody can be permitted to live a life of idleness, and in order to help preserve the health of the prisoners, it is a central requirement that all prisoners, regardless of rank, should be encouraged to willingly perform labor commensurate with their bodily strength and capabilities."[10]

The Hague Treaty prohibited the forced labor of POWs who were officers but not that of enlisted men and noncommissioned officers (NCOs), as did Japan's own 1904 "Rules concerning the Treatment of Prisoners of War." Hence Uemura's reference to the "willingness" of officers to perform labor. In reality, "encouraging" officers to work sometimes included the "inducement" of reducing their rations until they did so.

As we have noted, in using the labor of white POWs more was involved than economic advantage. The commander of Japanese forces in Korea, Itagaki Seishiro, judged the internment of white POWs to be "very effective in wiping out Anglo–American worship and instilling belief in our inevitable triumph," and in March 1942, even before Tojo's directive, Itagaki proposed sending white POWs to Korea. "*Hakujin*" POWs provided the army with potent war propaganda.[11]

The extensive use of POW labor was neither illegal under international law nor unique to Japan. Nazi Germany made extensive use of POW labor in both agriculture and industry, an estimated 2.7–3 million POW workers by the summer of 1941.[12] Japan followed German practice. By contrast, the United States, with its abundant resources of natural and human labor, made little use of POW labor.

## White POWs in Japan's Wartime Strategy

After traveling in a cramped ship for two weeks, American and British POWs arrived in Korea in late August 1942. A crowd of 120,000 Korean and 57,000 Japanese spectators turned out to view the 998 exhausted POWs in Pusan,

Seoul, and Inchon. The chief of General Staff in Korea, Ihara Junjiro, reported to the Ministry of the Army and the Headquarters of the General
Staff on the local reception of these POWs, noting "the exceedingly favorable
benefit" the POWs would bring to "Japanese rule in Korea." The report cited
comments made by Koreans such as "I almost cried with joy when I saw a fellow Korean youth guarding the POWs as a member of the Japanese Imperial
Army" and "It is like a dream seeing as prisoners those Americans and British
who have denigrated us as inferior beings. The sight generated a new pride
among the Koreans at having become Japanese." The Japanese army thus
hailed the psychological benefits of having white POWs in Korea. While
commissioned officers were to "voluntarily" carry out administrative and
other indoor assignments, noncommissioned officers and soldiers were assigned to work in agriculture, construction (roads, railways, seaports, airfields, and so forth), mining, collection of food and other supplies, and warehouse work.

## White POWs as Skilled Workers

The Japanese authorities knew that many white POWs had valuable skills.
Every prisoner was ordered to list special skills when filling out a registration
card. At the Zentsuji camp, outside Osaka, the authorities compiled a list of
skilled workers according to military rank. Among naval officers, for example,
twelve were health professionals and eight accountants; NCOs included
twenty typists, sixteen radio operators, and ten mechanics; and rank-and-file
soldiers included thirteen mechanics and twenty-seven drivers.[13]

Other camps similarly surveyed POW skills. On August 15, 1942, POWs
were assigned to priority areas, including mining, shipping, defense construction, and other types of construction.[14]

The prisoners reportedly worked seven hours a day and had Sundays off.
The POWs were paid one yen per day for their labor. However, operating fees
and military donations were deducted. What remained after these as well as
deductions for food, clothing, and shelter was deposited into individual POW
bank accounts. Some POWs received a little cash after the deductions, and
certain POW camps set up a shop where they could buy liquor and other
items. But when supplies became scarce, the authorities limited the purchase
of goods.[15]

The system, moreover, varied depending on the location of POW camps.
Hugh Clarke, an Australian POW, worked on the Thai–Burma Railway and in
1944 was transferred to the Kawanami shipyard on Koyagi Island in Nagasaki.
He stated that his salary was kept by the Japanese, who bought tangerines and
cigarettes for him out of this amount.[16]

Other POWs, however, report receiving no cash or goods. Their salaries were paid into bank accounts, but some did not have the bank statements in their possession. It appears that there was no uniformity in paying the POWs for their labor. The companies paid the army for POW labor, but after the army deducted operating costs and military donations, many POWs received little or no payment.

In the beginning, the POWs mainly worked as longshoremen in marine, coastal, and warehouse loading, or as workers in transport and loading. Later, individual companies specified the desired number of POWs and the content of their work. The prefectural government decided on the labor, location, and payment and negotiated with the army commander. Ultimately, permission to use POW labor required approval from the local army and the Ministry of the Army. A detailed list of rules for POW labor included specifications such as:

- Company authorities who supervise POWs must carry a pole rather than a weapon and must wear on their sleeves an armband (made of a white square cloth ten centimeters long and marked with the character "*fu*," indicating POW, in black;
- POWs must work separate from other workers; supervisors' interactions with POWs should be restricted to the utterance of work-related words only.

An October 21, 1942, report by the governor of Kanagawa prefecture underlined the positive impact of POW labor on Japanese workers' morale.[17] Observing the POWs at work, Japanese worked harder so as not to be outdone by them. The report stated that as a result, general productivity increased. Some Japanese workers even began to show up an hour earlier in the morning to assure completion of their work. Workers also refrained from demanding wage increases. The report concluded that use of POW labor not only increased domestic production but also helped to increase Japanese residents' will to work.

A Ministry of the Interior report attributed problems in the mining, freight, and construction industry not only to a labor shortage but also to the low productivity of Korean workers, who were said to be prone to protest and to escape from the forced labor conditions under which they worked.[18] White POWs provided an attractive alternative to employers, not only because they worked for extremely low wages and were controlled by the army, but also because they provided propaganda material to instill a sense of superiority and will to fight among Japanese and Korean workers.

On October 21, 1942, a new regulation allowed POWs to be dispatched outside the camp, closer to their work sites. Workstations were built near the factories and responsibility for the POWs living there fell to the companies that hired them. Prisoners were required to pledge that they would not escape.[19]

Other problems, however, arose. In Marugame on Shikoku Island, a group of schoolgirls asked a white POW for an autograph. This act was condemned as "being caused by subconscious worship of foreigners *(gaijin)*." The six girls were censured as a public lesson. At the Kanazawa train station, when POWs were served tea while waiting on the platform for a train, the military police severely warned station officials that "entertaining enemy prisoners with tea would lead to the loss of hostility toward them among the general public."[20]

## The "Banana Transport"

In 1942, 7,144 POWs were transferred to Japan from the Southern Region. In the beginning, 3.3 square meters were allotted to each two prisoners aboard ship. By the end of the year, ships became crowded with as many as six POWs occupying a space of 3.3 square meters. Many suffered from cold and diarrhea as a result of long travel and drastic change in climate and food.[21] Many POWs arrived in Japan seriously ill.

In 1943, the number of prisoners per 3.3 square meters climbed to 7.8 and it even reached ten in 1944. To make matters worse, ships originating in the Southern Region sometimes did not cook meals on board. The Japanese army called this the "banana transport" because prisoners were fed only bananas. Eventually, as many as twenty-nine prisoners were squeezed into a space of 3.3 square meters. They were arranged in two or three shelves in the hold. With poor air circulation, bad food, and sleep deprivation, many became ill.

The imbalance in resources available to the United States and Japan is illustrated by the difference in treatment of POWs. The United States appears to have provided its POWs with relief packages that included a bar of soap, canned tobacco, a bag of instant coffee, sugar, matches, cigarettes, toothbrush and toothpaste, vitamin pills, Hershey's tropical chocolate, Band-Aids, and a bottle of medicine.[22] The contrast to Japan's "banana transport" could hardly have been greater. No wonder many American, British, and Australian POWs experienced Japanese transport as blatant abuse.

White POWs also suffered in ways that had nothing to do with Japan's resource constraints. The Japanese soldiers who were in charge of enemy prisoners had been indoctrinated to choose death over capture by the enemy, a practice that many Japanese troops followed to the letter. For them, viewing the very existence of the white POWs as shameful, it was a small step from contempt to violent treatment. One thousand POWs from Indonesia's Macassar Island were temporarily interned at the Kawanami shipyard on Koyagi Island in Nagasaki prefecture. There were 215 British, 25 American, and 760 "racially mixed" Dutch POWs. In July 1984, the author met Anton Kromrin (this is a phonetic spelling) in Indonesia. The son of a Dutch father and an Indonesian mother, he had been captured by the Japanese navy on Macassar, having recently been drafted by the Dutch. He recalled:

> I was interned in Macassar for a while, but at the end of October was taken on board the *Asama maru*. I was in a dark hold. After seven days, I saw the land lit by bright sunlight. That was Nagasaki. I worked in the Kawanami shipyard on Koyagi Island until the end of the war.
>
> Our only day off was Christmas Day. For the rest of the year, we worked every day unloading cement and timber. The physical labor was hard on my empty stomach. We were given a meager ration of porridge made of rice and beans, or rice and potatoes. If we disobeyed, we were sent to a guardhouse, where we were beaten with clubs. We had to put our hands on our head, and they hit our buttocks. I also saw American and British POWs being beaten. Once I was caught smoking outside hours and was beaten with a gun. I was also hit for not bowing properly. They hit me with their fists.[23]

Anton was in Nagasaki at the time of the atomic bomb, but he was aboard a ship and was uninjured.

By late December 1942, 7,343 POWs were employed in Japan and 8,950 more were scheduled to arrive shortly. The productivity of some skilled workers reportedly exceeded that of their Japanese counterparts.[24]

The Japanese government and military agreed to apply the Geneva Treaty on POWs with necessary modifications in order to conform to Japan's domestic laws and regulations and in light of the (actual) war circumstances.[25] Japan's expression of its "intention to apply the treaty mutatis mutandis" was interpreted by the Allies to mean that Japan would abide by the restrictions imposed by the Geneva Treaty. The harsh treatment of POWs, therefore, would create a firestorm of contention between Japan and the Allied powers.

## Suitable Assignments for Different POWs

On December 15, 1942, Switzerland on behalf of the United States inquired about the labor conditions of interned POWs. The Japanese government responded that its fundamental policy was to observe the Geneva Convention *mutatis mutandis* and that the prisoners were working under safe conditions. Their work hours were said to be the same as those of Japanese workers and their salaries equivalent to those of noncommissioned officers and soldiers in the Japanese army. On February 20, 1943, Switzerland inquired again. The Japanese government again stated that the POWs were employed within the parameters of the Geneva Convention. Undiscussed was Japanese national and racial profiling of POWs. The POW Management Office guidelines for assigning work reflects official assumptions about race and skill as in the following discussion of assignments:

> Indonesian Dutch, Dutch, and people of other ethnicities possessing relatively low technical knowledge should preferably be assigned to simpler types of work such as construction, mining, or loading, while Americans and the British should be assigned to build ships, machines, and steel, and other types of work that require some technical knowledge. Intern POWs of the same ethnicity together in order to facilitate their management and increase their productivity.[26]

## The Gap in Food Supplies between Japan and the Allied Nations

There existed a vast difference between Japan and the United States with respect to the quality and quantity of food. After the end of the war, the director of Kamaishi POW camp was hospitalized at U.S. Army Hospital #361 when he contracted tuberculosis while detained under suspicion of war crimes. He was astonished by the plentiful food at the hospital.[27] He was given chicken casserole, two pieces of thickly buttered bread, boiled eggs, potatoes with ketchup, cake with apples and cream, coffee, and a small bottle of milk. Such a sumptuous meal was beyond the wildest dreams for Japanese, not to speak of POWs, during the late war years and after. These meals made him realize for the first time how starved the POWs must have been under the Japanese. He believed he had done his best to improve the food situation at the camp by buying fish and making powdered beef bones as a source of calcium during the war. He now understood POW complaints.

The International Red Cross sent relief packages to POWs during the war. In October 1943, Japan and the United States exchanged citizens who had been in each other's territories at a port in Portuguese Goa, and the ships that transported them carried many relief packages that were then distributed among different POW camps. In the same year, Japan also received relief goods for POWs from the United States at Vladivostok, for transshipment to China, Hong Kong, French Indochina, and Singapore via Kobe.[28]

At a time when Japan could barely feed its own soldiers—indeed, many of those who were fighting throughout Asia confronted starvation—Suzuki Tadakatsu, who oversaw the distribution of POW relief packages, was surprised that the United States continued to send packages to its POWs. Both their quantity and quality shocked him. Most Japanese had never seen instant coffee and most had not eaten chocolate in a very long time. These food packages came to symbolize the material wealth of America for those who saw them.

Conflicts intensified as the number of prisoners rose in inverse relation to the available food. At the Hakodate POW camp, internees reportedly attacked and cursed guards and skipped work by pretending to be sick.[29] One Dutch POW stole rice from the granary. He was sent to the black hole for seven days. At the eighth branch camp of the Fukuoka POW camp in Yamaguchi prefecture, British POWs reportedly attempted to "instigate" Korean independence by gesturing in a specific manner to five Korean laborers who worked with them at a coal mine. Interactions between POWs and Korean workers were also reported in Kumamoto, where 223 POWs, 1,823 Koreans, 1,522 Japanese, and 100 Japanese prisoners were working to build an airfield. Some POWs reportedly made contact with the Koreans and exchanged goods. Military police investigators concluded that no spy activities had taken place and that the POWs had exchanged goods with the Koreans solely "out of craving." Nishimatsu-gumi, the company in charge of this camp, was nonetheless ordered to tighten control. This incident shows that military police and the Foreign Affairs Police *(Gaiji Keisatsu)* kept close watch on the interactions between POWs and Chinese, Korean, and Japanese laborers.[30]

## "Emergency Measures" at the Branch Camps

The organizational structure of POW camps changed again in 1943, as companies again took charge of supervising POW workers. Previously, the military supervised branch camps established near where the POWs worked, but as the war situation worsened, officers and soldiers left the camps for the front. The only military officers who remained were the camp directors. Other officials were company employees. While Korean and Taiwanese civilian employees guarded POW camps in the occupied Southern Region, it was considered "inappropriate" for them to serve as guards in Japan. Injured Japanese military and civilian employees instead guarded "white" POWs in Japan. Instances of beatings and abuse were particularly frequent at camps that were guarded by wounded Japanese soldiers, many of whom became abusive toward the POWs. The bureau also stated that the guards hired by the companies to patrol the camps, as well as the Korean and Taiwanese guards who were hired by the army for camps overseas, often turned out to be "suspicious" characters. Japanese government officials attributed such abuses to failings of individual guards, while remaining silent on the responsibility of the army, the war ministry, and the companies that hired the POWs.[31]

## 1944: Working POWs to the Bone

As the war situation worsened for Japan in 1944, the transportation of POWs produced numerous tragedies. A U.S. submarine attacked and destroyed the *Arisan-maru,* which was carrying 1,782 POWs from Manila, only four of whom survived. But the Japanese kept transporting POWs from the Southern Region, despite the shortage of ships and the risk of attack. Sometimes they failed to identify the ships as carriers of POWs.

In 1944, many ships carrying prisoners to Japan were sunk en route. When the *Tamahoko-maru* was attacked by a submarine en route from Java, only 212 of the 772 POWs aboard survived. The *Toyofuku-maru,* carrying 1,287 passengers, lost 904 POWs. Similarly, on the *Kachidoki-maru,* carrying 950 POWs who had worked on the Thai–Burma Railway, 520 survived a submarine attack. In all, 12,737 POWs reached Japan in 1944. Even when the ships did arrive safely, many POWs had died on the journey.

A Japanese witness who requested anonymity recalled the coffins being carried out of the hold of a ship:

> It was the summer of 1944.
>     I was working on the first-floor medical room of the Shipping Headquarters of the Army located near the quay. I wanted to see outside, particularly since my boss told me not to look out the window. I still vividly recall the bizarre sight I witnessed after fifty years. I cannot erase it from my memory. On the quay, coffins were stacked on top of one another. Some were not fully closed, and I saw limbs hanging from them. The POWs were barely standing and walking, and their faces were yellow. They seemed just about dead, but they were grouped in file and were taken somewhere by Japanese soldiers.[32]

Hugh Clarke, an Australian POW, was aboard the *Rashin-maru* between June 6 and September 12, 1944, en route from Singapore to Nagasaki. He stated that the hold was so small that only 40 percent of the POWs could sleep at any given time, and that their daily ration consisted of five hundred grams of rice. About 90 percent became ill, but they received no medicine or treatment. By the time they arrived in Nagasaki, they were half dead and infested with fleas and lice. In his memoirs, Clarke describes the stifling smallness of the hold and the fear of beatings by Korean guards.[33]

The workload for POWs became heavier and their treatment harsher. In 1944, as their health deteriorated, resulting in a higher death rate, the vice minister of the army urged improving food and health care. He urged, for example, that sick and weak patients not be forced to do "harsh labor in order to make the employment rate appear high." But with defeat looming and Japanese forces desperately strapped for food and supplies, such directives concerning POWs would be honored in the breach.

## The Hell of Starvation

By 1944, food shortages led the Ministry of the Army to cut military rations and reduce the amount of rice and wheat in soldiers' diets.[34] Troops were also pressed to grow their own food. Camp directors were instructed to adjust daily rations for POWs. Noncommissioned officers and soldiers were provided with 570 grams of food grains per day, and commissioned officers with 390 grams per day. Officers received less food, the authorities explained, because they did light work.

Compared to 1942 rations, the amount allotted for commissioned officers decreased by thirty grams, and officers no longer received extra food when they worked as laborers. Moreover, instead of receiving side dishes, the POWs were given three sen to buy their own supplementary food. But what could one buy for three sen?

Food shortages translated into starvation. Fifty-six years later, in 2002, a reader in *Asahi shinbun* recalled the summer of 1945, when he was a junior high school student and worked alongside the POWs:

> Their upper bodies were tanned and red. Their heads were shaven, and their cheeks and eyes had sunken into their faces. Their bodies were emaciated, showing their rib cages. They looked just like the Jews at Auschwitz.
>
> At lunch, the POWs sat on rubble under the scorching sun, and, with a vacant gaze, silently ate black beans and a rice ball the size of a ping-pong ball.[35]

When camp employees, identifiable by their uniform, went shopping in the market, they were sometimes told, "we have no food to sell for POWs."

Asaka Toshinori, the director of the Eighth Tokyo POW Camp (the Osaruzawa mine of Mitsubishi Mining, later the Sixth Sendai POW Camp), described the food situation in this period during an interview with the author in 1985:

> I admit that it was not enough. But we went out of our way to buy food. Burdock had become a rare item unavailable for ordinary people by that time, but we went all the way to Sendai to get some. At other times, we implored the director of the Kamaishi camp to give us *konbu* kelp. But my indictment stated that I made them eat tree root and seaweed.
>
> Their diet at the time consisted of sorghum, which did not agree with the POWs, so we built an oven and baked them bread. This made them happy. We tried to give them meat on a regular basis by negotiating with the company [Mitsubishi Mining]. There was a Korean internment camp in the neighborhood with a slaughterhouse nearby. We negotiated with the slaughterhouse to obtain blood and insides of cows and horses. And meat, too. The POWs ate the insides, brains, animal blood—things the Japanese do not eat. They put blood in miso soup and happily ate animal brains by cooking them like fried eggs.[36]

Few POWs would later recall eating meat, animal brains or otherwise, during their internment.

The Zentsuji POW camp accepted relief packages from the Red Cross, which provided extra food for a while. But by November 1944, they had completely run out of soybeans, a staple food. Chestnuts, sorghum, green peas, azuki beans, and yams were substituted.[37] Securing food became so difficult that it was not possible to adequately feed the POWs, whatever the efforts of camp employees. Sergeant Sawamura Tadatoshi of the Osaka POW camp protested when I talked about what happened in the camps during the war in a 1998 public lecture at Itami City. He insisted "the POWs ate more food than the Japanese."[38]

There is insufficient evidence to compare the rations of white POWs and Japanese soldiers as the situation in Japan deteriorated. However, Japanese had other ways of alleviating hunger, such as shopping or growing their own food, whereas the POWs did not. Complementing his own experience with diaries written by fellow POWs, Hugh Clarke recalls in his memoirs that they ate burnt rice accompanied by an insipid soup. In June 1945, their rations were reduced to steamed rice mixed with beans and ropelike, dried vegetables with some potatoes. By this time, their rations had been cut in half.

Around this time, graffiti scribbled in English by the POWs was found in toilets at the camps in Tokyo, Osaka, and other places. Some drew the Union Jack and wrote: "This flag will never be destroyed. Our unity is strong like an oak tree." Other graffiti included "peaceful America," "I hate miso soup," "I hate the Japanese," "I want to go home," "I am hungry," and "I will return home this August."[39]

The camp authorities asked the military police to inquire into complaints about, and attitudes toward, the POWs among the local population, and to investigate any false rumors. Hugh Clarke observed that American POWs were treated worse than prisoners of other nationalities, especially after the American bombings of Tokyo and the U.S. recapture of the Philippines. The Americans were beaten most, then the Dutch and the British, while Australians received only light beatings.[40]

## Arousing Hatred toward the Enemy: The Demonic Americans

As the tide of the war turned against Japan, the media stirred hatred toward the enemy in ever more shrill tones. Newspapers and magazines that had previously featured hardworking American and British POWs docilely obeying their Japanese masters now characterized the enemy as demonic. One well-known instance of such media representation was a response to an article, published in the May 1944 issue of *Life*, that included a photograph of an American soldier sending home the skull of a Japanese soldier as a souvenir. On August 11, 1944, *Asahi shinbun* reproduced this photograph with the caption, "Demon Americans, you should be slain. . . . We must take revenge." The article concluded: "With our angry eyes wide open, we shall look straight into the true identity of the beast. . . . We . . . vow to "strike and destroy demonic Americans."

With the press covering the battles of Guadalcanal and Saipan, depiction of happy POW workers gave way to depiction of diabolical enemy soldiers. The Japanese army continued to exploit POW labor, even when faced with air raids and bombings, and regardless of POW hunger and sickness. Some camps evacuated to safer locations.[41] Local commanders, camp directors, and other local supervisors were empowered to decide whether to relocate POWs or to kill them.

## Nonwhite (Asian) POWs: POWs or *Romusha?*

## Japanese Prisoners and Laborers (*Romusha*) in Southeast Asia

The condition of Asians captured by Japanese forces in Southeast Asia in the years 1941–45 differed fundamentally from that of white POWs. Asian soldiers were generally forced to pledge loyalty to Japan as a condition for parole. They would then be "released," only to be employed as local laborers, often under coercive conditions. Captured Asian soldiers (see tab. 6.3) were of course defined as POWs under international law, but the Japanese military released them after anti-Anglo–American indoctrination and then employed

TABLE 6.3
The Number of Nonwhite POWs in August 1942

| Nationality | Count | Already Released |
|---|---|---|
| Indian | 75,466* | 641 |
| Indonesian (as of August 10) | 19,031 | 19,231 |
| Filipino | 42,539 | 4,167 |
| Burmese | – | 1,000 |
| Chinese | 135 | – |
| Malay | – | 11 |
| Others | 5 | – |
| Total | 137,176 | 25,050 |

*Source: Furyo geppo* (POW monthly) (August 1942).
*36,200 were not released. They were used by the Special Intelligence Agency and the army.

many of them as "*romusha*," or laborers. Under this policy, the POW Information Bureau released more than 153,200 Asian prisoners in 1942 alone. In 1943, 22,253 were released; in 1944, 1,352.[42]

## Chinese Prisoners and the POW Issue

The list of POWs compiled by the POW Information Bureau in 1942 included no Chinese, despite the fact that the Japanese army had fought in China for more than a decade beginning in 1931. Although many Chinese soldiers, guerrilla fighters, and militia were captured, they were not classified as POWs, since Japan styled its invasion and subsequent efforts to conquer China as an "incident," not a war. In the course of fifteen years of combat (1931–45), Japan never declared war (very much as the United States later in Vietnam) or set up a POW Information Bureau in China.

Many Chinese prisoners were managed by the Japanese-controlled government in Nanjing. Muto Akira, who headed the Military Affairs Bureau, testified during the Tokyo Tribunal that before the establishment of the Nanjing government in 1937, POWs were under the control of the (puppet) Chinese government in North and Central China.[43]

Although not officially classified as POWs, captured soldiers of Chiang Kai-shek's Guomindang army were classified by the Japanese media as POWs. For example, *Asahi shinbun* reported the number of Guomindang prisoners at forty-four thousand on June 10, 1942. But many other soldiers and local guerrilla forces, including those aligned with the Chinese Communists, were also captured.

To learn more about how these prisoners were treated, in 1995 the author distributed a questionnaire to members of "The Liaison Society of Returnees from China" *(Chugoku kikansha renrakukai),* which consisted of former Japanese soldiers who were captured and tried as war criminals in China. After their return to Japan in 1956, they publicly criticized Japanese wartime atrocities.

In the spring of 1943, a North China Army unit brought about one thousand Chinese Nationalist prisoners to a rendezvous. They were subsequently enlisted in the "Imperial Peace Preservation Army" *(Kokyo waheigun),* whose members worked on railroad construction. Chinese units that fought for Japan after being captured were generally known as the "Imperial Peace Preservation Army."

The former company commander of the Thirty-ninth Division cited a 1943 directive ordering that captured soldiers be used as prison labor. Japanese forces used Chinese prison labor to transport ammunition and food, and to carry injured soldiers in battle, as well as to farm and carry out various menial activities between battles. Clothed in old Japanese uniforms, the Chinese prisoners also wore a small red patch on their chest on which was written the character "*kyo*," which identified them as collaborators.

Some Asian prisoners confronted a degree of brutality far beyond anything that white POWs encountered. A corporal of the Thirty-ninth Division stated that he had killed some Chinese prisoners on the spot because they passed out while marching. They collapsed after being made to carry heavy loads on an empty stomach. Fearing that they might provide information to the enemy if left behind, he killed them. Many stated that they and others had bayoneted Chinese to death during training sessions. Others were killed by sword as practice targets for officers. Injured POWs were shot to death or had their heads cut off. A warrant officer of the Military Police stated that in Manchuria, captured Chinese soldiers were sent to biological warfare Unit 731, where they were murdered in medical experiments.

These responses vividly demonstrate how the Japanese army treated Chinese Nationalist and Communist prisoners, who they denied POW status. Japanese treatment of Chinese prisoners not only displayed blatant disregard for international law, but also ignored military discipline and Japan's own penal code.[44]

## Chinese Laborers in Japan

On November 27, 1942, the Tojo cabinet targeted men less than forty years of age in the North China region for transfer to Japan. Some former prisoners who were classified as reformed soldiers were sent. The decision to import Chinese labor is a clear indication of the seriousness of the labor shortage in Japan.[45]

A number of reformed soldiers were entrusted to the North China Industrial Labor Association *(Kahoku roko kyokai)*. After three months training, they were sent to Japan as "Chinese laborers" *(Kajin romusha)*.[46]

The Furukawa Mining Company intended to use three hundred Chinese at the Ashio mine. In the first group sent to Japan, two collapsed en route. Twenty-five others suffering from malnutrition and disease were unable to travel. By the time they got to Japan, many had swollen limbs and their faces were lifeless. The camp, which held more than two thousand released prisoners, had no doctors and the main food consisted of half-cooked buns. There were no water facilities, so the prisoners had to drink mud water. One hundred and nine Chinese died at Ashio, most from malnutrition.[47]

After the war, the Chinese Nationalist government protested that captured soldiers were taken to Japan as laborers and demanded reparations. Some Chinese workers made their own demands. After the war, Chinese workers protested at the Nanao Chinese Labor Management Office of the Japan Port Industry Association, demanding that the company "recognize their status as POWs and pay reparations." The negotiations escalated to violence and the U.S. Sixth Military Police arrested forty-two Chinese. No reparations were ever paid.

## Other Asian POWs

Many Indians were captured in Hong Kong, Shanghai, Malaya, Singapore, and other British occupied territories. The vice minister of the army, also the deputy head of the General Staff, stated Japan's policy concerning the treatment of Indian prisoners to the chief of the Southern Army General Staff on March 14, 1942. He called on the Indians to reject Indo–British unity and heighten commitment to a vision of "India for Asia." Captured Indians were interned separately from white POWs, and Japan intended to release those Indians who accepted reeducation and employ them as laborers. Japan also held out the prospect of Indian independence. As with Chinese prisoners, the status of the Indian captives was switched to that of contract workers. A number of Indian soldiers were transferred to the "Indian National Army," which was organized at the end of 1941 and fought the British at Inphal, Burma, together with Japanese forces. The rest were assigned to Labor Units and did menial work for the Japanese army or served as guards.

More than 100,000 Asians were captured by the Japanese army in Southeast Asia. After indoctrinating them with anti-Anglo–American ideas, Japan released most Indonesian, Filipino, Malay, Burmese, and Chinese prisoners. The official number of released Asian prisoners reported by the Japanese government was 153,200 in 1942, 22,253 in 1943, and 1,352 in 1944. As discussed earlier, many were used for the propaganda purpose of "Asian liberation" and featured in magazines such as *Asahi gurafu.*

When the war ended, the number of white POWs was 128,463. During the war, 38,135 white POWs had died.

Japanese sense of superiority over *hakujin,* fostered by the presence of white POWs laboring in Japan, would suffer a heavy blow with Japan's unconditional surrender. Replacing the "white POWs" were strong "white soldiers" who came to occupy Japan. The sheer size of the American soldiers, combined with the overwhelming material wealth of the U.S. Army and the fact that Japan was now in ruins, its cities destroyed and its economy a shambles, underlined the reversal of fortunes, lending weight to Japan's defeat.

Japan's POW policy brings out little-known dimensions of Japan's attempts at Asian conquest. These include the importance of racial categories in structuring Japanese international conduct, debates involving the Japanese foreign ministry and the military concerning international law and the treatment of POWs, and the uniquely heavy reliance on POW and other forced labor that lay behind Japan's desperate effort to pursue war simultaneously against China and the leading Western powers. The importance of these issues is underlined by the fact that POW treatment remains contested nearly six decades after the end of the war, with both Asian and Western POWs continuing to demand reparations from a Japanese government that steadfastly rejects any wrongdoing on its part.

## Notes

1. Yamada Futaro, *Senchu-ha mushikera nikki* (Diary of a Worthless Wartime Youth) (Tokyo: Chikuma Shobo, 1998), 10.

2. See, for example, "Nanpo ni okeru furyo no shori yoryo no ken" (Regulations concerning the treatment of POWs in the Southern Region), *Asahi Shinbun*, March 18, 1943.

3. Yamada Shoji, "Chosenjin kyosei renko" (The forced labor of Koreans), in *Kingendaishi no naka no Nihon to Chosen* (The modern and contemporary history of Japan and Korea) (Tokyo: Tokyo Shoseki, 1991), 178. Takematsu Teruo, *Renrakubo* (Communication notes). Takematsu, a former staff member of Mitsui company, researched forced labor at Mitsui's Miike mine and published the monthly report *Renrakubo*. According to *Renrakubo* no. 39, there were four tunnels at the Miike mine. The mine used Chinese laborers for three of the four; the fourth, the Mikawa tunnel, employed POWs for the dangerous task of using explosives to expand the tunnel. In Takematsu's opinion, Mitsui assigned the POWs to this particular task, assuming that they must have experiences in handling explosives from the army. During 1944 and 1945, when the Miike mine used Chinese laborers and POWs, it produced twice the amount of coal mined in previous years.

4. Court Evidence no. 3669-A, *Shorthand Notes for the International Military Tribunal for the Far East* (Tokyo: Yoshodo, 1968) no. 344, 7-8.

5. Court Evidence no. 3039, *Shorthand Notes*, no. 260, 18.

6. Notification from the commissar general of the War Ministry to the Southern Army entitled "Nanpo ni okeru furyo no shori yoryo no ken" (Regulations concerning the treatment of POWs in the Southern Region), May 5, 1942, included in the POW Information Bureau publication *Furyo ni kansuru shohoki ruishu* (Collection of orders and regulations relating to POWs) (reprint, Tokyo: Furyo Johokyoku, 1943), 168; Furyo Johokyoku, *Furyo geppo* (POW monthly), no. 4; *Rikuamitsu Dainikki*, no. 22 2/31. Military Archives of the National Institute of Defense Studies, Tokyo.

7. *Furyo toriatsukai no kiroku* (Records of POW Treatment) (Tokyo: Furyo Johokyoku, 1955), 6. In March 1942, the Ministry of the Army established the POW Management Office within the Military Affairs Bureau to deal with the large number of prisoners who were captured in the Southern Region. It appears that until this date, headquarters had not extensively studied the systematic utilization of POW labor.

Muto Akira, who headed the Military Affairs Bureau until April 1942, testified during the International Military Tribunal for the Far East (the Tokyo Tribunal) that the idea of using POWs as labor "had not at all been researched at the time. Court Evidence no. 3454, *Shorthand Notes*, no. 313, 13.

8. *Furyo toriatsukai no kiroku*, 6.

9. Furyo Johokyoku, *Furyo geppo* (POW monthly), no. 3 (May 1942), appendix 5, entitled "Hakujin furyo gaisu" (Estimated number of white POWs). Also see "Daini hakujin furyo ichiranhyo" (The second list of white POWs), *Furyo geppo* (POW monthly) (August 1942). Both are reprinted in *Tokyo saiban shiryo: furyo johokyoku kankei bunsho* (Materials from the Tokyo tribunals: documents relating to the POW Information Bureau), ed. Utsumi Aiko and Nagai Hitoshi (Tokyo: Gendai Shiryo Shuppan, 1999), 89, 179.

10. The Directives on the Labor of POW Officers and Warrant Officers from the POW Management Office (June 3, 1942 ), in *Tokyo saiban shiryo: furyo johokyoku kankei bunsho* (Materials from the Tokyo tribunals: documents relating to the POW Information Bureau), ed. Utsumi Aiko and Nagai Hitoshi (Tokyo: Gendai Shiryo Shuppan, 1999).

11. Court Evidence nos. 1973–1975, *Shorthand Notes*, no. 146, 16–17.

12. Koseisho Jinkomondai kenkyujyo (The Research Institute on Population in the Ministry of Health and Welfare), "Furyo no toriatukai ni kansuru shiryou" (Materials concerning the treatment of POWs) (Research Institute on Population in the Ministry of Health and Welfare, June 10, 1942), 9–17.

13. "Zentsuji Fuyroshuyojyo" (Zentsuji POW Camp), *Furyo shuyojo junpo* (The POW camp magazine), no. 1, IPS microfilm, reel no. 997.

14. Naimusho Keihokyoku Gaijika (Ministry of Home Affairs, Foreign Affairs Section), ed., *Gaiji geppo* (Foreign affairs monthly) (September 1942; reprint, Tokyo: Fuji Shuppan, 1994), 58–59.

15. Notification from the head of the POW Management Office to relevant units, "Furyo no shojikindaka ni kansuru ken" (On the amount of money in the possession of POWs), July 30, 1943, POW Management Office no. 6: 22. On the same day, relevant units were also notified of "Shuho hanbai seigendaka ni kansuru ken" (On the maximum sales amount of liquor vendors), the POW Management Office no. 6: 21. Both of these documents are printed in *Furyo ni kansuru shohoki ruishu*, 202–203.

16. Hugh V. Clarke, *Last Stop NAGASAKI!* (London: Allen & Unwin, 1984), 62.

17. Report from the Kanagawa Prefectural Governor Kondo Kaitaro to the Commander of the Eastern Army, "Furyo shuro ni kansuru ken" (On POW internment), October 6, 1942, presented as Court Evidence no. 1970A, *Shorthand Notes*, no. 146, 13.

18. Naimusho Keihokyoku, *Gaiji geppo* (November 1942), 84.

19. "Furyo haken kisoku" (Regulations concerning the dispatching of POWs), October 21, 1942, the Ministry of the Army Regulation no. 58, and "Haken furyo toriatsukai kisoku" (Regulations concerning the treatment of dispatched POWs), October 21, 1942, the Army Order no. 74. Both are printed in *Shohoki ruishu*, 30–38.

20. Naimusho Keihokyoku, *Gaiji geppo* (December 1942), 79, 81.

21. Hoda Haruo, *Furyo no shuyo ido ni tsuite* (On moving and interning POWs), National Archives, Washington D.C., RG 331, box 323. Also see *Gaiji geppo* (December 1942), 76.

22. The author obtained this information from an exhibit at the National Museum of Natural History, Washington D.C., on July 24, 1994.

23. Author interview at Baubau, Pulau Buton, Southeast Sulawesi, Indonesia, July 1984.

24. *Gaiji geppo* (December 1942), 76–78.

25. Matsumoto Shunichi, "Beikokujin taiguburi ni kansuru beikokuseifu kougi ni taisuru kaito ni kansuru ken" (The response to the protest by the U.S. government) May 1944; Furyo Johokyoku, "Furyo ni kansuru kogi ni kanshi Furyo jyohokyoku oyobi Furyo kanribu ga shorishitaru kogogara wo kirokushiaru shorui no utsushi" (Collection of POW Information Bureau and section of the POW Management Office against the protests pertaining to POWs maltreatment from allied nations) (reprint, Tokyo: Fuji shuppan, 1989), 159-161. *Gaiji geppo* (December 1942), *Shorthand Notes*, nos. 260, 261 (December 1942). Testimony of Matsumoto Shunichi, Chief of Treaties Bureau, Ministry of Foreign Affairs, *Shorthand Notes*, nos. 260, 17-18.

26. POW Management Office, "Furyo romu haichi no seiri ni kansuru ken" (On the organization concerning the arrangement of POW labor), July 7, 1943, printed in *Furyo ni kansuru shohoki ruishu*, 190.

27. Nakayama Kiyohei, *Ibara no kanmuri* (The crown of thorns) (Tokyo: Jiji Tsushinsha, 1976), 41.

28. Testimony of Suzuki Tadakatsu, Office in Charge of Detained Enemy Prisoners and Civilians (Zai Tekikoku Kyoryuumin-kankei jimusho), Court Evidence no. 3897, *Shorthand Notes*, no. 369, 8.

29. Naimusho Keihokyoku, *Gaiji geppo* (March 1943), 142–43.

30. Naimusho Keihokyoku, *Gaiji geppo* (May 1943), 178–80.

31. Court Evidence no. 3128, *Shorthand Notes*, no. 266, 15–16. Also see *Furyo tori-atsukai no kiroku*, 51–53. On the controversial issue of the work of interned commissioned officers, the Order by the Ministry of the Army was issued on May 20, 1943. The first clause of this law stipulated that commissioned officers could be employed if they displayed "such will" to work; commissioned officers were in fact required to work, even if it was on a "voluntary" basis.

32. Letter from "N" (she requested anonymity) to the author, May 8, 1998.

33. Clarke, *Last Stop*, 1.

34. From Tominaga Kyoji, vice minister of the army, "Shokuryotou no setsuyo ni kansuru ken" (On economizing food supplies), Confidential Telegram Directive No. 3827, May 6, 1944, reprinted in *Shohoki ruishu*, 208–209.

35. "Koe no ran" (The reader's column), *Asahi shinbun*, August 5, 2000.

36. Author interview with Asaka Toshinori in Shinjuku, August 27, 1985.

37. *Zentsuji furyo shuyojo geppo* (Zentsuji POW Camp monthly) (November 1944), presented as Court Evidence no. 3126, *Shorthand Notes*, no. 266, 14.

38. "Tokubetsu Koto Keisatsu," *Tokko Geppo* (The special high police monthly) (June 1944); *Gaiji Geppo* (June 1944), 3–4.

39. Clarke, *Last Stop*, 36.

40. *Tokko Geppo* (August 1944): 46; Clarke, *Last Stop*, 36.

41. Notification from Shibayama Kenshiro, vice minister of the army to relevant units, "Josei no suii ni osuru furyo no shori yoryo ni kansuru ken" (On the treatment

of POWs according to the change in war situations), March 17, 1945, printed in *Shohoki ruishu*, 186–88.

42. Court Evidence no. 255, the interrogation of Muto Akira, Chief of Military Affairs Bureau, No. 3897, *Shorthand Notes*, no. 44, 19.

43. An affidavit presented to the International Prosecutor Parkinson at the Tokyo Tribunal on June 29, 1946, 48. "The 1944 Plan of National Mobilization" (issued on August 16, 1944) urged increasing the number of Korean and Chinese workers. The vice-ministerial meeting on February 28, 1944, ordered the transfer of about forty thousand Chinese laborers, mainly targeting trained former POWs and reformed soldiers."

44. The 2002 Japanese film *"Japanese Devils"* (Riben Guizi) contains testimony by other members of the Liaison Group documenting many of these atrocities.

45. The Ministry of Foreign Affairs Management Bureau, "Kajin romusha shuro jijo chosa hokokusho" (Report on the condition of Chinese laborers), vol. 1, reprinted in Tanaka Hiroshi and Matsuzawa Tetsunari eds., *Chugokujin kyosei renko shiryo* (Materials on Chinese forced laborers) (Tokyo: Gendai Shokan, 1995), 212–15.

46. Maeda Hajime, *Tokushu romusha no romu kanri* (On managing the labor of special laborers) (Tokyo: Sankaido, 1943), 207.

47. Tanaka Hiroshi, Utsume Aiko, and Ishitobi Jin, eds., *Shiryo: Chugokujin kyosei renko* (Materials on Chinese forced labor) (Tokyo: Akashi Shoten, 1987), 233, 255, 258.

# 7

# The Waters Covered the Earth: China's War-Induced Natural Disasters

## Diana Lary

HUAYUANKOU IS A TINY PLACE, not much more than a name on the map, on the southern dike of the Yellow River in Henan Province. In English, the name means "flower garden mouth."[1] There was once a flower garden there, and during the Ming Dynasty the "mouth" was added when a ferry crossing was established. But the recent historical association could not be further removed from the images of lovely colors and scents the name evokes. Huayuankou is associated with horror, the place where one of the greatest natural disasters of all time took place. Huayuankou is where the dike of the Yellow River was deliberately breached in June 1938.

The flood that followed killed hundreds of thousands of people. It was one of the first mass killings in what became World War II, and one of the largest of the whole war, but unlike many of the later killings, this disaster was not the result of a state policy of slaughter, not the deliberate, brutal extermination of the Nazi death camps. Nor were the flood deaths the "collateral damage" of military actions; the breaching of the dike was not part of an attempt by an aggressor to bring an invaded country to its knees. Instead the flood that started at Huayuankou was a man-made disaster that grew out of the despair of the Chinese government and army, driven to a desperate act by the Japanese invasion of their country and the defeat of Chinese armies. In the face of the relentless Japanese advance, the Chinese high command decided to "use water as a substitute for soldiers" (*yishui daibing*), to turn the Yellow River into a strategic weapon to stop the enemy advance.

In military terms, this strategy can be seen as a variant of a strategy of scorched earth—the destruction of natural resources to deny them to the enemy—in this case drowning the earth rather than scorching it. But given the awful human consequences, it is hard not to see it as a state acting against its own people, by using an integral aspect of civilian life, a river, as a weapon of war. In the post-9/11 world, we see turning a normal part of civilian life (an airplane) into a weapon as terrorism. In China in 1938, a military action, conducted by the state, turned out to be an act of terror against that state's own civilians, in short, terror conducted by and in the name of the Chinese state, for the protection of China.

The huge flood unleashed through the breach in the dike at Huayuankou achieved the military target of preventing Japanese armies from taking Zhengzhou, the provincial capital of Henan and the key railway junction between the north–south railway line, the PingHan, between Beiping (Beijing) and Wuhan, and the east–west LongHai line. The dike was cut in the nick of time—the Japanese had already occupied Kaifeng and their vanguard was only thirty miles from Zhengzhou when the dike was cut. But the strategic gain was limited, because it only blocked the Japanese advance on one route. Japan's goal was not Zhengzhou, but Wuhan, the temporary capital of China and the hub of Central–South China; it could be reached by other routes. The Japanese command redirected their attack on Wuhan up the Yangzi. Zhengzhou did not fall, but Wuhan was captured in October 1938. The Japanese failure to take Zhengzhou did mean that until late in the war the Japanese could not use the PingHan line, a major inconvenience for north–south connections.

## The Flood

After it leaves the mountains that fringe the North China Plain, the silt-laden Yellow River flows between man-made dikes, which loom high above the plain. When the River[2] is in spate, in the early summer, it flows between three and twelve meters above the surrounding land. For much of the rest of the year it shrinks to a modest flow, deep within its dikes.[3] The dikes, huge structures of stone, earth, and wattle up to sixty feet tall at their crests, are built to withstand the force of the River in spate.

The River has never liked being controlled; it broke its dikes at least 1,500 times between 600 B.C. and 1949 A.D. and changed its course twenty-six times; the great majority of these breaches and course changes—one thousand of the breaches and all of the course changes—took place in Henan.[4] The dikes need constant maintenance, always one of the key tasks of Chinese governments since the mythical ruler, the Great Yu, first won control over the waters of the

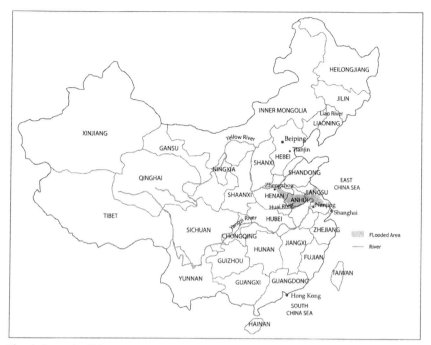

**Flooded area in China**

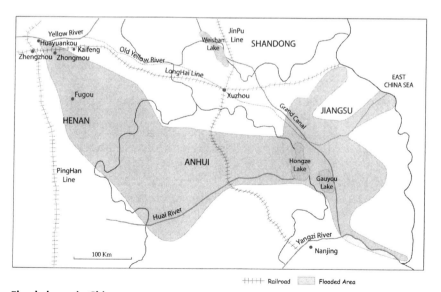

**Flooded area in China**

River. Teams of laborers and engineers stood duty on the dikes throughout China's history, carrying out maintenance and repair and closing breaches when the River broke through. In 1887, for example, a breach ten miles east of Huayuankou was closed within two years.[5]

Official and popular tradition has it that the dikes failed only when a government was negligent and corrupt; failure to maintain the dikes was a sign of a government's decline. A Yellow River flood was a sign of the waning of a government's competence to rule China, a sign of the ending of its mandate. There was a complete association between the solidity of the dikes and the good health of a government. But "solidity" meant the dikes' capacity to withstand the attacks of raging waters. The idea of a government deliberately opening the dikes was inconceivable. Yet this is what the Chinese high command decided to do in late May 1938.

The military situation was critical. After a bitter nine-month campaign to stop the Japanese advance into China, Japanese armies had taken almost all of the railway lines and most of the major cities of northern and eastern China. Chinese troops had been forced to withdraw, at the end of the Xuzhou (Jiangsu) Campaign, whose high point was a Chinese victory at Taierzhuang in early April. The victory could not be sustained and by mid-May a vast Chinese army was fleeing southwestward from Xuzhou, into Anhui, making for Wuhan.

Henan is bisected by the River, which flows east across the province and then turns northeast toward the sea. At this point, the province was already partially under Japanese occupation. Most of the northern part of the province, above the River, had fallen in the winter of 1937–38. The towns on the northern bank of the River had been occupied in February and March, and Japanese troops appeared soon after on the northern dikes, separated only by the width of the River from the Chinese defenders. Henan south of the River was still defended, but the morale of the troops was low, and it sank further when the Japanese started to advance westward along the LongHai railway.

Their approach filled the people to the south of the River with terror. The Japanese invasion of China was accompanied by terrible atrocities against civilians, the most infamous incident being the Nanjing Massacre (December 1937–January 1938). Stories of atrocities brought near panic to China's civilians. The *Henan Minjian Ribao* (Henan popular daily) published in Zhengzhou carried frequent and grim reports of atrocities committed by Japanese troops in the occupied north of the province.[6] The people living south of the River, caught between anguish at what was happening to their people across the River and fear at the thought of the fate that awaited them when the Japanese army reached them, were ready to help Chinese forces to resist, but nothing prepared them for the catastrophe about to befall them.

In late May 1938, the situation was critical: Japanese troops on the south bank were about to take the ancient city of Kaifeng; Zhengzhou was threatened next; Japanese troops on the north bank had been prevented from crossing the River at Zhengzhou only by blowing up the railway bridge; Chinese troops under General Shang Chen were still holding firm on the south bank, but had no hope of reinforcement and were in danger of being overwhelmed. In this desperate situation, the decision was made by army command in Wuhan to open the Yellow River dike.

There is no doubt that the decision came directly from Chiang Kai-shek; he did not deny responsibility for it at the time, as commander in chief, or later. Nor is there any evidence of division or opposition within the upper echelons of the Chinese military. At the time, the decision seems to have been quietly accepted as a desperate strategy in a desperate situation, but one with a deeply symbolic meaning—using the ultimate symbol of China to defend the country.

Later on, a division of opinion as to Chiang's rationale for making the decision did develop. Most commentators from the Guomindang side (GMD) hold that the order to breach the dike was given for strictly military reasons, and that it was a desperate strategy, though understandable in the context of the time.[7] Chiang's detractors are more critical. Some focus on his state of mind. Frank Dorn, an American military attaché in China at the time, spoke of Chiang panicking and turning to an impossible strategy, that is, Dorn put the blame for what subsequently happened on Chiang's psychological state.[8] Chinese Communist Party (CCP) sources are equally critical of Chiang, but on a class basis; they pay no attention to the war situation and accuse Chiang of utter callousness, a total lack of concern for the common people of China. This view has been echoed by other commentators. Lynn Pan, in her book on the Yellow River, says, "I doubt if Chiang ordered this [cutting the dike] lightly, but then I also doubt if it cost him much remorse. It was a strategy necessitated by war, that was all."[9] The comment is not false—but the last three words, "that was all," ignore quite how desperate China's military situation was in late May. China had lost the best of her armies and had nothing to counter Japan's air, naval, and materiel superiority. All her major cities except Wuhan and Guangzhou had been lost, and further defeats seemed inevitable. From a strategic point of view, so much awfulness had already happened that any strategy, however far-fetched, seemed worth trying. Civilians in the occupied areas had already suffered so much that, if the outcome of the breach for the peasants of the North China Plain was thought through at all, it must have been balanced against the likely costs of occupation—horrors in themselves.

Once the order to open the dike came from Wuhan, Cheng Qian, the commander of the First War Zone and governor of Henan, ordered men under his command to prepare to destroy the southern dike, just west of Kaifeng. Chen Weirui, as the civilian in charge of the dike, was in daily discussions with Cheng in late May and early June. He informed Cheng that the work of mining the dike would have to be done by soldiers; the men who worked under him lived in the shadow of the dike, and would be incapable of destroying it.[10]

The first two attempts to breach the dike, at Zhaokou, were unsuccessful. Soldiers dug cavities into the dike and placed explosives in them. On June 4 and again on June 6, the explosives were set off and the dike was holed, but the holes were too shallow and too high up the dike to make serious breaches.[11] Water from the River trickled through at one point for two hours before the breach was silted up by the sand in the water.[12] This failed effort increased the sense of desperation. The soldiers working on the dike were coming under sporadic Japanese shelling and had to do a lot of the work at night. It seemed impossible that a breach could be made before the Japanese arrived. The pressure from Wuhan was intense. Chiang Kai-shek telephoned again and again to the commanders in Zhengzhou and at the site to insist that the orders be carried out.[13]

The third attempt was at Huayuankou. Soldiers hacked away at the surface of the dike with spades, picks, hoes, drills, and hammers, excavating the dike from the top downward. No explosives were used at this stage. The dike was too strong and too wide to be destroyed by conventional explosives, unless it was first mined right through. It was widely assumed at the time and later on that the dike had been destroyed quickly, with explosives, or even that it had been bombed, but such a huge structure would have been almost impossible to blow up without mining. There was no time left to mine the dike; it had to be excavated.

On June 9, early in the morning water finally flowed through the dike and onto the plain below. The water flowed slowly at first, and the soldiers continued to dig away at the sides of the breach to increase its width. Some explosives, possibly mortar rounds fired into the sides of the breach, were used at this stage. Then the water started to gush. Over the following days and weeks, the current widened the breach steadily, until it was hundreds of feet across.[14] The main current of the River now flowed out toward the southeast, taking three quarters of its flow away from main course, pouring across the flat plain. When David Barrett, a U.S. assistant military attaché, flew over the site several weeks later, on a tour arranged by the Japanese military spokesman in Beijing, the breach was already three hundred yards wide and a great sheet of water spread out as far as the eye could see from a plane flying at a thousand feet.[15]

To halt the Japanese advance along the LongHai railway line, the flood only needed to cut the line itself, which ran just south of the River. But the flood had its own momentum, as any local or anyone who glanced at a topographical map must have known it would. The breach was at the head of a vast alluvial fan that spread out to the south and east.[16] The flood waters flowed toward the southeast, into the shallow, sandy beds of hundreds of streams and rivers that flowed toward the Huai River. The flood filled these watercourses, broke their banks, and poured out over the land to the east and west, inundating much of southeast Henan. The waters advanced with slow, inexorable deliberation, moving forward about ten miles a day. By the beginning of July, they had crossed into Anhui Province and entered the headwaters of the Huai River.[17] Once the flood entered the Huai, it turned northeast, cut the north–south JinPu railway line, and then poured into the Hongze Lake. The lake filled up quickly, and then the flood burst out in to Jiangsu Province. It flowed in three streams toward the sea. The northernmost branch flowed northeast across the plain. The middle stream moved into the old, pre-1855 Yellow River bed. The third poured through a series of small lakes and streams into the Grand Canal and turned south toward the Yangzi. The pressure of the waters broke the banks of the Grand Canal and flooded much of Jiangsu east from the canal to the sea.[18] Eventually seventy thousand square kilometers of land were flooded.[19]

As the flow of water coming down the River increased in the "normal" summer flood season, so the flooding increased. By cruel coincidence, the summer of 1938 was one of the wettest on record. Throughout June and July, the flooded area was under an almost continuous, unprecedented downpour, the rain only making the flood situation worse. The Yellow River flood was manmade, but other rivers were overflowing from natural flooding. The Yangzi was so full that it was expected to flood, too, though in the end it did not.[20]

The impact of the flood on the population south and east of the breach was almost beyond imagining. The Chinese military authorities had no means to warn the dense agricultural population in villages and small towns strung out across the plain that the flood was coming. In the days before radios and loudspeaker systems, only telephone messages to government offices and then word of mouth could warn people of what was coming. The offices were in chaos, many of the officials (and the local gentry) had already fled. Even if warned, peasants were unwilling to leave their land and their crops; the flood came at the peak season of the agricultural year, and the main crops were almost ready to harvest. This was the least likely time a peasant would flee willingly.

Warnings would have made little difference in helping people to escape from the flood. There was no refuge out on the flat plain, no hills, not even any high buildings, in an area where most houses were single-story adobe buildings. The only high structures that rose clear above the plain were the dikes of the River themselves. They became the temporary refuge for tens of thousands of people from the area immediately south of the breach.[21] Further south, there were no high places for refuge, except the walls of county towns.

The flood waters were quite shallow—seldom more than two or three feet deep—but they were implacable. With nowhere to escape to, and no rescue in sight, at least 800,000 peasants died in the flood itself. Others who survived the immediate flood died of hunger or illness over the next weeks and months. Millions of people on the western edge of the flood became refugees, fleeing in to West Henan and Shaanxi Province, both very poor areas. At the end of the war in 1945, there were six million refugees from the flood zone *(huangfanqu)* still in the places they had originally fled to, some receiving subsistence aid from the GMD government, others not.[22] Virtually no one fled to the east, the terror of the Japanese occupiers so great that flight in that direction was unthinkable. Some people managed to flee the area altogether, to the southwest and Wuhan, joining the hundreds of thousands of refugees who had already fled there from other parts of eastern China.[23] But most peasants could not afford this long-distance flight. This was a region of bare subsistence, where tough, stoical peasants scarcely grew enough to feed their families, let alone had money to spare for flight.

The River was an enormous danger in its new course. It gradually dug itself into a clear channel, but was still much more menacing in its southern course than it had been in its northern one, because it had no dikes to protect the surrounding land during periods of high water. As long as the River had no dikes, there was a chronic danger of flooding; much of the land was waterlogged. In earlier floods, government authorities would have moved immediately to close the breach. But the breach was the front line between invader and defender. It was inconceivable that either the Chinese or the Japanese would think of doing such a thing; in any case, neither side had the expertise necessary to do the work; the experts of the Yellow River Conservancy had fled.[24] The breach would stay open as long as the war lasted.

To the north and east of the flood zone, other civilians suffered indirectly from the breach. In the Xuzhou area, immediately to the northeast, large numbers of Japanese troops, whose advance westward had been stalled, took up permanent occupation and kept the local population under a reign of terror that endured into 1939.[25] Civilians still further north, living along the old course of the River, lost the part of their livelihood that depended on the River. All water-born traffic ceased. "On the lower course of the river, now carrying little more than a trickle, hundreds of craft were stranded with their tall masts pointing at crazy angles."[26] These people were not direct victims of the flood, but their incomes were affected dramatically. Some people along the old course actually benefited from the flood. They moved in to the dry riverbed and brought much of it under cultivation. But the "beneficiaries" were far fewer (about 200,000 by the end of the war) than the losers. The majority of the people living along the lower reaches of the old course were devastated by the sudden loss of the River, a catastrophe that turned their world upside down. But they, like the survivors of the flood zone, were without a voice, and had no means of finding help. They were abandoned souls.

## The Casualties

In the months following the breach, the scale of the casualties was scarcely recognized. Joseph Stilwell, the senior U.S. military attaché in China, noted in his situation report for the period May 22 to June 25 that Japanese military sources put the number of casualties at 100,000, but himself estimated that the numbers were much lower.[27] David Barrett, in a report based on his trip over the flood in July, doubted that many people had drowned.[28] Then the question of numbers disappeared until the Chinese government published statistics in early 1943 that claimed that twelve million people in forty counties had been either killed or severely affected by the flood. These figures might be looked at with some skepticism, since they were compiled in wartime by an administration that was hundreds of miles away from the scene, in the wartime capital of Chongqing.[29] It was 1948 before the Ministry of Administration (Xingzhengyuan) put out detailed statistics on the casualties of the flood, for each county inundated.[30] The statistics were listed without any indication of how they were collected, and they presented the information baldly in three categories: dead, refugees, and preflood population. But they are the only casualty figures ever presented on a place-by-place basis and they have some extra credence for that reason.

These figures show that the worst affected counties were the ones some distance from the breach, that caught the full force of the flood, before it subsided as it fanned out. In one of the worst affected counties, Fugou, due south of the breach, 79 percent of the population was reported either drowned or forced into flight: 78,600 (25 percent) were drowned, of a preflood population of 315,500, and another 169,800 (54 percent) fled.[31]

The global figures for the victims of the flood give the staggering number of more than 800,000 deaths and almost two million refugees in the two provinces of Henan and Jiangsu. The death rate can be assumed to be much higher, since the figures for Anhui do not distinguish between dead and refugees (see tab. 7.1).[32] Other figures have been given for how many people

## TABLE 7.1
### Deaths and Casualties of the 1938 Flood, by Province

|              | Henan     | Anhui     | Jiangsu   | Total     |
|--------------|-----------|-----------|-----------|-----------|
| Dead         | 325,589   |           | 529,900   | 855,498   |
| Refugees     | 1,172,687 |           | 687,470   | 4,840,460 |
| Dead/refugees |          | 2,980,303 |           | 2,980,303 |

died in the flood, ranging from a low of 400,000 to a high of 900,000.[33] The exact number will never be known, but lack of precision does not detract from the magnitude of the tragedy—and a tragedy so great that it is almost impossible to grasp its scale. The deeply cynical comment that "one death is a tragedy, a million deaths is a statistic" (attributed to Josef Stalin) is not completely false. Huge numbers have a numbing effect on even decent and caring people. The official war artist to the Canadian army, Alex Colville, has spoken often of the guilt he felt when he entered Belsen that he did not feel worse than he did in the presence of thirty thousand dead. He did not have the capacity to grasp the full horror that he saw with his own eyes and recorded on paper, because the scale was beyond his understanding.[34]

## A War-Induced Natural Disaster

The Huayuankou flood disaster was mysterious and inexplicable; it fell upon people who had no means to prepare themselves or to defend themselves. The army they had counted on to defend them was the agent of the disaster.

The sense of betrayal was enhanced by the absence of any organized help for the victims. The flood happened in a period of chaos and confusion brought on by the Japanese invasion, when there was almost no functioning civilian government in the flood zone and the people who might have intervened to stop panic and provide some relief, the local gentry and community leaders, had fled. The victims were helpless. They had no external, impersonal source to turn to for help or compensation. The insurance industry in China was in its infancy, and no peasants on the North China Plain would have had coverage. The traditional local mutual aid associations had largely broken down in the chaos of invasion and defeat. Many Western missionaries stayed on, especially in the large cities (Kaifeng and Zhengzhou) just north of the flood zone, but they had few material resources to help the victims.

The surviving victims could find no one to blame, either at the time or later. The flood was clearly not the fault of vindictive gods or of any other supernatural force. The attacking enemy did not commit the act of destruction, though their aggression precipitated it. The victims were not killed as a result of direct military actions; they were not victims of bombing or of enemy atrocities. They were the victims of the inadvertent consequences of a Chinese military strategy, of a catastrophic reaction to a brutal invader.

The Chinese army may have been driven to breach the dike in an effort to save the nation from being completely overrun. But the absence of any calculation of civilian casualties, the lack of warning, and the lack of relief work after the flood started make it difficult not to see the breach as an act of terror, terror derived from desperation rather than deliberate callousness. On the ground, the difference between being the victim of premeditated terror or of terror that resulted from a desperate strategy was not perceptible.

One way found to offset the perception of responsibility on the part of the Chinese state was to credit the decision to create the flood to Alexander von Falkenhausen, the chief German adviser.[35] As Japan's pressure on China increased during the 1930s, he had advocated ceding land to Japan to avoid war; he believed that no attempt should be made to defend China north of the Yellow River, and he did suggest that China prepare to hold up the enemy through a "systematic inundation" of the Yellow River Valley.[36] It was one step further to blame him for a tragic mistake, one that as a man given to bombast and self-aggrandizement he was unlikely to deny; he took credit for almost any military action taken in China while he was there.[37] But the explanation is not convincing. It was too neatly convenient to blame a foreigner—and one whose later career as a Nazi *Gauleiter* in Europe condemned him to disgrace and imprisonment as a war criminal—for one of China's worst disasters.

The much more banal explanation is that there was no deliberate intent in the Chinese high command to kill vast numbers of civilians, but that huge miscalculations—or rather a lack of calculations—of the outcome of the breach and its impact on civilians turned a defensive strategy into inadvertent state terror.

## A Silent Disaster

In the summer of 1938, the disaster unfolded in silence. Huayuankou was barely covered in the media in the weeks and months after the breach, either in China or abroad. It seems incredible that such an enormous catastrophe should escape public attention, but it did, though less out of callousness than because of the conditions of war. There was no one left in the region to report the flood. The Chinese newspapers had abandoned their prewar offices in Nanjing and Shanghai, and were unable to send journalists in to cover a story that would have put them in danger of falling in to Japanese hands. Two of China's best journalists, Fan Changjiang and Tao Juyin, covered the Xuzhou

Campaign, but then left with the retreating Chinese forces.[38] Several foreign journalists and writers (Peter Fleming, Jack Belden, W. H. Auden, Christopher Isherwood, and Israel Epstein, to name a few) covered the campaign, but they, too, either moved southwest with the retreating Chinese forces or went directly to Wuhan. None of them made any detailed mention of the flood. The famous war photographer Robert Capa took some photographs of people walking through the flood waters, but then he, too, moved to Wuhan, where the story of the war was still unfolding.[39]

The Chinese government made a brief effort to get some publicity out of the breach, but in such a cack-handed way that nothing came of it. The ploy was to blame the breach on Japanese bombing. An event was staged (after the breach had been made) that showed Chinese soldiers trying to fill in the breach. This event was filmed by official filmmakers, but if the film was ever shown it has since disappeared.[40] There were no further attempts to make propaganda after this—the silence almost a tacit recognition of how dreadful the outcome was turning out to be.

The catastrophic course of the war during the summer of 1938 explains why so little coverage was given to the flood. Japanese forces were advancing up the Yangzi, and at the same time bombing Guangzhou to the far south. Chinese resistance seemed to have crumbled. The papers were full of nothing but the terrible anxiety that Wuhan and Guangzhou would soon fall, and that all of China would be in Japanese hands. The story of the Yellow River flood disappeared.

Floods of this type are difficult stories to cover, because they are not dramatic news stories; a huge area is slowly inundated, widely dispersed people cling to trees and rooftops until they lose the strength to hold on, animals are drowned in the fields—none of this has the drama of a battle or a wildfire or even of a flood coursing through a major city. Floods also prevent coverage, because they make an area inaccessible. The only way to get an impression of the scale and the damage of a flood is from the air, and in China at the time aerial coverage was out of the question. The *North China Herald,* the main English-language paper in China at the time, did cover the flood, but not as a major item. The whole-page spread of photographs of flooding published on June 22 was not of the Yellow River flood but of the streets of Shanghai, deluged by unprecedented rainfall.[41] Their weekly coverage continued into July—when the flood was still advancing—and then petered out.

The Japanese military was not sure how to interpret the disaster—as a strategy that had cost them access to Zhengzhou and the main north–south railway line or as a sign of the cruelty of the Chinese government, that is, a *casus belli* for themselves, as "protectors" of the Chinese from their cruel rulers. Their uncertainty meant that they said as little as possible. They took some

Western journalists and the U.S. military attaché Barrett on plane trips to see the devastation, claiming that the flood was an example of the Chinese government's "ruthless contempt for human life."[42] But they were on shaky ground talking about contempt for human life, and they soon abandoned their efforts to influence the Western media. The flood did worry them, however, as a strategy that might be repeated. A Japanese source told Joseph Stilwell in July that they feared the strategy might be repeated on the Yangzi when the attack on Wuhan was launched.[43]

None of the discussion elsewhere meant much to the peasants who drowned or those who were forced into flight. They were at best the victims of the god of national salvation. There has never been any hope for them of reparations or compensation, no possibility of a historical commission to recognize the horrors that people endured and give meaning to their suffering. Huayuankou meant almost total loss for the victims—those who did not lose their lives lost their homes, their fields, their animals, their crops, their tools, their temples, their graves.

## After the Flood

The flood zone remained a disaster area for many years after the breach of the dike. There was an immense problem of destruction of habitat. Many places were abandoned, the people gone, the livestock drowned, crops destroyed, houses, roads, bridges, public buildings all ruined. In many areas, the water scarcely subsided after the high water season had passed. In Fugou, one of the worst affected counties, much of the county town was still under water in 1946, and the town was almost empty of people.[44] Large parts of the flood zone were uninhabitable. Agriculture could not resume until the land itself was rehabilitated; the banks of the irrigation channels had been eroded by the flood, the channels were silted up. Where the water did go down, much of the land itself was destroyed, covered in hard baked mud and sandy silt. According to GMD figures at the end of the war, two million acres of farmland had been out of production since 1938.[45] The work of rehabilitation and resettlement did not start until after the war was over. The 1946 population of the twenty counties affected in Henan was still 19 percent below that of the 1936 population—that is, less by 1,250,000 people.[46]

The flood zone was without effective government for a long time. As in much of North China formally occupied by the Japanese, there was no real authority to take control. Over the whole occupied area, the first years after the Japanese arrival were marked by total confusion, with GMD and CCP guerrillas and regular forces, local militias, bandits, and secret societies involved in intricate patterns of competition and cooperation with each other against Japan. One such arrangement was between the CCP's New Fourth Army and bands of Red Spears, one of the leading local secret societies. This was the start of a fruitful collaboration that led to the CCP becoming the most influential force in the area, especially after 1940, when the united front between the GMD and the CCP broke down.[47] Much of the flood zone was gradually incorporated into a major guerrilla base, the Yuwansu Base Area, which was dominated by the CCP.[48]

After the war was over in 1945, the GMD government resumed control over the whole of China, in theory, though not in fact. Their control of North China was sketchy at best, and the clouds of civil war were gathering. Nevertheless, one of the returned government's first tasks was to put the Yellow River back into its old course. In 1946, the government asked for the help of the United Nations Relief and Rehabilitation Administration (UNRRA) to close the breach at Huayuankou. At the start of a civil war, this might have seemed a distraction from the fighting, but the control of the Yellow River was too important a symbol of legitimacy and authority to neglect the obligation to close the breach. Planning for the closure had started long before the war was over, in 1942. By the end of the war detailed plans were ready.[49]

UNRRA also recognized the importance of the task, not least because it would bring a vast area of land back into cultivation. UNRRA opened an office in Chongqing in 1944 to prepare for work on the Yellow River and on seven other major flood control projects. In 1946, O. J. Todd, an American engineer who had worked in China for twenty years in famine control, was appointed to head the project. Almost fifty thousand workers were recruited to work on the closure.[50] The cost was astronomical—almost 40 billion yuan, in the wildly inflated Chinese currency,[51] and hundreds of millions in U.S. dollars.[52]

The work was successful. A lavish ceremony was held at Huayuankou, on top of the breach, now sealed, on May 4, 1947—the sacred day of Chinese nationalism—not to commemorate the victims of the flood, but to celebrate the closure of the breach.[53] There was a sense of unreality to the ceremony (and in the gorgeous volume that records it). The CCP controlled much of the rural areas north of the River and all of the 550 villages that had sprung up in the dry north course of the River—with 160,000 people in them. The CCP's representative had protested vociferously from the start at the plans for the closure—which would make their own people homeless—and had occasionally actually fired at workers at the breach from their positions on the north bank.[54] But their opposition and their protests were ignored. They were not represented at the closure ceremonies, though their ghosts were, since they seemed destined to control the area very soon.

In less than two years after the breach was closed, the CCP *did* control North China, and by the end of 1949 the GMD government had been ousted from mainland China. The victorious Communists did not take up the story of Huayuankou. Their concern was not to dwell on the past but to look to a glorious future. That future turned out to include other disasters and yet more human casualties. These displaced attention from earlier disasters. Huayuankou was consigned to silence.

## Strategic Floods

The breaching of the dike at Huayuankou was a rare example of a defensive flood, in which a government or an army deliberately floods its own land to deny it to an invading enemy, a watery form of scorched-earth tactics. The strategy has occasionally been tried elsewhere. In the Eighty Years War against the Spanish (1566–1648) the Dutch breached their own dikes on several occasions to deny movement to the Spanish cavalry. This sacrifice is a key part of the mythology of Dutch independence, a proof of what price the Dutch nation was willing to pay to throw off a foreign yoke.

Attempts at offensive dam breaching and flood creation are more common. In 1943, the Royal Air Force came up with a scheme to reduce the industrial capacity of the Ruhr by cutting off its water supply. The plan was a harebrained but brilliant product of the mind of a "boffin,"[55] Barnes Wallis, to bomb the dams holding the Ruhr's reservoirs. The dams would be destroyed by bombs that would bounce across the surface of the reservoirs like ducks and drakes (skipping stones) and crash into the dams at their crests. Dropping the bombs required great courage and skill from the "Dam Busters," the gallant pilots of RAF 617 Squadron who had to fly the night missions against the heavily defended dams. The raids, in May 1943, only succeeded in part—two of the three dams were destroyed, but the largest, the Eder Dam, withstood the bombs. Eight of the nineteen bombers that carried out the raids were lost, with their crews.[56] In the Dam Busters saga, there was no mention of German civilians who might have drowned, though at that stage of the war Britain had suffered so much from German bombing that concern for enemy civilians was not an issue in strategic planning—as the continuing and bitter dispute over the destruction of Dresden late in the war shows.

One of the most infamous cases of dike breaching was neither offensive nor defensive, but simply vicious. This was the German destruction of Dutch dikes in 1944 and 1945. Before the Allied landings in France in June 1944, the Germans had expected that the landings would come in occupied Holland, not in Normandy. In preparation for the landings, they mined the major dikes and pumping stations throughout the country and flooded 230,000 hectares of western Holland.[57] After June, when it was clear there would be no landings on the Dutch coast, and that the fighting would not come into northern or central Holland, the German army of occupation instigated a systematic program of dike destruction; by early 1945, 20–30 percent of Holland's arable land was under water and the country was in the grips of the Hunger Winter, a terrible period of starvation and malnutrition brought on in part by the loss of cultivable land.[58] Almost to the end of the war, when the fighting was well into Germany, the Germans continued to destroy dikes; the first polder reclaimed from the sea by the Dutch, the Wieringermeerpolder, was flooded in April 1945. Twenty thousand hectares of land were submerged and seven thousand people were evacuated.[59] These gratuitous acts left a deep well of bitterness at what seemed to be a deliberate strategy to starve the Dutch population.

## The Second War-Induced Natural Disaster: The North China Famine

The peasants of North China had their own ghastly experience with starvation during the war. The Huayuankou flood was the first of two massive "natural disasters" to afflict North China during the war. The worst, in terms of casualties, was not the flood but the North China Famine of 1942 to 1943.

Hunger and famine are two of the most common "natural disasters" induced by warfare. Some of the worst wartime famines occur when cities are besieged—when an urban population is deprived of food. The siege of Xi'an in 1926 lasted eight months and claimed between fifteen thousand and thirty-five thousand lives, before the besieging army was defeated by reinforcements sent to the aid of the besieged.[60] The siege of Leningrad lasted nine hundred days, from 1941 to 1944, and took the lives of a million and a half Russians. In both these cases the besieging army used the starvation of civilians as a deliberate strategy and went to enormous lengths to prevent food from getting in to the city.

The connection between warfare and rural famine is less clear-cut, less a matter of a deliberate military strategy. It takes many forms. Sometimes, warfare interrupts agricultural work, no crops can be planted (or harvested), and months later famine appears, caused by the harvest shortfall. In much of China, there was a strong seasonal correlation between warfare and the busy agricultural seasons. Wars were fought in spring or autumn, between the paralyzing cold of winter and the enervating heat of summer. This was especially true of North China, where the majority of military campaigns, whether the warlord battles in the 1920s or the war following the Japanese invasion of 1937, were concentrated in the spring and autumn. These were the critical agricultural seasons—for planting and harvesting, respectively. When peasants were unable to work in their fields because of fighting, their harvest yields declined dramatically. This is what happened during the Xuzhou Campaign in the late spring of 1938. The peasants could not plant their crops because of the fighting. Even though the military campaign was over by the early summer, cultivation during the key early stages had been so inadequate that in the autumn the crops were much reduced.

Another form of war-related damage to rural areas that often led to famine occurred when soldiers seized crops, standing or harvested, to feed themselves and their animals, or when they requisitioned animals or peasants to act as porters. In these circumstances, agriculture could be so severely disrupted that hunger or famine would be the eventual outcome. Even worse was the seizure of able-bodied men—that is, field-workers—by armies, either as porters or as soldiers. The single term used for such acts, *lafu* (dragging off men), had a terrifying sound in any Chinese village because it foretold not only present loss but also future destitution.

None of these forms of military depredation is sufficient reason alone to explain the coincidence of famines and warfare. Other factors enter in to the grim equation, one of which is that warfare creates a climate of fear, which leads to strongly negative effects in almost every aspect of life. In the administrative sphere, the threat of warfare leads to confusion, uncertainty, and anxiety, which is accentuated as war gets closer. Bureaucrats are not suited to making rapid, creative responses to fluid situations; they become impotent or make bad decisions. In the economic sphere, the immediate reaction to the threat of war is for people to look after themselves, to hoard whatever they can get their hands on. Merchants respond to the onset of a buying frenzy by jacking up prices and even withholding goods from the market until the prices have risen even higher.

The most frightful coincidence of war-induced fear and administrative bungling came in the Bengal Famine of 1943–44, in which 3.5 million people died. The famine was not the result of invasion or military action, or of crop failure, or of government requisitioning of grain. It was the product of a string of factors that emerged in a climate of general anxiety over the strong possibility of the outbreak of war—in the form of a Japanese invasion. The anxiety produced a serious disruption in the rice market, which the Bengal government tried to control by manipulating the wholesale prices. These steps led to a freezing of the market, which accelerated hoarding. This in turn paralyzed the market; merchants simply withheld their grain from sale. Within months, a terrible famine gripped a land where there was still plenty of grain.[61]

The Bengal Famine has become a watchword for administrative incompetence and callousness. It has been studied in great detail, particularly by Amartya Sen.[62] The North China Famine, which occurred at almost the same time, has not. It remains almost unknown, the best account of it still one written by a young journalist, Theodore White, fifty-five years ago.

In North China, a region that, unlike Bengal, was always poor, the conditions of warfare tipped over a situation of chronic poverty into absolute disaster. This disaster encompassed a huge area, one part of it the flood zone. The military situation had not changed much since 1938. In 1942, the Japanese controlled the cities and lines of communication in most of North China, and the region south of the Yellow River and north of the Yangzi as far west as the flood zone. The GMD military controlled the main points south of the Yellow River to the west of the flooded area.

The territorial divisions were not neat and tidy. GMD regular forces held large pockets of land that were virtually surrounded by the Japanese, for example, in the Dabieshan north of the Yangzi, while GMD guerrilla units, sometimes former regular units, were active in many areas that appeared to be under Japanese control, but where the Japanese only held the towns. The CCP had base areas, regular units, and guerrilla units throughout north China, sometimes cooperating with the GMD, sometimes not.

Most of what became the famine area was under some form of military control. What was missing was a competent civilian administration, one that might have been able to help the people of the North China Plain when, in 1942 and 1943, they were hit by a series of natural disasters—locusts, floods, drought—all of which were common phenomena in the region, though they seldom occurred in such concentration or on such a scale. These disasters came on top of a series of poor harvests. The area had few internal resources or reserves to deal with hunger, and it gradually fell into the grips of famine.

The intrepid Theodore White went into the region in February 1943, as the famine was taking hold. He traveled to Zhengzhou, still in GMD military hands and the epicenter of the famine:

> When we awoke in the morning, the city was a white sepulcher peopled with grey ghosts. Death ruled Chengchow [Zhengzhou], for the famine centered there. Before the war it held 120,000 people; now it had less than 40,000. The city had been bombed, shelled and occupied by the Japanese, so that it had the half-destroyed air of all battlefront cities. Rubble was stacked along the gutters, and the great buildings, roofless, were open to the sky.[63]

White traveled for three weeks through the famine area and wrote an account as compassionate and as graphic as any description of a famine anywhere. He described a silent world peopled by the quick and the dead, the living weak and emaciated. Only the elderly, the weak, and the young were left; all the strong and youthful were long gone, either to fight in the war or to seek refuge elsewhere.

White was appalled by how little had been done by government authorities to stop the famine as it was taking hold. It was clear to him that the preconditions for famine had been present in late 1941 and early 1942, when the spring wheat crop had failed. And yet there was no government reaction, not even a reduction in taxation. In the summer of 1942, when a severe drought gripped the region, no relief supplies were brought in until the very end of the year. Even then what arrived was a trickle, not enough to help even a fraction of the people beset by starvation. In the end, Henan was devastated. Of 30 million people in Henan before the famine, two to three million fled from the province; another two to three million died of hunger and disease.[64] And Henan was not only the worst affected area. There were terrible casualties right across the plain, as far east as Shandong.

White may have been unfair in blaming the Chinese civilian authorities for their failure to halt or to alleviate the famine. He was at the time based in Chongqing, where he had become disgusted with what he saw as the incompetence and the corruption of the GMD. Corruption and incompetence were not the only contributors to the misery. The war situation meant that military demands in the famine region took priority—requisitioning supplies for army units or seizing young men as recruits or as coolies—far above any concern for civilians. The political split between the GMD and the CCP meant that there was no cooperation between the two sides, even to help famine victims.

The weaknesses and inaction on the Chinese side were real enough, but they were only part of the context of the famine. The Japanese invasion had precipitated the breakdown of civil society in North China, and the Japanese military had not, as occupiers, been able to reestablish it in many areas, particularly rural ones. The puppet civilian administrations did very little to care for the populations under their control; their main concern was control itself. The Japanese military did even less to help. They renewed their attacks in China in 1942, after the United States entered the war, in an effort to tidy up the "China Incident" before the Pacific War started in earnest. Eastern Henan was the scene of frequent small-scale, but deadly, operations against local opposition. In 1941 and 1942 alone, there were more than five hundred "mopping-up" operations in the Japanese-occupied part of the province.[65]

North China peasants were inured to hardship. Their life was never easy, never comfortable. But they did, by tradition, expect that at a minimum the state would intervene to help them in times of real need. The existence of state-run granaries was a promise of help in need, an implied contract between the people and the state that the state would help them when they were hit by disasters.⁶⁶ In a time of war, these contracts were nullified. During the war, no authority, either civilian or military, Chinese or Japanese, was concerned with the relief of famine, with the alleviation of suffering. The guerilla units operating behind the lines knew most about the suffering of the victims, but they had no access to relief supplies of grain, and no access to supplies beyond the famine area.

The conditions of warfare added a new dimension to famine—they made it much more difficult for people to flee from the famine areas, as many would have done traditionally. Fleeing meant moving from one zone of military control to another, across de facto boundaries. No armed force wanted to see flocks of people moving about, and they often prevented them from doing so. All forms of transport were disrupted for the duration of the war, and often stopped completely at the internal "borders" between the zones of control. When peasants did flee, they often did so on foot. In Linqu, a beautiful county high in the central massif of Shandong, on the eastern edge of the area affected by famine, many people fled to join relatives who had long since migrated to Manchuria, where there was still plenty of food. But only the young and healthy were able to make the journey. Others—the elderly, the sick, women and young children—could not, and they stayed at home to die. More than forty years after the famine, it was remembered in the county as a far worse disaster than the Japanese invasion; Linqu was high in the hills and seldom saw Japanese soldiers, but the famine marked the villages forever, killing as much as half the population.⁶⁷

## Natural Disasters and Modern Warfare

The natural disasters of the Anti-Japanese War had a horrible irony to them. Floods and famines had afflicted China since the beginning of her history; they had an archaic cast and yet they occurred at a time when some aspects of the modern world had arrived in China and had changed the country dramatically—not by improving the lot of the people but by making warfare easier.

China's new railway lines are a sad example of the damage a modern technology can bring. They were the symbols of modernity in China; they were supposed to enhance the movement of people and goods, help to develop a market economy and even bring relief to regions in need. But the railways also provided strategic targets in warfare and served as means of troop transport. They helped the Japanese invaders to conquer much of China. They brought the war to the North China Plain but did nothing to help the peasants of the plain to avoid or to survive the two successive catastrophes that hit them during the war.

Both the Huayuankou flood and the North China famine were the products of a society in chaos—a chaos created by the state of war. There is a stark equation that connects war and natural disaster:

> War brings chaos
> Chaos is the handmaiden of natural disaster
> Natural disasters fall most heavily on civilians

Wartime disasters are left to run their own course; a state of war means that it is very difficult to help victims, because the relief mechanisms available in peacetime have largely ceased to function.

Natural disasters are horrible experiences. There is no place for heroism or courage; dignity is stripped away. The common individual responses to catastrophes are greed, theft, panic, followed by stoicism and apathy. Historically, in peacetime Chinese local authorities and local elites provided some kind of relief for the afflicted. This was impossible during the war, because the chaos had led to a complete breakdown of these old systems (in decay in many places) and because the elites that might have administered relief had either fled or were working with the Japanese.

The sufferings of Chinese civilians in these two wartime "natural disasters" were immense and unrelieved. They received no government relief during the war, nor any compensation after it. They have not been considered war victims; the possibility of Japanese reparations to these victims and their descendants has not been raised. Though these disasters were directly linked to the conduct of the war, and to the huge disruptions it brought to every part of Chinese society, because they were "natural" there has been no formal recognition that the victims were the victims of war. The dead of Nanjing are seen as the victims of a Japanese atrocity, the dead of Hiroshima as victims of atomic warfare; the dead of North China remain the victims of age-old natural phenomena—the flood a visitation of "China's Sorrow" (the Yellow River), the famine another of many that have afflicted the country over the millennia.

And famine did recur. The North China Famine was not the last famine to hit the area. Two decades later, an even more devastating famine afflicted not only North China but practically the whole country as well—a result of the lunatic schemes of the Great Leap Forward. Credible estimates of Great Leap deaths range from 15 million to more than 30 million.[68] This figure is far larger—by five to ten times—than the toll for the Bengal Famine.[69] The dead this time were the victims of ideological extremism that led to total disruption of agriculture, which was compounded by the failure of the Communist government to admit to and rectify their mistakes. "Natural disasters" were blamed, in the few contemporary accounts of the misery that was stalking the

Chinese countryside. It would take more than two more decades before the truth came out—that this catastrophe was man-made. The absence of the kind of meticulous records that the Bengal authorities kept of the famine there mean that we may never know exactly what happened in China, let alone get an exact statement of the casualties.

## Civilians and War

In the twentieth century, the conduct of war came to present increasing risks to civilians; war expanded beyond the battlefield and came to affect whole societies. The proportion of civilian casualties rose dramatically from one world war to the next, from 15 percent in World War I to 65 percent in World War II. Most of these casualties derived from deliberate political and military strategies—the bombing of cities, the massacre of inhabitants of captured cities and towns, the extermination of designated categories of people, the use of slave labor.[70]

Bombing of civilian targets started in Shanghai in 1932 and continued throughout the war in China. In Europe, the Blitzkrieg and, later, the Allied bombing of Germany made the suffering of civilians a major focus. In Asia, Japan itself became the prime target of bombing; the bombings of Japanese cities in the last months of the war, conventional and nuclear, cost Japan half a million people dead and took 24 percent of the country's housing stock.[71] The war also brought a new horror—atomic bombs. The people of Hiroshima and Nagasaki became symbols of civilian suffering, the innocent victims of the brutality of war, almost as if there had been no civilian victims before them: "The civilian has been pronounced dead. His death knell, which was yet only faintly audible in 1940, sounded loudly for all at 8:15 A.M. on August 5th, 1945 in Hiroshima, Japan."[72]

The victims of the atomic bombs suffered in a new and horrible way, one that terrified the whole world. Awareness of their fate has been kept alive by the antinuclear debates and by the Japanese authorities who have made the two cities into shrines for peace. The nobility of this undertaking, however, does not nullify the fact that the millions of civilian victims of Japan's aggression in China, direct and indirect, are unknown and even, as in the case of the victims of the Huayuankou flood, forgotten.

The question of how to analyze, let alone understand, suffering on such a scale is almost impossibly difficult. There is a temptation to respect the silence that, until now, Chinese in the regions affected have kept about the flood. This was a tragedy so great and so unrelieved that silence may be the only way to cope with a pain so awful. Silence also spares the agonizing recognition that so many people should have died for so small a strategic gain. In the face of this silence it may seem facile to express outrage as an outsider, to try to understand what happened. Even more facile is to put this disaster and all other war-related disasters beyond analysis with sweeping denunciations of the military as a whole, with environmental and gender biases built in:

> [A]ll militaries, everywhere, wreak environmental havoc—even bit-players on the global militarized scene such as the Canadian military. Everywhere. Military strategy is shaped by common assumptions about the use of the physical environment as the stage for the exercise of male power. Everywhere militaries share a contempt for civilian environmental regulation, placing themselves and their "national security" priorities above the law.[73]

Such denunciations are a fine rhetorical way of explaining away suffering, but they are so generalized that they offer no explanations that might help us to understand specific events; nor do they dignify the victims with recognition or compassion.

## Disasterology

In the twentieth century, war brought immeasurable suffering to civilians, and the twenty-first century has started on the same note. Civilians are killed, become refugees, lose their homes and property. The wars in which they suffer are covered on television, and civilians are now part of the story. International relief agencies rush in to help them, even into war zones. Funding from government and nongovernmental organizations is made available to help them. But still the magnitude and the extent of what they suffer remains remote and vague, because there is no sense of the duration of their suffering or of the many forms it takes. The only suffering that is clear-cut is what can be shown on the screen, the direct impact of warfare—a bombed out house, a maimed child. The natural disasters that accompany warfare, the environmental damage, can scarcely be grasped at all.

It is difficult to convey the long-term damage that accompanies such disasters, because the ramifications come in so many forms and affect so many aspects of life. The loss of a family member means not only grief but also the long-term loss of labor; the loss of one year's crop means that there will be no seed for the next year's planting; the loss of draught animals means that a peasant family will not be able to plough their fields, or move themselves and their goods around; the loss of many people means the loss of community, the loss of an intricate structure that takes decades to replicate. The idea that warfare is a dreadful but transitory phenomenon, that ruffles only the surface of a society that is fundamentally continuous, is thrown into doubt when the worlds of many of the individual members of that society are destroyed forever.

In a world now obsessed with disasters, it seems that the long-term effects of war are consigned to a separate category from the suffering created by natural disasters, or by single acts of terrorism. War is seldom considered as a disaster. In the extensive literature on natural disasters and catastrophes, the effects of war get little attention. The academic and popular coverage of disasters looks at earthquakes, volcanic eruptions, typhoons, hurricanes, waterspouts, tsunamis, landslides, and other horrors, while the work on catastrophes focuses on air crashes, railway crashes, explosions, fires, nuclear accidents, dam failures, and other sudden, spectacular events.

Academic work on disasters and catastrophes has largely been done by geographers and sociologists. The more sober among them are forward-looking and are trying to establish why disasters occur in particular places and what can be done to avoid disasters. The usual dismal conclusion here is that too many people live in fragile environments.[74] There is a whole field of study on how to cope with disasters when they occur, how to provide relief for victims, how to deal with posttraumatic stress. It is axiomatic now that when a disaster occurs in the western world, psychologists will be part of the disaster team.

These sober approaches fade into the shadow of the often histrionic work of those who focus on the disasters yet to come. This work uses past disasters to present apocalyptic visions of the future. The chapter headings of a recent book by Bill McGuire, professor of geohazards at University College, University of London, give a flavor of the genre: "Waiting for Armageddon"; "Fire and Ice: The Volcanic Winter"; "Wave Goodbye: Death by Water"; "Shake, Rattle and Roll: The Great Quake to Come"; "God's Anvil: Hell on Earth."[75] McGuire and his fellow practitioners of disasterology (surely a contender for economics as the original dismal science) are in tune with a world increasingly obsessed with disasters and now, too, with terror, and terribly insecure about what horrors the future holds.

These compendia of disasters scarcely mention the victims of warfare. McGuire mentions almost in passing that in the second half of the twentieth century "more people were killed in wars, and more affected by drought and famine" than were killed in "real disasters."[76] Other writers include categories such as civil unrest and terrorism, but only as a very minor element.[77] This disinclination to deal with natural disasters that are the product of warfare is characteristic not only of Western disasterology but also of Chinese. The treatment of disasters in Chinese seldom mentions warfare as a cause of disaster. The Yellow River flood of 1938 is mentioned as one of the ten great disasters of modern Chinese history, but its connection to warfare is not stressed.[78]

Disasterology speaks to our anxieties about the future. It is distinct from another new field of academic work that studies issues of reparations, of compensation for past damage and suffering. This field looks at abuses such as massacres, torture, destruction of culture, all the tragedies of the recent past, and looks for ways to help victims. The victims of the physical damage of warfare, and the people who suffer from war-induced natural disasters, are seldom discussed. These people are so numerous that talk of compensating them becomes inconceivable.

No one has yet taken up the cause of those who died because of the terrible decision to use the Yellow River to defend China. The victims of the largest single disaster of the war are not commemorated. To mark the actual breach on the dike there are only "a pair of dusty pavilions, standing like bookends at the limits of a low splodged wall."[79] The sixtieth anniversary of the breach, in June 1998, passed almost without notice. The victims are still unknown—mere statistics, not human beings. My aim here has been to make sure that the story of this particularly horrible disaster is told, in as accurate way as possible—perhaps even with detachment—so that until the issue can finally be faced by surviving victims, and by later generations, there is a record.

## Notes

My deep thanks go to my colleagues, Sun Xiufu, Second Historical Archives, Nanjing, who helped me find key documents; Hans van de Ven, Cambridge University, who taught me Dutch history; Stephen MacKinnon, Arizona State University, who shared his great knowledge of China at war; and Timothy Cheek, University of British Columbia, who gave me valuable comments on the manuscript. I also give deep thanks to Mark Selden, who prompted me to expand my research on Huayuankou.

1. There is another, more pedestrian translation—"garden entrance." But the word "flower" is part of the Chinese name, and the word *kou* literally means "mouth."
2. The Yellow River has played such a key part in China's history that it is often referred to simply as "the River."
3. Dangdai Zhongquo congshu bianji bu, *Dangdai Zhongguo de Henan* (Beijing: Zhongguo shehui kexue chubanshe, 1990), 280.
4. Dangdai Zhongquo congshu bianji bu, *Dangdai Zhongguo de Henan*, 279.
5. O. J. Todd, "The Yellow River Reharnessed," *Geographical Review* 39 (1949): 40.
6. Chen Zhuanhuai et al., *Rijin huoYu ziliao* (Zhengzhou: Henan renmin chubanShe, 1986), 73–88.
7. See, for example, a volume edited by Paul Sih, *Nationalist China during the Anti-Japanese War* (Hicksville: Exposition, 1977).
8. Frank Dorn, *The Sino–Japanese War* (New York: MacMillan, 1974), 177. Dorn, like other American military personnel in China at the time, was critical to the point

of contempt of Chiang Kai-shek. His views, which mirrored those of Joseph Stilwell, have colored much of the debate on the conduct of the war in China, which tends to put almost as much blame for the course of the war on GMD incompetence and Chiang Kai-shek's failure of leadership as on Japanese aggression.

9. Lynn Pan, *China's Sorrow* (London: Century, 1985), 190.

10. Chen Weirui, "Huang He Huayuankou juti jingguo," *Henan wenshi ziliao* 4 (1980): 69. Chen was the head of the Henan Repair and Protection Branch of the Yellow River Conservancy (Huang He shuili weiyuanhui Henan xiufangqu). Wei Rulin was the general in command of the work on the dike, while Xiong Xianyu was part of the division responsible for the defense of the south bank of the Yellow River.

11. Wei Rulin, *Ershiji tuanjun canmouzhang Wei Rulin* (Chongqing, 1938).

12. Chen, "Huang He Huayuankou juti jingguo," 170.

13. Dorn, *Sino–Japanese War,* 177.

14. Wei, *Ershiji tuanjun canmouzhang Wei Rulin,* and Xiong Xianyu, "Lujun xinbashi Kangzhan shiqi," in *Huang He shizhi shiliao,* vol. 2 (Zhengzhou: Henansheng xinwen chubanshe, 1989), 10–11.

15. David Barrett, "The Yellow River Flood," *U.S. Military Intelligence Files,* January 31, 1939, 1–2.

16. Chen Weirui, for example, was able to predict the exact course of the flood based on earlier floods. Chen, "Huang He Huayuankou juti jingguo," 169–70.

17. *North China Herald,* July 13, 1938, 54.

18. *Zhengxian Huayuankou Zhongmoulou,* 1939.

19. Huang He dukou duti gongchengju, *Huang He Huayuankou helong jiniance* (Nanjing: Huang He dukou duti gongchengju, 1947), 1.

20. *North China Herald,* June 6, 1938, 536.

21. K. J. Eskelkund, "Flood Relief in Honan Province," *China Journal* 29 (1938): 130–32.

22. Todd, "Yellow River," 44.

23. Stephen MacKinnon, "Refugee Flight at the Outset of the Anti-Japanese War," in *The Scars of War,* ed. Diana Lary and Stephen MacKinnon (Vancouver: University of British Columbia Press, 2001), 118–35.

24. Chen, "Huang He Huayuankou juti jingguo," 171.

25. Rosario Renaud, *Le diocese de Suchow (Chine)* (Montreal: Editions Bellamin, 1982), 227.

26. Dorn, *Sino–Japanese War,* 178.

27. Joseph Stilwell, "Situation Report May 22nd–June 25th, 1938," *US Military Intelligence Files,* 4.

28. Barrett, "Yellow River Flood," 2.

29. Zhongyang shuili shiyanqu, *Huang He huayuankou juekou kaocha* (Nanjing: Zhongyang shuili shiyanqu, 1943).

30. Xingzhengyuan Shanhou qiuji congshu, *Huangfanqu sunshi tongji* (Nanjing: Xingzhengyuan Shanhou qiuji congshu, 1948).

31. Huangfan qu

32. Xingzhengyuan Shanhou qiuji congshu, *Huangfanqu sunshi tongji.*

33. Diana Lary, "Drowned Earth: The Strategic Breaching of the Yellow River Dyke, 1938," *War in History* 8, no. 2 (2001): 205–206.

34. Alex Colville, *Life and Times*, Canadian Broadcasting Corporation, August 4, 2002.

35. Bi Chunfu, *Kangzhan jianghe juekou mishi* (Taipei: Mingwen shuju, 1995), 13.

36. Liang Hsi-huey, "General Alexander von Falkenhausen," in *Die Deutsche Beraterschaft in China*, ed. Bernd Martin (Düsseldorf: Droste, 1980), 141.

37. The German advisers were recalled by Berlin in May 1938 and left Wuhan in early July, to the relief of many senior Chinese commanders, such as Bai Chongxi, who saw them as a nuisance and even as unreliable, the source of many leaks of military secrets. Stilwell, "Situation Report," 4.

38. Tao Juyin, *Jizhe shenghuo sanshinian* (Beijing: Zhonghua shuju, 1984), 228–33; and Fan Changjiang, *Tongxun yu lunwen* (Chongqing: Xinhua, 1981), 99–103.

39. Robert Capa, *Images of War* (New York: Grossman, 1964).

40. Wei, *Ershiji tuanjun canmouzhang Wei Rulin*, and Xiong, "Lujun xinbashi Kangzhan shiqi," 10–11.

41. *North China Herald*, June 22, 1938, 483.

42. Frank Oliver, *Special Undeclared War* (London: Cape, 1939), 210–11.

43. Stilwell, "Situation Report," 15.

44. Zhang Zhigang, "Lianheguo shanhou qiuji zongshu," *Henan wenshi ziliao* 20 (1986): 171.

45. Todd, *Huang He Huayuankou helong jiniance*, 40.

46. Odoric Wou, *Mobilizing the Masses* (Stanford, Calif.: Stanford University Press, 1994), 219.

47. Gregor Benton, *The New Fourth Army* (London: Curzon, 1999), 222.

48. Wou, *Mobilizing the Masses*, 219–20.

49. George Woodbridge, *United Nations Relief and Rehabilitation Agency* (New York: Columbia University Press, 1950), 428 ff.

50. Huang He dukou, *Huang He Huayuankou helong jiniance*, 3

51. Huang He dukou, *Huang He Huayuankou helong jiniance*, 21–22.

52. Woodbridge, *United Nations*, 371.

53. Huang He dukou, *Huang He Huayuankou helong jiniance*, 59.

54. C. Riviere, "Destruction et reconstruction de la digue," *Revue de geographie et d'ethnologie* 1 (1948): 76–79.

55. Boffins were the British scientists and engineers who produced the technological innovations of World War II that were crucial to victory—radar, code-cracking machines, sonar.

56. Paul Brickhill, *The Dam Busters* (London: Evans, 1977).

57. Henri Van de Zee, *The Hunger Winter* (London: Norman, 1982), 13.

58. Zee, *Hunger Winter*, 189.

59. Zee, *Hunger Winter*, 226.

60. James Sheridan, *Chinese Warlord* (Stanford, Calif.: Stanford University Press, 1966), 206–209.

61. Paul Greenough, *Prosperity and Misery in Modern Bengal* (Oxford: Oxford University Press, 1982), 261–62.

*Diana Lary*

62. Amartya Sen, *Poverty and Famine* (Oxford: Clarendon, 1981).
63. Theodore White and Annalee Jacoby, *Thunder out of China* (New York: Sloane, 1946), 170.
64. White and Jacoby, *Thunder,* 171–77.
65. Chen et al., *Rijin huoYu ziliao,* 239.
66. Pierre-Etienne Will and Bin Wong, *Nourish the People* (Ann Arbor: Center for Chinese Studies, University of Michigan, 1991).
67. Author interview in Linqu, Shandong, April 1984.
68. Jasper Becker, *Hungry Ghosts* (London: Murray, 1997), 270; Dali Yang, *Calamity and Reform in China: State, Rural Society, and Institutional Change since the Great Leap Famine* (Stanford, Calif.: Stanford University Press, 1996).
69. Jean Dreze and Amartya Sen, *Hunger and Public Action* (Oxford: Clarendon, 1989), 210.
70. Barbara Ehrenreich, *Blood Rites* (New York: Metropolitan, 1997), 206.
71. Thomas Havens, *Valley of Darkness* (New York: Norton, 1978), 176.
72. Richard Hartigan, *The Forgotten Victim* (Chicago: Precedent, 1982), 1.
73. William Thomas, *Scorched Earth* (Philadelphia: New Society, 1995), xi.
74. K. Hewitt, *Interpretations of Calamity* (Boston: Allen and Unwin, 1983).
75. Bill McGuire, *Apocalypse* (London: Cassell, 1998).
76. McGuire, *Apocalypse,* 42.
77. Lee Davis, *Man Made Catastrophes* (New York: Facts on File, 1993).
78. Li Wenhai et al., *Zhongguo jindai shi da zaihuang* (Shanghai: Renmin chuban-she, 1994).
79. Pan, *China's Sorrow,* 192.

# 8

# Drugs and Oil:
# The Deep Politics of U.S. Asian Wars

*Peter Dale Scott*

## Oil, Drugs, and American Third World Interventions

IN THE HALF CENTURY since the Korean War, the United States has been involved in four major wars in the Third World: in Vietnam (1961–75), in the Persian Gulf (1990–91), in Colombia (1991–present), and in Afghanistan (2001–2002).[1] All four wars have been fought in or near significant oil-producing areas. All four involved reliance on proxies who were also major international drug traffickers.[2] We shall see that this pattern is grounded in the opium-tinged intrigues in Asia and America that contributed to the survival of the Guomindang (GMD) in postwar Taiwan and also has its roots in the Korean War.

This pattern is further reinforced when we consider two of America's major indirect interventions of the same period: support for the Nicaraguan Contras (1981–88) and for the Afghan *mujahedin* (1979–1991). The Central Intelligence Agency (CIA) contracted for Contra support with a ringleader of the largest cocaine network in the region.[3] By providing funds for Gulbuddin Hekmatyar, a drug trafficker selected for support by Pakistani intelligence (the Inter-Services Intelligence Directorate, or ISI), the CIA helped propel Hekmatyar into becoming, for a while, the largest heroin trafficker in Afghanistan and perhaps the world.[4]

In every one of these instances, oil was among the factors shaping U.S. policy goals in the region, just as in every instance drug trafficking proxies figured prominently among the assets used for promoting U.S. interests. A point not usually recognized by U.S. historians is that every one of these interventions left drug traffickers an even more important factor in world politics than they had been before.

All empires since the Renaissance have been driven by the search for foreign resources, and nearly all imperial powers—including the British, the French, and the Dutch—used drugs as a cheap way to pay for overseas expansion. When the United States decided to preserve Western influence in Southeast Asia, it inherited a social structure of former colonial regimes that had coexisted in one way or another with powerful Chinese Triads engaged in the drug traffic.[5] In China also, the Western powers collaborated with drug-trafficking gangsters such as Du Yuesheng against the growing communist movement.

American postwar dependence on drug proxies can be traced to the CIA decision, in 1949–1950, to provide arms and logistic support to the residual forces of the GMD in Burma. This evolved into the much larger program of support for the opium-growing Hmong tribesmen in northeastern Laos. In the wake of the domestically unpopular Vietnam War, the United States, in asserting an increasingly explicit geostrategic interest in oil reserves throughout the world, has almost continuously sought out local drug proxies as a supplement or alternative to the use of U.S. armed forces.

I propose to show that this recurring convergence between oil and drugs is not a coincidence, but a feature of what I have called the deep politics of U.S. foreign policy—those factors in policy formation that are usually repressed rather than acknowledged. The role of oil in U.S. geostrategic thinking is generally acknowledged. Less recognized has been the role of drug proxies in waging and financing conflicts that would not have been financed by Congress and U.S. taxpayers. Less recognized still has been the role of U.S. interventions in preserving and expanding the global drug traffic. These anomalies will be explored in this chapter.

The phenomenon I am describing is sometimes characterized as blowback: the CIA's own term for unintended consequences at home of covert (and usually illegal) programs designed for abroad. But the term, by suggesting an accidental and lesser spin-off, misrepresents the dimensions and magnitude of the drug traffic that the United States helped relaunch after World War II. That drug traffic has multiplied and spread through the world like a malignant cancer. It has also branched out into other areas—notably money laundering and people smuggling—which like the drug traffic itself have contributed to the problem of terrorism we now face. Of course, the U.S. reliance on drug proxies, at risks that were always clear, was motivated by the desire to secure access to natural resources in the Third World—principally oil.

I prefer to characterize what is happening with a general proposition, which is that covert operations, when they generate or reinforce autonomous political power, almost always outlast the specific purpose for which they were designed. Instead, they enlarge and become part of the hostile forces the United States has to contend with. To put it in more precise terms, *parapolitics,* the exercise of power by covert means, tends to metastasize into *deep politics,* an interplay of unacknowledged forces over which the original parapolitical agent no longer has control. This is the heart of the analysis.

## Heroin in Afghanistan

The clearest and most important case of consequential parapolitics was the decision of the United States in April and May 1979 to arm *mujahedin* guerrillas in Afghanistan, at least one of whom was already known as a drug-trafficker with his own heroin refineries. In the subsequent years, Afghan–Pakistani opium production soared. Almost no heroin from this area reached the United States before 1979, yet according to official U.S. sources it supplied 60 percent of U.S. heroin by 1980.[6]

Yet this scandal was kept out of the mainstream U.S. press until the CIA support was winding down. Belatedly, in 1990, the *Washington Post* reported that U.S. officials had failed to investigate drug trafficking by Pakistan's intelligence service (ISI) and Gulbuddin Hekmatyar, the top CIA–ISI client in Afghanistan, "because U.S. narcotics policy in Afghanistan has been subordinated to the war against Soviet influence there."[7]

CIA collaboration with and support for Islamists such as Osama bin Laden dates back at least to 1971, when the CIA joined Saudi intelligence in backing the Muslim Brotherhood and its allies in a worldwide campaign against communism.[8] During the Afghan resistance to the Soviet Union in the 1980s, bin Laden became the financier and logistics expert in Afghanistan for the Saudi-financed Makhtab al-Khidamat, the Office of Services, an organization that through the Muslim Brotherhood recruited foreign volunteers from all over the world, including the United States.[9] There are contested allegations that the CIA, directly or through intermediaries, assisted this recruitment campaign.[10] Simon Reeve also heard from a retired CIA officer that U.S. emissaries to Pakistan "met directly with bin Laden, and that it was bin Laden, acting on advice from his friends in Saudi intelligence, who first suggested the mujaheddin should be given Stingers."[11] French and Italian newspapers have alleged a contact between bin Laden and a CIA officer as late as July 2001.[12]

Bin Laden had been linked by many sources to the global drug trade. Why then did the United States and its dutiful media not proclaim the war against him to be a war on drugs? Partly because the primary U.S. target was the Taliban, which by 2001 had already responded to U.S. and UN demands that it halt opium cultivation. As *Jane's Intelligence Review* noted on October 22,

2001, "the ban imposed by Taliban supreme leader Mullah Mohammad Omar in July 2000 . . . resulted in some 70% of the world's illicit opium production being wiped out virtually at a stroke." And our drug proxy allies were the Northern Alliance, who responded to the Taliban ban on opium cultivation in 2000 by trebling output in their sector of northeastern Afghanistan.

The United States was not waging a war *on* drugs, in short, but a war helped *by* drugs. It is true that previously the Northern Alliance had only controlled less than 5 percent of the Afghan opium traffic, compared to the Taliban's 75 to 80 percent. But even before the onset of the U.S. bombing, that was changing. On October 22, 2001, *Jane's Intelligence Review* reported that, while "poppy cultivation has almost totally disappeared" from the areas of Afghanistan under Taliban control, "a rising tide of narcotics—both opium and the heroin refined from it"—was flooding out of the northeast corner of Afghanistan under the control of the Northern Alliance.[13]

A subsequent article in the London *Observer* attributed the shift in opium supplies to the Taliban ban on cultivation in 2000: "During the ban the only source of poppy production was territory held by the Northern Alliance. It tripled its production. . . . Alliance fields accounted for 83 per cent of total Afghan production of 185 tons of opium during the ban. Now that the Alliance has captured such rich poppy-growing areas as Nangarhar, production is set to rocket."[14]

## The Emerging Patterns from Vietnam to Afghanistan

### Dramatic Boost to Drug Trafficking with Each War

*With each of these wars, there has been a dramatic boost to international drug trafficking, including a rise in U.S. drug consumption.*

In short, the U.S. military intervention in Afghanistan in 2001 was accompanied by restoration of opium for the world market, a re-creation of what happened with the earlier U.S. intervention of 1979–80, and before that with the U.S. interventions in Indochina after 1959 and Southeast Asia in 1950.

Consider the pattern of drugs and oil that emerged in Southeast Asia following the victory of the Chinese Revolution and the exile of the GMD to Taiwan. The U.S. drug proxies in Laos, principally the former GMD armies operating in Burma since the late 1940s, were by 1961 major drug traffickers. They were also principal agents in inducing the U.S. Indochina War and then in building up Laotian drug production, from an estimated 50 tons in 1953 to 100–150 tons in 1968.[15]

When the CIA began its covert involvement in Burma and Laos in the early 1950s, local opium production was in the order of 80 tons a year. Ten years later, thanks to GMD warlords and Hmongs supported by CIA and Civil Air Transport (later Air America), the region produced 300–400 tons a year.[16] During the Vietnam War, production at one point reached 1,200 tons a year. By 1971, there were also seven heroin labs in the region, just one of which, close to the forward CIA base of Ban Houei Sai in Laos, was estimated to produce 3.6 tons of heroin a year.[17]

With the waning of the Vietnam War, opium production in the Golden Triangle also declined. In the case of Laos, it plummeted, from 200 tons in 1975 to 30 tons in 1984.[18] Heroin consumption in the United States also declined. Although the decline in Laotian production has been attributed to drought conditions, a related factor was clearly the increase in cultivation in the so-called Golden Crescent along the Pakistani–Afghan border, from 400 tons in 1971 to 1,200 tons in 1978.[19]

The strengthening of the global narcotics traffic has fueled other smuggling and related criminal activities, leading to the consolidation of an international criminal milieu. Chinese Triads, Japanese yakuza, Russian gangs, and the mafias of Italy, the United States, and Colombia have now combined into a "worldwide criminal consortium" that is, according to experts, "growing exponentially."[20] Writing in 1997 of his experience in exposing the Bank of Credit and Commerce International (BCCI), Senator John Kerry concluded that "today globalized crime can rob us not only of our money but also of our way of life."[21]

We can take his words as a prophecy now fulfilled. Although Al Qaeda and the Taliban might appear on the surface to exemplify a "clash" of civilizations, their activities were paid for, as noted above, by heroin and other transactions at the very heart of this global crime milieu.

## Accelerating U.S. Dependency on Oil and Petrodollars

*The U.S. dependency on international oil and petrodollars has been accelerated, in the context of globalization and war.*

At the height of the Vietnam War, with inflation threatening to wreck his domestic program for a "great society," Lyndon Johnson relaxed the import quota system that had been introduced by Eisenhower to protect domestic U.S. oil production.[22] This increased U.S. vulnerability to the pressure of Organization of Petroleum Exporting Countries (OPEC) oil boycotts in the 1970s, a vulnerability further heightened after Nixon abolished quotas altogether in 1973.

The United States handled the quadrupling of oil prices in the 1970s by arranging, by means of secret agreements with the Saudis, for the recycling of petrodollars back into the U.S. economy. The first of these deals assured a special and ongoing Saudi stake in the health of the U.S. dollar; the second secured continuing Saudi support for the pricing of all OPEC oil in dollars.[23] These two deals assured that the U.S. economy would not be impoverished by OPEC oil price hikes. The heaviest burdens would be borne instead by the economies of less-developed countries.[24]

From these developments emerged the twin phenomena, underlying 9/11, of triumphalist U.S. unilateralism on the one hand and global Third World indebtedness on the other. The secret deals increased U.S.–Saudi interdependence at the expense of the international comity that had been the base for U.S. prosperity since World War II. They also increased Saudi leverage on U.S. foreign policy, as was seen in the 1979 sale of F-15 fighter planes to Saudi Arabia, against strong Israeli opposition.[25] In particular, they explain why George Bush moved so swiftly in 1990 to counter the threat posed by Saddam Hussein to U.S.–Saudi security in the Persian Gulf. The threat was not just that the United States itself would lose oil from the Gulf, against which the United States was partially insured by the redundancy in world oil supplies. A bigger threat was a shrinkage of the OPEC oil whose sales were denominated in U.S. dollars.[26]

The U.S.–Saudi deals also increased the dependence of the United States on oil- and drug-funded Arab assets such as BCCI, which in the 1980s became a chief paymaster for the anti-Soviet Afghan *mujahedin,* and even ran arms directly to them from Karachi.[27] (The failure of the U.S. government to investigate and prosecute BCCI reflected not only the extent of BCCI penetration of U.S. ruling circles, but also the dependency of the U.S. economy on the continued influx of petrodollars and narcodollars. As a former National Security Council (NSC) economist commented, Treasury Secretary James Baker "didn't pursue BCCI because he thought a prosecution of the bank would damage the United States' reputation as a safe haven for flight capital and overseas investments."[28]

Some had expected that the successful OPEC revolt in the 1970s against Washington's and London's economic policies would presage a "new economic order" that would strengthen the South vis-à-vis the North. The secret Saudi–U.S. deals led to a different outcome: a new world order that saw increasing U.S. military dominance combined with increasing economic instability and occasional crises elsewhere. Statistics reveal the change in direction. Between 1960 and 1980, per capita income grew 73 percent in Latin America and 34 percent in Africa. Between 1980 and 2000, income grew less than 6 percent in Latin America and declined by 23 percent in Africa.[29]

This loss of economic stability and momentum, combined with political impotence in the face of U.S. military hegemony, are of course root factors to be addressed in any serious effort to combat terrorism.

## U.S. Wars in the Light of the International Drug Trade

The examples cited above, of drug factors underlying U.S. interventions, illustrate what I mean by deep politics. The point is not to suggest that the increase in drug consumption was a conscious aim of high-level U.S. planning, but that it was a direct consequence of policy decisions. There are grounds, however, for considering a different question: Did successive crises in the illicit drug traffic induce some drug-trafficking U.S. interest groups and allies to press successfully for U.S. involvement in an Asian war?

I have no evidence that the U.S. government intervened militarily as a conscious means of maintaining control over the global drug traffic. However, conscious decisions were definitely made, time after time, to ally the United States with local drug proxies. The U.S. motives for doing so were usually to minimize the costs and exposure of direct engagement. However, the drug proxies appear to have exploited these conditions of nonaccountability with escalations to meet their own drug agendas, particularly at moments when the survival of the drug traffic was threatened.

For decades after World War II the United States was involved with a Far Eastern drug-trafficking proxy—the GMD—that through the China Lobby had obtained or purchased significant support within the U.S. political establishment.[30] Although the picture is a complex one defying reduction, one can certainly see the role of the China Lobby as a factor in the events leading to America's first war on the Asian mainland—the Korean War in 1950.[31] This was right after the victorious armies of Mao Zedong began to eliminate Chinese opium, the source of 85 percent of the world's heroin.

The following sections examine three moments in which U.S. wars deeply intertwined with the world drug traffic, beginning with the most recent.

## 2001

In October 2001 a UN report confirmed that the Taliban had successfully eliminated the year's opium production in Afghanistan, which in recent years had supplied 90 percent of Europe's heroin. However, it appears that what would have been the world's largest curtailment of opium production in half a century has now been reversed. Following the defeat of the Taliban, farmers began replanting wheat fields with opium poppies. It is now estimated that the 2002 opium crop was about 3,400 metric tons (3,700 tons), surpassing Afghan production in 2000 and amounting to 75 percent of production in the record year of 1999.[32]

On October 16, 2001, the United Nations Office for Drug Control and Crime Prevention released its Afghanistan Annual Opium Poppy Survey for

2001. It reported that the Taliban ban on opium in 2000 was almost universally enforced. The estimated 2001 crop of 185 metric tons was only 6 percent of Afghanistan's 2000 total of 3,276 tons, which had been more than half the world's output. Over 90 percent of the 2001 crop came from provinces under the control of America's eventual allies, the Northern Alliance, where the area under cultivation radically increased. Helmand Province under the Taliban, the area of the highest cultivation in 2000, recorded no poppy cultivation in the 2001 season.[33]

As the Taliban was ousted from province after province in 2001, starving farmers everywhere started to replant the one lucrative crop available to them, often at the behest of local commanders. The crop augured a return of warlordism to Afghanistan—regional commanders and armies financed by the opium in their area, jealously refusing to relinquish such a lucrative income source to a central government. Thus there could be a revival of the vicious internecine feuds that took so many civilian lives in the 1990s, after the Soviet withdrawal.

On February 18, 2002, the *Financial Times* of London reported: "The US and United Nations have ignored repeated calls by the international anti-drugs community to address the increasing menace of Afghanistan's opium cultivation, threatening a rift between Europe and the US as they begin to reconstruct the country."

The initial failure of the U.S. press to report or comment on these developments was an ominous sign that the U.S. government might be prepared to see its former protégés finance themselves once again through the drug traffic. More ominous was active disinformation by officials of the U.S. government. The Taliban's drastic reduction in opium cultivation was ignored, and indeed misrepresented, by CIA director George Tenet in his report to Congress on February 7, 2001, in a speech that threatened retaliatory strikes against the Taliban: "Production in Afghanistan has been exploding, accounting for 72 percent of illicit global opium production in 2000. The drug threat is increasingly intertwined with other threats. For example, the Taliban regime in Afghanistan, which allows Bin Laden and other terrorists to operate on its territory, encourages and profits from the drug trade."[34]

On January 17, 2002, Afghanistan's new leader, Hamid Karzai, issued a new ban on opium poppy cultivation and promised to work with donors to assure it could be implemented. However, as the State Department reported, "Whether factions will follow a ban on poppy cultivation, issued by the Interim Authority is uncertain. The Northern Alliance, for example, has, so far as the U.S. is aware, taken no action against cultivation and trafficking in the area it controls."[35] The result has been that drugs have continued to flow north into Tajikistan and Kyrgyzstan, where they finance Islamist radical groups.[36]

We are still waiting for a clearer American resolve to deal with the restored drug flows it has created, for adequate funds to restore the shattered Afghan economy, and for a firm commitment to address the problem of warlordism. Until then, one has to believe that once again the United States is unprepared to challenge the drug politics of its proxies in the region.

## 1979

The situation in 2001 re-created many elements of the 1980s, when in the words of the *Washington Post* U.S. officials ignored heroin trafficking by the *mujahedin* "because U.S. narcotics policy in Afghanistan has been subordinated to the war against Soviet influence there."[37]

The consequences of that official toleration of trafficking have been summarized vividly by Michael Griffin:

> By the mid-1980s, the processing and export of heroin had created a black economy in Pakistan of about $8 billion—half the size of the official one—and Pakistan's military administration was showing signs of evolving into a fully-blown narco-government. . . . The number of Pakistani addicts, meanwhile, had spiraled from nil in 1979 to between 1.2 and 1.7 million at the end of 1988. Such a rapid rate would have been impossible without the protection or active collaboration of the ISI which, empowered by CIA funding and arms deliveries, had grown from a small military department into a modern intelligence network with a staff of 150,000 and hundreds of millions of dollars a year at its disposal. . . . The U.S. colluded in the development of this new heroin source for fear of undermining the CIA's working alliance for the *mujahedin*.[38]

Many authors besides Griffin have seen this enormous expansion of the drug trade as a by-product of the anti-Soviet war. But there are signs that opium traffickers did more than just profit from the war: they may have helped induce it. It is certain that the buildup of opium and heroin production along the Afghan–Pakistani frontier was not a consequence of the war: it preceded it. What particularly catches the eye is that in 1979, just as in 2001, the war helped avert what would otherwise have been an acute drop in world opium production from earlier heights.

In his important book, *The Politics of Heroin*, Alfred McCoy notes that heroin from South Asia had been insignificant in the global market until in the late 1970s there was a two-year failure of the monsoon rains in the Burma–Laos area. It was in response to this drought that Pakistan cultivation increased and heroin labs opened in the Northwest Frontier region by 1979 (a fact duly noted by the Canadian *Maclean's Magazine* of April 30, 1979).

McCoy notes the subsequent increase: "By 1980 Pakistan–Afghan opium dominated the European market and supplied 60 percent of America's illicit demand as well."[39] He also records that Gulbuddin Hekmatyar controlled a complex of six heroin laboratories in the Koh-i-Sultan district of Baluchistan, a region (we are told elsewhere) "where the ISI was in total control."[40]

This timetable raises the same question as events in 2001. What forces led the CIA in May 1979, armed with an NSC authorization from Brzezinski one month earlier, to work with the Pakistani ISI and their protégé Hekmatyar, in the context of an already burgeoning heroin trade that would come to dominate the activities of the ISI–Hekmatyar connection.[41]

Before that time, the CIA had already cultivated Pakistani assets that would become an integral part of the Afghan arms pipeline. One was the Gulf Group shipping line of the Gokal brothers, a firm that was heavily involved in shipping goods to Third World countries for American aid programs.[42] Another, allegedly, was BCCI, the biggest backer of Gulf Group.[43] BCCI's chairman Agha Hasan Abedi had been suspected of links to U.S. intelligence even before he founded BCCI in 1972.[44] BCCI's inside connection to the CIA appears to have been strengthened in 1976, when under director George Bush "the CIA strengthened its relationships with so-called friendly Arab intelligence agencies. One of the most important of these was Saudi Arabia's intelligence service [the Istakhbarat], run by Kamal Adham, Prince Turki [al-Faisal al-Saud], and Abdul-Raouf Khalil, all of whom were BCCI insiders."[45]

In Pakistan, meanwhile, Abedi was extremely close to General Mohammed Zia-ul-Haq, who seized power in 1977. Abedi and Zia also met frequently with Fazle Haq, or Huq, the man whom Zia appointed military governor of the Northwest Frontier Province and allegedly the patron of the Pakistani heroin refiners who bought the *mujahedin* opium.[46] Like Abedi, Fazle Haq developed a reputation as a CIA asset, as well as a reputation with Interpol by 1982 as an international narcotics trafficker.[47]

Drugs may have been at the heart of this relationship from the outset. A BCCI informant told U.S. authorities that Abedi's influence with Zia "benefited from the backing of a Pakistani named Fazle Haq, who was . . . heavily engaged in narcotics trafficking and moving the heroin money through the bank."[48] DEA headquarters in Washington told reporters they knew nothing about Fazle Haq; but a highly placed U.S. official explained to *Time* correspondent Jonathan Beaty that this was because Haq "was our man. . . . [E]verybody knew that Haq was also running the drug trade," and "BCCI was completely involved."[49]

Carter's national security adviser, Zbigniew Brzezinski, subsequently claimed responsibility for the CIA–ISI intervention in Afghanistan.[50] But in a 1989 interview, Fazle Haq maintained that it was the Pakistanis (including himself) who pressured Brzezinski to back the ISI clients in Afghanistan: "I told Brzezinski you screwed up in Vietnam and Korea; you better get it right this time."[51] In his book *Drugs in South Asia,* M. Emdad-ul Haq speculates further that Fazle Haq was the "foreign trained adviser" who, according to the *Hindustan Times,* had suggested to General Zia that he use drug money to meet the Soviet challenge.[52]

It is clear that in May 1979, months before the Soviet invasion, the ISI put the CIA in contact with Hekmatyar, the ISI protégé who would become the central figure in *mujahedin* drug trafficking.[53] The CIA did so at a time when the international heroin trade had suffered a major drop-off in opium from the Golden Triangle and thus needed to build up a new source. After Pakistan banned opium cultivation in February 1979 and Iran followed suit in April, the absence of legal controls in the Pashtun areas of Pakistan and Afghanistan "attracted Western drug cartels and 'scientists' [including "some 'fortune-seekers' from Europe and the US"] to establish heroin processing facilities in the tribal belt."[54] All this new attention from "the international drug syndicates" was apparently *before* either the CIA active intervention in Afghanistan in August 1979 or the Soviet invasion in December.[55]

No one can doubt the importance of drug trafficking to the ISI, both as an asset in support of policy goals and (for some) as a source of personal profit. Through the 1980s and 1990s, the ISI clearly allowed Hekmatyar to use drugs to increase his influence vis-à-vis other Afghan commanders over which the ISI had less control.[56]

Control of drug flows appears to have become part of the CIA–ISI strategy for carrying the Afghanistan War north into the Soviet Union. As a first step, Casey appears to have promoted a plan suggested to him by Alexandre de Marenches that the CIA supply drugs on the sly to Soviet troops.[57] Although de Marenches subsequently denied that the plan went forward, there are reports that heroin, hashish, and even cocaine from Latin America soon reached Soviet troops, and that the CIA–ISI-linked bank, BCCI, along with "a few American intelligence operatives were deeply enmeshed in the drug trade" before the war was over.[58] Maureen Orth heard from Mathea Falco, head of International Narcotics Control for the State Department under Jimmy Carter, that the CIA and ISI together encouraged the *mujahedin* to addict the Soviet troops.[59]

But the plans went farther. According to Ahmed Rashid, "In 1986 the secret services of the United States, Great Britain, and Pakistan agreed on a plan to launch guerrilla attacks into Tajikistan and Uzbekistan."[60] The task "was given to the ISI's favorite *mujahedin* leader," Gulbuddin Hekmatyar,[61] who by this time was already supplementing his CIA and Saudi income with the proceeds of his heroin labs "in the Koh-i-Sultan area [of Pakistan], where the ISI was in total control."[62]

Casey was an oil man, and his Central Asian initiative of 1984 was made at a time when oil interests in Texas already had their eyes on Caspian Basin oil. His cross-border guerrillas, recruited from ethnic Uzbeks and Tajiks, evolved in time into heroin-financed Islamist groups, such as the Islamic Movement of Uzbekistan (IMU), who are the scourge of Central Asia today.[63]

But we need also to ask: How far back did this use of Hekmatyar and drugs go, and who originated it? Did the CIA initiate the May 1979 contact with Hekmatyar as part of Carter and Brzezinski's national policy? Or did Abedi, Haq, and company, enjoying a special relationship with pro-Saudi elements in the CIA, arrange the contact on behalf of drug interests that would soon profit handsomely?[64] Or did the CIA strengthen the drug-trafficking position of its friends, such as BCCI and Fazle Haq, because it feared the Soviet-backed and heroin-financed intelligence activities among Muslims of men such as Rifaat Assad, who controlled the drugs and laboratories of Lebanon's Bekaa Valley?[65]

If that question cannot yet be definitively answered, it is clear that BCCI and its affiliates, the Gokal shipping interests and Global International Airways, soon formed the backbone of the CIA–ISI arms pipeline to Gulbuddin Hekmatyar. And the United States, fully conscious of Hekmatyar's drug trafficking and anti-Americanism, never exerted pressure to have the ISI deny him U.S. aid.[66] This inaction is the more striking because of Hekmatyar's conspicuous failure to contribute to the *mujahedin* military campaign.[67]

## 1959

In 1959, drug-trafficking elements in Southeast Asia, facing a loss of their traditional opium bases and routes in Burma, had simulated a phony war crisis in Laos. After researching the issue in 1970, I suspected, but could not prove, that the GMD did so in order to secure a new basis for drug operations in that country with a CIA airline they partly controlled, Civil Air Transport (known after 1959 as Air America).[68] This simulation involved collusion with elements in the CIA and U.S. armed forces who shared the GMD goal of using the drug armies of Burma as a base for reconquering China. It is certain that in 1959, as again in 1979 and 2001, the GMD drug trade was threatened by political developments; and that the threat vanished with a CIA-backed escalation.[69]

The chief pressures were coming from Burma. Since 1958, GMD forces, under pressure in Burma, had been gradually expelled to towns such as Ban Houei Sai and Nam Tha in northwestern Laos that would soon become opium centers and CIA bases. By March 1959, they were being supplied in Laos by what Bernard called "an airlift of 'unknown planes'"—almost certainly a euphemism for the Taiwanese airline Civil Air Transport (CAT), which fronted for the CIA proprietary known since 1959 as Air America.[70] The CIA owned 40 percent of the airline; GMD bankers owned 60 percent.[71] The planes had been supplying the GMD opium bases in Burma continuously since 1951, until the GMD were expelled in 1959.

In 1959, the GMD connection to Thailand was also challenged. In the 1950s, GMD drugs from Burma had been routinely "seized" by Thai border police and then sold locally or to Hong Kong traffickers, to the profit of the CIA's puppet in Thailand, Phao Sriyanon.[72] This came to an abrupt end on July 1, 1959, when "Field Marshal Sarit [Thanarat of Thailand] unleashed a full military assault on the opium trade."[73]

However, the CAT planes that could no longer land in Burma soon began to land in Laos, thanks to a conspiratorial "crisis" that began there only two weeks later, on July 16, 1959. Ouane Rathikone, a drug-dealing Laotian general, announced a phony North Vietnamese "invasion," and his story was duly promoted in Washington by Allen Dulles and others in the CIA and Defense Department.[74] Although most Western journalists did not fall for Ouane's story, it was vigorously promoted by Joseph Alsop, a reporter with CIA connections who for years had also been close to CAT's founder, General Claire Chennault. The result was to obtain eventual White House sanction for a continuous CAT/Air America airlift to Laos, which began on August 23, 1959.[75]

Soon, Air America planes were mounting a major airlift to Hmong (Meo) camps in northern Laos. They began exporting the Hmong's traditional cash crop, opium, and by 1968 were carrying heroin as well. Apparently, most of this ended up in traditional GMD networks leading through Hong Kong to the United States.

The 1959 "crisis" was the first of a series that between 1961 and 1964 would lead to greater and greater U.S. involvement in Laos and then Vietnam. Air America's support for Ouane Rathikone and another GMD-backed rebel Laotian leader, Phoumi Nosavan, both drug dealers, contributed to these crises. But clearly the "crises" combined a stimulus from outside Washington with high-level support inside it. We know now that a plan for a GMD reinvasion of South China, a plan first authorized by President Truman in 1951, continued to be supported long after the Korean War by some high-level generals and CIA officials. These ranged from extremists such as Air Force general Curtis LeMay, who wrote privately about "nuking the chinks," to CIA deputy director Ray Cline, who had served as CIA station chief in Taipei.[76] The plan was revived by right-wing oppositionists in the 1959–62 period, when to the old McCarthyite question, "Who lost China?" was added a new one, "Who lost Cuba?"[77]

Perhaps the most vocal advocate of the plan from 1959 to 1965 was the GMD-sponsored Asian People's Anti-Communist League (APACL; after 1966, the World Anti-Communist League), whose member agency at its Taiwan headquarters also sponsored the airlift to the GMD opium camps of western Laos.[78] As I wrote in 1971,

> The GMD's [GMD] stake in the CAT airlift to its troops in the "fertile triangle" became obvious in 1961, when Fang Chih, a member of the GMD [GMD] Central Supervisory Committee and secretary-general of the Free China Relief Agency (FCRA), admitted responsibility for an unlisted CAT plane that had just been shot down over Thailand by the Burmese Air Force. . . . The unpublicized visit to Laos of Fang Chih, in the weeks immediately preceding the phony Laos "invasion" of 1959, suggests that the narcotics traffic, as well as Pathet Lao activity, may have been a reason why CAT's planes inaugurated their flights in that year into the opium-growing Meo [Hmong] areas of Sam Neua province.[79]

But GMD machinations fomenting a Laotian crisis in 1959 would have gone unheeded had it not been for support from men such as Allen Dulles in Washington.

We should not be surprised that the CIA and its friends took steps to help protect and strengthen the GMD drug traffic in 1959, at a time when that traffic was being threatened. Since 1950, the CIA and its part-owned proprietary CAT had played a key role in building up the drug-trafficking GMD presence as the most dependable CIA asset in East and Southeast Asia.

## 1950

After World War II, it should have been possible to contain the global opium traffic, which had been severely weakened by the interruption of maritime commerce. The expulsion of the Guomindang from mainland China in 1949 and the founding of the People's Republic were followed by the elimination of the opium crops in Yunnan and Sichuan, which had been perhaps the chief source of world supply, as well as a major source of local income for the GMD regime.[80]

But the Shan States of eastern Burma, which for decades had been increasing their illegal local opium production to meet British tribute requirements, became an even more important international source with the displacements of World War II. Thai prime minister Phibun's wartime alliance with the Japanese had secured for Thailand the right to occupy and annex the eastern Shan States in 1943; and a major reason for this occupation was to secure opium for the Thai government opium monopoly, now cut off from its traditional sources in India.[81]

The occupying Thai general, Phin Choonhavan, became both rich and powerful through his involvement with the drug trade. So did his son-in-law

Phao Sriyanon, who became the dominant opium figure in Thailand in the 1950s. Phao was supplanted by General Sarit Thanarat, who reached political prominence by his association with General Phin in the Shan occupation. Phin, Phao, and Sarit together organized the coup in 1947 that ousted the left-wing Prime Minister Pridi and ensured that Thailand would remain a drug polity for years.

As it became more and more evident that Japan would lose the war, General Phin took steps in April 1944 to preserve his Shan drug connection. He did so by complex negotiations with both the Japanese and the GMD 93d Division in Yunnan, in a meeting attended also by the brilliant but ruthless Japanese war criminal, Colonel Tsuji Masanobu.[82]

General Phin's postwar connections to the Shan opium economy owed much to GMD connections in Bangkok and Hong Kong, and also to Chiang Kai-shek's supporters in Washington, including Chiang's personal friend General Claire Chennault. Chennault was an early advocate of a plan to attack the communists from the west (Lanzhou) and south (his wartime base of Yunnan), using American military advisers and logistic support from his postwar airline, Civil Air Transport.[83]

Even before the outbreak of the Korean War in June 1950, there was support in Washington for Chennault's plan to strengthen the remnant GMD armies in Burma. On April 10, 1950, the Joint Chiefs of Staff, noting the "renewed vitality" of the Chinese Nationalist forces, proposed implementing a "program of special covert operations designed to interfere with Communist activities in Southeast Asia."[84] The program was entrusted to the Office of Policy Coordination (OPC) to supply the Chinese Nationalist forces in Burma of Li Mi, who was working for the CIA by May 1950, if not earlier.[85]

General Li Mi's army soon proved itself to be no threat to the new Chinese People's Republic. Its two attempts at invasions in 1951 and 1952 were easily repulsed by Yunnanese militia, after advances of only sixty miles.[86] As a force to restore the supply of opium to the GMD, however, Li Mi and his army were so successful that Burma's total annual harvest of opium increased from less than 40 tons before World War II to 300–400 tons by 1962. "By the end of the 1950s, Burma, Laos, and Thailand together had become a massive producer, and the source of more than half the world's present illicit supply of 1,250 to 1,400 tons annually."[87]

OPC, later merged into the CIA, was vital to this surge in production. Starting in February 1951, airplanes of the CIA-refinanced airline CAT supplied the troops with arms from another CIA proprietary, Sea Supply, at an OPC-built airbase, Mong Hsat. "After delivering the arms to the GMD in Burma, an unknown number of CAT's American pilots was loading the GMD's opium for the return flight to Bangkok."[88] But after being flown south, most of the

GMD opium was sold to Thai Police Chief Phao Sriyanon, who by what McCoy calls a "coincidence" was "the CIA's man in Thailand."[89] (The "coincidence" was deeper than this, because the same proprietary, Sea Supply, Inc., supplied both the GMD and the Thai border police.)

The CIA's continuing support for the GMD's opium enterprise in Burma can be at least partly explained by the U.S. desire to (in McCoy's words) "combat the growing popularity of the People's Republic among the wealthy, influential overseas Chinese community throughout Southeast Asia."[90] The GMD reached these communities through Triads and other secret societies that had traditionally been involved in the opium traffic. Thus the restoration of an opium supply in Burma to replace that lost in Yunnan had the result of sustaining a social fabric that was traditional, albeit corrupt.[91] It also financed the GMD sabotage of and opposition to the People's Republic.

This explanation assumes that the OPC and CIA were using the GMD and organized crime. But one can also ask the deep political question whether the opposite was not also true. In other words, did forces determined to restore the prewar opium trade manipulate postwar U.S. government policies in order to restore that traffic?

We have to look, first of all, at the events leading up to the outbreak of the Korean War in June 1950 (the key to launching the CAT airlift to the GMD troops in Burma). As Bruce Cumings notes, Chiang Kai-shek "may have found the fulcrum on the Korean peninsula, the provocation of a war that saved his regime for two more decades, and bid fair to bring Nationalist troops back to the mainland."[92]

These events were marked by extraordinary intrigues that drew, at the time, multiple charges of diverse and opposing conspiracies.[93] At this time, according to Cumings, the definitive chronicler of these complex intrigues, "The China Lobby infiltrated the CIA, and vice versa, and insiders knew by mid-1950 that the war would soon be coming."[94] It was in this context that, in mid-June 1950, Whiting Willauer of CAT flew to Washington to negotiate the final takeover of the airline by the U.S. government's Office of Policy Coordination (OPC). Cumings assembles much evidence to suggest that the war suited people in high places, not only in Taipeh and Seoul but also in Washington.

However, it is symptomatic of what might be called Cumings's archivist inclination that he does not mention Paul Helliwell, the man who arranged for Chennault to meet with Wisner and gain support for his plan.[95] Helliwell was obviously a key figure. He was a veteran of the Office of Strategic Services (OSS) Kunming station, which in World War II worked on the one hand with General Chennault and on the other with opium warlords, regularly making payments in opium. Helliwell dealt with Dai Li, the GMD police chief whose bureau was composed largely of Green Gang drug traffickers; and like Dai Li, he went on to become the architect of a governmental intelligence–drug connection.[96] As an OPC official, Helliwell not only arranged with Chennault for the creation of CAT, Inc., but he also formed Sea Supply, Inc., the proprietary that supplied arms to Chiang despite State Department disapproval. After 1949, Sea Supply shipped arms via CAT to both the GMD drug forces in Burma and the Thai border police of Phao Sriyanon—the two main arms of the GMD–Burma–Thai drug connection.[97]

But Helliwell was not just an OSS and CIA officer; he was also for years counsel for the money-laundering Miami National Bank, controlled by Meyer Lansky.[98] Helliwell also went on to invest in Florida real estate and to represent Phao's government in the United States, at a time when "Kuomintang [GMD] money from Thailand and Burma came via Hong Kong to be washed through Lansky-related property firms."[99] Still later, he helped establish the Castle Bank in the Bahamas, which laundered funds for both the CIA and organized crime.[100] Castle Bank was only one of a series of banks in this double role; it had complex links to both the analogous Nugan Hand Bank in Australia and to the Washington banker (George Olmsted) whose firm (Financial General Bankshares) was eventually taken over by BCCI.[101]

Helliwell's career is symptomatic of a web of extragovernmental connections centered on the business and laundering activities of organized crime. With respect to these extragovernmental intrigues, Cumings's archival history has little to say. In a book containing 102 page references to Chiang Kai-shek and 15 to the China Lobby, he does not mention what I consider to be the key to their power in U.S. politics, as shown in the charges made by Ross Koen in 1960 "that a number of [Nationalist] Chinese officials engaged in the illegal smuggling of narcotics into the United States" and "further that the narcotics business has been an important factor in the activities and permutations of the China Lobby."[102]

This silence is in keeping with Cumings's failure to explore the tongs and secret societies that were the true sociological underpinnings of the GMD and the China Lobby—in China, in Southeast Asia, and above all, in the United States. He speaks narrowly of "China Lobby types who were fixated on Taiwan," ignoring those whose existence depended only marginally on Taiwan, or even mainland China, but had everything to do with the preservation and restoration *of the opium traffic itself.*[103]

These secret societies were older by far than the GMD, and have continued to function until the present, long after the GMD ceased to be historically important. We now know from a number of excellent histories of the opium trade that in Southeast Asia since the middle of the nineteenth century "the opium farms were almost always connected to the secret societies that flourished in Chinese communities."[104] It is now also generally recognized how

Chiang Kai-shek's seizure of both the GMD and of China was achieved with the help of the opium-trafficking Green Gang of Du Yuesheng, to the mutual profit of both.[105] By the mid-1930s, China was producing seven-eighths of the world's opium supply, and some of it came to Chinese tongs in the United States and their organized crime contacts such as Meyer Lansky and Lucky Luciano.[106]

These contacts with the U.S. mob were apparently not wholly broken by World War II.[107] They were clearly renewed after 1949, when Du Yuesheng and the remnants of the Green Gang fled to Hong Kong along with a rival secret society.[108] It is certain that a high-level drug bust in 1959 in San Francisco involved the same Hip Sing tong as an earlier organized crime drug bust in 1930. Significantly, U.S. officials arranged for the ringleader Chung Wing Fong, an official of the San Francisco Anti-Communist League (a GMD front) to escape to Taiwan before local arrests were made.[109]

The Hip Sing's dope and other criminal activities, like those of the On Leong, Bing Kong, and other American tongs, predated and outlasted by far the GMD linkup with the Green Gang in 1927. The 1905–1906 tong war in New York City was between the Hip Sing tong and its chief rival, the On Leong tong. Ninety years later, the organized crime of New York's Chinatown was still dominated by three tongs, two of which were the Hip Sing and the On Leong.[110] In 1996, long after the decline of the GMD as a political force in Taiwan, the Hip Sing tong was involved in yet another major San Francisco drug bust.[111] The GMD has faded, but the tongs and their drug connections are very much still with us, thanks in part to the efforts of the OPC in 1949–51.

These continuities lend a coherence to the intrigues leading up to the Korean War that would otherwise be missing. For example, Cumings notes that Satiris "Sonny" Fassoulis, a minor mob player who went on to major organized crime swindles in stolen securities, supplied half a million dollars as part of a China Lobby campaign to support Chiang Kai-shek (with army backing, but against State Department opposition).[112] Fassoulis was tapped by "one Col. Williams from the Army" to be part of the campaign. Almost certainly this was Colonel Garland Williams, the creator of the U.S. Army Counterintelligence Corps. After the war, Williams continued his intelligence career in the Federal Bureau of Narcotics as one of a small group of FBN officials who used their knowledge of the drug world to recruit mobsters for intelligence purposes.[113] A key example was Williams's former subordinate, George White, who with the aid of Meyer Lansky recruited Lucky Luciano during World War II for the OSS–Office of Naval Intelligence "Project Underworld," and who in 1959 arranged for the escape of Chung Wing Fong in the Hip Sing tong drug bust.[114]

In other words, the political efforts of the China Lobby were inseparable from their connections to the American mob, which had a bigger stake in the future of the drug traffic than in the outcome of Chinese politics. And these figures in turn could play a role because of their deep political connections to U.S. intelligence. No one was better located in this respect than Meyer Lansky, who by the 1960s enjoyed protection and virtual immunity from prosecution, both in the Federal Bureau of Investigation (FBI) and in the CIA.[115] If we look at these deep underpinnings to the intrigues of postwar U.S. politics in the Far East, it helps us understand how these could have led to the restoration of the world's chief opium source, just at the point when its prewar source of supply was about to be eliminated.

I am not suggesting that anyone in the highest levels of U.S. government made a conscious decision to restore or expand the global opium traffic. However, it is clear that elements in the U.S. government were prepared to work with GMD troops long after their drug activities were obvious. In 1949, even the relatively moderate and cautious Dean Rusk argued at a State Department meeting that the United States "should employ whatever means were indicated, . . . arms here, opium there, bribery and propaganda in the third place."[116] Such advice was perhaps only to be expected: as the United States took up the role in Asia of the colonial powers before it, the easiest line was to exert influence through the opium Triads that had helped in earlier years to support the colonies of the British and French.[117] And those outside government with the requisite skills to organize the global drug traffic knew very well that one of the most important of these requisites was the ability, which on occasion they clearly possessed, to manipulate governments.

## Conclusion

It is too early to determine whether the de facto restoration of the opium traffic in 2001 was the result of such manipulation. But as we look back in time to the U.S. interventions of 1979, 1959, and finally 1950, evidence of such manipulation becomes clearer and clearer. Clearest of all is the role of these interventions in fostering the opium traffic as a major international force.

The drug traffic today is bigger and more powerful than ever before. At the same time, there will be pressure for the U.S. presence in these regions to increase as well. As Paul Rogers has pointed out, U.S. oil reserves have declined to 2.8 percent of the world total, whereas the Gulf states now have 66.5 percent. Meanwhile, U.S. oil dependency continues to increase: in 1990, the United States imported 42 percent of its total oil requirements; ten years later this had risen to 60 percent.[118] And the national debate on foreign policy is increasingly dominated by geostrategists from both parties who link unilateral control of the world to control of its oil-producing areas.

These two factors—drugs and oil—virtually guarantee that the United States will be confronted with new crises in this region where the traditions of liberal democracy carry little weight, and where so many live in abject poverty in proximity to enormous fortunes from drugs and oil. This is especially true of the drug-ridden nations of Central Asia.

America's dependency on foreign oil has been much studied and criticized. Less attention has been paid to America's role in recurring interventions that have had the effect of preserving and strengthening the drug traffic. It is important to clarify whether this resulted from a series of past historical accidents or from a structural dependency, political, financial, or both, that is still active.

U.S. and European banks clearly profit from laundering the proceeds from the Afghan drug traffic. (The high-end profits are of course realized in the countries of destination, not where the opium originates.) The scholar Alain Labrousse, formerly editor of the respected *Geopolitical Drug Dispatch,* has estimated that 80 percent of the profits from drug trafficking end up in the banks of the wealthy countries or their branches in the underdeveloped countries where there is weaker legal control.[119] We have already seen the extent to which the current U.S. dependency on foreign oil has required a favorable flow of petro- and narcodollars.

The mechanics of the U.S. relationship to the drug trade remain mysterious. But when I first wrote this in 2002, there was serious talk of using Kurdish forces, long notorious for drug smuggling, as proxies in a new war against Iraq.[120] The Bush administration is also steering America into closer involvement with the drug-ridden countries of Central Asia, from Georgia to Uzbekistan and Kyrgyzstan. Some observers have long believed Russia has "close intelligence links" with the heroin trafficking IMU, in order to weaken these governments and increase their dependency on Moscow.[121] It is important that that U.S. agencies and corporations not play this game.

The State Department seems determined to see no problem in these Central Asian involvements, proclaiming on its website that "The United States . . . values Uzbekistan as a stable, moderate force in a turbulent region."[122] This recalls the absurd claims made once by the State Department about Diem's Republic of Vietnam. If in truth the United States has learned nothing since that war, one can predict confidently that U.S. troops will once again be shot at.

The American people must work to find better approaches to the social problems of the rest of the world, in which the mistakes of the past will not be repeated.

# Notes

1. There were of course a number of briefer military, paramilitary, and covert involvements. The discussion of drugs and oil in this chapter can be adapted to a number of these involvements, notably Indonesia and Panama. The U.S. invasion of Iraq in 2003, which occurred after this chapter was written, relied much less on local allies. However, the Kurds also qualify as drug proxies. As noted in footnote 120, the projected use of Kurds in this war never really occurred.

2. In this chapter, I shall not deal at length with the Gulf War, because the scheduled uprising by Kurdish proxies in 1991 never really took place. They have, however, been accused of drug trafficking (see footnote 120).

3. Peter Dale Scott, *Drugs, Contras, and the CIA: Government Policies and the Cocaine Economy* (Sherman Oaks, Calif.: From the Wilderness, 2000), 30. The ringleader was Juan Ramón Matta Ballesteros.

4. Alfred W. McCoy, *The Politics of Heroin: CIA Complicity in the Global Drug Trade* (New York: Lawrence Hill, 1991), 19.

5. See Carl A. Trocki, *Opium, Empire, and the Global Political Economy: A Study of the Asian Opium Trade, 1750–1950* (London: Routledge, 1999); Timothy Brook and Bob Tadashi Wakabayashi, eds., *Opium Regimes: China, Britain, and Japan, 1839–1952* (Berkeley, Calif.: University of California Press, 2000).

6. William French Smith, "Drug Traffic Today: Challenge and Response," *Drug Enforcement* (Summer 1982), 2–3; McCoy, *Politics of Heroin*, 447 (60 percent in 1980).

7. *Washington Post*, May 13, 1990; McCoy, *Politics of Heroin*, 459. For further examples, see Peter Dale Scott, *Drugs, Oil, and War: The United States in Afghanistan, Colombia, and Indochina* (Lanham, Md.: Rowman & Littlefield, 2003).

8. John K. Cooley, *Unholy Wars: Afghanistan, America and International Terrorism* (London: Pluto, 2000), 43.

9. Michael Griffin, *Reaping the Whirlwind: The Taliban Movement in Afghanistan* (London: Pluto, 2001), 133; Cooley, *Unholy Wars*, 243; Peter L. Bergen, *Holy War, Inc.: Inside the Secret World of Osama bin Laden* (New York: Free Press, 2001), 133.

10. Cooley, *Unholy Wars*, 87. Cf. Yossef Bodansky, *Bin Laden: The Man Who Declared War on America* (New York: Random House/Prima, 2001), 213; Richard Labévière, *Dollars for Terror: The United States and Islam* (New York: Algora, 2000), 102–4, 223–24.

11. Simon Reeve, *The New Jackals: Ramzi Yousef, Osama bin Laden and the Future of Terrorism* (Boston: Northeastern University Press, 1999), 167.

12. *Guardian* (London), November 1, 2001.

13. Anthony Davis, "Afghan Drug Output Wanes—But Only under Taliban," *Jane's Intelligence Report*, www.janes.com/security/international_security/news/jir/jir011022_3_n.shtml.

14. *Observer*, November 25, 2001.

15. McCoy, *Politics of Heroin*, 299.

16. McCoy, *Politics of Heroin*, 162.

17. McCoy, *Politics of Heroin*, 286–87.

18. Peter Dale Scott, "Honduras, the Contra Support Networks, and Cocaine: How the U.S. Government Has Augmented America's Drug Crisis," in *War on Drugs: Studies in the Failure of U.S. Narcotic Policy,* ed. Alfred W. McCoy and Alan A. Block (Boulder, Colo.: Westview, 1992), 126–27.

19. McCoy, *Politics of Heroin,* 446.

20. Claire Sterling, *Thieves' World: The Threat of the New Global Network of Organized Crime* (New York: Simon & Schuster, 1994), 44, citing a lecture by Italian judge Giovanni Falcone in November 1990.

21. John Kerry, *The New War: The Web of Crime That Threatens America's Security* (New York: Simon & Schuster, 1997), 18.

22. Daniel Yergin, *The Prize: The Epic Quest for Oil, Money and Power* (New York: Simon & Schuster, 1991), 538–39.

23. According to David E. Spiro, "In 1974 [Treasury Secretary William] Simon negotiated a secret deal so the Saudi central bank could buy U.S. Treasury securities outside of the normal auction. A few years later, Treasury Secretary Michael Blumenthal cut a secret deal with the Saudis so that OPEC would continue to price oil in dollars. These deals were secret because the United States had promised other industrialized democracies that it would not pursue such unilateral policies." David E. Shapiro, *The Hidden Hand of American Hegemony: Petrodollar Recycling and International Markets* (Ithaca, N.Y.: Cornell University Press, 1999), x. Cf. 103–112.

24. "So long as OPEC oil was priced in U.S. dollars, and so long as OPEC invested the dollars in U.S. government instruments, the U.S. government enjoyed a double loan. The first part of the loan was for oil. The government could print dollars to pay for oil, and the American economy did not have to produce goods and services in exchange for the oil until OPEC used the dollars for goods and services. Obviously, the strategy could not work if dollars were not a means of exchange for oil. The second part of the loan was from all other economies that had to pay dollars for oil but could not print currency. Those economies had to trade their goods and services for dollars in order to pay OPEC." Spiro, *Hidden Hand,* 121.

25. See also below. John Loftus and Mark Aarons, *The Secret War against the Jews* (New York: St. Martin's, 1994), 343, which does not mention the two secret financial deals with the Saudis, and which offers a different and, I think, one-sided account of the sale of the F-15s. Cf. Spiro, *Hidden Hand,* 123–24.

26. To achieve this defense of the dollar it was necessary to repel Saddam Hussein, but not to destroy him. Thus the United States in 1991 did not make much use of its drug proxy in the Gulf War, which was the badly divided Kurdish independence movement.

27. Cooley, *Unholy Wars,* 116–17.

28. Jonathan Beaty and S. C. Gwynne, *The Outlaw Bank: A Wild Ride into the Heart of BCCI* (New York: Random House, 1993), 357.

29. Greg Palast, *The Best Democracy Money Can Buy* (London: Pluto, 2002), 48. Palast supplies examples of how the International Monetary Fund (IMF), created at Bretton Woods in 1944 to promote economic stabilization and growth, has since 1980 promoted the opposite by policies that contract economies to preserve debt payments. Cf. the comments of Nobel-winning economist Joseph Stiglitz, formerly of the IMF

staff, on the IMF response to the Asian crisis of 1997: "It went to the countries and told them to be more contractionary than they wanted, to increase interest rates enormously. It was just the opposite of the economic analysis that was the basis of the founding of the IMF. Why? In order to make sure that creditors got repaid." Joseph Stiglitz, interview by Lucy Komisar, *Progressive*, June 2000, 34.

30. The GMD as such is no longer a visible player in the Asian drug traffic. However, its former assets such as the Wei brothers of the Wa Army in Myanmar are still heroin kingpins. The Wa Army traffics, especially in amphetamines, with the benign consent of the ruling SLORC in Myanmar and the benign neglect of the U.S. Drug Enforcement Agency. See Bertil Lintner, *Burma in Revolt: Opium and Insurgency since 1948* (Chiangmai, Thailand: Silkworm, 1999), 236, 380, 413.

31. Bruce Cumings, *The Origins of the Korean War, Vol. II: The Roaring of the Cataract 1947–1950* (Princeton, N.J.: Princeton University Press, 1990), 106–17, 599–602 (especially 601), and *passim*.

32. United Nations Office for Drugs and Crime (UNODC) *Afghanistan Annual Opium Poppy Survey for 2002*, www.unodc.org:80/pdf/afg/afg_opium_survey_2002 _exesum.pdf (accessed 2002); *New York Times*, October 28, 2002. The Taliban probably eliminated production in a mostly vain effort to gain international aid and assistance (they were rewarded with $43 million by the United States in May 2001).

33. United Nations International Drug Control Program, *Afghanistan Annual Opium Poppy Survey, 2001* (UNDCP, 2001), at www.unodc.org:80/pdf/afg/ report_2001-10-16_1.pdf.

34. Statement by Director of Central Intelligence George J. Tenet before the Senate Select Committee on Intelligence, February 7, 2001, at www.cia.gov/cia/public_ affairs/speeches/archives/2001/UNCLASWWT_02072001.html.

35. Department of State, *International Narcotics Strategy Report, 2001*, at www.state.gov/g/inl/rls/nrcrpt/2001/rpt/8482.htm.

36. Peter Dale Scott, "Poppy Paradox—U.S. War in Afghanistan Boosts Terror Funds," Pacific News Service, August 1, 2002, at news.pacificnews.org/news/view_ article.html?article_id=824.

37. *Washington Post*, May 13, 1990.

38. Griffin, *Reaping the Whirlwind*, 145–46. According to Christina Lamb, "The Afghan war had made Pakistan the world's largest supplier of heroin, and by 1989 drugs were bringing in at least $4 billion a year—more foreign exchange than all Pakistan's legal exports combined." Christina Lamb, *Waiting for Allah: Pakistan's Struggle for Democracy* (New York: Viking, 1991), 195. Lamb cites Pakistan Narcotics Control Board figures. Also see *Washington Post*, May 13, 1990. Giovanni Quaglia, the chief of operations for the UN Office of Drug Control, has estimated that the total contraband economy in Pakistan now amounts to $15 billion. Maureen Orth, "Afghanistan's Deadly Habit," *Vanity Fair* (March 2002): 178.

39. McCoy, *Politics of Heroin*, 447; cf. 446. For his production figures in Pakistan, Afghanistan, and Iran, McCoy cites U.S. State Department statistics. But according to other sources, including a 1986 U.S. congressional report, these statistics were politically manipulated to show a drop in Pakistan–Afghan production in the 1980s, accompanied

by an increase in Iranian production. (The State Department actually "claimed that due to climatic conditions opium production in Pakistan and Afghanistan dropped in the 1980s.") The reverse was almost certainly true. See M. Emdad-ul Haq, *Drugs in South Asia: From the Opium Trade to the Present Day* (New York: St. Martin's, 2000), 194–95.

40. Mccoy, *Politics of Heroin*, 458, Griffin, *Reaping the Whirlwind*, 148; Emdad-ul Haq, *Drugs in South Asia*, 189.

41. Lawrence Lifschultz, "Pakistan: The Empire of Heroin," in *War on Drugs: Studies in the Failure of U.S. Narcotic Policy*, ed. Alfred W. McCoy and Alan A. Block (Boulder, Colo.: Westview, 1992), 321; McCoy, *Politics of Heroin*, 451.

42. Peter Truell and Larry Gurwin, *False Profits: The Inside Story of BCCI* (Boston: Houghton Mifflin, 1992), 123.

43. John Kerry and Hank Brown, *The BCCI Affair: A Report to the Committee on Foreign Relations, United States Senate*, 102d Congress, 2d sess., December 1992, 318–19.

44. Kerry and Brown, *BCCI Affair*.

45. Truell and Gurwin, *False Profits*, 130.

46. Truell and Gurwin, *False Profits*, 160–61; McCoy, *Politics of Heroin*, 454; Lifschultz, "Pakistan," 342. Zia's role in appointing Fazle Haq is reported by Alain Labrousse, *La drogue, l'argent et les armes* (Paris: Fayard, 1991), 110.

47. Beaty and Gwynne, *Outlaw Bank*, 52; Lifschultz, "Pakistan," 342.

48. Beaty and Gwynne, *Outlaw Bank*, 48. The informant, named here as "Mirza," is identified as Amir Lodhi in James Ring Adams and Douglas Frantz, *A Full Service Bank* (New York: Pocket Books, 1992), 257, and Kerry and Brown, *BCCI Affair*.

49. Beaty and Gwynne, *Outlaw Bank*, 52.

50. In *Le Nouvel Observateur*, January 15–21, 1998.

51. General Fazle Haq, quoted in Christina Lamb, *Waiting for Allah*, 222 (cf. 206); cited in Emdad-ul Haq, *Drugs in South Asia*, 185.

52. *Hindustan Times*, October 1, 1994, cited in Emdad-ul Haq, *Drugs in South Asia*, 187. Fazle Haq's story (that the U.S. backing of the *mujahedin* was in response to a Pakistani initiative) is corroborated by Robert Gates of the CIA. Gates's memoir speaks of "an approach by a senior Pakistani official to an Agency officer" in March 1979, four months before Carter "signed the first finding to help the Mujahedin covertly." Robert M. Gates, *From the Shadows* (New York: Simon & Schuster, 1996), 144, 146. Haq's suggestion might explain the CIA-backed ISI decision to focus aid on Gulbuddin Hekmatyar, whose Hizb-i-Islami faction was allegedly ignored and "almost non-existent" during the formation of the first organized Afghan resistance in Pakistan in mid-1978.

53. McCoy, *Politics of Heroin*, 451: Lifschultz, "Pakistan," 321–23, 326.

54. Emdad-ul Haq, *Drugs in South Asia*, 188. The transnational drug presence in Afghanistan was even clearer by the 1990s, when a French journalist learned "that 'the Pakistanis'—presumably the ISI's clandestine operators— . . . had actually provided seed grains of a new and more productive species of poppy . . . said to have come from Burma . . . and Africa, probably Kenya." Stephane Allix, *La petite cuillère de Schéhérazade: sur la route de l'héroïne* (Paris: Editions Ramsay, 1998), 33–34; Cooley, *Unholy Wars*, 150. Cf. Griffin, *Reaping the Whirlwind*, 148.

55. According to a contemporary account, Americans and Europeans became involved in drug smuggling out of Afghanistan in the early 1970s. See Catherine Lamour and Michel R. Lamberti, *The International Connection: Opium from Growers to Pushers* (New York: Pantheon, 1974), 190–92.

56. Cf. Maureen Orth, "Afghanistan's Deadly Habit," *Vanity Fair*, March 2002, 170. As late as 2001, one ISI general was convicted in Pakistan for having "assets disproportionate to his known sources of income." Orth, "Afghanistan's Deadly Habit," 152.

57. Cooley, *Unholy Wars*, 128; Beaty and Gwynne, *Outlaw Bank*, 305–306.

58. Beaty and Gwynne, *Outlaw Bank*, 306 (cf. 82). See also Allix, *Petite cuillère*, 35, 95.

59. Maureen Orth, "Afghanistan's Deadly Habit," *Vanity Fair*, March 2002, 170–71. A Tajik sociologist added that she knew "drugs were massively distributed at that time," and that she often heard how Russian soldiers were "invited to taste."

60. Ahmed Rashid, *Jihad: The Rise of Militant Islam in Central Asia* (New Haven, Conn.: Yale University Press), 43.

61. Ahmed Rashid, *Taliban: Militant Islam, Oil and Fundamentalism in Central Asia* (New Haven, Conn.: Yale University Press, 2000), 129.

62. Emdad-ul Haq, *Drugs in South Asia*, 189.

63. Allix, *Petite cuillère*, 100.

64. For BCCI and drugs, see, for example, Kerry and Brown, *BCCI Affair*, 49–51; Truell and Gurwin, *False Profits*, 160.

65. Loftus and Aarons, *Secret War*, 381–82.

66. Bergen, *Holy War Inc.*, 67.

67. Bergen, *Holy War Inc.*, 70.

68. Peter Dale Scott, *The War Conspiracy* (Indianapolis: Bobbs-Merrill, 1972), chapters 1, 2, and 8; Scott, *Drugs, Oil, and War*, chapters 8, 9, and 11.

69. Scott, *War Conspiracy*, 10–15; Scott, *Drugs, Oil, and War*, 128–32.

70. Bernard Fall, *Anatomy of a Crisis* (Garden City, N.Y.: Doubleday, 1969), 99. Scott, *War Conspiracy*, 11, 204–205.

71. Scott, *War Conspiracy*, 197.

72. McCoy, *Politics of Heroin*, 162, 184–86; Scott, *War Conspiracy*, 202.

73. McCoy, *Politics of Heroin*, 190.

74. Scott, *Drugs, Oil, and War*, 129.

75. Scott, *Drugs, Oil, and War*, 128–32. Two key authorizations for the CAT/Air America airlift to Laos were made on presidential authority at a time when Eisenhower was in fact not in his office.

76. Scott, *War Conspiracy*, 64; Cumings, *Origins of the Korean War*, II, 102. LeMay's remark was made in the 1960s in a note to his friend, Whiting Willauer (one of the founders of CAT).

77. See Anthony Kubek, *How the Far East Was Lost* (Chicago: Regnery, 1963), which is discussed at greater length in Peter Dale Scott, *Deep Politics and the Death of JFK* (Berkeley: University of California Press, 1996), 292–93.

78. In April 1971, the French learned that a longtime APACL delegate, Prince Sopsaisana of Laos, had arrived at Orly with a suitcase of heroin "worth $13.5 million on the streets of New York." McCoy, *Politics of Heroin*, 283–84.

79. Scott, *War Conspiracy*, 204–205, Scott, *Drugs, Oil, and War*, 194. Today I would discount the "Pathet Lao activity" even more than I did in 1972.

80. Trocki, *Opium, Empire*, 134.

81. David K. Wyatt, *Siam in Mind* (Chiangmai, Thailand: Silkworm, 2002), 107–108.

82. Sterling Seagrave, *Lords of the Rim: The Invisible Empire of the Overseas Chinese* (New York: Putnam's, 1995), 160.

83. Scott, *Drugs, Oil, and War*, 2.

84. *Pentagon Papers*, Gravel edition (Boston: Beacon, 1971), 1:366, quoted in McCoy, *Politics of Heroin*, 165.

85. Joseph Burkholder Smith, *Portrait of a Cold Warrior* (New York: Ballantine, 1976), 66–67; Cumings, *Origins of the Korean War*, II, 533, 872.

86. McCoy, *Politics of Heroin*, 170, 177.

87. McCoy, *Politics of Heroin*, 191, citing a 1970 report from the U.S. Bureau of Narcotics and Dangerous Drugs.

88. William R. Corson, *The Armies of Ignorance: The Rise of the American Intelligence Empire* (New York: Dial, 1977), 320–22, cited in McCoy, *Politics of Heroin*, 178.

89. McCoy, *Politics of Heroin*, 173, 178.

90. McCoy, *Politics of Heroin*, 185. McCoy then quotes from a 1954 NSC position paper in the Pentagon Papers (1:438) in support of encouraging anticommunist activity in the overseas Chinese communities.

91. Scott, *War Conspiracy*, 201–3.

92. Cumings, *Origins of the Korean War*, II, 600.

93. For example, Cumings quotes a communication from General Hodge to Preston Goodfellow: "Either [Syngman] Rhee doesn't know developments here or he is guilty of heinous conspiracy against American efforts. I believe the latter." General Hodge to Preston Goodfellow, January 5, 1947, Hoover Institution Archives, Goodfellow Papers, box 1, cited in Cumings, *Origins of the Korean War*, II, 65.

94. "On Taiwan, the CIA funded pro-Chiang rollbackers. The brother of T. V. Soong mounted a corner on the soybean market timed for the outbreak of some unexpected event on the weekend of June 25, 1950; Joe McCarthy was reportedly a beneficiary." Cumings, *Origins of the Korean War*, II, 123. Cf. Scott, *War Conspiracy*, 196.

95. McCoy, *Politics of Heroin*, 167. Cf. Scott, *Deep Politics*, 165–66.

96. The importance of the Kunming OSS station to the postwar drugs–intelligence connection is illustrated by the subsequent careers of its members. Stationed there were Helliwell, who later set up CAT, Inc. and Sea Supply, Inc.; Lou Conein, who became the CIA's liaison to Corsican and other traffickers in Saigon; Ray Cline and John Singlaub, both part of the CIA's GMD connection and its offshoot, the drug-sponsoring Asian People's (later World) Anti-Communist League; Howard Hunt, who also helped set up what became the World Anti-Communist League; and Mitchell WerBell, an armorer for the CIA later indicted in an arms-for-drugs deal. WerBell was also involved in a questionable deal for the resettlement of Hmong tribesmen with the Nugan Hand Bank. Presiding over the Kunming station was George Olmsted, whose Washington bank was eventually acquired by BCCI.

97. McCoy, *Politics of Heroin*, 168–70; Scott, *War Conspiracy*, 194, 208, 211.

98. Penny Lernoux, *In Banks We Trust* (Garden City, N.Y.: Anchor Doubleday, 1984), 42–44, 84, which is discussed at greater length in Scott, *Drugs, Oil, and War*, 61, 207.

99. R. T. Naylor, *Hot Money and the Politics of Debt* (New York: Simon & Schuster, 1987), 292.

100. *Wall Street Journal*, April 18, 1980; Lernoux, *In Banks We Trust*, 82–88. Among those who had trust accounts at Castle Bank were Chiang Kai-shek's daughter and her husband. Lernoux, *In Banks We Trust*, 86. Another may have been Richard Nixon. Anthony Summers, with Robbyn Swan, *The Arrogance of Power: The Secret World of Richard Nixon* (New York: Viking, 2000), 253–57.

101. Peter Dale Scott and Jonathan Marshall, *Cocaine Politics* (Berkeley: University of California Press, 1998), 92–93; Lernoux, *In Banks We Trust*, 87.

102. Ross Y. Koen, *The China Lobby in American Politics* (New York: Macmillan, 1960), ix; Scott, *War Conspiracy*, 203–204; Scott, *Drugs, Oil, and War*, 193–94.

103. Cumings, *Origins of the Korean War*, II, 515. The role of Triads in preserving the GMD on Taiwan is noted in a book based largely on U.S. and foreign law enforcement sources: "When China, sinking under addiction, banned opium in nearly all its forms, . . . the Triads had a luxuriant black market in heroin all to themselves. When China fell to the communists after World War II, the Triads had the foresight to help a Triad brother named Generalissimo Chiang Kai-shek flee to Formosa (now Taiwan), taking along much of China's movable wealth." Sterling, *Thieves' World*, 45.

104. Trocki, *Opium, Empire*, 149. Cf. Brook and Wakabayashi, eds., *Opium Regimes*, 83, 92, 94, 97, 305, 309; John Butcher and Howard Dick, eds., *The Rise and Fall of Revenue Farming* (New York: St. Martin's, 1993), 90–91, 168–69, 179–80, 251–55, etc.; *War Conspiracy*, 201–202.

105. McCoy, *Politics of Heroin*, 262–68; Trocki, *Opium, Empire*, 133, Brook and Wakabayashi, 278, 327; Scott, *War Conspiracy*, 202–203.

106. Jonathan Marshall, "Opium and the Politics of Gangsterism in Nationalist China, 1927–1945," *Bulletin of Concerned Asian Scholars* 8, no. 3 (July–September 1976): 29–30, cited in Trocki, *Opium, Empire*, 133; Scott, *War Conspiracy*, 203.

107. The American pilots of Chennault's wartime Flying Tigers, suspected of drug trafficking on the side, would meet regularly with a mysterious Madame Chung in San Francisco, who in turn would meet with Bugsy Siegel's mistress, Virginia Hill. See Peter Dale Scott, "Opium and Empire: McCoy on Heroin in Southeast Asia" (a review of Alfred W. McCoy et al., *The Politics of Heroin in Southeast Asia*), *Bulletin of Concerned Asian Scholars* 5, no. 2 (September 1973): 49–56.

108. McCoy, *Politics of Heroin*, 270; Scott, *War Conspiracy*, 203.

109. Scott, *Deep Politics*, 167. Cf. Scott, *War Conspiracy*, 203; Scott, *Drugs, Oil, and War*, 193. A subsequent U.S. report to the UN on the incident noted that the tong's activities possibly paralleled "the operations of the Triad societies in Hong Kong."

110. *New York Times*, June 2, 1995, A1, A16. Claire Sterling estimated in 1994 that the "Triads were bringing in three-quarters of America's heroin." Sterling, *Thieves' World*, 43.

111. *San Francisco Chronicle*, February 6, 1996, February 7, 1996.

112. Cumings, *Origins of the Korean War*, II, 511–12.

113. Alan A. Block, "Failures at Home and Abroad: Studies in the Implementation of U.S. Drug Policy," in *War on Drugs: Studies in the Failure of U.S. Narcotic Policy*, ed. Alfred W. McCoy and Alan A. Block (Boulder, Colo.: Westview, 1992), 41; Alan A. Block and John McWilliams, "On the Origins of American Counterintelligence: Building a Clandestine Network," *Journal of Policy History* 1, no. 4 (1989), 353–72.

114. Scott, *Deep Politics*, 165–67.

115. Curt Gentry, *J. Edgar Hoover: The Man and the Secrets* (New York: Penguin, 1991), 531–32; Scott, *Deep Politics*, 145–46; Sally Denton and Roger Morris, *The Money and the Power* (New York: Knopf, 2001), 254, 424 n. (cf. 28).

116. Cumings, *Origins of the Korean War*, II, 872, note 93.

117. See McCoy, *Politics of Heroin*, 89–96; Scott, *War Conspiracy*, 201–202.

118. Rogers adds, "Moreover, the rate of discovery of new reserves in the United States was not keeping pace with demand, whereas discovery of reserves in the Gulf region was exceeding production." Paul Rogers, "Oil and the 'War on Terrorism': Why Is the United States in the Gulf?" *openDemocracy*, January 9, 2002, at www.opendemocracy.net/themes/article-2-82.jsp.

119. Alain Labrousse, interview with *El Pulso*, (La Paz, Bolivia) at www.narconews.com/pressbriefing21september.html. Labrousse also agreed "absolutely" with the statement by Carlos Fuentes that for each dollar earned in the business of drugs, two thirds stays in the banks of the United States.

120. A well-placed Washington observer (Anthony Cordesman) observed that "The only military skill the Iraqi Kurds have ever demonstrated is the ability to fight each other over smuggling rights." *Los Angeles Times*, November 19, 1998. Thanks in part to a falling out with Turkey, the United States did not mount a major northern front in Iraq as contemplated, in which Kurds would have played a larger role.

121. Rashid, *Jihad*, 216; cf. 178.

122. State Department, Bureau of European and Eurasian Affairs, "Background Note: Uzbekistan," www.state.gov/r/pa/ei/bgn/2924.htm.

# 9

# War, Genocide, and Resistance in East Timor, 1975–99: Comparative Reflections on Cambodia

*Ben Kiernan*

## Cambodia, East Timor, and the United States

ON JULY 5, 1975, TWO MONTHS AFTER the communist victories in Cambodia and Vietnam, Indonesia's President Suharto visited Washington for his first meeting with U.S. President Gerald Ford and Secretary of State Henry Kissinger. The conversation ranged over Southeast Asian affairs. Suharto assessed the U.S. defeat in Vietnam: "It is not the military strength of the Communists but their fanaticism and ideology which is the principal element of their strength"—something he said Vietnam's anticommunists had not possessed. Suharto continued: "Despite their superiority of arms in fighting the Communists, the human factor was not there. They lacked this national ideology to rally the people to fight Communism." But Indonesia was different, he said: "We are fortunate we already have this national ideology *[Panca Sila]*. The question is, is it strong enough?"[1]

On December 6, Ford and Kissinger in turn called on Suharto in Jakarta. Ford told him that "despite the severe setback of Vietnam" seven months earlier, "[t]he United States intends to continue a strong interest in and influence in the Pacific, Southeast Asia and Asia. . . . [W]e hope to expand this influence." Ford was returning from China, where, he said, "we made it clear that we are opposed to the expansion of any nation or combination of nations." The United States aimed this message not at China but at its rivals. Kissinger informed Suharto: "We believe that China does not have expansionist aims now. . . . Their first concern is the Soviet Union and their second Vietnam." Ford agreed, saying, "I had the impression of a restrained Chinese foreign policy." Suharto asked whether the United States believed that Cambodia, Laos, and Vietnam would "be incorporated into one country." Ford replied: "The unification of Vietnam has come more quickly than we anticipated. There is, however, resistance in Cambodia to the influence of Hanoi. We are willing to move slowly in our relations with Cambodia, hoping perhaps to slow down the North Vietnamese influence although we find the Cambodian government very difficult." Kissinger then explained Beijing's similar strategy: "the Chinese want to use Cambodia to balance off Vietnam. . . . We don't like Cambodia, for the government in many ways is worse than Vietnam, but we would like it to be independent. We don't discourage Thailand or China from drawing closer to Cambodia."[2]

Even as Ford and Kissinger aimed to strengthen the independence of Pol Pot's Cambodian communist regime, another Southeast Asian humanitarian disaster was in the making. In that same December 1975 conversation, Suharto now raised "another problem, Timor." He needed U.S. support, not condemnation, for planned Indonesian expansion into the small Portuguese colony. "We want your understanding if we deem it necessary to take rapid or drastic action." Ford replied, "We will understand and will not press you on the issue." Kissinger then added: "You appreciate that the use of U.S.-made arms could create problems. . . . It depends on how we construe it; whether it is in self-defense or is a foreign operation. It is important that whatever you do succeeds quickly. We would be able to influence the reaction in America if whatever happens happens after we return. This way there would be less chance of people talking in an unauthorized way. . . . We understand your problem and the need to move quickly. . . . Whatever you do, however, we will try to handle in the best way possible. . . . If you have made plans, we will do our best to keep everyone quiet until the President returns home."[3] U.S. policy opposed Vietnamese expansion and supported Indonesian expansion. Washington approved the independent existence of the Khmer Rouge regime, but not the independence of East Timor. It was prepared to sacrifice that independence to strengthen U.S. influence in Jakarta.

Suharto saw the green light, and Indonesian paratroopers landed in Dili the next day. The Cambodian genocide had already begun, and the Timor tragedy now commenced. The death toll from the Indonesian invasion and occupation of East Timor from 1975 to 1999 would reach approximately 150,000, a fifth of the territory's population.[4] This is much lower in absolute numbers but proportionately comparable to the 1975–79 Cambodian toll of 1.7 million in a population of 7.9 million.[5] There are other similarities. In each country, an initial, small-scale civil war preceded major international interventions. The two genocides that began in 1975 were also each in turn followed by extended foreign occupation and, finally, by United Nations intervention.

## War and Genocide in Cambodia and East Timor

The first Cambodian civil war, from 1967 to 1970, had pitted a few thousand insurgents of the Communist Party of Kampuchea (CPK, or "Khmer Rouge") against the independent regime of Prince Sihanouk. The war became internationalized after Lon Nol's coup of March 18, 1970, when the Vietnam War smashed across the border. Vietnamese communist and anticommunist forces, and U.S. ground troops and air fleets, turned Cambodia into a new battleground. More than 100,000 Khmer civilians were killed by U.S. B-52 bombardments alone.[6] Sihanouk joined forces with the now rapidly growing Khmer Rouge in a wider civil and international war. The Khmer Rouge defeated Lon Nol's Khmer Republic and entered Phnom Penh in April 1975, two weeks before the Vietnamese communists took Saigon.

Pol Pot's victorious Khmer Rouge immediately attacked into Vietnamese territory, only to be rebuffed there by the newly triumphant communists. Cambodia renewed its border attacks in January 1977 and escalated them over subsequent months.[7] Phnom Penh declared war at year's end and rejected the Vietnamese offer of mutual pullback and negotiations. In mid-1978, the Khmer Rouge regime put down a mutiny in Cambodia's Eastern Zone, and its massacres of Cambodians and ethnic minorities reached their peak. In December 1978, Vietnam invaded and quickly drove the Khmer Rouge army across the country to the Thai border. Hanoi's occupying forces established a new Cambodian government and army, headed from 1985 by Prime Minister Hun Sen. Khmer Rouge troops continued their attacks from sanctuaries in Thailand. Vietnam's withdrawal in 1989 was followed by the UN-sponsored elections of 1993. These brought to power an uneasy coalition of Hun Sen's People's Party and the royalist Funcinpec, led by Sihanouk's son Prince Ranariddh. This coalition, dominated by Hun Sen, finally defeated the Khmer Rouge insurgency in 1999.

Two months later, a UN-appointed Group of Experts concluded that the surviving Khmer Rouge leaders should be prosecuted by an International Tribunal "for crimes against humanity and genocide."[8] The events of 1975–1979, the legal experts reported, fit the definition of the crime outlawed by the UN Genocide Convention of 1948. In addition to committing "war crimes" against Vietnam and Thailand, the Khmer Rouge regime had also "subjected the people of Cambodia to almost all of the acts enumerated in the Convention." Did it carry out these acts with the requisite intent and against groups protected by the convention? According to the UN experts,

> [T]he existing historical research justifies including genocide within the jurisdiction of a tribunal to prosecute Khmer Rouge leaders. In particular, evidence suggests the need for prosecutors to investigate the commission of genocide

against the Cham, Vietnamese and other minority groups, and the Buddhist monkhood. The Khmer Rouge subjected these groups to an especially harsh and extensive measure of the acts enumerated in the Convention. The requisite intent has support in direct and indirect evidence, including Khmer Rouge statements, eyewitness accounts and the nature and numbers of victims in each group, both in absolute terms and in proportion to each group's total population. These groups qualify as protected groups under the Convention: the Muslim Cham as an ethnic and religious group, the Vietnamese communities as an ethnic and, perhaps, a racial group; and the Buddhist monkhood as a religious group.

The UN legal experts added that "the intent to destroy the Cham and other ethnic minorities appears evidenced by such Khmer Rouge actions as their announced policy of homogenization, the total prohibition of these groups' distinctive cultural traits, their dispersal among the general population and the execution of their leadership."[9] Of the Cham population of 250,000, for example, approximately 90,000 perished in four years, many of them deliberately killed because of their ethnicity. Under such conditions, combined with utopian Maoist forced labor programs and Stalinist exterminations of "class enemies" among the majority Khmer population, 1.7 million Cambodians perished.[10]

While recognizing these crimes against humanity, some legal experts doubt that the legal definition in the UN Genocide Convention—attempted destruction "in whole or in part" of "a national, ethnical, racial or religious group, as such"—covers either the Khmer Rouge mass murders of Cambodia's noncommunist political groups and defeated officer class or Indonesia's mass murder of political groups in East Timor from 1975 to 1999.[11] Objections to a legal interpretation protecting "political groups" also exclude the Indonesian army's mass extermination of its domestic Communist Party (PKI), over half a million of whose members were killed in 1965–66.[12] But the crimes committed a decade later in East Timor, with a toll of 150,000 in a population of 650,000, clearly meet a range of sociological definitions of genocide used by most scholars of the phenomenon, who see both political and ethnic groups as possible victims of genocide.[13] The victims in East Timor included not only that substantial "part" of the Timorese "national group" targeted for destruction because of their resistance to Indonesian annexation—along with their relatives, as we shall see—but also most members of the twenty-thousand-strong ethnic Chinese minority prominent in the towns of East Timor, whom Indonesian forces singled out for destruction, apparently because of their ethnicity "as such."

As in Cambodia, a small-scale civil war preceded the Timor tragedy. In mid-1975, a short conflict in the Portuguese colony led to unexpected victory for its independence movement, Fretilin. Jakarta's armed forces invaded the territory on December 7. Full-scale war raged until 1980. The occupation continued to take lives for another twenty years, even after a 1999 UN-organized referendum demonstrated that 79 percent of East Timorese wanted independence. Then, in a preplanned operation, Indonesian occupation forces sacked the territory, destroying 80 percent of the homes, deporting hundreds of thousands of people to West Timor, and killing possibly one thousand. U.S. President Bill Clinton insisted that Indonesia "must invite" an international peacekeeping force to take over East Timor. Australian troops led in the UN forces, as Indonesian soldiers left much of the territory in ruins. In UN-organized parliamentary elections in 2001, Fretilin won 57 percent of the vote. In the April 2002 presidential elections, Fretilin's former leader, Xanana Gusmao, won 79 percent and its founding president, Xavier do Amaral, won 17 percent.[14] On May 20, 2002, after more than two years of transitional rule, the UN handed over responsibility to the new independent state of East Timor.

The two cases of genocidal mass murder in Southeast Asia thus share a roughly contemporaneous time frame and a combination of civil war, multiple international intervention, and UN conflict resolution. But ideological crosscurrents abound. Jakarta pursued anticommunism; the Khmer Rouge were communists. In East Timor, the major Indonesian goal was conquest. In Cambodia, the Khmer Rouge goal was revolution. Maoism influenced Pol Pot's CPK regime, but it also influenced the Fretilin resistance to Indonesia. U.S. policy makers supported the invading Indonesians in Timor, as well as the indigenous Khmer Rouge in Cambodia. Both perpetrator regimes exterminated ethnic minorities, including local Chinese, as well as political dissidents. How did Indonesian anticommunist counterinsurgency and Cambodian communist revolution both lead to such horrific results?

As I will argue, the genocides were in part products of international alliances and impositions. But they also reflected and provoked indigenous divisions, both ideological and regional. Were these divisions in both cases also ethnic? Domestic coalitions formed and ruptured over time. The CPK's Maoist ideology combined explosively with its virulent Khmer racism and expansionism, leading it to seek to eliminate both political and ethnic enemies and to launch attacks on all neighboring states. Fretilin Maoists, by contrast, fought Indonesian aggressors, but they also fell out with other Fretilin leaders, local elites, regional coalitions, and military professionals. Was this in part for ethnic reasons, as in Cambodia? Regional and political differences plagued the Khmer Rouge, too. The 1978 rebellion by the Eastern Zone CPK forces against the Party Center constituted the major armed resistance to the genocidal regime.[15] In East Timor, from the start, political and regional divisions also debilitated the pro-Indonesian cause, not just the Fretilin resistance. But to understand fully the conditions in which these divisions emerged, and to what extent they were comparable, it is first necessary to examine the international forces that abetted both the Suharto and Pol Pot regimes.

## Green Lights from Ford and Kissinger

Suharto had first raised the issue of the Portuguese decolonization of East Timor at his July 5, 1975, meeting with Ford and Kissinger at Camp David. Describing Indonesia as "a unified nation without any territorial ambition," which "will not commit aggression against other countries . . . [or] use force against the territory of other countries," Suharto nevertheless pointed out that for East Timor, "an independent country would hardly be viable," and that "the only way is to integrate with Indonesia." However, "The problem is that those who want independence are those who are Communist-influenced." Suharto concluded that "Indonesia doesn't want to insert itself into Timor self-determination, but the problem is how to manage the self-determination process with a majority wanting unity with Indonesia."[16]

In this way, six months before ordering the December 1975 invasion, Suharto secured U.S. acquiescence in the territory's prospective incorporation by Indonesia. The expansionist impulse would be denied; the excuse, the communist threat. While the U.S. Department of State called the Timorese independence movement, Fretilin, "a vaguely leftist party,"[17] Kissinger labeled Fretilin "a Communist government in the middle of Indonesia."[18] Suharto considered its members "almost Communists."[19] Jakarta saw a "Communist wing" of Fretilin in Timorese Maoist students educated in Lisbon during the 1974 revolution there.[20]

From March to July 1975, the Portuguese authorities organized local village elections throughout East Timor. Fretilin won 50–55 percent of the vote.[21] Its main rival, the Timorese Democratic Union (UDT), favoring gradual progress toward independence, received slightly fewer votes. Apodeti, a small party favoring union with Indonesia, came in a distant third. Fretilin had managed to bring a nationalist message to a population of 650,000 divided into possibly thirty ethnic groups speaking fourteen distinct languages.[22] This multicultural success, which included members of Dili's one-thousand-strong Muslim Arab community in Fretilin's largely Catholic ranks, would remain one of the party's strengths.[23] Fretilin did remain suspicious of the local Chinese, a largely urban entrepreneurial community that failed to find a voice within Fretilin, which cited reasons of class but not race.

Suharto announced following his return from the United States on July 8, 1975, that East Timor lacked the economic basis for viable independence.[24] This was the backdrop to an attempted coup in Dili by Fretilin's rival UDT on

August 11.[25] In Washington the next morning, Philip Habib told Henry Kissinger that authorship of the coup was still unclear: "[I]f it is an Indonesian move, or the Indonesians move against it . . . we should just do nothing. It is quite clear that the Indonesians are not going to let any hostile element take over an island right in the midst of the Indonesian archipelago." Only if the coup proved to be a pro-independence move would the U.S. act—that is, against independence. Kissinger said, "[T]he Indonesians are going to take over the island sooner or later," ensuring merely "the disappearance of a vestige of colonialism." Habib added that "we should not get ourselves sucked into this one by having opinions."[26]

## Civil War

In mid-June 1975, Fretilin forces led by a former Portuguese soldier, Hermengildo Alves, had briefly seized power in Oecusse, a small enclave of Portuguese territory within West Timor. Jill Jolliffe reports that "the Portuguese regained control after sending a negotiating force from Dili as a result of which Alves was gaoled for twenty days and UDT and Fretilin agreed to rule jointly." This coalition prevailed in the Oecusse enclave for the next few months.[27]

However, within four days of their August 11 coup in the capital, UDT leaders arrested more than 80 Fretilin members, including future leader Xanana Gusmao. UDT members killed a dozen Fretilin members in four locations. The victims included a founding member of Fretilin, and a brother of its vice president, Nicolau Lobato.[28] Fretilin responded by appealing successfully to the Portuguese-trained East Timorese military units.[29] UDT's violent takeover thus provoked the three-week civil war, pitting its fifteen hundred troops against the two thousand regular forces now led by Fretilin commanders.

By the end of August, UDT remnants were retreating toward the Indonesian border. A UDT group of nine hundred crossed into West Timor on September 24, followed by more than a thousand others, leaving Fretilin in control of East Timor for the ensuing three months. The death toll in the civil war reportedly included four hundred people in Dili and possibly sixteen hundred in the hills.[30] In the aftermath, "numerous UDT supporters were beaten and jailed" by the Fretilin victors.[31]

Indonesia stepped up its plans for invasion. In early September, as many as two hundred special forces troops launched incursions, which were noted by U.S. intelligence, and in October, conventional military assaults followed.[32] Indonesian forces murdered five Australian journalists in the border town of Balibo on October 16.

In September, the leader of the pro-Indonesian Apodeti party, Osorio Soares, remained "freely able to move about,"[33] but as Indonesian incursions escalated, Fretilin took Soares and several hundred other Apodeti and UDT members into custody.[34] Political positions had hardened. Fretilin had begun as the Timorese Social Democratic Association, led by Jose Ramos-Horta and former Jesuit seminarian Xavier do Amaral. Since the UDT coup, however, what Jolliffe calls "a discernible shift in power" had brought the ascendancy of a more "inward-turning" nationalist Fretilin faction led by Nicolau Lobato. They blended notions of "revolutionary African nationalism, pragmatism and conservative self-reliance," but, according to Jolliffe, "operated from a solely nationalist framework with the stress on meeting local needs by whatever means necessary, whether socialization or foreign investment." Fretilin's left wing, too, "did not regard themselves as Marxists but as nationalists who believed they could draw on Marxism and adapt it to nationalist ends." As Jolliffe puts it, "The consequence of the marriage of these two streams was a Timor-isation of the leadership following the coup period, accompanied by an emphasis towards black nationalism rather than social democracy."[35] Helen Hill suggests this meant African-style politics rather than "black nationalism." Beyond an anti-Chinese or anticapitalist undercurrent, evidence of indigenous racist ideology is sparse.[36]

A full-scale Indonesian invasion loomed. Portugal had evacuated its officials offshore. Fretilin formally declared East Timor's independence on November 28, 1975, and a Fretilin cabinet took office. Its eighteen members included a Portuguese and two Arabs, all members of the party's Central Committee (CC). Jolliffe writes of the new government's leadership, Xavier do Amaral, Nicolau Lobato, and Mari Alkatiri, that "The two principal figures were practicing Catholics, the third a practicing Moslem."[37] There were no ethnic Chinese members.

## Invasion, Genocide, and Resistance, 1975–80

### Political Turmoil and Division

Jakarta had secured the support of some of the defeated UDT leaders as well as the Apodeti party. Two East Timorese chiefs from the West Timor border area also proclaimed the support of their small Kota and Trabalhista parties for integration with Indonesia. Kota was a monarchist group established by a number of *liurai* (district rulers, or "petty kings") with several hundred members. It "appeared to be a racially pure satellite of Apodeti, based on an inner circle of tribal leaders with access to the mystical rites of the traditional culture." Trabalhista had "a dozen or so members, many of whom came from the same family."[38] This lineup enabled Suharto, in his talk with Ford and Kissinger on December 6, to claim the support of "four parties" from East Timor, adding: "The local kings are important, . . . and they are on our side."[39]

Following the Indonesian invasion the next day, retreating Fretilin forces released a number of their Apodeti and UDT prisoners. But in the hills several weeks later, they summarily executed eighty Apodeti members, including the party's leader, Osorio Soares, and possibly seventy UDT prisoners, including Secretary General Fernando Luz.[40] To compound the tragedy, as the Indonesians landed in Dili, according to James Dunn, "a large number of Apodeti supporters, who had just been released from internment by Fretilin, went out to greet their liberators, to be machine-gunned in the street for their trouble." Indonesian troops shot down thirty Apodeti supporters in cold blood. An Apodeti member "was shot while presenting his party identification card to a group of soldiers."[41] As we shall see, Indonesian force would soon also be turned against other non-Fretilin groups, such as the ethnic Chinese.

The Indonesians soon appointed the Kota leader, Jose Martins, son of a *liurai* from Ermera in western East Timor, to a prominent position. However, Jakarta's constituency even among anti-Fretilin Timorese quickly collapsed. During a March 1976 visit to the United Nations, Martins defected and criticized Jakarta's intervention.[42] Another initially pro-Indonesian Timorese official, UDT's founding president, Mario Carrascalao, was placed under house arrest in West Timor and repatriated to Portugal in mid-1976. A third "prointegration" Timorese official also defected to Portugal. Indonesia announced on January 31, 1976, that all Timorese political parties had now "dissolved themselves."[43] Just in case, Jakarta banned them on February 3.[44] It then turned to traditional rulers from the western part of East Timor. After formal "integration" of the territory in mid-1976, the *liurai* of Atsabe became the Indonesian provincial governor and the *liurai* of Maubara became chair of the new province's legislature.[45] Thus the strength of pro-Indonesian feeling was limited to traditional rulers in the west of the territory.

Differences quickly emerged in Fretilin ranks as well. On the morning of the Indonesian invasion, Fretilin's founding president, Xavier do Amaral, allegedly set out for the capital, telling his cabinet minister, Eduardo dos Anjos, "I am going to Dili to ask the Javanese why they [are] invading our homeland."[46] The next day, dos Anjos told Fretilin Central Committee member Xanana Gusmao that do Amaral had threatened to "speak with the invaders to ask them to retreat immediately!" Xanana recalls that "Eduardo managed to convince him to stop such strange and daring behaviour!"[47] A month later, in January 1976, do Amaral approached Fretilin's vice president, Nicolau Lobato, suggesting they "ask the United Nations to hold a referendum on self-determination." Lobato and the chief of staff of Falantil (Fretilin's army) "categorically rejected" this proposal, arguing that the issue was now closed, since independence had been unilaterally proclaimed on November 28.[48]

## The War

According to Australian intelligence, by April 1976 Indonesia had 32,000 troops engaged in East Timor and another 10,000 in reserve in West Timor.[49] Against these, Fretilin deployed 2,500 regular troops and 7,000 part-time militia, and could draw upon 10,000–20,000 reservists, all trained by the Portuguese.[50] Suharto acknowledged in August 1976 that "the Fretilin movement is still possessed of strength."[51] Indonesian intelligence reportedly estimated in September that Fretilin still fielded as many as 5,000 guerrillas.[52] Australian sources reported by late 1976 that Indonesia had lost 10,000 troops killed, wounded, or missing.[53] In early 1977, a senior Indonesian officer conceded that Fretilin had inflicted up to 5,000 casualties.[54] But the invaders took a much greater toll on Fretilin forces, and by 1978 had also organized two Timorese battalions of their own.[55]

A discernible regional pattern began to emerge. Indonesia was able to count on *liurai* and other leaders from the northwestern part of East Timor. Within the resistance, as we shall see, moderate or conciliatory factions of Fretilin appeared strongest in the north-central sector. The Fretilin resistance would find its firmest support base in the remote eastern sector of the half-island.[56]

There were also ideological divisions. In 1984, Carmel Budiardjo and Liem Soei Liong described three major issues that had divided Fretilin's resistance since 1975. These were: "compromise with the enemy, the nature of the war, and the implementation of Fretilin's social and political programs." Firstly, from the start the majority of Fretilin's fifty-two-person CC opposed negotiations or compromise with Indonesia.[57] But in early 1977, "the leadership split over the question," leading to do Amaral's dismissal. The CC was committed to a Maoist-inspired self-reliant strategy for the achievement of independence. Secondly, there was further division over the nature of "people's war," a strategy Fretilin adopted at its national meeting at Soibada in May–June 1976. Many of the professional army officers who joined Fretilin in 1975 had been trained by the Portuguese to keep the army out of politics. They differed with those leftist Fretilin leaders who insisted that "the political line prevail over the military line" and that peasant militia be trained. Army officers also tended to resist overall military and political coordination, retreating into and thus strengthening regionalism. Thirdly, Fretilin's political leaders emphasized rural development and egalitarian social policies that conflicted with local, traditional, hierarchical structures in some communities and regions.[58]

In the first year and a half of the resistance war (1975–77), Fretilin president Xavier do Amaral worked sporadically with his vice president and prime minister, Nicolau Lobato. Both were reportedly shocked at the scale of Indonesian brutality. As pressures escalated, however, differences between the two men grew, and in September 1977 Lobato had his superior do Amaral arrested for "high treason." In an extended denunciation speech broadcast by Fretilin radio on September 14, 1977, Lobato acknowledged that "for over a year, the Radio Dili of the Javanese invaders has spread the story that there is a serious confrontation" between himself and do Amaral. "There was some truth in all this," Lobato now announced.[59] As we shall see, divisions in Fretilin ranks were not only regional and ideological, but also rather volatile, as circumstances and opinions changed over time.

Fretilin's minister of information and national security, Alarico Fernandes, reflected this changing pattern in the different positions he adopted during 1975–78. A former meteorologist and noncommunist social democrat, he had originally seen Austria and Scandinavia as political models for Fretilin.[60] But after the UDT's violent coup, Xanana Gusmao says, Fernandes became a "real executioner" with "a frenzied thirst for vengeance." Before the Indonesian invasion, Fernandes announced, "I'll continue to stay [in] Fretilin but I will not accept communism." Gusmao implies, but does not clearly state, that Fernandes was responsible for the execution of the UDT prisoners after the invasion. As the war against Indonesia ground on, Fernandes hoped for assistance from socialist countries, which never came.[61] In mid-1976, he aligned himself with the professional military faction, but now also proclaimed, "I accept Marxism as the only way of liberating our people."[62] Initially opposed to negotiations, Fernandes finally lost hope of international support in 1977–78, when he "began to waver and slowly shifted" toward compromise with Indonesia.[63] By then, internecine purges were escalating. The soldier Hermengildo Alves, second deputy secretary for defense and, according to Gusmao, an "incorrigible drunk," had also become a "real executioner."[64] And the Maoist left wing of Fretilin, Gusmao later wrote, was also responsible for "purging waves of massacres of nationalists" whom it "assassinated as reactionaries and traitors."[65]

Despite internal violence and instability, for the first years of the war Fretilin mounted a highly successful resistance to Indonesia.[66] About forty of its fifty-two CC members escaped death or capture during the initial invasion.[67] (Jose Ramos–Horta and Mari Alkatiri, who were abroad, took up the diplomatic struggle at the UN and elsewhere.) Nicolau Lobato's rambling speech of September 1977, revealing the intense political and regional differences, also conveys an impression of great mobility on the part of the Fretilin leaders, of often free movement of forces and units, of mass meetings and assemblies in the hills, and of large areas and populations under Fretilin administration, despite occasional serious harassment from the Indonesian occupiers.[68] A report from Indonesian Catholic Church sources in late 1976 estimated that "80% of the territory is not under the direct control of the Indonesian military forces."[69] A foreign diplomatic delegation, which visited East Timor in May 1977, reported that Indonesia still controlled only one-third of the territory, while Fretilin controlled another third and was able to move freely in the remaining third.[70] The next month, Alarico Fernandes claimed in a radio broadcast that Fretilin "control[led] most parts of the country, 80% of the national soil, defeating the vandal Indonesian invaders on all fronts."[71] Nicolau Lobato added that "all over the country the resistance is still very strong despite the continuous raids deeply launched by the enemy to the large areas under our forces' control."[72] As Dunn has pointed out, "an indication of the extent of Fretilin's control is that it was able to hold the town of Remexio, only 15 kilometres from the capital, almost without interruption for more than three years."[73]

Of the territory's 1974 population of approximately 650,000,[74] an Indonesian-attempted census in October 1978 returned a population estimate of only 329,000. Possibly 200,000 more may still have been living in Fretilin-held areas in the hills.[75] In the east, for instance, Indonesian officials later acknowledged that in 1975–76, "a large part of the population in this region fled to the mountains."[76] As late as November 1979, Indonesian foreign minister Mochtar conceded that only half of East Timor's pre-1975 population had been brought under Indonesian control.[77] Jakarta's hope of a quick victory had foundered.

But Nicolau Lobato's prediction of triumph over "senile Javanese expansionism" was also premature.[78]

## The Genocide

Indonesian massacres of Timorese began on the first day of the December 1975 landing. Dunn calls the assault on Dili "one of the most brutal operations of its kind in modern warfare. Hundreds of Timorese and Chinese were gunned down at random in the streets." The Bishop of Timor watched from his window as 150 people, including at least twenty women, were systematically shot on the town's jetty. Five hundred Chinese were killed on December 8 alone. About forty unarmed Timorese men were murdered in the south of the capital on December 9. A priest reported that the invaders killed about two thousand people in the first few days, including seven hundred Chinese.[79] John Taylor reports many testimonies "of entire families being shot for displaying Fretilin flags on their houses, of groups being shot for refusing to hand over their personal possessions, of grenades being rolled into packed houses, and of Fretilin sympathizers singled out for immediate execution."[80] The latter included the wife of Vice President Nicolau Lobato, shot dead on the dock. Her sister saved their infant son at the last minute.[81]

The massacres then spread to the coastal and hill towns. Dunn continues: "When they finally forced Fretilin to withdraw from Aileu, Indonesian troops, in a brutal public spectacle, machine-gunned the remaining population of the town, except for children under the age of four, who were sent back to Dili in trucks." The killings at Aileu even distressed Tomas Goncalves, son of the *liurai* of Atsabe, a leading supporter of integration with Indonesia.[82] Citing Dunn, Taylor reports that "in the villages of Remexio and Aileu, south of Dili, everyone over the age of three was shot." Taylor adds, "When Indonesian troops entered Aileu in February 1976, it contained 5,000 people. When a group of Indonesian relief workers visited it in September 1976, only 1,000 remained—they were told that the remainder had moved to the mountains."[83] A visitor found no Timorese in Ainaro in late 1975. Of Baucau's population of 85,000, 32,000 met the arriving Indonesian troops on December 10, 1975, but by the end of February 1976 most had fled the exactions of the occupiers, leaving a population of only 9,646. In mid-1976, "When the towns of Liquica and Maubara were eventually wrested from Fretilin's control the Indonesians put to death nearly all members of their Chinese communities."[84] Twenty-six people were executed in Liquica in May 1976 alone. Some survivors did remain in these towns, while many others fled to Fretilin-held mountain areas. But the Indonesian massacres took a heavy toll. A Timorese guide for a senior Indonesian officer told Dunn that "in the early months of the fighting, as the Indonesian forces moved into the central regions, they killed most Timorese they encountered."[85]

Perhaps the worst massacre took place just inside Indonesian West Timor. At Lamaknan in June 1976, Dunn reports, "Indonesian troops who had been badly mauled by Fretilin units took their vengeance on a large refugee settlement which housed some 5000 to 6000 people." After setting fire to several houses, the troops fired at the refugees for several hours, "shooting down men, women and children." According to a Timorese truck driver for the Indonesian forces, about two thousand people died.[86]

The president of the pro-Indonesian provisional government of East Timor, Lopes da Cruz, announced on February 13, 1976, that 60,000 people had been killed "in the six months of civil war in East Timor," suggesting a toll of more than 55,000 in the two months since the invasion.[87] A late 1976 report from the Indonesian Catholic Church estimated that 60,000 to 100,000 Timorese had perished.[88] In March 1977, Indonesian foreign minister Adam Malik conceded that "50,000 people or perhaps 80,000 might have been killed during the war in Timor, but we saved 600,000 of them."[89] On November 12, 1979, Indonesia's new foreign minister, Mochtar Kusumaatmadja, estimated that 120,000 Timorese had died since 1975.[90]

The pressures of full-scale invasion and ongoing genocide initially brought to the fore Fretilin's harshest and most radical elements, who began to predominate in the resistance. As we shall see, Indonesian military forces successfully targeted them for destruction in 1977–79, but still could not eliminate Fretilin, which soon reemerged and rebuilt itself under Xanana Gusmao as the relatively moderate nationalist movement of its early years. In 1987, Xanana condemned the "senseless radicalism" that had "paid no attention to our concrete conditions" and "made us intolerably overbearing and led us to put many compatriots on the same footing as the criminal aggressor." But he also lamented that "humanity had closed its eyes to the extermination of the Maubere people, a genocide carried out by the assassinating forces of the Indonesian occupation."[91] More than $1 billion in military equipment, supplied to Indonesia mostly by the United States, but also by Britain, France, and Australia, had made this genocide possible.[92]

## The Resistance

How did resistance continue and function under conditions of Indonesian-imposed famine and genocide? And how did moderate Fretilin leaders regain the initiative in a movement under such a siege? The primary evidence of internal Fretilin division, both regional and ideological, only underscores the remarkable persistence and survival of East Timorese nationalism, despite regional differences but with minimal ethnic conflict.

In his September 1977 denunciation, Nicolau Lobato claimed that do Amaral had "forged a racist theory, attributing the cause of the war to the *mesticos*."[93] Lobato's accusation of do Amaral's racism against those of partial Portuguese descent is a rare suggestion of a politics of ethnicity within Fretilin. It certainly betrays political animosities. With partial fairness, do Amaral may have complained of Fretilin being run by a small non-Chinese *mestico* elite rather than the indigenous Timorese majority. He may even have considered that Lobato's "black nationalist" posture was an educated pretension disguising undemocratic exclusiveness, and that Fretilin's multiregional national identity was urban in origin. But such political characteristics alone do not constitute racial persecution. Do Amaral's complaint seems as much against top-down political domination. Lobato, acknowledging and denying that complaint, in turn accused do Amaral, son of a *liurai*,[94] of drawing upon regionalism, traditionalism, and indigenous nativism to shore up his own political support. Such regionalism would indeed pose a ready challenge to nationalist imposition.

As nominal resistance leader in 1975–77, according to Lobato, do Amaral "never attempted to call a Fretilin Central Committee meeting." "He created and fomented divisionism among Commands, among the rank-and-file, among different zones, among the different ethnic groups." According to Lobato, do Amaral's stronghold was an arc of territory in north-central East Timor, from the mountains south of Dili to the coastal area to its west. "His feudal fiefs were Turiscai-[Ainaro]–Remexio-Lekidoe–Manatuto and part of Maubisse."[95]

What kind of regime prevailed in this north-central area run by do Amaral in 1976–77? Xanana recalls that in early 1976, "We traveled through Turiskai. Xavier was in his kingdom leading a carefree life under the feudalistic care of his brother."[96] Lobato, claiming that do Amaral "installed his relatives and friends," also faulted "his protection of feudal institutions, like the *rajahs*, *sucos* [tribal groups], *povoacaos* [village units]." "These chiefs, together with the secretaries, some commanders and the major part of the other authorities are among his more loyal followers." Do Amaral "spread through the mouths of his relatives and feudal bosses, the wrong theory that Turiscai was the fount of politics in East Timor." Lobato called all this "an authentic feudal authority."[97]

Locally, do Amaral seems to have made rather successful use of many of the traditional techniques of *liurai* rule. Lobato accused him of "recourse to use of corporal punishment, trials by Councils of Elders, . . . support for the feudal relations of parenthood, *balaques* (arranged marriages)," as well as *lulics* (animist sacred objects) "and other superstitious practices." Do Amaral made "visits to festivities with big noise and big banquets; long voyages in cavalcade with the noise of numerous guards"; and "big colonial-style dances lasting all night and sometimes for a whole week."[98]

Significant political issues also emerge from these crosscurrents of rivalry, regionalism, and traditional leadership. Lobato envisioned "a new society, free from all forms of exploitation of man by man." He considered "democratic centralism" to be "a fundamental principle . . . on which our politics are based." He used the slogan, "Put Politics in Command," by which he meant, "Between a civilian and a soldier, no wall exists . . . easily in practice, a civilian can become a soldier and a soldier, a civilian. The civilian tasks as well as the military tasks, are all political tasks. . . . [A]ll our acts must be oriented and directed to reach a political objective." The CC meeting in Soibada from May 20 to June 2, 1976, which adopted the people's war strategy, emphasized organizational as well as military tasks.[99] Budiardjo and Liong report, "It was concluded that it would be suicidal to continue to engage in frontal combat against the numerically superior and much better equipped Indonesian army units. As a result the leadership decided to switch to more appropriate guerrilla tactics."[100] Maoist influence was now on the rise. It may also have been at this meeting that the CC created the Supreme Council of Resistance to oversee a protracted people's war.

By contrast, Lobato said, do Amaral believed in separating the military struggle from the civilian sphere, giving the war precedence over state organization and economic tasks, and diverting scarce seed and human resources to the military on "the strange theory that in time of war there was no time to make politics" and "no place" even for military preparations. "Now, we have only to fight anyhow." Thus, Lobato claimed, many "disorganized soldiers . . . were put unprepared in the frontline around Turiscai and Maubisse." Do Amaral allegedly interpreted "Put Politics in Command" to mean placing his own civilian appointees in charge of the armed forces in his region. He turned his Zone Political Bureau into "a sort of mini-Central Committee, like little heads leading the people in the zone." This threatened Lobato's authority as prime minister and the Supreme Council's overall control of Fretilin's still substantial territory. As Lobato put it, "only one vanguard exists: the Fretilin Central Committee—as in a person's body there is only one head."[101] This was clearly a political standoff.[102]

The rivals took their battle to Alarico Fernandes' radio transmitter. Do Amaral supposedly gave "erroneous orders" that broadcasts were "not to attack any further . . . imperialism and its lackeys." But Fernandes and Lobato broadcast that "the principal enemy of the people is imperialism." Then "do Amaral started and sustained a very sharp polemic" with Fernandes.[103] Meanwhile, Fretilin's Maoists also opposed do Amaral, as well as Fernandes and the military officers, who all wished to seek external support for their resistance. Xanana recalls hearing an anti-Soviet Maoist slogan: "'Imperialism [equals] social imperialism' was the reason the politicians gave for rejecting the request for help to the Soviet Union. 'I don't want to know if it is imperialism or social imperialism. I don't care if the help comes from America, the Soviet Union, China, or whatever. All I need is help. Isn't that what we need?' yelled Xavier, dazed and defeated."[104]

Strikingly, this partly political, partly regional internal conflict never became a racist crusade. In each political incarnation, the struggle remained nationalist and inclusive. The political divisions debilitated Fretilin, but did not prevent its eventual recovery across the territory, from a solid regional base in the east.

## Implosion

Internecine conflict seems to have broken out first in March 1976, during a meeting of the CC Standing Committee at Fatu Berliu, the first of three Fretilin gatherings in the south-central sector. Fernandes "started to follow very closely the tracks of Xavier do Amaral." Then the CC rejected do Amaral's proposed candidates for membership.[105] In April, at a meeting in nearby

Barique, civilian–military relations soured; "it became obvious that the military had an aversion towards those of us who were politicians. . . . Silence and an obvious dissatisfaction characterized the climate of argument. . . . Outside the meetings, the soldiers avoided the politicians." However, "many" professional officers were promoted to the CC, "avoiding a rebellion of the soldiers."[106] Perhaps a deal had been struck to permit the establishment of the Supreme Council of Resistance.

At the CC meeting held at Soibada from May 20–June 2, 1976, initial ideological discussions turned to Marxist concepts of the state. Do Amaral declared the state to be "eternal, coming from God." In what Xanana calls "a revolutionary avalanche of minds," the CC adopted its strategy of people's war, with most favoring "self-reliance"—except the army officers.[107] Do Amaral left the meeting "after only attending three days of its work, with the excuse of the National Celebration of May 20." He planned "a big concentration of the masses in his feudal fief of Turiscai" in June. From then on, do Amaral allegedly "did not follow the resolution made in the May 1976 meeting." He asserted rather "that the organizational work must come after the war."[108] He may also have objected to being subordinated to the Supreme Council. Moreover, Alarico Fernandes "aligned himself with the soldiers" and also walked out on the Soibada meeting, taking the radio transmitter. "The soldiers did not indicate any consternation," which worried Xanana. "Xavier had lost control because he knew so little about politics. Nicolau was on the other side, the soldiers continued to form a separate nucleus, and the majority of us, the members of the FCC [Fretilin Central Committee], were unpoliticised."[109]

The Soibada meeting saw other divisions, too. Some of the student leftists who had returned from Portugal, Xanana says, "tried to influence our thinking about 'free love,'" while others, such as Vicente Sa'he, advocated a lifestyle of "puritanism" that earned more popular trust. Sa'he also gave Xanana a copy of *Historical Materialism*, "but I informed him I had already heard enough 'isms' in Barique."[110] More ominously, conflict continued between the CC majority and a group of Timorese sergeants led by Aquiles Soares, a *liurai* from the central-eastern region. These conservative nationalists, professional soldiers, rejected national political oversight. Soares later reportedly disobeyed CC orders to provide food to other zones and transfer populations to more secure areas. He began moves to purge Fretilin nationalists from his region, and may have contacted Indonesian forces. In November 1976, Soares and three associates were arrested by neighboring Fretilin commanders and subsequently executed.[111] One of those executed was a pro-Fretilin *liurai* in the central-eastern sector; several other local *liurai* were Apodeti members. According to Xanana, "Our commanders constantly arrested the Apodetis and I kept freeing them. Finally they got tired of arresting them."[112]

The CC Standing Committee, which met on September 20, 1976, may have authorized the repression. It is not known if do Amaral attended. Again the ranks diverged. In mid-December, do Amaral allegedly met secretly with commanders in the absence of the local political cadres and "tempted them to disobey" central directives.[113]

The ideological gap widened, too. "At the end of 1976," Xanana recalls, "I managed to get hold of a copy of *The Thoughts of Chairman Mao.* I read and re-read it, trying to understand Mao's simple way of describing complex things." By May 1977, "In groups we studied the 'strategic questions' of Mao and a change of war theory. The theory excited us in the planning of ideas and in strategic thinking, but it was a theory that required a heavy loss of life."[114]

The internal divisions came to a head. Rejecting invitations from "all members" of the CC, President do Amaral boycotted the conference of the Supreme Council of Resistance of the CC Political Committee, held at Laline from May 8 to 20, 1977.[115] Xanana says that "Xavier was happy in his kingdom and did not want to go to any more meetings."[116] Despite his absence, "sharp debate centered on a proposal to declare Fretilin a Marxist movement." Xanana recalls that "we were still dazzled by a vision of a miraculous process of human redemption."[117] At mealtimes between political discussions, Nicolau Lobato "stopped talking. . . . 'No one prays to thank God for this food that the people have sweated to collect,' Nicolau said." Xanana recalls: "I understood how he was upset because although he was a Marxist he continued to be a religious person. . . . Nicolau stopped going to the meetings. He said he was sick." He donated his family's coffee plantations to the state. Hermengildo Alves complained, "Any day now, the state will get my wife's gold earrings too," while the "inveterate bohemian," dos Anjos, told "endless anti-revolutionary jokes, which did not amuse the Department of Political and Ideological Orientation." Finance Minster Sera Key "debated issues, making an effort to demonstrate his abilities as a political theorist. In fact he was the only one who livened up the meeting, until all the political commissars were told to sit around the same table and get organized. After that there was no more debate."[118]

As Fretilin leaders debated Marxism, heavy Indonesian aerial bombardments began. Debate was apparently unresolved when approaching Indonesian troops prevented ratification of the proposal.[119] According to Xanana, "Marxism was acclaimed," but apparently this was done without formation of a revolutionary party.[120] Indonesian military pressure only widened Fretilin's internal divisions. The result was what Lobato would soon call a "profound crisis that has shaken our nation, hit our people, threatened our young state and undermined the unity of the Front."[121]

Heightening differences seem reflected in successive statements by do Amaral, Lobato, and Fernandes, all broadcast by Fretilin radio and recorded in northern Australia. On May 20, 1977, the third anniversary of Fretilin's founding, do Amaral, absent from the Laline meeting, claimed that his government had "organised the people to defend their country, so that they were not bunched up to be captured, but were spread out to contain the invasion. They did very well with only guns, bows and arrows, and no heavy artillery. Today, the fight continues against colonialism and neo-colonialism."[122] Do Amaral thus emphasized the military and regional aspects of the struggle, and apparently avoided criticism of "imperialism." Nor did he mention the Maoist notion of Soviet "social-imperialism." By contrast, in a recorded interview broadcast the next month, Nicolau Lobato stated: "Always politics is [in] command. We don't make war by war. Our armed struggle has a deeply political form and sense." He called for "liberation of our people from the colonialists and imperialists."[123] This difference appears to have given rise to another issue, whether to seek negotiations. In successive interviews conducted by radio from Australia on June 18 and 19, 1977, Alarico Fernandes insisted on a slogan that may have required reaffirmation in recent debate: "negotiations with the corrupt Jakarta government, never," and "negotiations with the enemy, never."[124] Who had called for negotiations was still unclear.

Ideological discussions continued. In nightly meetings during August 1977, Vicente Sa'he and Xanana prepared "for the time when a revolutionary party would be formed." Xanana recalled, "We would be Maoists. At least they were Maoists." Sa'he, who admired Albania and Cuba, asked Xanana if he would agree to join the party. Xanana says he replied, "No."[125]

On August 7, 1977, "the traitor Domingoes Simoes" tried to assassinate Alarico Fernandes. Do Amaral got the blame, and on September 7, 1977, he was arrested by Lobato and Fernandes, possibly after avoiding another Supreme Council meeting.[126] "In circumstances that are still far from clear, he had apparently sought to arrange a compromise with the occupying forces."[127] Lobato announced: "Against the mistakes of comrades, we use the weapon of criticism. Against the enemies, traitors and sellers of the homeland, we use the criticism of weapons. To do that we must strengthen the repressive apparatus of our State."[128] Attacking do Amaral's group as "loyal slaves of the Javanese expansionists," Lobato's faction expelled two CC members from central East Timor and five cadres from the same region.[129] Other cadres and an alleged agent "infiltrated in the Department of Information and National Security" were arrested and "seriously interrogated." Lobato announced that confessions had been "dragged out of the prisoners" and that the Remexio Zone secretary was "a traitor already under our control in a safe place."[130]

At a meeting of the CC Political Committee in Aikurus, Fretilin education minister Hamis Basserwan now assumed "responsibility for the ideological training of the Fretilin Central Committee members." Xanana Gusmao recalls Basserwan earlier confiding: "Don't think, Xanana, that we are well-versed in theory. In Lisbon, I spent most of my time with the Portuguese Communist Party painting slogans on the walls!"[131]

In the east, CC member Sera Key returned from Aikurus and told his subordinate Xanana of the purges and atrocities committed there. Confused but apparently convinced of the need for "revolutionary violence," Key launched an investigation of local "counter-revolutionaries." But at a meeting of four CC members, Xanana reports challenging him: "I cannot accept this violence. I cannot accept that a member of the Central Committee would inflict torture." Xanana claims that he managed to persuade Key to let him conduct his own investigations, and that he eventually freed the prisoners.[132]

Despite the violent purge of his followers, do Amaral and his associate Arsenio Horta survived nearly a year in Fretilin custody. On August 30, 1978, they were captured by Indonesian troops during the battle for Remexio.[133] Do Amaral was taken to Dili, where he called on Fretilin to surrender.[134] (He spent the next twenty-two years in Bali and Jakarta.)[135] Then came the capture or surrender of his former rival, Information Minister Fernandes, on December 2, 1978.[136] One of Fernandes' last radio transmissions announced that he and several others had broken with the CC.[137] In turn, Fretilin now also accused him of plotting a coup with "a correlation of forces in the central-north sector."[138] This region had been Amaral's stronghold. Close to Dili and to the center of Indonesian power, in 1977–78 the north-central sector appears to have favored a succession of local and national leaders seeking compromise with Jakarta.

At his surrender, Fernandes named the six "intransigent" leaders of the continuing Fretilin resistance: President Lobato, the new vice president and justice minister Mau Lear, National Political Commissioner Vicente Sa'he, Education Minister Hamis Basserwan, Economy Vice Minister Helio Pina, and Commissioner Carlos Cesar.[139] One of their last bases was Mt. Matebian in the Eastern Zone, where thirty thousand people were holding out.[140] Xanana arrived there with many others from the island's eastern tip in September 1978. He describes what he saw: "I visited all the front lines engaged in combat. There was no room for the people. There were bombardments, explosions, death, blood, smoke, dust, and interminable queues of people waiting for their turn to try to get a bit of water for the children. . . . There was total lack of control. . . . The fighter planes were sowing the seeds of death all day long."[141]

The base fell to Indonesian encirclement on November 22, 1978. That night, Xanana and some troops fought their way out to the east.[142] Others escaped west. Fretilin was now unable to defend its even larger base area, the Natarbora plain, with a population of sixty thousand people near the south coast, commanded by Vice President Mau Lear and Vicente Sa'he. Indonesian forces occupied Natarbora in December.[143] Then, Nicolau Lobato was surrounded near Maubisse. On December 31, the Fretilin president was killed after a six-hour battle with Indonesian forces led by Suharto's future son-in-law, Prabowo. Twenty other Fretilin leaders and troops fell with him, including Deputy Defense Minister Guido Soares.[144] Mau Lear took his place as Fretilin president. Vicente Sa'he took command of its military wing, Falantil—after escaping the battlefield with Hamis Basserwan.[145] Mau Lear was tracked down and executed on February 2, 1979. Later that month, pursuing Indonesian troops wounded Sa'he in the leg. He ordered his fleeing comrades to leave him behind.[146] Basserwan, Pina, and Cesar all disappeared.[147] In the east, Xanana sent a young Falantil commander, Taur Matan Ruak, to the central sector to "find the Resistance Executive," but his unit was betrayed and trapped near Viqueque. Ruak surrendered on March 31. He managed to escape after twenty-three days and would later become Falantil deputy chief of staff.[148]

From September 1977 to February 1979, the Fretilin Central Command was virtually destroyed. Only three of the fifty-two CC members survived, all in the Eastern Zone: minister of finance and political commissar Sera Key, Xanana Gusmao (chief of the eastern sector, Ponte Leste), and Mau Hunu (deputy secretary of the eastern region command).[149] David Alex, who had commanded elite companies until the fall of Mt. Matebian, also remained active in the east, his forces intact, including fourteen troops from his native village there.[150] Budiardjo writes, "Although losses suffered by Fretilin in the eastern sector were enormous, the resistance movement there was in better shape than in the border and central regions."[151]

It was here that Xanana now began the slow, painful process of rebuilding. In December 1978–January 1979, he recalls, "for a month and a half I traveled through the hamlets, making contact with the people." An Indonesian-appointed village official hosted a secret meeting with a former Fretilin CC member, Joao Branco, and they "settled a few ideas on the continuity of the struggle. In February 1979 I summoned Txay and Kilik so we could assess the situation." Also, "The Commanders who were supposed to be in the Centre Region joined me." They reported that the center was in "chaos," as was Viqueque region, where the violent Hermengildo Alves had treated them with characteristic "suspicion." A CC member from the center-east, Solan, and his ill wife, as well as "Olo Kasa and his weak wife, and Sera Key and his wife," along with their escorts, were all "isolated from each other and abandoned by their forces. Sera Key recommended to his two commanders that the forces that had returned from the Centre Region, and those that could not get through, be put under my charge. He would go to the Centre to try to find the Resistance Executive." Xanana toured the east, locating bands led by Mau Hodu, Taur Matan Ruak, Mauk Muruk, David Alex, Lay Kana, Olo Gari, Fera Lafaek, and Sabica. But the Indonesians captured Solan and Olo Kasa. They massacred Lay Kana, "the best commander" in the east, with his company and other defectors.[152]

In March 1979, the top five surviving Fretilin military officers (Falantil operational commander Mauk Muruk, Kilik Wae Gae, Olo Gari, Nelo, and Freddy) met with the five senior political leaders (Xanana, Mau Hunu, Mau Hodu, Bere Malay Laka, and Txay) at Titilari–Laivai in the central-eastern sector, "to analyse the causes and consequences of the military collapse, and to devise adequate measures for the reorganization of the resistance."[153]

Sera Key set out from the east in April to make contact with the remaining resistance bands in the central sector. He and his wife were soon captured, "sick, abandoned and betrayed by the last forces from the East Centre sector which had also surrendered." Indonesian troops reportedly took Sera Key to Dili by helicopter and dumped him in the sea. In July and December, Xanana and Mau Hunu sent out further missions, but both returned without encountering surviving resistance groups further west.[154] In May 1980, Xanana took half a company of sixty troops from the east to the western border and back. A Fretilin unit staged a spectacular attack on the Dili TV station on June 10. By October, Xanana had made contact with continuing resistance forces in Kablake near the border and in the central sector. On Christmas Day, Falantil attacked Baucau, the territory's second city.[155]

Fretilin was eventually able to organize a national conference, from March 1 to 8, 1981, at Lacluta in the central-east region. Xanana was elected president, Kilik Wae Gae became chief of staff, and Mau Hunu became deputy chief of staff. Bere Malay Laka was named secretary of information. They reported to the conference that Fretilin had lost 79 percent of the members of its Supreme Command, 80 percent of its troops, 90 percent of its weapons, all its population bases, and all the channels of communication between its scattered groups and with the outside world.[156]

## Famine and Mass Murder

According to Indonesian documents that Fretilin forces captured in 1982, "as a result of all the unrest, many village heads have been replaced, whilst many new villages have emerged." The experience of two eastern villages is instructive: "With the upheavals," the inhabitants "fled into the bush," returning only in May 1979, when they were "resettled" in a district town. "But this led to their being unable to grow food on their own land, so that food shortages have occurred."[157] Famine ravaged East Timor in 1979. Indonesian aerial bombardment of their homes and cultivated gardens in the hill areas had forced many Timorese to surrender in the lowlands, but food was scarce there. Indonesia's control eventually expanded, and its counts of the Timorese population rose from 329,000 to as many as 522,000 in mid-1979.[158] More than 120,000 Timorese remained missing, mostly victims of the famine and the continuing Indonesian-instigated massacres and repression. Taylor reports that on November 23, 1978, Indonesian troops shot five hundred people who surrendered to them the day after the fall of Mt. Matebian; soon afterward there was a similar massacre of three hundred in Taipo, and in two further incidents in the east in April–May 1979, Indonesian forces murdered 97 and 118 people.[159] Also in the east, Indonesians massacred Joao Branco and forty others at the end of 1979.[160] In a September 1981 massacre southeast of Dili, four hundred people died, mostly women and children.[161] In August 1983, sixty men, women, and children were tied up and bulldozed to death at Malim Luro near the south coast. On August 21–22, troops burned alive at least eighty people in the southern village of Kraras, and then made a "clean-sweep" of the neighboring area, in which another five hundred died. Of East Timor's twenty-thousand-strong ethnic Chinese minority, survivors numbered only "a few thousand" by 1985.[162]

As fighting continued, Indonesia's special forces worked to recruit Timorese paramilitary combat teams, predecessors of the militias responsible for widespread massacres in the 1990s. In the first two months of 1982, the team Railakan I, comprising fifty-two troops, killed eight Falantil rebels and captured thirty-two. In an attack on Xanana's forces in September, Railakan I killed nine more Fretilin troops.[163]

## Regional Resurgence

In the early 1980s, despite devastating blows, Timorese resistance still challenged Jakarta's forces, who termed Fretilin "gangs of security disruptors" (Gerakan Pengacau Keamanan, or GPK).[164] In 1982, Indonesian commanders in Dili acknowledged in confidential documents that "despite the heavy pressure and the disadvantageous conditions under which they operate, the GPK has nevertheless been able to hold out in the bush." For instance, from just six villages of the Eastern Zone, 293 inhabitants were "still in the bush." After seven years of occupation, Fretilin "support networks" still existed "in all settlements, the villages as well as the towns." These "underground networks are closely related to customs and to the family system." Jakarta aimed "to obliterate the classic GPK areas" and "crush the GPK remnants to their roots."[165]

The conquered territory must "eventually be completely clean of the influence and presence of the guerrillas." Deportations continued; in one sector of the Eastern Zone, thirty more villages were resettled in 1982.[166]

The Indonesian commander in Dili, Colonel A. Sahala Rajagukguk, revealed to his officers that nine Fretilin bands continued to operate. Of four "small, unorganized groups," one even operated near West Timor and Dili, "in the border district of Ermera, and in the districts of Dili, Liquica, and Ailiu." Summarizing the activities of all these groups, Colonel Rajagukguk concluded that "they can meet together at predetermined places. . . . Meetings in the eastern region can be held in the regions of Koaliu, Matabean, Macadique or Builo. On such occasions there is a very sizeable concentration of forces in one place." He went on: "It is in the eastern sector that people's support is most militant and most difficult [for Indonesian forces] to expose. This is because of the very strong, close family ties and also because it has been possible for the GPK to consolidate its political leadership in this region for several years. This is also because a large part of the population in this region fled to the mountains and only came down to the new villages at the beginning of 1979. In such circumstances, the GPK has consciously chosen the eastern region as its hinterland and reserve base."[167]

## Normalizing the Occupation, 1983–99

In 1982, Indonesian intelligence knew most of the surviving Fretilin leaders, naming Mauk Muruk, Mau Hunu, David Alex, Kilik, Txay, and Loro Timur Anan.[168] If Jakarta was as yet unaware of Xanana's leadership position, they learned of it within a year. A new Indonesian army commander, General Mohammed Yusuf, agreed to a cease-fire and negotiations with Fretilin. Xanana then held two days of talks with his Indonesian counterparts, on March 21 and 23, 1983. Jakarta later abandoned the negotiations, but the cease-fire was a temporary acknowledgment of Fretilin's continuing military challenge. Fighting resumed, with Falantil estimated to be fielding up to one thousand guerrillas in several areas. Indonesian reinforcements in 1984 brought troop levels back up to fourteen thousand to twenty thousand. Railakan I, a locally recruited special forces paramilitary team, increased in size from fifty-two to ninety men. From March to December 1984, this team alone killed thirty-two Falantil rebels and captured twelve. As the war raged on, Suharto declared a state of emergency in East Timor on September 9, 1985.[169]

Douglas Kammen sees the 1983 cease-fire as Jakarta's "tentative, indeed abortive, first attempt" to normalize its control of East Timor and secure foreign recognition for its integration of the territory. However, this was accompanied by "alternative forms of violence," such as increasing Indonesian use of East Timorese combat "teams." Suharto made a second attempt in 1988, when he declared East Timor's "equal status" with Indonesia's other twenty-six provinces. Jakarta announced the "opening" of the territory and the introduction of Operation Smile. The 1989 papal visit followed. But, Kammen says, "greater openness was accompanied by the heightened use of covert operations and terror," especially against Fretilin's new strategy of nonviolent urban protest, but also a new rural offensive aiming to capture Xanana, who moved secretly into Dili in February 1991.[170] In August 1991, Indonesian forces in East Timor totaled 20,700, including 11,000 "external" troops on rotation there from other provinces, 4,800 "territorial" or local troops, and other members of the Indonesian armed forces. Samuel Moore writes, "The East Timorese continued to live under one of the most intensive military occupations of modern history," with ten to fourteen troops stationed in each village and neighborhood, a soldier for every thirty-eight civilians. In Dili on November 12, 1991, the army gunned down and bayoneted three hundred Timorese funeral marchers at the Santa Cruz cemetery, an event secretly filmed by a journalist, bringing East Timor to world attention. A year later, Xanana was discovered and arrested.[171] Still the resistance continued, and urban unrest mounted.

In May 1990, Jakarta had replaced its combat Security Operations Command (Koopskam) with a new East Timor Operations Implementation Command (Kolakops). In response to international condemnation of the Santa Cruz massacre, external battalions began to be withdrawn and replaced by local territorial troops, and a third attempt at normalization was made with the liquidation of Kolakops in April 1993. All security responsibilities, including command of the nine external battalions then on rotation in the territory, were now assigned to the local territorial command, Korem 164, headquartered in Dili but "entirely under the direction of non–East Timorese."[172] By April 1994, when the number of battalions under Korem 164 was reduced to seven, the military had begun forming paramilitary units such as the "Young Guards Upholding Integration" (Gada Paksi), which had eleven hundred members by 1996. These militia forces expanded rapidly. By 1995, the former commander of the Railakan I paramilitary team headed a three-hundred-strong militia. By 1997–98, there were twelve such paramilitary teams with four thousand to eight thousand members. Also in 1997–98, the number of regular battalions under Korem 164 again increased, to thirteen.[173] By August 1998, the total number of Indonesian troops in the territory was 21,600, including 8,000 external troops.[174]

Suharto fell from power in May 1998 and pressure mounted on Jakarta to hold a referendum in the territory. This brought a sharp increase in militia activity. The army sponsored the creation of several new militia forces at the end of 1998.[175]

The Fretilin leadership had suffered major losses by the time of Suharto's fall. Falantil's Operational Commander Mauk Muruk, who had surrendered in July 1985, spent the next four years in the psychiatric isolation ward of a Jakarta military hospital.[176] In June 1990, Mau Hudo became Fretilin vice chairperson, but he was captured in January 1992. After the arrest of Xanana in November the same year, David Alex became deputy chief of staff of Falantil. He was wounded and captured by Indonesian troops in June 1997 and is presumed dead. His successor was Konis Santana, who was killed in an accident in March 1998 and replaced by Taur Matan Ruak, who had been deputy chief of staff in the mid-1980s.[177] But despite these setbacks, six hundred to nine hundred veteran Fretilin troops fought on in the hills, joined by six hundred recruits in 1998 alone. Taur Matan Ruak's force of fifteen hundred welcomed the United Nations peacekeepers when they arrived in the territory in September 1999.[178]

Despite its military losses, Fretilin maintained a broad political base. In 1992, an Indonesian intelligence report entitled "Data on Disturbed Villages" categorized only 163 of East Timor's 442 villages as peaceful and secure. Seventy-nine villages were coded "Red," or "disturbed" (possibly Fretilin-controlled). In 1997, Korem 164 intelligence estimated that the GPK "clandestine front" had about fifteen hundred members in the capital, and in 1999 they were estimated to have six thousand members throughout the territory.[179]

In September 1998, in a historic reconciliation, all five East Timorese parties involved in the civil war of 1975 joined forces under the new umbrella organization, the Timorese Council of National Resistance (CNRT), and elected the political prisoner Xanana Gusmao as president.[180] A year later, 79 percent of Timorese voted for independence in the UN-organized referendum.

## Genocidal Counterinsurgency

Jakarta was unable to achieve its goal of conquest. But what underlying ideology justified genocide in the attempt? In Remexio and Aileu, where "everyone over the age of three was shot" in early 1976, Indonesian forces explained that the local people had been "infected with the seeds of Fretilin." After the September 1981 Lacluta massacre, a soldier allegedly explained, "When you clean your field, don't you kill all the snakes, the small and large alike?" In 1984, a new territory-wide military campaign aimed at what one commander called the obliteration of Fretilin "to the fourth generation."[181] The mixture of biological and agricultural metaphors is common in genocidal regimes.[182] While the killings of more than 500,000 communists in Indonesia in 1965–66 had not been accompanied by ethnic massacres targeting minorities, in the territorial expansion a decade later, Jakarta's repressive forces did single out the Chinese of East Timor for "selective killings."[183]

Indonesia's targeting of Fretilin as a multigenerational kinship group also resembles genocide. In early 1999, as the UN referendum approached, Indonesian military and militia commanders threatened to "liquidate . . . all the pro-independence people, parents, sons, daughters, and grandchildren."[184] At a meeting in Bali in February 1999, Indonesian commanders Adam Damiri and Mahidin Simbolon ordered militias "to eliminate all of the CNRT leaders and sympathizers."[185] On February 16, meeting with militia leaders, Lieutenant Colonel Yahyat Sudrajad called for the killing of pro-independence leaders, their children, and their grandchildren. "Not a single member of their families was to be left alive, the colonel told the meeting."[186] Jakarta's governor of the territory, Abilio Soares, ordered that "priests and nuns should be killed."[187] (In 2002, Soares was convicted in a Jakarta court.) Militia leaders called on their followers to "conduct a cleansing of the traitors of integration. Capture them and kill them."[188] Tono Suratman, Korem 164 commander in Dili, warned, "if the pro-independents do win . . . all will be destroyed. It will be worse than 23 years ago."[189] A May 1999 Indonesian army document ordered that "massacres should be carried out from village to village after the announcement of the ballot if the pro-independence supporters win." The East Timorese independence movement "should be eliminated from its leadership down to its roots."[190]

## Conclusion

Cambodia and East Timor were both subjected to genocide in 1975–79. Foreign occupying forces from Indonesia perpetrated the genocide in East Timor, while foreign occupying forces from Vietnam ended the indigenous Khmer Rouge genocide in Cambodia. The perpetrator regimes in Jakarta and Phnom Penh enjoyed diplomatic support from the United States, which continued after the genocides, including training and arming the Indonesian military. Until the 1990s, Washington supported Indonesia's occupation of East Timor and voted in the UN for the exiled Khmer Rouge to represent Cambodia. Maoist ideological influence on Fretilin in East Timor and on the Khmer Rouge in Cambodia produced political purges, repression, and murder in both cases. Yet in the Cambodian case, Khmer Rouge military aggression against Vietnam, supported by China for geopolitical reasons, combined with a virulent Khmer Rouge racism that targeted foreigners and minorities for extermination, resulting in genocide. To the Maoist-influenced Fretilin regime, however, genocide came from without, in the name of anticommunism. East Timor did not attack Indonesia, but was the victim of aggression. Maoism functioned there within a multicultural nationalist party resisting foreign invasion and genocide. The political and geopolitical factors favoring genocide varied, and in each case regionalisms undercut the genocidists and the resistance, while racism and expansionism played major roles in both tragedies.

## Notes

1. Memorandum of Conversation between Ford, Suharto, and Kissinger, July 5, 1975, in W. Burr et al., eds., *East Timor Revisited: Ford, Kissinger and the Indonesian Invasion,* National Security Archive, Electronic Briefing Book 62, December 6, 2001, at www.gwu.edu/~nsarchiv/NSAEBB/NSAEBB62.

2. Ford–Kissinger–Suharto discussion, Embassy Jakarta Telegram 1579, December 6, 1975, in W. Burr et al., eds., *East Timor Revisited: Ford, Kissinger and the Indonesian Invasion,* National Security Archive, Electronic Briefing Book 62, December 6, 2001, at www.gwu.edu/~nsarchiv/NSAEBB/NSAEBB62.

3. Ford–Kissinger–Suharto discussion.

4. John G. Taylor, *East Timor: The Price of Freedom* (London: Pluto, 1999).

5. Ben Kiernan, *The Pol Pot Regime: Race, Power and Genocide in Cambodia under the Khmer Rouge, 1975–1979* (New Haven, Conn.: Yale University Press, 2002), 458.

6. Kiernan, "The Impact on Cambodia of the U.S. Intervention in Vietnam," in *The Vietnam War,* J. Werner et al., eds. (Armonk, N.Y.: M. E. Sharpe, 1993), 216–29.

7. Kiernan, *Pol Pot Regime,* 103–11, 357–68.

8. United Nations, AS, General Assembly, Security Council, A/53/850, S/1999/231, March 16, 1999, Annex, *Report of the Group of Experts for Cambodia Established Pursuant to General Assembly Resolution 52/135,* 19–20, 23, 57.

9. *Report of the Group of Experts,* 19–20. S. Heder says this *Report* "cautioned that it might be a 'difficult task' to prove that the CPK carried out acts 'with the requisite intent' to destroy such ethnic and religious groups 'as such.'" S. Heder, "Seven Candidates for Prosecution" (Washington: unpublished manuscript, 2001), 14 n. 24.

10. Kiernan, *Pol Pot Regime,* 458.

11. R. Clark, "Does the Genocide Convention Go Far Enough?" *Ohio Northern Law Journal* 321 (1981): 8; B. Saul, "Was the Conflict in East Timor 'Genocide'?" *Melbourne Journal of International Law* 2 (2001): 477–522.

12. Robert Cribb, ed., *The Indonesian Killings, 1965–66* (Clayton, Australia: Monash Centre of Southeast Asian Studies, 1990).

13. Leo Kuper, *Genocide* (New Haven, Conn.: Yale University Press, 1981), 174–75, 186, 241; F. Chalk and K. Jonassohn, *History and Sociology of Genocide* (New Haven, Conn.: Yale University Press, 1990), 408–11; I. W. Charny, ed., *Encyclopedia of Genocide* (Oxford: ABC-Clio, 1999), 191–94; James Dunn, "East Timor," in *Genocide,* ed. G. Andreopoulos, 171–90 (Philadelphia: University of Pennsylvania Press, 1994).

14. *New York Times,* April 17, 2002.
15. On the Eastern Zone, 1970–78, see Kiernan, *Pol Pot Regime,* 14–15, 46–47, 65–68, 205–10, 323–25, 369–76, 392–405; M. Vickery, *Cambodia 1975–1982* (Boston: South End, 1984), 131–39; Ben Kiernan, *How Pol Pot Came to Power* (London: Verso, 1985), 270–84, 310–12, 320–21, 340–41, 358, 363–68; Ben Kiernan, "Wild Chickens, Farm Chickens and Cormorants: Kampuchea's Eastern Zone," in *Revolution and Its Aftermath in Kampuchea,* ed. D. P. Chandler et al. (New Haven, Conn.: Yale Southeast Asia Council, 1983), 136–211; Ben Kiernan, *Cambodia: The Eastern Zone Massacres* (New York: Columbia Center for the Study of Human Rights, 1986); S. Heder, "Racism, Marxism, Labelling and Genocide," *Southeast Asia Research* 5, no. 2 (1997): 117–23.
16. Conversation between Ford, Suharto, and Kissinger, July 5, 1975, in W. Burr et al., *East Timor Revisited: Ford, Kissinger and the Indonesian Invasion,* National Security Archive, Electronic Briefing Book 62, December 6, 2001, at www.gwu.edu/~nsarchiv/NSAEBB/NSAEBB62.
17. State Department, "Indonesia and Portuguese Timor," c. November 21, 1975, W. Burr et al., *East Timor Revisited: Ford, Kissinger and the Indonesian Invasion,* National Security Archive, Electronic Briefing Book 62, December 6, 2001, at www.gwu.edu/~nsarchiv/NSAEBB/NSAEBB62.
18. Memorandum of Conversation, December 18, 1975, Washington, D.C., "Departmental Policy," at www.etan.org/news/kissinger/secret.htm.
19. Conversation between Ford, Suharto, and Kissinger, July 5, 1975, in W. Burr et al., *East Timor Revisited: Ford, Kissinger and the Indonesian Invasion,* 6, National Security Archive, Electronic Briefing Book 62, December 6, 2001, at www.gwu.edu/~nsarchiv/NSAEBB/NSAEBB62.
20. Jill Jolliffe, *East Timor: Nationalism and Colonialism* (St. Lucia, Australia: University of Queensland Press, 1978), 84, 115; Xanana Gusmao, *To Resist Is to Win!* (Melbourne: Aurora, 2000), 28 n. 51; Helen Hill, *Stirrings of Nationalism in East Timor: Fretilin 1974–1978* (Sydney: Otford, 2002), 66.
21. James Dunn, *Timor: A People Betrayed* (Milton, Australia: Jacaranda, 1983), 88; Taylor, *East Timor,* 45 n. 52.
22. Dunn, *Timor,* 3; G. Gunn, *Timor Loro Sae* (Macau: Oriente, 1999), 4041; R. Tanter et al., eds., *Bitter Flowers, Sweet Flowers: East Timor, Indonesia, and the World Community* (Lanham, Md.: Rowman & Littlefield, 2001), 254–56.
23. Jolliffe, *East Timor,* 70, 220; Hill, *Stirrings,* 36, 133–35.
24. Dunn, *Timor,* 166.
25. UDT leader Joao Carrascalao acknowledged responsibility for the coup. Gusmao, *To Resist,* 23 n. 36.
26. State Department, "The Secretary's Principal's [*sic*] and Regional Staff Meeting, August 12, 1975," 2–4, in W. Burr et al., *East Timor Revisited: Ford, Kissinger and the Indonesian Invasion,* National Security Archive, Electronic Briefing Book 62, December 6, 2001, at www.gwu.edu/~nsarchiv/NSAEBB/NSAEBB62.
27. Jolliffe, *East Timor,* 273.
28. Gusmao, *To Resist,* 29, 26.
29. Dunn, *Timor,* 177; Gusmao, *To Resist,* 22–31.

30. Dunn, *Timor,* 177–80, 321; Denis Freney, *Timor* (Nottingham, England: Spokesman, 1975), 24; Gusmao, *To Resist,* 30–31.

31. Sarah Niner, "A Long Journey of Resistance," in *Bitter Flowers, Sweet Flowers: East Timor, Indonesia, and the World Community,* ed. R. Tanter, M. Selden, and S. R. Shalom (Lanham, Md.: Rowman & Littlefield, 2001), 17.

32. Dunn, *Timor,* 181–82.

33. Australian senator Arthur Gietzelt reported meeting Apodeti secretary general Fernando Osorio Soares in Dili in September 1975. Hansard, April 7, 1976, 1171. Fretilin killed Soares two weeks after the invasion. Dunn, *Timor,* 305.

34. Jolliffe, *East Timor,* 156.

35. Jolliffe, *East Timor,* 152–53, 72.

36. Hill, *Stirrings.*

37. Jolliffe, *East Timor,* 219–20.

38. Jolliffe, *East Timor,* 67; Dunn, *Timor,* 75.

39. U.S. Embassy Jakarta Telegram 1579, December 6, 1975, in W. Burr et al., *East Timor Revisited: Ford, Kissinger and the Indonesian Invasion,* paragraphs 39, 51, National Security Archive, Electronic Briefing Book 62, December 6, 2001, at www.gwu.edu/~nsarchiv/NSAEBB/NSAEBB62.

40. Gusmao, *To Resist,* 32; Dunn, *Timor,* 305; D. Ball and H. McDonald, *Death in Balibo* (Sydney: Allen & Unwin, 2000), 175; Paulino Gama (Mauk Muruk), "A War in the Hills, 1975–85: A Fretilin Commander Remembers," in *East Timor at the Crossroads,* ed. P. Carey and G. C. Bentley (New York: SSRC, 1995), 98–99; Niner, "Long Journey," 19.

41. Dunn, *Timor,* 283–85.

42. Dunn, *Timor,* 296; "Intervention of the Republic of Indonesia in the Life of Portuguese Timor," Kota internal document, March 23, 1976, cited in R. Tanter, "The Military Situation in East Timor," *Pacific Research* 8, no. 2 (1977): 1–6; Jolliffe, *East Timor,* 282–87.

43. Dunn, *Timor,* 60, 296–97.

44. Taylor, *East Timor,* 72.

45. Dunn, *Timor,* 5.

46. "Full Text of Speech of Nicolau Lobato, Reading Statement of the Permanent Committee of Fretilin Central Committee on the High Treason of Xavier do Amaral, over Radio Maubere September 14, 1977," *East Timor News Agency* (*ETNA*), Sydney, September 17, 1977, 13 pp. typescript, 4.

47. Gusmao, *To Resist,* 49; Carmel Budiardjo et al., *The War against East Timor* (London: Zed, 1984), 61.

48. "Speech of Nicolau Lobato," 4–5.

49. Tanter, "Military Situation."

50. Taylor, *East Timor,* 70; Dunn, *Timor,* 291–92.

51. *Age* (Melbourne), August 26, 1976, cited in Tanter, "Military Situation."

52. Tanter, "Military Situation," 10, citing Peter Monckton, *AM,* ABC radio, September 20, 1976, and *Sydney Morning Herald.*

53. Tanter, "Military Situation," citing *National Times,* September 27, 1976, and *Australian,* September 20, 1976.

54. Dunn, *Timor*, 310.

55. Douglas Kammen, "The Trouble with Normal: The Indonesian Military, Para-militaries, and the Final Solution in East Timor," in *Violence and the State in Suharto's Indonesia*, ed. B. R. O'G. Anderson (Ithaca, N.Y.: Cornell University, Southeast Asia Program, 2001), 159.

56. Gusmao, *To Resist*, 29 n.

57. Budiardjo et al., *War*, 60; Jolliffe, *East Timor*, 270.

58. Budiardjo et al., *War*, 60–65.

59. "Speech of Nicolau Lobato," 9–10.

60. Jolliffe, *East Timor*, 56, 72; Taylor, *East Timor*, 47.

61. Gusmao, *To Resist*, 22 n. 31; 32; 39 n. 68; 43; Budiardjo et al., *War*, 61.

62. Gusmao, *To Resist*, 42–43.

63. Budiardjo et al., *War*, 61.

64. Gusmao, *To Resist*, 32, 47. See also Jolliffe, *East Timor*, 220, 154, 273.

65. Gusmao, *To Resist*, 134, statement dated December 7, 1987.

66. For accounts by priests living in Fretilin areas until 1979, see Taylor, *East Timor*, 81–82.

67. Jolliffe, *East Timor*, 270.

68. "Speech of Nicolau Lobato," *passim*.

69. *Age*, November 19, 1976, cited in Tanter, "Military Situation," 5; Jolliffe, *East Timor*, 300–301; Dunn, *Timor*, 310.

70. Dunn, *Timor*, 307.

71. "Fretilin Secretary for Information Answers Journalists' Questions," June 18, 1977, *ETNA*, June 21, 1977.

72. "Prime Minister Nicolau Lobato Answers Questions," June 30, 1977, *ETNA*, July 4, 1977.

73. Dunn, *Timor*, 309. Indonesian forces attacked Remexio in June 1978; "Offensive Near Dili," *East Timor News* 36, June 29, 1978, 1. From September 1977, Indonesian offensives began conquering wide areas. Budiardjo et al., *War*, 57–58, 63.

74. Estimates for 1974 are 635,000 (Jill Jolliffe, *Cover-Up* [Melbourne: Scribe, 2001], 46), and 689,000 (the Timorese Catholic Church). Taylor, *East Timor*, 89–90, 98, 203.

75. Taylor, *East Timor*, 89–90.

76. Budiardjo et al., *War*, 201.

77. Taylor, *East Timor*, 201.

78. "Speech of Nicolau Lobato," 13.

79. Dunn, *Timor*, 283–85; Taylor, *East Timor*, 68–69.

80. Taylor, *East Timor*, 69.

81. Jolliffe, *East Timor*, 8.

82. Dunn, *Timor*, 286, 303.

83. Taylor, *East Timor*, 70, 81.

84. Dunn, *Timor*, 293, 286; Taylor, *East Timor*, 80–81.

85. Dunn, *Timor*, 303, 293.

86. Dunn, *Timor*, 303.

87. Dunn, *Timor*, 302–303; Taylor, *East Timor*, 201; Jolliffe, *East Timor*, 278.

88. Dunn, *Timor*, 310, based on "Notes on East Timor," in Dunn's possession.

89. *Age*, April 1, 1977. See also N. Chomsky and E. Herman, *The Political Economy of Human Rights*, vol. 1 (Boston: South End, 1979), 175–76.

90. Taylor, *East Timor*, 203.

91. Gusmao, *To Resist*, 132. The statement was made December 7, 1987.

92. Budiardjo et al., *War*, 8–11; Taylor, *East Timor*, 84, 133–34, 174–75, 203; Ball and McDonald, *Death*, 182; Tanter, ed., *Bitter Flowers*, 135–36, 163–72.

93. "Speech of Nicolau Lobato," 4.

94. Dunn, *Timor*, 4, 63.

95. "Speech of Nicolau Lobato," 4–6.

96. Gusmao, *To Resist*, 40.

97. "Speech of Nicolau Lobato," 6–9.

98. "Speech of Nicolau Lobato," 7, 4, 6.

99. "Speech of Nicolau Lobato," 2, 13, 5, 7–8.

100. Budiardjo et al., *War*, 26.

101. "Speech of Nicolau Lobato," 6–8, 10.

102. Here we must rely largely on accounts of do Amaral's rivals and successors, not all of whom survived. Hopefully do Amaral will provide a memoir of 1974–77.

103. "Speech of Nicolau Lobato," 10.

104. Gusmao, *To Resist*, 41–42.

105. "Speech of Nicolau Lobato," 11.

106. Gusmao, *To Resist*, 41–42.

107. Gusmao, *To Resist*, 42–43.

108. "Speech of Nicolau Lobato," 5, 11, 8.

109. Gusmao, *To Resist*, 43.

110. Gusmao, *To Resist*, 49, 42.

111. Taylor, *East Timor*, 95–96; Niner, "Long Journey," 19; Gusmao, *To Resist*, 42, 44–46, 50.

112. Gusmao, *To Resist*, 44.

113. "Speech of Nicolau Lobato," 8–9.

114. Gusmao, *To Resist*, 47, 49.

115. "Speech of Nicolau Lobato," 5.

116. Gusmao, *To Resist*, 47.

117. Niner, "Long Journey," 19.

118. Gusmao, *To Resist*, 47–58; 25 n. 42; Jolliffe, *East Timor*, 219.

119. Gusmao, *To Resist*, 52 n. 83; Niner, "Long Journey," 19.

120. Gusmao, *To Resist*, 47, 66.

121. "Speech of Nicolau Lobato," 11.

122. "President F. Xavier do Amaral on Radio Maubere May 20 1977," *ETNA*, June 8, 1977.

123. "Prime Minister Nicolau Lobato Answers Questions," June 30, 1977, *ETNA*, July 4, 1977.

124. "Fretilin Secretary for Information Answers Journalists' Questions," June 18, 1977, *ETNA*, June 21, 1977; "Answers by Minister Alarico Fernandes, . . . June 19, 1977," *ETNA*, July 12, 1977.

125. Gusmao, *To Resist,* 66.

126. "Speech of Nicolau Lobato," 9, 3.

127. Niner, "Long Journey," 19.

128. "Speech of Nicolau Lobato," 11–12.

129. The CC members were from Manatuto and Lakular; the zone cadres were Laclo and Remexio secretaries and their deputies, and the Laklubar secretary. "Speech of Nicolau Lobato," 1, 3.

130. "Speech of Nicolau Lobato," 3, 11.

131. Gusmao, *To Resist,* 66, 47. Jolliffe says Basserwan was "Hata." Jolliffe, *East Timor,* 219.

132. Gusmao, *To Resist,* 49–52; Niner, "Long Journey," 19.

133. "Traitors Escape, Xavier Rescue," *East Timor News* 41, September 14, 1978, 1; Niner, "Long Journey," 19; 27 n. 20.

134. Melbourne *Herald,* December 5, 1978; *East Timor News* 47, December 28, 1978.

135. Niner, "Long Journey," 27 n. 20. In the 1990s, do Amaral joined a group favoring autonomy within Indonesia. He returned to East Timor in 2000.

136. Melbourne *Herald,* December 8, 1978; *East Timor News* 47, December 28, 1978; Taylor, *East Timor,* 96.

137. Gusmao, *To Resist,* 58 n. 91.

138. "Betrayal Not End of Struggle," *Tribune* (Sydney), December 13, 1978; *East Timor News* 47, December 28, 1978. On fellow CC member Redentor, see "Speech of Nicolau Lobato," 9.

139. *East Timor News* 48, January 18, 1979; Jolliffe, *East Timor,* 219–20.

140. Budiardjo et al., *War,* 33.

141. Gusmao, *To Resist,* 56.

142. Gusmao, *To Resist,* 57.

143. Budiardjo et al., *War,* 33, 66.

144. Gusmao, *To Resist,* 25 n. 40; Dunn, *Timor,* 317; Budiardjo et al., *War,* 36; Jolliffe, *East Timor,* 220.

145. *East Timor News* 48, January 18, 1979, 3, citing Indonesian reports.

146. Dunn, *Timor,* 317; Taylor, *East Timor,* 97.

147. Xanana received a report that "Cesar Maulaka was in the South Centre region, in the area of Alas, but much of the information was contradictory." Gusmao, *To Resist,* 63.

148. Gusmao, *To Resist,* 60 n. 94; 57 n. 89.

149. Gusmao, *To Resist,* 25 n. 42; 152. Gusmao says Txay was the third surviving CC member. Budiardjo et al., *War,* 67, 70, says it was Sera Key.

150. Gusmao, *To Resist,* 59 n. 92; 60; Budiardjo et al., *War,* 196, 213.

151. Budiardjo et al., *War,* 67; Taylor, *East Timor,* 115; Gusmao, *To Resist,* 29 n. 51.

152. Gusmao, *To Resist,* 51, 58–59.

153. Gama, "War in the Hills," 101.

154. Budiardjo et al., *War,* 67; Taylor, *East Timor,* 115; Gusmao, *To Resist,* 62; 25 n. 42.

155. "Instruction Manual No. Juknis//05/I/1982: System of Security," English translation in Budiardjo et al., *War,* 183; Taylor, *East Timor,* 115; Gusmao, *To Resist,* 64–65.

156. Budiardjo et al., *War*, xii, 67–70.

157. Budiardjo et al., 201, 243, 212–13.

158. Taylor, *East Timor*, 98.

159. Taylor, *East Timor*, 88.

160. Gusmao, *To Resist*, 53–54 n. 89.

161. Taylor, *East Timor*, 101–102; Gama, "War in the Hills," 102.

162. Taylor, *East Timor*, 102–103, 142, 206, 68–70, 164, 207 (citing *Far Eastern Economic Review*, September 8, 1985).

163. Kammen, "Trouble," 159–60.

164. Captured Indonesian documents, English translations of which are in Budiardjo et al., *War*, 82.

165. Budiardjo et al., *War*, 176, 215, 222, 227, 194–96, 216, 242, 193.

166. Budiardjo et al., *War*, 242–43, 193, 228, 241, 213.

167. Budiardjo et al., *War*, 196, 201; Gusmao, *To Resist*, 29 n. 51.

168. Budiardjo et al., *War*, 177, 196.

169. Taylor, *East Timor*, 136, 151, 206; Dunn, *Timor*, 319; Kammen, "Trouble," 159–60.

170. Kammen, "Trouble," 160–62; Samuel Moore, "The Indonesian Military's Last Years in East Timor: An Analysis of Its Secret Documents," *Indonesia* 72 (October 2001): 14.

171. Kammen, "Trouble," 164–65; Moore, "Indonesian Military," 24–25, table 2.

172. Kammen, "Trouble," 162–65; Moore, "Indonesian Military," 28.

173. Kammen, "Trouble," 166, 168–69, 180, 174.

174. Moore, "Indonesian Military," 25, table 2.

175. Kammen, "Trouble," 182–83.

176. Gama, "War in the Hills," 103.

177. Gusmao, *To Resist*, 43–44, 57–60. Moore names other 1990s leaders: Sabica, Lere Anan Timur, Ular, and Falur. Moore, "Indonesian Military," 14.

178. Moore, "Indonesian Military," 13.

179. Moore, "Indonesian Military," 13–14, 16. A 1982 Indonesian document describes the "Red Zone" as areas of Fretilin control. Budiardjo et al., *War*, 203.

180. Kammen, "Trouble," 173.

181. Taylor, *East Timor*, 70, 102, 151.

182. Kiernan, "Genocide and 'Ethnic Cleansing,'" in *Encyclopedia of Politics and Religion*, ed. R. I. Wuthnow (Washington, D.C.: Congressional Quarterly, 1998), 294–99.

183. Taylor, *East Timor*, 69.

184. Andrew Fowler, "The Ties That Bind," Australian Broadcasting Corporation, February 14, 2000, quoted in N. Chomsky, *A New Generation Draws the Line: East Timor, Kosovo, and the Standards of the West* (London: Verso, 2000), 72. For details, see A. Evans, "Revealed: The Plot to Crush Timor," *South China Morning Post*, September 16, 1999.

185. Quoted in Kammen, "Trouble," 183.

186. Tomas Goncalves, former head of the PPPI militia, quoted in Evans, "Revealed," 54. Andrew Fowler reported that in early 1999, pro-Indonesia commanders

threatened to "liquidate . . . all the pro-independence people, parents, sons, daughters, and grandchildren." Chomsky, *New Generation*, 72.

187. Evans, "Revealed"; Kammen, "Trouble," 184.

188. Kammen, "Trouble," 184.

189. Brian Toohey, "Dangers of Timorese Whispers Capital Idea," *Australian Financial Review*, August 14, 1999; John Aglionby et al., "Revealed: Army's Plot," *Observer*, September 12, 1999.

190. Chomsky, *New Generation*, 74.

# 10

# Resisting State Terror: The Anti-Vietnam War Movement

## Marilyn B. Young

THE NOTION THAT North Vietnam won the Vietnam–American war because of the actions of the American peace movement pleases both the Left and the Right. The Left because it testifies to its own efficacy: never before in the history of warfare has a domestic peace movement forced the government to call a halt to an unjust war. The Right because it means that U.S. arms remain invincible; only betrayal can explain American defeat.[1]

Judgments about whether the antiwar movement was responsible for U.S. military defeat are, of necessity, *post facto*. A quite different task is to suspend such questions and ask more directly what role the U.S. antiwar movement played over the course of the war. Did it shorten or prolong the war? Demoralize U.S. fighting forces? Influence military tactics? Give essential aid and comfort to the enemy? The first question cannot be answered historically with any certainty. Adam Garfinkle, in his book, *Telltale Hearts: The Origins and Impact of the Vietnam Antiwar Movement,* offers a somewhat idiosyncratic version of the proposition that the movement prolonged the war. His argument rests on a set of interdependent counterfactual propositions. Antiwar public opinion, Garfinkle believes, would have appeared earlier and increased massively had the movement not aroused so much hostility by its militant behavior. In partial consequence, so would the "impulse" of Democratic Party members to "betray their party leadership and their president." Had those impulses been allowed free rein, rather than withdraw his candidacy for reelection in 1968, Lyndon Johnson would have yielded to pressure, reversed the course of the war earlier, and gone on to win the presidential election. The antiwar movement gave Johnson "more time to fail" and in so doing "contributed at least something to the conditions under which American soldiers were being killed by the thousands each and every year."² Thus the antiwar movement, because it was ineffective, was culpable for taking so long to bring the war to an end.

However, had the movement been effective, it would also have been guilty. Assuming the war was winnable, as Garfinkle and others who blame the movement do, "then a hypothetically effective antiwar movement was the agent of unnecessary catastrophe in Vietnam, and worse, mocked the purposes for which more than 58,000 American soldiers died." The analysis does not consider that, for many, perhaps for most, protesters, the problem was not winning the war but fighting it at all. Garfinkle's proposition implies that victory in war *ipso facto* makes the war itself just, the lives lost in its pursuit meaningful. But an American victory in Vietnam would not have given the 58,000 deaths purpose; it would only have meant those lives were lost in the prosecution of a successful, rather than an unsuccessful, but still illegitimate war. Nor would victory have justified the millions of Vietnamese dead, who seem to trouble Garfinkle far less than they did the antiwar movement at the time. Indeed, it was the entire panoply of organized state terror that fueled the moral outrage of most of those opposed to the war: its systematic assault on the civilian population of Vietnam by saturation bombing, the deliberate creation of refugees, and the poisoning of the land itself with chemical defoliants so that the very fabric of village life was shredded.

There are two further problems with Garfinkle's judgments of the antiwar movement, problems common to all those who believe that but for the protest movement, the United States would have won. First, like many others, Garfinkle separates "public opinion" from the antiwar movement, reading protesters out of the American body politic in much the same way the U.S. government defined the National Liberation Front as somehow not South Vietnamese, or as the Bush administration in 2003 seeks to read protest against its policies as outside the American political consensus. Whatever percentages Gallup may have gathered over the years, the fact remains that hundreds of thousands of ordinary citizens took to the streets in unprecedented opposition to an ongoing war. Those who participated *were* the public; not all of it, certainly, but not outside of it, either. And included in that public were significant numbers of the troops assigned to fight it. Second, there is the notion that the domestic political impact of the war on the United States can be separated from its military course. "If only there were no protests and if only those protests had not influenced Congress," this line of analysis suggests, "we would have won." Such a separation makes little historical sense. No war is a purely military endeavor. The domestic response to the war was not an independent variable, open to government manipulation, but a direct response by Americans of every variety, including politicians and soldiers in the field, to the escalating violence in Vietnam.

Lecturing to a college audience after the publication of his most recent reconsideration of the war, former secretary of defense Robert McNamara reminded an aging veteran of the antiwar movement that "your people weren't in the majority. Most Americans supported the war [here he pounded the table with the flat of his hand], supported escalation [another pound], supported the bombing [a final, yet more decisive pound that made the water glasses jump]. "At least until 1968," he added—and his hand was still. And he may be right. Depending on how you read the statistics, the public remained committed to, or at worst ambivalent about, the Vietnam War throughout much of its course. Benjamin Schwartz of the RAND Corporation has argued that, while figures indicating public disapproval for having gotten into Vietnam in the first place rose steadily throughout the war, 77 percent of those questioned favored escalation to either withdrawal or a continuation of wherever the current level of military operations stood. "There is a tendency," Schwartz concludes, "for war to become absolute." Anger at having gotten into the war in Vietnam (or Korea, for which the figures are similar) was massive but the desire to "finish it once and for all" was also great. However, it might be more significant to consider the traceable shifts in opinion as government policy changed. Thus, in 1965–66, when Hanoi and Haiphong were off-limits as bombing targets, only 30 percent of those polled thought they should be bombed; when they *were* bombed in July 1966, 85 percent thought it was an excellent thing to have done. There are similar statistics on support for seeking negotiations through bombing halts. Support for such a policy, which stood at 37 percent in September 1967, rose to a remarkable 64 percent once Johnson had decided on just such a halt.[3] The shifts reveal as much, perhaps more, about the timing of polls, the framing of questions, and the willingness of most of the people to trust their government until demonstrably betrayed, as they do about public opinion.

In any event, the statistics don't tell us enough. By the numbers, in the absence of other information, Korea was a more unpopular war than Vietnam. If popularity ended wars, the Korean War should have been over before it began. "The data suggest," John E. Mueller concluded in an essay comparing popular support for the two wars, "that while *the opposition to the war in Vietnam may have been more vocal than that in Korea, it was not more extensive*" (emphasis in original).[4] A vocal opposition may not be the same as a mass movement, but an opposition in full public voice means that attention, on the part of the press, politicians, and pundits, had to be paid. And once attention was paid, questions could be asked, questions that would lead to the unraveling of some, though hardly all, of the dominant ideology of the day. Senator

William J. Fulbright, who had shepherded the Gulf of Tonkin resolution
through the Senate only a year and a half earlier, by the end of January 1966
was ready to hold public hearings on the war. The hearings, in turn, provided
the antiwar movement with an abundance of information and an evident re-
spectability. Fulbright explicitly validated the protests in his initial question-
ing of Secretary of State Dean Rusk, when he said, "It seems to me that something is wrong or there would not be such great dissent, evidenced by
teach-ins, articles and speeches by various responsible people." The hearings
were covered live by network television and, David Halberstam observed, they
"ended more than a generation of assumed executive branch omniscience in
foreign policy and congressional acquiescence to that omniscience."[5] In late
April, Fulbright gave the Christian A. Herter Lectures at Johns Hopkins University and, in words that resonate forcefully in the current era of unrivaled
American power, warned against the "arrogance" of American power: "Power
confuses itself with virtue and tends also to take itself for omnipotence. . . .
The cause of our difficulties in Southeast Asia is not a deficiency of power but
an excess of the wrong kind of power."[6]

General William Westmoreland and other military leaders and administration spokespersons often claimed that the U.S. peace movement prevented the
military from unleashing the necessary power to win the war. The repetition
of the idea that U.S. soldiers fought with "one arm tied behind their backs" obscured the reality of the war in Vietnam, where the military fought with both
hands, both feet, and all its teeth. There were more than half a million American troops, an equal number of regular Republic of South Vietnam forces,
and more than sixty thousand Allied soldiers. The military alone set targets in
South Vietnam and the bombing, which began in 1962, continued without
presidential interference for the whole of America's war. In the North, targets
were more restricted in light of the risks of Soviet or Chinese retaliation, but
the relationship between bombing the North and "victory" in the South was
always tenuous.

Connected to the notion of a hobbled military was the claim that when the
United States finally exerted appropriate power, as in the Christmas bombing
of 1972, Hanoi was, at last, forced to negotiate. "Just imagine," General
William Westmoreland mused in the early days of the Gulf War, "what would
have happened if we had used that kind of bombing after our military victory
at Tet." Apart from the devastation, what indeed? The Christmas bombing had
no effect on the negotiations and Hanoi had been bombed before. In 1966,
Harrison Salisbury had already reported on the damage to residential areas of
Hanoi and Haiphong; the city of Vinh and many other cities and towns had
been leveled long before 1972, and then the rubble was bombed again. In
some areas of the North, people lived entirely underground in the late 1960s,

emerging at great risk to transplant and then harvest their rice. "A grain of rice, a drop of blood," was a common saying. Between 1963 and 1973, 15 million tons of explosives (about half from the air) were dropped on Vietnam, Laos, and Cambodia, the equivalent of seven hundred Hiroshima-strength nuclear bombs. Three tons of bombs were dropped on just one village in Long An Province in 1966. Two years later, Long An served as the staging area for the Tet attack on Saigon.

Rhodri Jeffrey–Jones, in his recent book, *Peace Now,* argues that the serial nature of the peace movement made it more effective, as it expanded from student groups to include churches, civil rights leaders, and the nascent women's movement and made modest gains in the ranks of organized labor and among the troops themselves. "The protests had a cumulative effect that sapped the resistance power of the policy makers."[7] A 1967 Central Intelligence Agency (CIA) assessment, while silent on the power of policy makers to resist, draws a remarkably similar picture of the movement itself: "The American peace 'movement' is not one but many movements; and the groups involved are as varied as they are numerous. The most striking single characteristic of the peace front is its diversity." In a rolling set of paired opposites, some of which antiwar organizers might have used to describe themselves, the CIA report unfurled a "peace umbrella" under which it said could be found "pacifists and fighters, idealists and materialists, internationalists and isolationists, democrats and totalitarians, conservatives and revolutionaries, capitalists and socialists, patriots and subversives, lawyers and anarchists, Stalinists and Trotskyites, Muscovites and Pekingese, racists and universalists, zealots and nonbelievers, puritans and hippies, do-gooders and evildoers, nonviolent and very violent." Indeed, "anti-war sentiment has taken root in separate sectors of society having little else in common. In addition to the professional pacifists, activists come from the student world, from militant elements of the Negro and other minority communities, from the labor movement, and from the intellectual sphere." The degree of diversity, the CIA noted, brought with it "confusion and more than a little disagreement." After all, the analysts observed, not unsympathetically, the task of "coordinating a program of joint action, first within the US and then internationally, is an enormous one." And yet, despite the "strains and complications," the coordinators had done an "impressive" job. Moreover, "we see no significant evidence that would prove Communist control or direction of the US peace movement or its leaders."[8] The longer the war lasted, the more diverse the opposition, until by the early 1970s, it embraced significant numbers among the House, the Senate, the business community, the federal bureaucracy, family members of high government officials, and the Democratic Party, which in 1972 nominated a peace candidate, George McGovern, for president.

It is useful to recall the sheer variety of activity in which opponents of the war expressed their views: draft counseling; draft-card burning; sit-ins at draft centers; draft resistance, through flight to Canada or Europe or surrendering oneself to arrest; nonviolent demonstrations (local, regional, national); demonstrations with violence against property; teach-ins; movements to remove ROTC and war research from university campuses; barring or removing from campuses recruiters for the CIA, DOW Chemical, and other companies involved in war-related industries; sanctuary and support for military deserters at home and abroad; antiwar coffeehouses and underground newspapers near army bases; support for the movement against the war inside the military; and so on. The protests, Gabriel Kolko has observed, "fixed to the war an unprecedented social price."[9] A recent critical assessment of the antiwar movement by Edward Morgan comes to a similar conclusion: for all its weaknesses, "movement militance and the ensuing social chaos may have forced the Nixon administration's hand, helping to bring the war to an end on terms that fell somewhat short of the total destruction of Indochina."[10] In short, it increased to unacceptable levels the political price to the government of continued prosecution of the war.

Part of that price was paid by the army. Acts of resistance to the war within the military began as early as 1965 in step with the dispatch of U.S. forces, and they increased in tempo and variety with each year the United States remained in Vietnam. "The morale, discipline and battleworthiness of the U.S. Armed Forces are, with a few salient exceptions, lower than at any time in this century and possibly in the history of the United States," Colonel Robert D. Heinl wrote in 1971. "By every conceivable indicator," his article for the *Armed Forces Journal* warned, "our army that now remains in Vietnam is in a state approaching collapse, with individual units avoiding or having refused combat, murdering their officers and noncommissioned officers, drug-ridden, and dispirited where not near-mutinous." As Heinl tolled the woes of the military, his prose turned apocalyptic: the armed forces reflected the country, with its "agonizing divisions and social trauma," and disclosed the depths of society's problems "in an awful litany of sedition, disaffection, desertion, race, drugs, breakdown of authority, abandonment of discipline, and, as a cumulative result, the lowest state of military morale in the history of the country." Between 1968 and 1971, desertion rates had doubled and stood at twice the peak rate for Korea; there were 788 confirmed cases of fragging (deliberately killing an unpopular officer with a hand grenade) for the period 1969–72, 252 chargeable acts of insubordination in 1968, and double that number in 1971; and often violent racial conflict.[11] In addition, there was organized protest within the military, including between 141 and 245 underground newspapers; underground radio stations (more difficult to quantify); fourteen dissident GI organizations, two of which were made up of officers; and six antiwar veterans' groups. Heinl was especially concerned about the connections that had been forged with the civilian antiwar movement. Three organizations of lawyers specialized in aiding GIs in antiwar trouble, including one that operated in Vietnam itself, set up in Saigon in 1970 to offer free legal services for dissident soldiers being court-martialed.[12] Vietnam Veterans against the War (VVAW) and similar dissenting groups were never large, but their existence, along with more informal acts of protest in all three services, indicated a state of crisis in the military establishment.[13] The antiwar movement did not demoralize the armed forces, the war itself did. The movement did aid and abet antiwar soldiers and veterans when it could, but more important, the existence of visible, vocal protest at home normalized the act of protest itself, making it available to soldiers as to all citizens.

At minimum, most historians who have studied the antiwar movement conclude that "the continuous decline of support for the war among the general population was, in part, a result of the well-organized campaigns that countered the line from Washington."[14] President Johnson's bombing halts and the opening of peace talks in Paris were the result of a combination of domestic pressure at home, international pressure abroad, and military pressure in the field. Richard Nixon, like Lyndon Johnson before him, was extremely sensitive to the antiwar movement and monitored it closely. "Realizes," Haldeman noted in his diary for September 29, 1969, referring to the president, that "war support is more tenuous every day and knows we have to maintain it somehow." Fearful of the coming October Moratorium to end the war in Vietnam, Nixon considered scheduling a press conference that would "preempt coverage of the day's activities." The point, Haldeman told his diary, was to "try to make the innocents see they are being used. . . . Hard to do much because momentum is tremendous and broad based." The November Moratorium disturbed Nixon even more. He thought hard about it and had "helpful ideas like using helicopters to blow their candles out." Much in the style of his superior's later observation of the Great Wall of China, that it was a great wall, Haldeman noted that "the big march turned out to be huge."[15] In a backhanded compliment to the power of the antiwar movement, both Johnson and Nixon thought it sufficiently threatening to warrant major covert efforts to infiltrate and disrupt its activities. Operation CHAOS, whose mandate was to uncover connections between the antiwar movement and foreign, especially communist, governments, was initiated by the CIA on Johnson's orders in 1967.[16] Operation COINTELPRO (Counter-Intelligence Program), instituted by the Federal Bureau of Investigation (FBI) in 1967 and expanded by Nixon, also sought to link the protest movement to communists, domestic and foreign. Its undercover agents acted as agents provocateurs while regular

FBI agents engaged in more traditional acts of intimidation by photographing participants in demonstrations.

The marches were to grow larger. When its initial effort to detail U.S. war crimes in Vietnam received little public attention, VVAW organized a week-long "limited incursion into the country of Congress," from April 19 to April 23, 1971. More than a thousand veterans set up camp in Potomac Park, performed guerrilla theater, lobbied Congress, and marched. But VVAW owed its most dramatic moment to the misguided security effort of the Nixon administration. Foiled in their effort to return their medals and battle ribbons to Congress, the veterans stood one by one before a microphone, announced their names and their citations, and then tossed them over the high fence protecting the Capitol building. Inside, a navy veteran, John Kerry, testified before the Senate Committee on Foreign Relations: "In our opinion and from our experience, there is nothing in South Vietnam which could happen that realistically threatens the United States of America. And to attempt to justify the loss of one American life in Vietnam, Cambodia or Laos by linking such loss to the preservation of freedom . . . is to us the height of criminal hypocrisy, and it is that kind of hypocrisy which we feel has torn this country apart."[17] On April 24, the veterans were joined by more than 500,000 protesters for the largest single demonstration of the war.

Joan Hoff, a historian of the Nixon administration, has argued that Nixon never changed his attitudes or policies on Vietnam because of protests"; but she concedes that "he was forced to consider the timing and publicity given to his military and diplomatic moves more carefully than otherwise would have been the case for a wartime president." The bombing of North Vietnam was ruled out by the administration in February and March 1969, in part because of the attention Nixon paid to "general public opinion."[18] I have already addressed the artificial distinction between the "general public" and the antiwar movement, but putting that aside, Hoff's conclusion is too grudging. Other historians show a firm link between public protest and White House policy. At issue in 1969 was not just bombing North Vietnam, but radically escalating the war through an all-out offensive against Hanoi (Operation Duck Hook). Nixon was dissuaded by numerous advisers who predicted a dire public response both at home and abroad. "Put cynically," Stephen Ambrose has written, "after having proclaimed that he would not let policy be made in the streets, Nixon let policy be made in the streets."[19] Larry Berman's massively documented account of Nixon's war reaches the same conclusion: the major demonstration planned for October 15, 1969, "played an important role in the cancellation of Duck Hook. With hundreds of thousands of demonstrators taking to the streets of Washington, D.C., it was apparent that Nixon's attack would face a groundswell of opposition. In the end, Nixon cancelled Duck

Hook because it would have been very difficult to pursue an open military solution while the country was ostensibly beginning its disengagement from
Vietnam. In short, American public opinion already had him over a barrel,
and he knew it."[20]

The really huge marches were not limited to the United States. There were
demonstrations across the world against U.S. policy that merged with broader
efforts for social equity and justice in France, Mexico, Japan, West Germany,
Great Britain, Scandinavia, Italy, the Netherlands, Mexico, Canada, and Australia. In 1968, when the forces of the National Liberation Front and Hanoi
launched the series of attacks that have been summarized by the single word
for the Vietnamese New Year, Tet, it seemed as if the streets of the capital cities
of the globe were themselves exploding in sympathy. In many countries,
including France, Canada, Sweden, and Japan, there was also direct aid to deserters and draft evaders, which constituted a defiant challenge to the U.S. effort in Vietnam. The movements in Europe and elsewhere were both local and
international, joining domestic issues to an anti-imperialist passion, and they
provided international support that strengthened the U.S. movement. When
demonstrators arrested at the Democratic Convention in Chicago in 1968
claimed that the whole world was watching, they were just being accurate.[21]
The effort of the Nixon administration in particular to isolate the movement
and lead a putative "silent majority" to reject not his policies but those who
demonstrated against them, foundered on the sense of a wider, sympathetic
audience.

Did the antiwar movement aid and comfort the enemy, as Johnson and
Nixon both charged? The force of the accusation was sufficient to discourage
Martin Luther King Jr., one of the most eloquent civil rights leaders in criticizing the war, from traveling to Paris to meet with North Vietnamese representatives.[22] And certainly Hanoi and the National Liberation Front were convinced the American and international antiwar movement could make a
contribution to their victory. But given the long and determined history of
Vietnamese nationalism and resistance, it is an act of arrogance to imagine
that without the antiwar movement the Vietnamese would have fought less
hard or less long. The point rather is that, in the face of the absolute military
superiority of the United States, the international antiwar movement added to
the weight of direct military and economic aid from the Soviet Union and the
People's Republic of China a moral force untainted by state power or ideology,
a force the Vietnamese recognized, welcomed, and used. Throughout the war,
Hanoi hosted delegations of sympathetic Americans, released prisoners of war
directly to representatives of the antiwar movement, sent delegates to international conferences, and with the help of the alternative news media publicized
their diplomatic initiatives.[23] The effort was to inform and persuade the

American public of their war aims and their desire for peace, and the antiwar movement played an important role in this endeavor. Although their resources were miniscule in comparison to those available to the government, publications and news services such as *Ramparts, Viet Report, Liberation,* the Liberation News Service, the proliferating GI underground journals, and the underground press in the United States disputed the government's account of the origins and progress of the war and disseminated Vietnamese peace proposals in the face of the silence, or worse, distortion, of the mainstream press. Through Third World Newsreel, documentaries filmed in both South and North Vietnam were distributed in the United States and, together with American-made antiwar films, became a regular feature of college teach-ins.

The antiwar movement benefited as well from the work of the U.S. press corps in Vietnam. Reporters quickly learned to treat military press briefings with the respect they deserved: the 5 o'clock follies they were called and they were widely mocked. Reporters understood it was the task of the military to report victory; it was the reporters' task to find out what was going on. This is not to romanticize the role of the press in Vietnam. The majority of reporters supported the war and their criticisms were rarely based on principle but rather on tactics. Even so, the reporters made clear the cavernous abyss between what the U.S. military and State Department wished the public to believe and what they saw to be the case. The abyss was called the "credibility gap," and it meant that people began to treat government handouts with an unprecedented degree of skepticism. In 1971, the *New York Times* printed secret documents leaked by Daniel Ellsberg and Anthony Russo (the *Pentagon Papers*) and throughout the conflict TV and photojournalists took pictures that gained iconic status—the burning Buddhist monk in 1963, the execution of an unarmed guerrilla in Saigon in 1968, the flaming body of a child racing down a road in 1971—their power enhanced by their broadcast on network news or their publication in the *New York Times, Washington Post,* and indeed the entire mainstream press, rather than *Ramparts.* The antiwar movement, these documents and images implied, wasn't making it up.

For some time now, the antiwar movement has become a footnote in essays, documentaries, novels, and films that focus on that amorphous proper noun, The Sixties. In contrast to Nixon, Haldeman, and the CIA, who recognized the power and broad base of the political movement that annually deposited tens of thousands of citizens on their doorstep, the latter-day media and popular historical treatment of the Sixties trivialize and depoliticize the decade, representing it largely in terms of styles of consumption. The war, insofar as it has any presence at all in these renderings, is reduced to a peace sign—displayed by preference in multicolored ink on the flat belly of a topless young woman swaying to the music at an endless Woodstock festival. More generous critics, themselves often veterans of the era, suggest that the Sixties were best characterized by utopian politics that died of their own excesses—factionalism, romantic revolutionary violence, blind anti-Americanism—their only legacy the identity politics, individualism, and consumerist greed of the decades that followed.

The separation between political, social, and cultural movements these analyses insist upon distorts the history of the period. The movements overlapped in terms of personnel, practices, and anticapitalist yearnings and tactics; they were mutually reinforcing. Skepticism about constituted authority—governmental, philosophic, historical, political, pedagogical, scientific—marked the counterculture, the civil rights movement, and such political groups as Students for a Democratic Society or, more broadly, the New Left.[24]

An important source of this skepticism was the legacy of the political and cultural movements of the late 1950s and early 1960s, which preceded the antiwar movement and continued after the war had ended, in particular the movement for civil rights. Its criticisms couched initially in the familiar rhetoric of the Cold War, the movements quickly developed in entirely new directions, introducing the country to a set of tactics, and the images that went with them, that raised different questions: What was the nature of the federal government's commitment to universal suffrage? Would it use federal troops to enforce equal rights for all its citizens? Questions about contemporary racial arrangements led inevitably to historical ones and an uneasy recognition of the contradictory nature of the entire national narrative, from Founding Fathers to nation-building in Vietnam.

Early on in the war, some leaders of the civil rights movement made the connection between racial justice at home and the war abroad. Malcolm X, for example, denounced the war in December 1964 and, before the year was out, he was joined by James Forman, executive secretary of the Student Non-Violent Coordinating Committee (SNCC). In 1965, the McComb, Mississippi, branch of the Freedom Democratic Party explicitly called for draft resistance: "No one has a right to ask us to risk our lives and kill other Colored People in . . . Vietnam so that the White American can get richer. We will be looked upon as traitors to the Colored People of the world if Negro people continue to fight and die without a cause. . . . We can write our sons and ask if they know what they are fighting for. If he answers Freedom, tell him that's what we are fighting for here in Mississippi. And if he says Democracy tell him the truth—we don't know anything about Communism, socialism, and all that, but we do know that Negroes have caught hell under this American democracy."[25]

Chicano draftees, like African Americans, for whom the military had always offered economic mobility and who possessed far less access to safe ways to evade the draft than did their white counterparts, nevertheless joined the ranks of resisters. The first Chicano draft resister was Ernesto Vigil, who refused to fight against his "brown brothers in Vietnam."[26] And by 1967, white America's favorite civil rights leader, Martin Luther King Jr., had not only endorsed draft resistance, but had expressed an unexpected empathy for the "desperate, rejected and angry young men" who had set ghettos from Watts to Washington, D.C., on fire: "As I have walked among [them] I have told them that Molotov cocktails and rifles would not solve their problems. . . . But they asked—and rightly so—what about Vietnam? . . . Their questions hit home, and I knew that I could never again raise my voice against the violence of the oppressed in the ghettos without having first spoken clearly to the greatest purveyor of violence in the world today—my own government."[27] A May 1967 FBI report on the potential for racial violence in the summer of that year noted the link between the civil rights movement and anti–Vietnam War movement with considerable alarm: "King has now joined [Stokely] Carmichael [of SNCC], [Floyd] McKissick [of the Congress of Racial Equality], and other civil rights extremists in embracing the communist tactic of linking the civil rights movement with the anti–Vietnam-War protest movement. . . . King's exhortation to boycott the draft and refuse to fight could lead eventually to dangerous displays of civil disobedience and near-seditious activities by Negroes and whites alike."[28] The assassinations of King and Malcolm X short-circuited what might have been a powerful, united movement against the war and for fundamental social change. For the overwhelming majority of the antiwar movement, it was enough to try to end the slaughter.

Finally, Ho Chi Minh *did* win. His colleagues and heirs had defeated the world's preeminent military power. And the antiwar movement had succeeded as well, if not in ending the war then at least contributing to its end. It took more than a decade to achieve this modest good, but the legacies of the antiwar movement, like the legacies of the war itself, linger. The mantra of every administration since Nixon has been the necessity for broad public support of any military intervention abroad, as if such support could be separated from the goal of the intervention itself. Since the case for intervention has frequently been unconvincing in the numerous American wars since Vietnam, these administrations have labored to make their wars exceedingly brief, over almost before they have properly begun, and virtually free of American casualties. Nevertheless, the echo of the antiwar movement continues to trouble the war makers and haunt the dreams of politicians. In the face of Bush administration plans for a war against Iraq in 2002, some members of a Congress otherwise acquiescent in the face of terrorist threats to the United States roused themselves to admonish the president. "I recall all too well the nightmare of Vietnam," Senator Robert C. Byrd (Democrat, West Virginia), told his colleagues. "I recall too well the antiwar protests and demonstrations, the campus riots, and the tragic deaths at Kent State. . . . And I remember all too well the gruesome daily body counts in Vietnam. The United States was a deeply divided country."[29] On the day President Bush launched the war, Byrd, with some piece of this nightmare realized, told a near empty Senate chamber, "Today, I weep for my country."

Post-Vietnam administrations may have learned how to control the American body count, but their hubris in seeking to control world forces through the application of overwhelming military power has, if anything, increased in the interim. Martin Luther King Jr.'s observation of 1967 that the United States was the "greatest purveyor of violence in the world" remains true thirty-six years later. Nevertheless, the memory of successful protest in the past and the potential for its repetition continues to haunt the Bush administration as it has all others since the American defeat in Vietnam.

## Notes

An earlier version of this chapter appeared in Marc Gilbert, ed., *Why the North Won the Vietnam War* (New York: Palgrave, 2002).

1. There is another position, also attractive to both left and right, to which the role of the peace movement is irrelevant: North Vietnam did not win the war at all, the U.S. did. Noam Chomsky, contemplating the destruction of the semiautonomous insurgency in South Vietnam along with the rural society out of which it grew, the illustration the war provided to rebel movements elsewhere in the world of the costs of defying the United States, and the acquiescence of postwar Vietnam to the exigencies of global capitalism, has concluded that it is hard to describe the outcome as a victory for Hanoi. General William Westmoreland agrees, for the same reasons. See Edward S. Herman and Noam Chomsky, *Manufacturing Consent: The Political Economy of the Mass Media* (New York: Pantheon, 1988), 246–47. See also, Chomsky, "Visions of Righteousness," *Cultural Critique* 3 (1986), 30 ff.

2. Adam Garfinkle, *Telltale Hearts: The Origins and Impact of the Vietnam Anti-war Movement* (New York: St. Martin's, 1995), 18, 19.

3. Benjamin Schwartz, "Casualties, Public Opinion and US Military Intervention," (Santa Monica, Calif.: RAND Corporation, 1994).

4. John E. Mueller: "Trends in Popular Support for the Wars in Korea and Vietnam," *American Political Science Review* 65 (June 1971): 358–75.

5. William Fulbright and David Halberstam, quoted in William Conrad Gibbons, *The U.S. Government and the Vietnam War: Executive and Legislative Roles and Relationships, Part IV: July 1965–January 1968* (Princeton, N.J.: Princeton University Press), 224, 227.

6. Quoted in Gibbons, *U.S. Government*, 306, 307.

7. Rhodi Jeffrey–Jones, *Peace Now! American Society and the Ending of the Vietnam War* (New Haven, Conn.: Yale University Press, 1999), 224. See also, Tom Wells, *The War Within: America's Battle over Vietnam* (Berkeley, Calif.: University of California Press, 1994); Todd Gitlin, *The Sixties: Years of Hope, Days of Rage* (New York: Bantam, 1993); and Paul Berman, *Tale of Two Utopias: The Political Journey of the Generation of 1968* (New York: Norton, 1996).

8. I am grateful to Marc Gilbert for bringing the document to my attention. The summary section of the forty-six-page report was analyzed and reprinted in Charles DeBenedetti, "A CIA Analysis of the Anti-Vietnam War Movement: October, 1967," *Peace and Social Change* 9, no. 1 (Spring 1983): 31–41. The entire report, with a cover letter from Richard Helms, director of the CIA, dated November 15, 1967, can be found on the Declassified Documents Research Search website at www.ddrs.psmedia.com.

9. Gabriel Kolko, *Vietnam: Anatomy of War* (New York: Pantheon, 1985), 174.

10. Edward Morgan, "From Virtual Community to Virtual History: Mass Media and the American Antiwar Movement of the 1960s," *Radical History Review* 78 (Fall 2000): 85–122.

11. Racial tension was especially marked after the assassination of Martin Luther King Jr. in 1968. King's assassination, Michael Herr wrote, "intruded on the war in a way that no other outside event had ever done." Michael Herr, *Dispatches* (New York: Avon, 1977), 169. For an account of race and race relations during the war, see James E. Westheider, *Fighting on Two Fronts: African Americans and the Vietnam War* (New York: New York University Press, 1997), and George Mariscal, *Aztlan and Viet Nam: Chicano and Chicana Experiences of the War* (Berkeley: University of California Press, 1999). On class and the war, see Christian Appy's classic, *Working Class War: American Combat Soldiers and Vietnam* (Chapel Hill: University of North Carolina Press, 1993).

12. Robert D. Heinl Jr., "The Collapse of the Armed Forces," *Armed Forces Journal* (June 7, 1971). Reprinted in Marvin E. Gettleman et al., eds., *Vietnam and America: A Documented History* 2d. rev. ed. (New York: Grove, 1995).

13. See Gerald Nicosia, *Home to War: A History of the Vietnam Veterans' Movement* (New York: Crown, 2001); Richard Moser, *The New Winter Soldiers: GI and Veteran Dissent during the Vietnam Era* (New Brunswick, N.J.: Rutgers University Press, 1996), Richard Stacewicz, *Winter Soldiers: An Oral History of the Vietnam Veterans against the War* (New York: Twayne, 1997), and Andrew E. Hunt, *The Turning: A History of Vietnam Veterans against the War* (New York: New York University Press, 1999).

14. Melvin Small, "The Impact of the Antiwar Movement on Lyndon Johnson, 1965–68: A Preliminary Report," *Peace and Change* 10, no. l (Spring, 1984): 2.

15. H. R. Haldeman, *The Haldeman Diaries: Inside the Nixon White House* (New York: Berkley, 1995), 110, 129. The call for a day of protest during which ordinary activities would be suspended originated with a Massachusetts peace group and was quickly adopted by the New Mobilization Committee to End the War in Vietnam. Millions of people across the country participated in a variety of protest events, including church services, teach-ins, marches, and vigils.

16. The operation violated the CIA charter and was terminated in 1972. See Melvin Small, *Antiwarriors: The Vietnam War and the Battle for America's Hearts and Minds* (Wilmington, Del.: Scholarly Resources, 2002), 101–102.

17. John Kerry, reprinted in Gettleman et al., *Vietnam and America*, 458.

18. Joan Hoff, *Nixon Reconsidered* (New York: Basic, 1994), 220, 227.

19. Stephen Ambrose, "Nixon and Vietnam: Vietnam and Electoral Politics" (Third Dwight David Eisenhower Lecture on War and Peace, Kansas State University, April 19, 2001), at www.ksu.edu/history/specialevents/Eisenhowerlecture/eisenhower3.htm.

20. Larry Berman, *No Peace, No Honor: Nixon, Kissinger, and Betrayal in Vietnam* (New York: Free Press, 2001), 57.

21. See, for example, Ronald Fraser, ed., *1968: A Student Generation in Revolt* (New York: Pantheon, 1988), but also Todd Gitlin, *The Whole World Is Watching: Mass Media in the Making and Unmaking of the New Left* (Berkeley: University of California Press, 1980).

22. See Cable, FBI (Hoover) to President, CIA, May 13, 1967, Declassified Documents CD-Rom ID#1986030100866/fiche#1986-76. An informant close to Stanley Levinson reported a conversation in which King expressed concern that he would lend force to the notion that Hanoi based its policy toward negotiations on an assessment of the strength of the peace movement in the United States.

23. See Robert Brigham, *Guerilla Diplomacy: The NLF's Foreign Relations and the Vietnam War* (Ithaca, N.Y.: Cornell University Press, 1999), 90–91.

24. One of the most interesting interpretations of post-1945 American political and cultural history is Tom Engelhardt's *The End of Victory Culture: Cold War America and the Disillusioning of a Generation* (New York: Basic, 1995). For an account of the role of the Cuban revolution in the early days of the New Left, see Van Gosse, *Where the Boys Are: Cuba, Cold War America, and the Making of the New Left* (London: Verso, 1993).

25. Student Nonviolent Coordinating Committee, "Statement on Vietnam, January 6, 1966," *Black Protest, History, Documents and Analysis, 1619–Present*, ed. Joanne Grant, 415–16 (New York: Fawcett World Library, 1969).

26. Ramon Ruiz, "Another Defector from the Gringo World," *New Republic* (July 27, 1968): 11. See also early issues of the Chicano journal *La Raza* and George Mariscal, *Aztlan and Vietnam: Chicano and Chicana Experiences of the War* (Berkeley: University of California Press, 1999).

27. Martin Luther King Jr., "A Time to Break Silence," *I Have a Dream: Writings and Speeches That Changed the World*, ed. James Melvin, 135–52 (San Francisco: Harper-San Francisco, 1992).

28. Federal Bureau of Investigation, "Racial Violence Potential in the US This Summer" May 23, 1967, at www.ddrs.psmedia.com (accessed May 23, 1967).

29. Paul J. Nyden, "Byrd Challenges Bush's Ideas on War," *Charlestown Daily Gazette Online*, June 20, 2002, at www.truthout.org/docs_02/07.04A.byrd.war.htm (accessed March 19, 2003).

# 11

# Resisting Nuclear Terror: Japanese and American Antinuclear Movements since 1945

## Lawrence S. Wittner

I F THE DELIBERATE MURDER of noncombatants is a form of terror, then two of the largest and most effective antiterrorist organizations of the postwar era have been the Japanese and American antinuclear movements. During World War II and thereafter, most nations continued their traditional practice of amassing and using military might to protect what they defined as their interests. This military might soon included nuclear weapons, which held great promise as devices that could be employed to massacre the populations of "enemy" nations and thus intimidate their governments. Indeed, nuclear weapons could provide the ultimate form of state terror. Within only a few weeks of developing the first atomic bombs, and with World War II virtually at an end, the U.S. government dropped them on Japanese cities. Inspired by this example, the governments of nearly all the great powers subsequently deployed atomic bombs and, later, thermonuclear weapons, to enhance their power in world affairs. But, challenging this postwar trend, the Japanese and American movements—together with dozens of antinuclear movements in other lands—registered some surprising victories. In the face of a murderous international system, both during the Cold War and after it, they set limits on nuclear terror by helping to stigmatize nuclear weapons, curb the nuclear arms race, and prevent nuclear war.[1]

## The Descent into Barbarism

As numerous studies have shown, the use of airpower in World War II grew increasingly indiscriminate during the course of the war, ending the distinction made in previous decades between attacks upon military forces and attacks upon civilians.[2] Indeed, bombing raids upon urban centers became popular with belligerent governments precisely because they would terrorize civilians and thereby, they hoped, undermine the will of the enemy to resist. U.S. officials placed the atomic bomb in this category, hoping that the urban devastation it produced would be so horrendous that it would shock the Japanese into surrender. The innocuously named Interim Committee, which pulled together top U.S. officials for discussions of the weapon's use, recommended that it be employed without warning, upon a city, with the goal of making "a profound psychological impression on as many of the inhabitants as possible." The "most desirable target" would include "workers' houses." Habituated to terror bombing, which they had already conducted on a broad scale in Europe and Japan, top Allied leaders felt thoroughly comfortable with employing the atomic bomb to massacre Japanese civilians. According to Churchill, when he and Truman chatted at Potsdam about the successful testing of the new atomic bomb, "there was never a moment's discussion" or hesitation about its use. The future seemed "fair and bright."[3]

The U.S. atomic bombing of Hiroshima and Nagasaki opened the gates for a full-fledged nuclear arms race. Although all the great powers had initiated nuclear programs during World War II, with the exception of the U.S. and British government's Manhattan Project they were quite small and produced negligible results.[4] But the nuclear attack upon Japan proved that the Bomb could be built, that the U.S. government possessed it, and that the weapon could be employed with impunity. Not surprisingly, then, Stalin immediately called together Soviet leaders and ordered them to develop atomic weapons "in the shortest possible time." Directed by Lavrenti Beria, chief of the secret police, the Soviet nuclear project produced atomic bombs by August 1949 and hydrogen bombs—a thousand times more powerful—by 1954. When the Truman administration dropped the British from the Anglo–American nuclear weapons program, they, too, opted to develop their own Bomb. "We have got to have this thing over here whatever it costs," declared Foreign Secretary Ernest Bevin. "We've got to have the bloody Union Jack flying on top of it." Britain tested its first atomic bomb by October 1952 and its first H-bomb by 1957. In the midst of this great power scramble for position, the U.S. government was not idle. It continued nuclear testing and built up its stockpile of atomic weapons. In 1950, responding to the test of the Soviet atomic bomb, President Truman ordered the development of a hydrogen bomb—a feat accomplished by 1954.[5]

Powered by the Cold War and other international disputes, conflicts, and wars, the nuclear arms race went on and on. France joined the nuclear club in 1960, China in 1964. Israel, South Africa, India, and Pakistan also began nuclear programs and, over the following decades, developed their own nuclear weapons. To secure the Bomb, declared Pakistan's prime minister, Zulfikar Ali Bhutto, his people would be willing to "eat grass."[6] Furthermore, along with nuclear proliferation went the development of new "delivery" systems: advanced bombers, intermediate range missiles, intercontinental ballistic missiles. The U.S. government developed a strategic "triad" of nuclear striking forces—on the land (in missile silos), in the air (in bombers), and under the sea (in nuclear submarines). Even when nations did not themselves develop nuclear weapons, the U.S. and Soviet governments used their soil for weapons deployment, and thus countries such as Canada, Belgium, the Netherlands, West Germany, Italy, Turkey, South Korea, East Germany, and Czechoslovakia were turned into nuclear-armed nations—and targets. Furthermore, numerous nonnuclear nations were plunged into aspects of the nuclear arms race through the berthing of nuclear armed warships in their ports and the testing of nuclear weapons on their soil or nearby. By 1974, nuclear weapons were located all over the world, and the combined U.S. and Soviet nuclear arsenals possessed the force of more than one million times the atomic bomb that had annihilated Hiroshima.[7]

On numerous occasions, nations came perilously close to using these vast and devastating nuclear arsenals. The Eisenhower administration adopted a policy of "massive retaliation," threatening to initiate full-scale nuclear war against what it defined as communist aggression. NATO made plans to respond to a Soviet conventional attack on Western Europe by unleashing nuclear war. During the Korean conflict, the Indochina War, and the confrontation with China over offshore islands, the U.S. government gave serious consideration to the use of nuclear weapons. For its part, the Soviet Union, though rejecting the inevitability of nuclear war, threatened on occasion to initiate it, as during the Suez crisis of 1956. The Cuban missile crisis provided both nations with a nuclear confrontation that narrowly missed getting out of hand. And it was not the last time. Even in October 1973, at the zenith of Soviet–American détente, U.S. national security officials, responding to disagreeable talk from the Russians about the Israeli–Egyptian war, ordered a worldwide alert of U.S. military forces, including U.S. nuclear forces. Shocked by this U.S. behavior, Soviet officials eased the situation. In the early 1980s, Soviet leaders, convinced that the Reagan administration was preparing a nuclear attack upon them, placed some of *their* nuclear forces on alert.[8]

And yet there is a curious ambiguity about this apparent march to Armageddon. Since 1945—despite Cold War confrontations and later international conflicts—the erstwhile nuclear enthusiasts have grown more subdued and nuclear war has not occurred. Ideological hawks have argued that this nuclear restraint reflects nuclear deterrence, even nuclear intimidation. But, if deterrence "works," why have nuclear armed nations bothered negotiating nuclear arms control and disarmament treaties? Why have nations capable of building nuclear weapons (i.e., dozens of advanced industrial powers) not built them? Why have nonnuclear nations refused to accept the deployment of nuclear weapons by their allies on their territory? Why have nuclear nations not attacked nonnuclear nations with nuclear weapons? A better explanation of these kinds of nuclear restraint is that they result from citizen activism against the nuclear arms race. Let us explore this alternative hypothesis by examining the history of two of the most powerful antinuclear movements: the Japanese and the American.

## The Japanese Antinuclear Movement

At its inception, the Japanese movement was deeply marked by the idea of Japan's victimization at the hands of the United States. To be sure, the atomic bombings—capping the disastrous outcome of World War II, including the deaths of three million Japanese—fostered a sharply critical view of war and of the nation's wartime militarist leaders. Japan became one of the few nations in which pacifist sentiment strongly shaped popular worldviews, and the only one with a constitution that explicitly renounced war and the maintenance of military forces.[9] In addition to pacifism, however, the fact that Japan was the only nation to have experienced the horrors of nuclear war played a key role in fostering a popular outcry against nuclear weapons. Particularly among the *hibakusha* (surviving victims of the atomic bombing) there arose the idea that their terrible ordeal could acquire a transcendent meaning if they warned a war-making world of the fate that awaited it. In early 1946, citizens' groups in Hiroshima began to commemorate the sufferings of the population and to agitate against the nuclear arms race. By 1949, thanks to the efforts of the Reverend Kiyoshi Tanimoto and of the Hiroshima Peace Association, August 6 had become World Peace Day, with antinuclear actions held in nations around the globe.[10] Although antinuclear sentiment was contained to some degree by the U.S. occupation regime, which banned or selectively censored accounts of the atomic bombings and limited what might be said publicly about nuclear weapons,[11] revulsion against the Bomb nonetheless provided a deep-seated component of Japanese life and thought.

In March 1954, only two years after the end of the occupation, that antinuclear sentiment was strengthened substantially by the first U.S. H-bomb tests, conducted in the Marshall Islands. Although the Atomic Energy Commission had staked out an official danger zone of fifty thousand square miles around the test site, the blast on Bikini atoll proved more than twice as powerful as expected. It generated vast clouds of radioactive fallout, which landed on Marshall Islanders, U.S. weather station personnel, and the crew of a Japanese fishing boat, the *Lucky Dragon*—all outside the danger zone. By the time the ill-fated fishing boat had reached its home port of Yaizu, the twenty-three crew members were experiencing advanced stages of radiation sickness. Most of the crew recovered, but the *Lucky Dragon's* radio operator died that September. Naturally, this well-publicized disaster once again struck the chord of Japan's nuclear victimization by the United States.[12]

As these events unfolded, an antinuclear storm swept through Japan. Polls that spring found overwhelming public opposition to further nuclear testing. Indeed, they revealed that 78 percent of the public opposed all nuclear testing under any circumstances, while only 2 percent approved it unconditionally. That May, middle-class housewives in the Suginami ward of Tokyo began an anti-H-bomb petition campaign. Expanding into a nationwide movement, the petition drive sparked national debate and eventually drew 32 million signatures.[13] Most cities, towns, and villages across Japan passed resolutions calling upon the United States to ban nuclear weapons. On August 6, 1955, when tens of thousands of delegates—most of them Japanese—met in Hiroshima for the First World Conference against Atomic and Hydrogen Bombs, it was an event with widespread appeal throughout Japan. Out of it grew the Japan Council against Atomic and Hydrogen Bombs (Gensuikyo), which assumed leadership of the Japanese antinuclear campaign. Although the Socialist Party and the Communist Party played important roles in Gensuikyo, the organization did not have a particularly partisan tone, for antinuclear activism spanned the political spectrum. In Japanese cities, Gensuikyo staged antinuclear demonstrations of twenty to thirty thousand people.[14]

Nevertheless, in subsequent years, increasingly sectarian behavior led to the disintegration of the movement. Although nations on both sides of the Cold War participated in the escalating nuclear arms race, the Japan Communist Party—ever ready to assail American imperialism and to excuse Soviet nuclear armament and aggressive policies—insisted upon portraying the United States as the sole villain. At Gensuikyo's world conferences in the late 1950s, Communist activists forced through sharply anti-American resolutions while avoiding any criticism of the policies of Communist nations. Alienated by these developments, centrist elements withdrew from Gensuikyo, forming Kakkin Kaigi (the National Council for Peace and against Nuclear Weapons). Meanwhile, Socialist Party–led groups launched a campaign against Communist domination of the organization at the 1961 world conference. But the Communists managed to cling to power, and when the Soviet Union resumed nuclear testing in late August, they defended the action as provoked by U.S.

belligerence—despite the fact that, only a few weeks before, the 1961 conference had voted to condemn the first nation to resume nuclear testing.[15]

Subsequently, Gensuikyo was torn by bitter dissension between those who criticized all nuclear testing and those who criticized only the Western variety, as the opposing camps staged walkouts at the two world conferences in 1962. Although the Socialists and Sohyo, the Socialist-led labor federation, boycotted the 1963 world conference, the signing of the atmospheric test ban treaty by the United States and the Soviet Union plunged the conference into another crisis. Acceptance of a test ban treaty would block Chinese development of nuclear weapons, and this fact, added to a widening split between China and the Soviet Union in world affairs, led to a showdown at the world conference between supporters of the rival Communist nations. Swept up in bitter invective and organized violence, the conference proved a disaster.[16]

For years thereafter, the Japanese antinuclear movement remained sharply divided and debilitated. Led largely by the Socialists and Sohyo, noncommunist groups officially launched their own antinuclear organization, Gensuikin (the Japan Congress against Atomic and Hydrogen Bombs), in February 1965. It promised to oppose the testing, development, and use of nuclear weapons "by any country." For its part, Gensuikyo reduced to a largely Communist rump, claimed that it retained "the only correct policy in the movement against nuclear weapons."[17] Kakkin Kaigi remained aloof from both organizations. This political division of Japan's antinuclear movement seriously undermined public confidence and participation in the antinuclear campaign, which came to be seen as a partisan activity. During the late 1960s and early 1970s, when the Japanese people demonstrated in large numbers against the Vietnam War, it was under the auspices of a new organization, Beheiren, formed in part to avoid the political meddling that had proved so disastrous to the antinuclear struggle. Furthermore, the emphasis upon the Vietnam War during these years diverted resources and popular attention from resistance to nuclear weapons.[18]

Even so, the Japanese people considered the struggle against the Bomb too important to abandon, and the movement underwent a gradual recovery. Antinuclear agitation continued during the early 1970s, but at a reduced level. Japanese activists protested against nuclear testing, demonstrated against the arrival of nuclear-armed U.S. warships, and held rival world conferences each August.[19] In January 1975, the president of Soka Gakkai, a Buddhist reform movement, presented the UN secretary-general with the names of 10 million Japanese signers of a petition calling for the abolition of nuclear weapons. Recognizing that a fractured movement was failing to provide effective leadership for Japan's antinuclear public, seven concerned organizations began reunification talks that year. But the talks went badly, with the groups divided not only over the old issue of nuclear weapons in the hands of Communist nations, but also over newer ones such as nuclear power (supported by Gensuikyo and opposed by Gensuikin). Finally, in May 1977, the two feuding organizations agreed to work together in preparation for the 1978 UN Special Session on Disarmament, to hold a united world conference in August, and to strive toward organizational unity.[20]

For a time, this organizational cooperation, coupled with the revival of the Cold War and the rise of antinuclear activism around the world, gave the movement renewed impetus and strength. A Liaison Committee to Promote a National Movement (LCPNM) was established in 1981 to bring together not only the two major antinuclear organizations, but also *hibakusha*, labor, women's, youth, consumer, and religious groups—in all, twenty-seven national organizations—around the demand for the abolition of nuclear weapons. Meanwhile, independently, professional associations, centrist groups, and large numbers of independent peace groups threw themselves into antinuclear efforts. In March 1982, some 200,000 antinuclear demonstrators turned out in Hiroshima; that May, 400,000 people participated in an antinuclear protest in Tokyo—the largest peace rally ever held in Japan. Numerous municipalities declared themselves nuclear free. In June, the LCPNM sent a disarmament petition, signed by some 29 million Japanese, to the second UN Special Session on Disarmament.[21]

Subsequently, however, the movement went into another decline. In December 1982, under the cloud of further conflict between Gensuikyo and Gensuikin, the LCPNM was dissolved; and after 1985 the two organizations abandoned their joint world conferences.[22] Gensuikyo reverted to many of its traditional ventures: staging demonstrations, running petition campaigns, dispatching *hibakusha* worldwide, and holding its own world conferences. None of these, however, had the mass backing of the movement's halcyon days, and most were discounted by broad sectors of the public as Communist Party ventures.[23] Gensuikin, too, faced difficult times, especially as Sohyo underwent membership losses and as the Japan Socialist Party sought alliances with centrist parties in preparation for elections and a governing role. Even so, Gensuikin carved out new political territory in Japan by breaking with the notion of Japan's unique nuclear victimization and emphasizing the disastrous effects of the nuclear arms race upon people the world over.[24]

Given the limited public confidence in the old-line peace organizations, much of the momentum in Japan's antinuclear campaign passed to newer groups during the 1980s and 1990s. Among them were the National Movement for Nondeployment of Tomahawk Missiles, the Peace Boat, and the Peace Office—all quite independent, but rather weak.[25] Antinuclear activism fared somewhat better among Japan's local governing authorities and, by

1987, 1,104 of them (about a third of the total) had proclaimed themselves nuclear free. At least some of these local governments did introduce regulations that raised serious challenges to the presence of nuclear weapons on board U.S. warships.[26] During the 1990s, especially, independent grassroots antinuclear groups began to network with one another and with organizations outside the country. One of the most successful of them was Peace Depot, which blended collection, analysis, and dissemination of nuclear information with advocacy work. As for the Japanese public, it remained overwhelmingly opposed to nuclear weapons. According to polls in the fall of 1998, 78 percent of Japanese respondents thought that all nuclear weapons should be destroyed.[27] Thus, despite the decline in mass protest, Japanese society offered few opportunities for pronuclear policies.

## The American Antinuclear Movement

Like its Japanese counterpart, the American antinuclear movement had its roots in World War II, when substantial numbers of scientists working in the Manhattan Project began to question and, eventually, to protest plans for the use of the atomic bomb. Their participation in this wartime venture was based upon their hope that they could outpace German scientists in developing nuclear weapons, thus preventing Nazi leaders from conquering the world. With Germany's surrender in the spring of 1945, another nightmare loomed: U.S. employment of the Bomb against Japan. This would not only constitute an act of aggression, they felt, but unleash a postwar nuclear arms race. Their protests along these lines, conducted "within channels," included the famous "Franck Report" and petitions among Manhattan Project scientists. In conversations with U.S. president Franklin Roosevelt and Britain's Winston Churchill, the Danish physicist Niels Bohr also warned of a postwar nuclear arms race and emphasized the need for developing nuclear arms controls. But U.S. and British officials ignored their advice.[28]

The vast destruction wrought by the atomic bombings of Hiroshima and Nagasaki caused an enormous stir in the United States. Part of this concern was based upon revulsion at the callous massacre of a civilian population. Pacifist groups and some religious bodies—among them the Federal Council of Churches—protested the inhumanity of the action.[29] Privately, some top U.S. military officers, as well as many scientists and intellectuals, agreed with their critique. These officers included General Dwight Eisenhower, General George Marshall, and Admiral William Leahy.[30] Nevertheless, early polls found that up to 85 percent of the American public approved of the atomic bombings, a reflection of the hatred (including racial hatred) and the dulling of humane sensibilities produced by the war. Although U.S. opposition to the bombings grew significantly in subsequent decades, as their full horror became manifest, it never reached majority proportions.[31] But if a feeling of *guilt* did not disturb most Americans, a sense of *anxiety* did. "Seldom, if ever," remarked CBS radio commentator Edward R. Murrow, "has a war ended leaving the victors with such a sense of uncertainty and fear." Many thought that a future war, fought with nuclear weapons, would be suicidal. In May 1946, a poll reported that 75 percent of Americans believed that, if their country fought another war within the next twenty-five years, nuclear weapons would be used to annihilate U.S. cities. Haunted by this prospect, large numbers of Americans favored banning nuclear weapons. A poll that same month found that 72 percent of U.S. respondents supported UN action "so that no country in the world can make atomic bombs."[32]

Riding this wave of public dismay, a variety of groups emerged in the late 1940s, championing the need for nuclear arms control and disarmament. Concerned scientists organized themselves into the Federation of Atomic Scientists (soon renamed the Federation of American Scientists) and the Emergency Committee of Atomic Scientists. Leaders such as Albert Einstein—who called for "a new way of thinking" in the nuclear age—provided these elite groups with substantial influence and credibility. In addition, the United World Federalists grew into an organization of more than fifty thousand members, while pacifist groups such as the Fellowship of Reconciliation, the War Resisters League, and the Women's International League for Peace and Freedom made a comeback after their decline during World War II. Arguing that the choice was "One World or None," these organizations often worked together to spur opposition to the nuclear arms race. By contrast, a Communist-led nuclear disarmament movement, run by the tiny Peace Information Center, spurned these emphases and, instead, stressed the 1950 Stockholm Peace Appeal and other ventures that avoided criticizing Communist bloc militarism. Thanks to this one-sidedness, plus the rising tide of anticommunism in American life, the Communist-led movement remained isolated, largely confined to sympathizers with Soviet foreign policy.[33] Overall, though, the U.S. movement during these years was larger and more visible than its Japanese counterpart.

However, as the Cold War intensified from 1949 to 1953, the American movement declined precipitously. Membership in the Federation of American Scientists, the United World Federalists, and pacifist groups plummeted. With the general public caught up in Cold War alarms, it became increasingly difficult to voice or mobilize public opposition to U.S. military programs. In addition, the hysterical crusade against domestic "subversion" not only wrecked the Communist-led antinuclear movement, but badly damaged its nonaligned counterpart as well.[34]

In the late 1950s and early 1960s, however, the American movement re-gained momentum. The immediate cause was the surge of H-bomb tests con-ducted by the great powers. These nuclear explosions not only served as grim reminders of the suicidal nature of nuclear war, but also created vast clouds of radioactive fallout that ever-widening sectors of the public believed would produce cancer and genetic damage. In the fall of 1957, Norman Cousins— who had earlier brought the "Hiroshima Maidens" (a group of young women badly disfigured by the atomic bombing) to the United States for reconstruc-tive surgery—organized the National Committee for a Sane Nuclear Policy (SANE), which soon claimed some twenty-five thousand members. Initially focused on international agreements to halt nuclear testing, SANE moved be-yond this in later years to demand broad nuclear arms control and disarma-ment measures.[35] Antinuclear students flocked either to SANE's student wing or to another new group, the Student Peace Union. In November 1961, out-raged by the resumption of Soviet and American nuclear testing after a three-year hiatus, a group of women activists organized a nationwide women's protest—drawing tens of thousands of participants—that led to the establish-ment of Women Strike for Peace. Like SANE, these groups melded the de-mand to halt the nuclear arms race with a call to ban the Bomb.[36] Although smaller than Gensuikyo, the new U.S. peace and disarmament movement was America's largest and most popular since the 1930s. By the early 1960s, U.S. opinion surveys consistently found that supporters of international agree-ments to end nuclear testing and secure nuclear disarmament outnumbered opponents.[37]

Politically, there were some important differences between the American and Japanese movements. From the start, the organizers of SANE sought to build a broadly based majority movement by appealing to middle-of-the-road opinion. Their focus upon international (rather than unilateral) action and their willingness to campaign for arms control measures (e.g., a test ban treaty) en route to nuclear disarmament reflected their self-consciously "mod-erate" appeal. In fact, despite their efforts, SANE never managed to woo many centrists (much less conservatives) into activist roles. Accordingly, its mem-bership remained predominantly liberal (and sometimes left-wing), and in-fluenced American politics through the liberal wing of the Democratic Party. Even so, the "moderate" emphasis provided the U.S. movement with credibil-ity within the parameters of American party politics. In 1960, both major party presidential candidates supported a test ban, and in 1963 a Democratic administration negotiated and secured the ratification of the atmospheric test ban treaty, with opposition coming only from the conservative wing of the Re-publican Party.[38] In contrast to the leading role played by the Japan Commu-nist Party in the Japanese movement, the American Communist Party did not constitute a powerful—or even significant—component within the U.S. movement. When hawkish forces did seek to discredit the movement by leveling charges of Communist participation, SANE responded by stating that Communists were unwelcome in its ranks, while Women Strike for Peace ridiculed the Red hunters. Thus, despite some difficult moments over the issue,[39] the movement survived and persisted.

Indeed, although the U.S. antinuclear movement—like its Japanese counterpart—declined in the late 1960s and early 1970s, anticommunism had little to do with it. Ironically, one key factor behind the movement's waning energy was its partial success. With the signing of the atmospheric test ban treaty and subsequent arms control measures, substantial portions of the American public, including many activists, felt overly confident that the problem posed by nuclear weapons was being solved. Furthermore, within the movement, there was a widespread sense of exhaustion. Finally, the U.S. government's escalation of the Vietnam War inspired fervent opposition on the part of the nation's peace and antinuclear constituency. By contrast to the bloody conflict in Indochina, the nuclear issue—apparently resolved through great power arrangements—seemed to lack urgency.[40]

With the end of the Vietnam War in 1975, the U.S. antinuclear campaign began a slow revival. Peace groups turned their energies to stopping the nuclear-capable B-1 bomber and closing down nuclear weapons facilities—projects that developed substantial support.[41] As in Japan, the 1978 UN Special Session on Disarmament helped to channel peace groups toward the nuclear issue.[42] Although antinuclear activists welcomed some policies of the Carter administration (e.g., the president's call for the abolition of nuclear weapons and the Strategic Arms Limitations Treaty, or SALT II), they were dismayed by plans for a neutron bomb, by the dangers of nuclear power plants, and by the administration's increasingly hawkish posture.[43] A new group, Mobilization for Survival, paired opposition to nuclear weapons with opposition to nuclear power, while the charismatic Helen Caldicott resurrected an older group, Physicians for Social Responsibility.[44] Inspired by Randall Forsberg, a defense and disarmament analyst, a broad range of peace groups issued a "Call to Halt the Nuclear Arms Race," which proposed a Soviet–American agreement to halt testing, production, and deployment of nuclear weapons.[45]

Forsberg's "Nuclear Freeze" proposal served as the centerpiece of the U.S. antinuclear effort during the early 1980s. Although pacifist and Communist-led groups were unenthusiastic about the Freeze campaign—the former charging shallowness of a movement that left nuclear stockpiles intact and the latter complaining of anticommunism[46]—its moderate formula catapulted the nuclear issue into public discussion and U.S. politics more effectively than ever before. Hundreds of thousands of Americans joined SANE, the Nuclear

Weapons Freeze Campaign, and Physicians for Social Responsibility,[47] while an estimated one million turned out for a New York City rally against the nuclear arms race—the largest political demonstration up to that time in American history. Indicative of the breadth of its appeal, the Freeze drew the backing of major unions, professional organizations, religious groups, and the Democratic Party. During his 1984 campaign for the presidency, Democratic candidate Walter Mondale pledged that, on his first day in the White House, he would call upon the Soviet Union to freeze the arms race.[48]

In part, this upsurge reflected the new Reagan administration's unabashed hawkishness, including its revival of the Soviet–American Cold War confrontation, plans for a nuclear buildup, and provocative talk of nuclear war. Yet the antinuclear campaign also thrived because its alternative to nuclear escalation—a Soviet–American agreement to halt the nuclear arms race—seemed thoroughly reasonable to most Americans. Although the Reagan administration succeeded in blocking a Freeze resolution in the U.S. Senate, the resolution was passed by an overwhelming vote in the House of Representatives and endorsed by eleven state legislatures and more than two hundred city councils. According to the polls, the Freeze had the support of some 70 percent of Americans.[49]

Beginning in the latter half of the 1980s, the American movement waned. For a few years, the decline was quite modest, and antinuclear groups retained a powerful presence in American life. In 1987, when SANE (possessing 150,000 members) merged with the Nuclear Freeze (possessing no formal membership, but some eighteen hundred local chapters) to form Peace Action, the new peace group was by far the largest in American history. Nevertheless, antinuclear activism gradually ebbed, thanks to the signing of Soviet–American arms control agreements, the end of the Cold War, and the demise of the Soviet Union.[50] Although the movement campaigned for a shutdown of U.S. nuclear facilities, to secure the adoption and ratification of the Comprehensive Test Ban Treaty, and for the abolition of all nuclear weapons, it proved unable to recapture the central focus and mass mobilization of the early 1980s.[51] Furthermore, the general public, though lacking in enthusiasm for nuclear weapons, seemed increasingly complacent about the ongoing nuclear arms race. Jeremy Stone of the Federation of American Scientists complained that "the fear of nuclear weapons is falling faster than the danger."[52] Like its Japanese counterpart, the American movement, while visible on occasion and possessing a measure of political clout, evolved into but one of many citizen action campaigns.

## The Issue of Efficacy

Although it is clear enough that the Japanese, American, and other antinuclear campaigns have not banned the Bomb, that does not mean that they have been ineffective. Indeed, there is substantial evidence—which can only be sketched in this brief account—that, together with the antinuclear sentiment they have mobilized, they have been very effective, indeed.

During the Korean War, for example, there was no compelling military reason for the U.S. government *not* to use nuclear weapons. The Soviet Union did not enter the conflict and, furthermore, had only recently developed an atomic bomb and lacked an effective delivery system for the new weapon. In addition, during the early years of the war, U.S. forces came close to military defeat at the hands of nonnuclear powers. In these circumstances, numerous U.S. political and military leaders urged a U.S. nuclear attack.[53] But their entreaties were countered, effectively, by others who argued that nuclear war had become politically impossible. Use of the Bomb on an Asian population would cause "a revulsion of feeling" to "spread throughout Asia," warned the State Department's Far East specialist. "Our efforts to win the Asiatics to our side would be cancelled and our influence in non-Communist nations of Asia would deteriorate to an almost non-existent quantity." Militarily, the Bomb would probably be effective, commented Paul Nitze, head of the State Department's policy planning staff, but its use "would help arouse the peoples of Asia against us."[54] Responding to a claim that the atomic bomb was America's "political ace," Secretary of State Acheson retorted that it was a "political liability." Recalling General MacArthur's demand for all-out nuclear war within and beyond the borders of Korea, Dean Rusk, the assistant secretary of state for the Far East, recalled that, if it had been accepted, "we would have worn the mark of Cain for generations to come. The political effect would have been devastating." General James Gavin, complaining of the failure to employ nuclear weapons in Korea, recalled that "the situation in the summer of 1950 offered us a number of well worth-while tactical nuclear targets if we had had the moral courage to make the decision to use them."[55] Truman, though, a nuclear enthusiast in 1945, was a chastened man by 1950 and refused to give the green light for nuclear war.[56]

When the Eisenhower administration came to office, it was quite ready to resort to nuclear weapons, particularly when it came to the war in Korea. According to NSC 162/2, the new administration's statement of national security policy, "In the event of hostilities, the United States will consider nuclear weapons to be as available for use as other munitions." In early 1953, Dulles complained about "the inhibitions on the use of the A bomb," and Eisenhower asserted that he and Dulles were in complete agreement that "somehow or other the tabu [*sic*] which surrounds the use of atomic weapons would have to be destroyed."[57] But, despite Eisenhower's repeated suggestions for employment of nuclear weapons in Korea, this proved politically inexpedient. In discussions with the president, Dulles reported that, "in the present state of world opinion we could not use an A-bomb," although "we should make every effort now to dissipate this feeling, especially since we are spending such vast sums on the production of weapons we cannot use."[58] In the summer of 1953, shortly after the end of the Korean War, Admiral Arthur Radford, chair of the Joint Chiefs of Staff, complained of the administration's nuclear weapons policy, pointing out that the U.S. government was "holding back on their use because of our concern for public opinion."[59]

He was quite correct. During the Vietnam War—a conflict in which the U.S. government accepted military defeat rather than employ nuclear weapons—there was no lack of nuclear targets or advocates of U.S. nuclear attacks. Also, there was virtually no fear of nuclear counterattack from China or the Soviet Union. But the existence of widespread antinuclear sentiment constrained U.S. officials. Objecting strongly to the use of nuclear weapons, George Ball pointed to the "profound shock" that would ensue, "not merely in Japan but also among the nonwhite nations on every continent." It would also mobilize domestic "resentment against a Government that had gotten America in a position where we ... again ... use nuclear power to our own world discredit."[60] In 1965, a RAND weapons analyst, enthusiastic about the employment of small nuclear weapons in Vietnam, was dismayed to find State Department officials "adamantly opposed to the development and use of such weapons from a political point of view." Taking office a few years later, Richard Nixon and Henry Kissinger also began as nuclear enthusiasts, but could not rid themselves of external constraints. Had he bombed North Vietnamese dikes or used nuclear weapons, Nixon recalled bitterly, "the resulting domestic and international uproar would have damaged our foreign policy on all fronts."[61] Kissinger, too, though an early advocate of nuclear threats and warfare, found to his regret that they could not be employed in Vietnam. Nations armed with nuclear weapons "could not necessarily use this power to impose their will," he wrote ruefully. "The capacity to destroy proved difficult to translate into a plausible threat even against countries with no capacity for retaliation." Recalling the "irrelevance of nuclear weapons" in the Vietnam War, McGeorge Bundy—a key war planner—attributed it to U.S. government fear of a massive negative "reaction" in nations around the world, including the United States, where "no president could hope for understanding and support from his own countrymen if he used the bomb."[62]

Popular pressures also helped curb nuclear tests. So great was the antinuclear campaign's clamor against nuclear weapons testing that, in 1958, when the Soviet Union halted its tests and dared the United States to follow its example, the Eisenhower administration very reluctantly did just that. Explaining his decision to a group of nuclear testing enthusiasts, Eisenhower declared: "The new thermonuclear weapons are tremendously powerful; however, they are not ... as powerful as is world opinion today." Thereafter, the U.S. government looked forward to resuming nuclear testing, but felt constrained from doing so by public opinion.[63] Even when the Soviet government resumed nuclear testing in August 1961, Kennedy—concerned about the domestic and foreign reaction to a U.S. resumption of atmospheric nuclear testing—resisted holding such tests for another seven months. According to the minutes of a November 1961 NSC meeting, "the President voiced doubts that we could ever test in Nevada again for domestic political reasons," while UN ambassador Adlai Stevenson "pointed up the difficulty of testing at Eniwetok."[64] Subsequently, determined to move nuclear test ban negotiations forward, Kennedy leaned heavily on Norman Cousins, founder and chair of SANE, who—as Kennedy's emissary—made important breakthroughs in discussions with Khrushchev. After the atmospheric test ban treaty was signed in 1963, Cousins became the White House's unofficial coordinator of the Senate ratification campaign.[65]

Antinuclear agitation played a key role in securing the Comprehensive Test Ban Treaty (CTBT), as well. Although the Reagan administration—convinced that a halt to nuclear testing would inhibit its nuclear buildup—ended U.S. participation in CTBT negotiations, the movement forced the issue back upon the great power agenda. Responding to the urgings of nuclear disarmament group leaders, Soviet Communist Party secretary Mikhail Gorbachev began an eighteen-month moratorium on Soviet nuclear testing in August 1985, designed—like the Soviet moratorium of 1958—to get the U.S. government to stop nuclear testing. Reagan refused to halt U.S. tests, but he did resume discussions with the Soviet government over a test ban.[66] Meanwhile, congressional Democrats, working closely with disarmament groups, introduced a variety of bills to halt U.S. nuclear testing. In 1991, at the behest of U.S. disarmament groups, a freshman House member from Oregon, Mike Kopetski, masterminded a new congressional attempt to terminate test funding. This carefully crafted legislation, passed in September 1992, halted underground nuclear testing for nine months, sharply limited testing thereafter, and established a timetable for phasing out tests entirely. Although President George H. W. Bush threatened to veto the measure, he ultimately signed it because it was attached as a rider to other legislation that he keenly desired in that election year.[67] Subsequently, after antinuclear forces won a struggle within the Clinton administration to block resumption of nuclear testing, the administration extended the testing moratorium, pressed other powers to join it, and began worldwide efforts to secure a test ban treaty. In September 1996, representatives of nations around the world signed the CTBT. Secretary of State Madeleine Albright remarked, "This was a treaty sought by ordinary people everywhere, and today the power of that universal wish could not be denied."[68]

Other key nuclear arms control and disarmament measures also owed a great deal to antinuclear activism. The Anti–Ballistic Missile treaty of 1972 would probably never have emerged without the efforts of antinuclear U.S. scientists, who—arguing that defensive measures were just as likely to accelerate the nuclear arms race as offensive ones—convinced U.S. officials, Soviet scientists, and (through the Soviet scientists) Soviet officials of this fact.[69] Similarly, the insertion of the disarmament track into NATO's December 1979 "two track" decision for cruise and Pershing II missile deployment was politically motivated, designed to appease antinuclear opinion.[70] Even during the hawkish Reagan administration, missile removal could not be ignored, leading to the "zero option"—the U.S. proposal to forgo deployment of Western intermediate-range missiles if the Soviets would remove their SS-20s. "We got the idea from your banners," a State Department official told a leading antinuclear campaigner.[71] Although, for most Western officials, the "zero option" represented a propaganda gesture rather than a serious offer, key antinuclear activists, meeting with Gorbachev, convinced the Soviet leader to accept it.[72] Consequently, NATO leaders were stuck with a nuclear disarmament measure that they could not justifiably refuse. As Secretary of State George Shultz recalled, "If the United States reversed its stand now . . . such a reversal would be political dynamite!"[73] Ultimately, to the dismay of the Republican right, the U.S. government signed the Intermediate Nuclear Forces Treaty with the Soviet Union.[74]

As these incidents indicate, Gorbachev played a very significant role in promoting the antinuclear movement's agenda. Becoming party secretary in March 1985, he represented a breakthrough for the reform wing of the Soviet Communist Party and brought with him reform intellectuals who had been involved for years in efforts to defuse the nuclear confrontation. Gorbachev trumpeted what he called the "new thinking"—ideas drawn from the disarmament-oriented intellectuals and movements in the West. These included the inadmissibility of nuclear war, "reasonable sufficiency" in defense, "common security," and the need for nuclear disarmament. Typically, his phrase "new thinking" had its roots in the rhetoric of the postwar atomic scientists' movement, which had warned humanity that a new way of thinking provided the only alternative to nuclear catastrophe. In his book *Perestroika*, Gorbachev praised antinuclear movements lavishly, arguing that "it is impossible to ignore what these people are saying," for "what they are saying and what they do is prompted by accurate knowledge and a passionate desire to warn humanity about the danger looming over it."[75] Gorbachev met with antinuclear leaders on numerous occasions, including all the American–Soviet summit conferences, and often took their advice on arms control and disarmament issues. In turn, they were delighted with him.[76] This informal alliance between Gorbachev and the movement put added pressure on the U.S. government, contributing to the 1989 decision to scrap plans for modernizing NATO's short-range nuclear missiles in Europe and to the removal of all short-range missiles in 1991.[77]

In Japan, too, accommodations to public pressure are clear enough. Over time, the Japanese government provided increasing attention to and compensation for the *hibakusha*. This was not always an easy policy for Japanese officials to adopt, as their nation's Cold War alliance with the United States made an emphasis upon the disastrous effects of the U.S. atomic bombing of Hiroshima and Nagasaki politically embarrassing.[78] In addition, the Japanese government was forced to become a public critic of nuclear testing and of the nuclear arms race—once again, an embarrassment to the government, given the key role played in both of these ventures by its U.S. ally. Behind the scenes, it apologized to U.S. officials, pointing out that its public protests were "largely a public opinion matter." In September 1957, the Japanese foreign minister told Dulles that "the psychological situation in Japan compels the government to stand for disarmament . . . and against the manufacture and use of all nuclear weapons."[79] Although it could be claimed that, in these situations, nothing was lost but honor, the constant apologies, as well as the public critiques, attest to the influence of the antinuclear movement and the widespread acceptance of its ideas.

The greatest concession to antinuclear pressure, however, was the Japanese government's December 1967 proclamation of the "three nonnuclear principles." Later approved by a unanimous resolution in Japan's House of Representatives, the proclamation meant that the government would not possess, manufacture, or introduce nuclear weapons into Japan. This total renunciation of nuclear might was a bitter pill for any nation accustomed to great power status to swallow; and in fact no others did swallow it. Furthermore, Japan certainly possessed the advanced scientific and industrial capabilities to enable it to develop nuclear weapons fairly easily.[80] To be sure, the government apparently violated the third of the principles, by making secret concessions that permitted the U.S. government to keep nuclear weapons on board U.S. warships as they entered Japanese harbors.[81] At the same time, the Japanese government could not have been happy about sticking to public support of this third principle, for such support encouraged local governments to proclaim themselves nuclear free, thus provoking constant controversies over the visits of U.S. warships.

## Conclusion

What, then, are we to conclude about the efforts of the Japanese and American nuclear disarmament campaigns? In some ways, they have been quite similar. In the aftermath of the atomic bombings of Hiroshima and Nagasaki, each created mass movements with broad public support. Their efforts, in conjunction with the efforts of antinuclear campaigns in dozens of other nations, have set limits on their own and other governments' nuclear policies. These governments almost certainly would have pursued more ambitious programs—and might have employed nuclear weapons after 1945 to attack other nations—had these movements not existed. Furthermore, although both campaigns have receded substantially from their mobilization peaks of the early 1980s, they continue their efforts today with substantial memberships, a significant financial base, experienced staff, and important allies in politics. If they are currently down, they are not out, and may yet prevail against the remaining policies of nuclear terror.

This chapter has also highlighted some significant differences between the two antinuclear efforts. From the start, the Japanese campaign focused on Japan's unique victimization and America's unique villainy, and did so for years with considerable effect. Even so, over the years this emphasis proved out of touch with international realities, and sectors of the movement, such as Gensuikin, began to develop a more balanced and universal approach. By contrast, the American campaign began in what was then the world's only nuclear-armed nation—as well as in the only nation to have used nuclear weapons—and, therefore, faced a more difficult task in promoting disarmament. Not surprisingly, it quickly gravitated toward discussing nuclear dangers in universal terms. To some degree, the U.S. campaign managed to bring the nuclear issue home to Americans by focusing on nuclear fallout and stressing the dangers of annihilation in a Soviet–American nuclear war. Even so, there are limits to the effects of this kind of emphasis, particularly with an atmospheric test ban in place and with the Soviet Union eliminated from the world scene. Another difference pivots around the key role of the Communist Party in the Japanese movement—a fact that tended to marginalize the movement and keep it more divided than its American counterpart. To be sure, the American movement has been close, at times, to the liberal wing of the Democratic Party. But the Democrats do not control the American movement. Also, they occasionally govern the United States and, therefore, are able to deliver on their antinuclear promises.

By focusing on the differences between the Japanese and American movements, however, we risk missing their common elements, interrelations, and broader significance. Both emerged in the context of an international system that, over the past century, has grown ever more devastating, massacring millions of civilians in pursuit of what national power wielders have defined as national interests. Despite the unprecedented destructiveness of nuclear weapons, they are but the latest instruments in the hands of an irrational system of armed, competing nation-states. Recognizing that, with the advent of nuclear terror, this system was careening toward disaster, the Japanese and American antinuclear campaigns sought to foster "new thinking" and new policies pertaining to nations, weapons, and people that will ensure human survival. Admittedly, they did not succeed in banning the Bomb or ending the vast carnage produced by conventional weapons. But through their efforts they did help to set limits on the nuclear arms race and on the opportunities for nuclear war. In this sense, they have been a vital part of what the novelist H. G. Wells predicted for the future: a "race between education and catastrophe."[82]

# Notes

1. These points and many other observations in this chapter are developed at greater length in my trilogy on the antinuclear movement: *The Struggle against the Bomb: One World or None. A History of the World Nuclear Disarmament Movement Through 1953* (Stanford, Calif.: Stanford University Press, 1993); *Resisting the Bomb: A History of the World Nuclear Disarmament Movement, 1954–1970* (Stanford, Calif.: Stanford University Press, 1997); and *Toward Nuclear Abolition: A History of the World Nuclear Disarmament Movement, 1971 to the Present* (Stanford, Calif.: Stanford University Press, 2003).

2. See, for example, chapter 2 in this volume, by Mark Selden.

3. Ronald Schaffer, *Wings of Judgment: American Bombing in World War II* (New York: Oxford University Press, 1988); "Notes of the Interim Committee Meeting, May 31, 1945," in Martin J. Sherwin, *A World Destroyed: Hiroshima and the Origins of the Arms Race* (New York: Vintage, 1987), 302; Winston S. Churchill, *Triumph and Tragedy* (Boston: Houghton Mifflin, 1953), 638–39.

4. Richard Rhodes, *The Making of the Atomic Bomb* (New York: Simon & Schuster, 1986).

5. David Holloway, *The Soviet Union and the Arms Race* (New Haven, Conn.: Yale University Press, 1983), 19–20; Alan Bullock, *Ernest Bevin: Foreign Secretary, 1945–1951* (London: Heinemann, 1983), 352; Ronald Powaski, *March to Armageddon* (New York: Oxford University Press, 1987), 50–59.

6. Gordon Edwards, "Canada's Nuclear Industry and the Myth of the Peaceful Atom," in *Canada and the Nuclear Arms Race*, ed. Ernie Regehr and Simon Rosenblum (Toronto: Lorimer, 1983), 134–35.

7. Alva Myrdal, *The Game of Disarmament: How the United States and Russia Run the Arms Race* (New York: Pantheon, 1976), 178.

8. Richard Ned Lebow and Janice Gross Stein, *We All Lost the Cold War* (Princeton, N.J.: Princeton University Press, 1994), 246–88; Anatoly Dobrynin, *In Confidence* (New York: Times Books, 1995), 300; Ronald E. Powaski, *Return to Armageddon* (New York: Oxford University Press, 2000), 41–42.

9. Nobuya Bamba and John F. Howes, eds., *Pacifism in Japan: The Christian and Socialist Tradition* (Vancouver: University of British Columbia Press, 1978), 269–70; Kazuko Tsurumi, *Social Change and the Individual: Japan before and after Defeat in World War II* (Princeton, N.J.: Princeton University Press, 1970), 258–59, 263–65, 271–73, 280–83.

10. Robert J. Lifton, *Death in Life: Survivors of Hiroshima* (New York: Simon & Schuster, 1967), 211–52; *The Meaning of Survival: Hiroshima's 36 Year Commitment to Peace* (Hiroshima: Chugoku Shimbun and the Hiroshima International Cultural Foundation, 1983), 57, 60–61, 64, 67, 69–70, 76–79; Committee for the Compilation of Materials on Damage Caused by the Atomic Bombs in Hiroshima and Nagasaki, *Hiroshima and Nagasaki: The Physical, Medical, and Social Effects of the Atomic Bombings* (New York: Basic, 1981), xxxix–xl; *Peace News*, May 21, 1948; September 10, 1948; February 18, 1949; September 23, 1949.

11. Monica Braw, *The Atomic Bomb Suppressed: American Censorship in Japan* (Malmo, Sweden: Liber, 1986); Robert J. Lifton, *History and Human Survival* (New York: Vintage, 1971), 140; *Meaning of Survival*, 64–65, 68, 87, 195; Laura Hein and Mark Selden, "Commemoration and Silence: Fifty Years of Remembering the Bomb in America and Japan," in *Living with the Bomb: American and Japanese Cultural Conflicts in the Nuclear Age*, ed. Laura Hein and Mark Selden (Armonk, N.Y.: M. E. Sharpe, 1997), 9, 19, 25–27.

12. Robert A. Divine, *Blowing on the Wind: The Nuclear Test Ban Debate, 1954–1960* (New York: Oxford University Press, 3–13; Ralph E. Lapp, *The Voyage of the Lucky Dragon* (New York: Harper & Row, 1958).

13. Sunao Suzuki, "Japanese Attitudes toward Nuclear Issues," in *Peace Research in Japan*, ed. Japan Peace Research Group (1974–75), 114; Yasumasa Tanaka, "Japanese Attitudes toward Nuclear Arms," *Public Opinion Quarterly* 34 (1970): 29.

14. *Meaning of Survival*, 117, 122; George O. Totten and Tamio Kawakami, "Gensuikyo and the Peace Movement in Japan," *Asian Survey* 4 (May 1964): 835; Invitation to the 2nd World Conference against Atomic and Hydrogen Bombs, August 6–15, 1956, Japan (April 1, 1956), folder 333, War Resisters' International Records, International Institute for Social History, Amsterdam, the Netherlands (hereafter cited as WRI Records); J. A. A. Stockwin, *The Japanese Socialist Party and Neutralism* (Carleton, Australia: Melbourne University Press, 1968), 88; Signe Hojer, "Japan United against Nuclear Weapons," *Pax et Libertas* 22 (December 1956): 8–9.

15. *Peace News*, August 28, 1959; *Manchester Guardian*, August 21, 1959; Committee for the Compilation of Materials, *Hiroshima and Nagasaki*, 580–81; Totten and Kawakami, "Gensuikyo," 836–37.

16. *Meaning of Survival*, 158–59, 163, 166–67; *Sanity* (October 1962): 6; *Peace News*, August 23, 1963.

17. *Meaning of Survival*, 170, 176; "Basic Principles of the Movement against Atomic and Hydrogen Bombs," *Information*, no. 1 (May 20, 1965): 3, Japan Congress against A & H Bomb Records, Swarthmore College Peace Collection, Swarthmore, Pennsylvania (hereafter cited as SCPC); Yushin Hosoi et al. to War Resisters' International, June 10, 1965, folder 333, WRI Records.

18. Glenn D. Hook, "The Ban the Bomb Movement in Japan: Whither Alternative Security?" *Social Alternatives* 3 (March 1983): 35; Committee for the Compilation of Materials, *Hiroshima and Nagasaki*, 581–82; Ohtori Kurino and Katsuya Kodama, "A Study on the Japanese Peace Movement," in *Towards a Comparative Analysis of Peace Movements*, ed. Katsuya Kodama and Unto Vesa (Hants: Dartmouth, 1990), 121–23; Yoshiyuki Tsurumi, "Beheiren," *Japan Quarterly* 16 (October–December 1969): 444–48.

19. *Meaning of Survival*, 237; Takako Tatematsu to Ethel Taylor, October 16, 1974, box 13, series A, 3, Women Strike for Peace Records, SCPC (hereafter cited as WSP Records); Ichiro Moritaki to Raymond Wilson, June 1, 1972, Japan Congress against A & H Bomb Records, SCPC.

20. Daisaku Ikeda, "A Ten-Point Proposal on Nuclear Disarmament" (1979), 6, Soka Gakkai International Records, SCPC; J. Victor Koschmann, "Postwar Democracy and Japanese Ban-the-Bomb Movements" (unpublished manuscript), 16–17; *Japan Times*, May 20, 1977; author interview with Koichi Akamatsu, May 15, 1999.

21. Hitoshi Ohnishi, "The Peace Movement in Japan," *International Peace Research Newsletter* 21 (1983): 26–30; "The Japanese Disarmament Movement on the Upsurge," *Japan Quarterly* 29 (July–September 1982): 287–90; Hook, "Ban the Bomb Movement in Japan," 35–39.

22. Ohnishi, "The Peace Movement in Japan," 30, 33; Katsuya Kodama, "Red vs. Green: A Comparative Study on Peace Movements in Japan, Denmark, and Finland" (paper presented at the Lund Conference on Peace Movements, Lund, Sweden, August 17–20, 1987), 3; author interview with Ikuro Anzai, May 15, 1999.

23. Yuko Yamaguchi to Dear Friends, July 25, 1986, Japan Council against A & H Bomb Records, SCPC; author interview with Koichi Akamatsu; Glenn D. Hook, "The Anti-Nuclear Discourse in Japan: Implications for Praxis," in *Towards a Comparative Analysis of Peace Movements*, ed. Katsuya Kodama and Unto Vesa (Hants: Dartmouth, 1990), 116.

24. Kodama, "Red vs. Green," 11; John R. Miller, "Japanese Politics: Antimilitarism on the Rise?" *Nonviolent Activist* 6 (December 1989): 4; "The Japanese Peace Movement: Beyond Hiroshima and Nagasaki," *Gensuikin News*, no. 113 (Summer 1986): 1–3, and Mikio Haruna, "Breaking Away from the Mentality of 'the Only Hibakusha Country,'" *Gensuikin News*, no. 113 (Summer 1986): 3–8.

25. Joanne Landy to Horst Stasius, December 31, 1986, in author's possession; Junko Yamaka, "Japan's Anti-Tomahawk Movement," *Freeze Focus* 4 (November 1984): 15; "Rally Report: 'No Tomahawk/Asia Pacific Day,'" *AMPO* 17, no. 2 (1985): 16–17.

26. Takao Takahara, "Local Government Initiatives to Promote Peace," *Peace and Change* 12, nos. 3–4 (1987): 51–58; Naoki Kamimura, *Japanese Civil Society, Local Government, and U.S.–Japan Security Relations in the 1990s: A Preliminary Survey* (Osaka: Japan Center for Area Studies, 2001), 9; "No Nukes in Japan," *Greenpeace* 13 (November–December 1988): 5.

27. Kamimura, *Japanese Civil Society*, 11–13; Elizabeth Hann Hastings and Philip K. Hastings, eds., *Index to International Public Opinion, 1998–1999* (Westport, Conn.: Greenwood, 2000), 608.

28. This story is recounted in Rhodes, *Making of the Atomic Bomb;* Sherwin, *World Destroyed;* and Wittner, *One World or None,* 8–36.

29. A. J. Muste, Memorandum on the Atomic Bombing (August 15, 1945), box 23, Fellowship of Reconciliation Records, SCPC; Sydnor H. Walker, ed., *The First One Hundred Days of the Atomic Age* (New York: Woodrow Wilson Foundation, 1945), 15; Federal Council of the Churches of Christ in America, *Atomic Warfare and the Christian Faith* (New York: n. p., 1946).

30. Dwight D. Eisenhower, *Mandate for Change, 1953–1956* (Garden City, N.Y.: Doubleday, 1963), 312–13; William D. Leahy, *I Was There* (New York: McGraw-Hill, 1950), 441; Alice Kimball Smith, *A Peril and a Hope: The Scientists' Movement in America, 1945–47* (Chicago: University of Chicago Press, 1965), 78–79.

31. George H. Gallup, ed., *The Gallup Poll: Public Opinion, 1935–1971* (New York: Random House, 1972), 521–22; Thomas W. Graham, *American Public Opinion on NATO, Extended Deterrence, and Use of Nuclear Weapons* (Lanham, Md.: University Press of America, 1989), 7, 32.

32. Paul Boyer, *By the Bomb's Early Light* (New York: Pantheon, 1985), 7, 13–32; "The Quarter's Polls," *Public Opinion Quarterly* 10 (Summer 1946): 247.

33. Wittner, *One World or None,* 59–76, 202–209; Smith, *Peril and a Hope;* Wesley T. Wooley, *Alternatives to Anarchy: American Supranationalism since World War II* (Bloomington: Indiana University Press, 1988), 3–59.

34. Smith, *Peril and a Hope,* 507–13, 523; Wooley, *Alternatives to Anarchy,* 60, 72–74, 80; Membership Statistics (1954), box 4, Fellowship of Reconciliation Records, SCPC; Gallup, ed., *Gallup Poll,* 839, 895, 929; Stanley K. Bigman, "The 'New Internationalism' Under Attack," *Public Opinion Quarterly* 14 (Summer 1950): 235–61; Jessica Wang, *American Science in an Age of Anxiety: Scientists, Anticommunism, and the Cold War* (Chapel Hill: University of North Carolina Press, 1999).

35. "A Short History of SANE," box 1, series 1, SANE Records, SCPC; Donald Keys to J. David Bowen, August 29, 1958, box 2, series 5, SANE Records, SCPC; *SANE World,* April 15, 1964.

36. "Student Peace Groups," *New University Thought* 1 (Spring 1961): 75–80; Ken Calkins, "The Student Peace Union," *Fellowship* 26 (March 1, 1960): 5–7; Amy Swerdlow, *Women Strike for Peace: Traditional Motherhood and Radical Politics in the 1960s* (Chicago: University of Chicago Press, 1993), 15–96; "Women—Strike for Peace" (January 1, 1962), box 1, series I, WSP Records.

37. Eugene J. Rosi, "Mass and Attentive Opinion on Nuclear Weapons Tests and Fallout, 1954–1963," *Public Opinion Quarterly* 29 (Summer 1965): 283; Arthur M. Schlesinger Jr., *A Thousand Days: John F. Kennedy in the White House* (Boston: Houghton Mifflin, 1964), 913; Gallup, ed, *Gallup Poll,* 1691, 1839.

38. Author interview with Homer Jack, June 12, 1988; Lynn Z. Bloom, *Dr. Spock: Biography of a Conservative Radical* (Indianapolis: Bobbs-Merrill, 1972), 248; *New York Times,* October 10, 1960; Theodore C. Sorensen, *Kennedy* (New York: Harper & Row, 1965), 736–39.

39. Wittner, *Resisting the Bomb,* 324–31; Amy Swerdlow, "Ladies' Day at the Capitol: Women Strike for Peace Versus HUAC," *Feminist Studies* 8 (Fall 1982): 493–520.

40. Author interview with Homer Jack; author interview with Sanford Gottlieb, July 19, 1998; G. B. Kistiakowsky and H. F. York, "Strategic Arms Race Slowdown through Test Limitations," *Science* 185 (August 2, 1974): 404; Swerdlow, *Women Strike for Peace*, 129–42, 164.

41. Author interview with Terry Provance, July 20, 1999; American Friends Service Committee press release, January 7, 1974, box 10, series II, American Friends Service Committee Records, SCPC (hereafter cited as AFSC Records); "Fact Sheet on History of Rocky Flats Campaign," box 1, American Friends Service Committee–Rocky Flats Project Records, Norlin Library, University of Colorado, Boulder; Tom Rauch, "Pioneering Work against Nuclear Weapons Plants," *Quaker Service Bulletin* 70 (Winter 1989): 1, 7.

42. Author interview with Robert Musil, July 20, 1998; author interview with David Atwood, June 1, 1999; "United Nations Special Session on Disarmament: Bulletin #1—1/12/78," box 2, section IV, series A, 6, Women's International League for Peace and Freedom Records, SCPC (hereafter cited as WILPF Records).

43. Bernard Feld, "The Way to Begin Is to Stop," *Bulletin of the Atomic Scientists* 33 (March 1977): 9; author interview with Harold Willens, May 11, 2000; "Resolutions and Statements" (June 27–July 1, 1979), box 25, series A, 2, WILPF Records; Elizabeth S. French to Mary Boyer, January 13, 1978, WSP Records; "SANE Opposes Carter Renomination" (September 14, 1979), box 60, series G, SANE Records; "The Nuclear Connection" (1979), box 11, series II, AFSC Records.

44. "A Call to Action" (June 1977), Mobilization for Survival Records, SCPC; "Statement of the National Coordinating Committee, Mobilization for Survival" (1977), Mobilization for Survival Records, SCPC; Barbara Day and Howard Waitzkin, "The Medical Profession and Nuclear War: A Social History," *Journal of the American Medical Association* 254 (August 2, 1985): 647–48.

45. Author interview with Randall Forsberg, July 7, 1999; "Call to Halt the Nuclear Arms Race," box 15, Nuclear Weapons Freeze Campaign Records, Western Historical Manuscript Collection, Thomas Jefferson Library, University of Missouri, St. Louis.

46. Author interview with Randall Kehler, August 20, 1999; David McReynolds to Wim Bartels, August 26, 1983, box 134, series G, SANE Records; "The New 'Red Scare': An Open Letter" (1982), U.S. Peace Council Records, SCPC.

47. Author interview with Robert Musil, July 20, 1998; author interview with Randall Kehler, August 20, 1999; author interview with Helen Caldicott, February 27, 1999.

48. Gene Carroll to Brother/Sister, October 11, 1984, Nuclear Weapons Freeze Campaign Records; *New York Times*, June 16, 1983, Sept. 6, 1984; Renata Rizzo, "Professional Approach to Peace," *Nuclear Times* 4 (July–August 1986): 6–7.

49. Author interview with John Isaacs, July 20, 1999; "The Nuclear Weapons Freeze Campaign," *Freeze Newsletter* 3 (August 1983): 2; Karin Fierke, "Overwhelming Victory for the Freeze in the House," *Freeze Newsletter* 3 (June 1983): 5; Chaplain Morrison, "The Freeze in Congress: Past and Present," *Freeze Focus* 4 (April 1984): 6–7; "Nuclear Arms," *Gallup Report*, no. 208 (January 1983): 10.

50. "SANE Votes to Merge with Freeze," *SANE World* (Spring 1987): 3; author interview with Helen Caldicott, February 27, 1999.

51. Author interview with Robert Musil, July 20, 1998; Daryl G. Kimball, *The 1993 Campaign for a Nuclear Test Ban* (Washington: Physicians for Social Responsibility, 1993); "People's Pledge: From a Nuclear Test Ban to Nuclear Abolition" (September 24, 1996), in author's possession; "Abolition 2000 Statement," in author's possession; author interview with David Krieger, May 14, 1999.

52. George Gallup Jr., *The Gallup Poll: Public Opinion 1998* (Wilmington, Del.: Scholarly Resources, 1999), 77, 79–80; author interview with Jeremy Stone, July 22, 1999.

53. Rosemary Foot, *The Wrong War: American Policy and Dimensions of the Korean Conflict, 1950–1953* (Ithaca, N.Y.: Cornell University Press, 1985), 114–15, 157; Memorandum of Conversation, May 25, 1951, 711.5611/5-2551, U.S. Department of State Records, National Archives, Washington, D.C. (hereafter cited as State Department Records); Forrest C. Pogue, *George C. Marshall: Statesman, 1945–1959* (New York: Viking, 1987), 488; Dean Rusk, *As I Saw It* (New York: Penguin, 1990), 170.

54. John K. Emmerson to Dean Rusk, November 8, 1950, 711.5611/11-850, State Department Records; *Foreign Relations of the United States, 1950* (Washington, D.C.: Government Printing Office, 1976), 7:1041–42 (hereafter cited as *FRUS*).

55. Roger Dingman, "Atomic Diplomacy during the Korean War," *International Security* 13 (Winter 1988–89): 69; John Newhouse, *War and Peace in the Nuclear Age* (New York: Knopf, 1989), 84; James M. Gavin, *War and Peace in the Space Age* (New York: Harper & Brothers, 1958), 116.

56. Harry Truman, "Memorandum" (April 24, 1954), in *Off the Record: The Private Papers of Harry S. Truman,* ed. Robert Ferrell (New York: Harper & Row, 1980), 304; Rusk, *As I Saw It,* 170.

57. *FRUS, 1952–1954* (Washington, D.C.: Government Printing Office, 1984), 2:593; *FRUS, 1952–1954,* 15:770, 827.

58. *FRUS, 1952–1954,* 15:827, 977; Nina Tannenwald, *The Nuclear Taboo: The United States and the Nonuse of Nuclear Weapons since 1945* (Cambridge: Cambridge University Press, forthcoming), 143.

59. *FRUS, 1952–1954,* 2:447.

60. McGeorge Bundy, *Danger and Survival* (New York: Random House, 1988), 536; Tannenwald, *Nuclear Taboo,* 220–21.

61. Samuel Cohen, *The Truth about the Neutron Bomb* (New York: Morrow, 1983), 84, 93–94; Richard Nixon, *No More Vietnams* (New York: Arbor House, 1985), 102.

62. Henry Kissinger, *White House Years* (Boston: Little, Brown, 1979), 66–67; Bundy, *Danger and Survival,* 536–37.

63. A. J. Goodpaster, "Memorandum of Conference with the President, August 12, 1958" (August 14, 1958), box 3, Alpha Subseries, Subject Series, Office of the Staff Secretary, White House Office Records, Eisenhower Library; Wittner, *Resisting the Bomb,* 172–83, 407–409.

64. Oral history interview with Adrian Fisher, May 13, 1964, 10, John F. Kennedy Library, Boston; *FRUS, 1961–1963* (Washington: Government Printing Office, 1995), 7:220.

65. Norman Cousins, *The Improbable Triumvirate: John F. Kennedy, Pope John, Nikita Khrushchev* (New York: Norton, 1972); Glenn T. Seaborg, *Kennedy, Khrushchev,*

*and the Test Ban* (Berkeley: University of California Press, 1981), 207; Norman Cousins, "August 7, 1963," Norman Cousins Papers, Beverly Hills, Calif.; McGeorge Bundy to Cousins, August 30, 1963, "RS 2/" folder, box 889, Subject File, White House Central File, Kennedy Papers, Kennedy Library.

66. Author interview with Bernard Lown, July 6, 1999; Matthew Evangelista, *Unarmed Forces: The Transnational Movement to End the Cold War* (Ithaca, N.Y.: Cornell University Press, 1999), 270–88.

67. "Clamor for a Test Ban," *Greenpeace Examiner* 11 (October–December 1986): 5; author interview with Peter Bergel, August 3, 1999; author interview with Robert Musil, July 20, 1998; author interview with Daryl Kimball, July 21, 1998; author interview with James Baker III, September 15, 1999.

68. Kimball, *1993 Campaign*, 1–23; author interview with Daryl Kimball, July 21, 1998; author interview with Thomas Graham Jr., August 23, 1999; *New York Times*, September 11, 1996.

69. Evangelista, *Unarmed Forces*, 194–232; author interview with Sergei Kapitza, June 28, 1990; author interview with Joseph Rotblat, July 11, 1994.

70. Cyrus Vance, *Hard Choices: Critical Years in America's Foreign Policy* (New York: Simon & Schuster, 1983), 392; author interview with Zbigniew Brzezinski, July 21, 1999; author interview with Harold Brown, August 16, 1999; author interview with Paul Warnke, July 20, 1999; Bundy, *Danger and Survival*, 568, 570.

71. Ronald Reagan, *An American Life: The Autobiography* (New York: Simon & Schuster, 1990), 295–96; Caspar W. Weinberger, *Fighting for Peace: Seven Critical Years in the Pentagon* (New York: Warner, 1990), 339; author interview with Richard Perle, June 29, 1999; author interview with Robert McFarlane, July 21, 1999; author interview with Mary Kaldor, June 7, 1999.

72. Mikhail Gorbachev, *Perestroika* (New York: Harper & Row, 1987), 153; Evangelista, *Unarmed Forces*, 329.

73. George P. Shultz, *Turmoil and Triumph: My Years as Secretary of State* (New York: Scribner's, 1993), 984–85.

74. Colin L. Powell, with Joseph Persico, *My American Journey* (New York: Random House, 1995), 377–78; Shultz, *Turmoil and Triumph*, 899–900, 988, 990–91, 1007–1008; 1081–85.

75. Robert D. English, *Russia and the Idea of the West: Gorbachev, Intellectuals, and the End of the Cold War* (New York: Columbia University Press, 2000), 117–240; George Arbatov, *The System: An Insider's Life in Soviet Politics* (New York: Random House, 1992), xii, 304, 309–12; Gorbachev, *Perestroika*, 154, 197.

76. Author interview with Robert Musil, July 20, 1998; author interview with Bernard Lown, July 6, 1999; author interview with Helen Caldicott, February 27, 1999.

77. James A. Baker III, *The Politics of Diplomacy: Revolution, War and Peace, 1989–1992* (New York: Putnam's, 1995), 82–96, 526; Powell, *My American Journey*, 541; author interview with James A. Baker III, September 15, 1999.

78. *Meaning of Survival*, 129–30.

79. Howard L. Parsons, "Nuclear Tests in the Pacific," May 3, 1956, 711.5611/5-356, State Department Records; *FRUS, 1955–1957* (Washington, D.C.: Government Printing Office, 1988), 23:495.

80. Tsuneo Akaha, "Japan's Three Nonnuclear Principles: A Coming Demise?" *Peace and Change* 11 (Spring 1985): 75; Mitchell Reiss, *Without the Bomb: The Politics of Nuclear Nonproliferation* (New York: Columbia University Press, 1988), 118–19.

81. Glenn D. Hook, "The Erosion of Antimilitaristic Principles in Contemporary Japan," *Journal of Peace Research* 25 (December 1988): 387–88; Reinhard Drifte, *Japan's Rise to International Responsibilities: The Case of Arms Control* (London: Athlone, 1990), 23–26; Reiss, *Without the Bomb*, 119.

82. David Smith, *H. G. Wells: Desperately Mortal* (New Haven, Conn.: Yale University Press, 1986), 458.

# Index

# About the Contributors

**Bruce Cumings** teaches international history, modern Korean history, and East Asian political economy at the University of Chicago. His books include the two-volume study, *The Origins of the Korean War, Korea's Place in the Sun: A Modern History*, and *Parallax Visions: Making Sense of American East Asian Relations*. He is a frequent contributor to *The Nation, Current History*, and the *Bulletin of the Atomic Scientists*.

**Richard Falk** was Milbank Professor of International Law at Princeton University until his retirement in 2001. At present, he is teaching in the Global Studies Program of the University of California at Santa Barbara. He is chair of the board of the Nuclear Age Peace Foundation and a member of the editorial board of *The Nation*. His most recent books are *Religion and Humane Global Governance* and *The Great Terror War*.

**Ben Kiernan** is the A. Whitney Griswold Professor of History and founding director of the Genocide Studies Program at Yale University (www.yale.edu/gsp). He is the author, among other works, of *How Pol Pot Came to Power: A History of Communism in Cambodia, 1930–1975*, and *The Pol Pot Regime: Race, Power, and Genocide in Cambodia under the Khmer Rouge, 1975–1979*. He is coeditor of *The Specter of Genocide: Mass Murder in Historical Perspective* and is currently writing a global history of genocide since 1492.

**Diana Lary** is professor of history at the University of British Columbia, and director of the Centre of Chinese Research there. She works on regionalism in China, migration, and the effect of war on society. Her most recent publication is *The Scars of War: The Impact of War on Chinese Society* (with Stephen MacKinnon).

**Peter Dale Scott** is a former Canadian diplomat and professor of English at the University of California, Berkeley. His books include *The War Conspiracy, Deep Politics, and the Death of JFK* and, most recently, *Drugs, Oil, and War: The United States in Afghanistan, Colombia, and Indochina*. In 2002, he received the Lannan Poetry Award for his poetic trilogy *Seculum*.

**Mark Selden** teaches sociology at Binghamton University and is a professorial associate in the East Asia Program at Cornell University. His recent books include *The Resurgence of East Asia: 500, 150 and 50 Years Perspectives* (with G. Arrighi and T. Hamashita); *Censoring History: Citizenship and Memory in Japan, Germany, and the United States* (with L. Hein); *Bitter Flowers, Sweet Flowers: East Timor, Indonesia, and the World Community* (with R. Tanter and S. Shalom); and *Islands of Discontent: Okinawan Responses to Japanese and American Power* (with L. Hein). He is the editor of the War and Peace Library series at Rowman & Littlefield Publishers.

**Alvin Y. So** teaches at the Division of Social Science of the Hong Kong University of Science and Technology. His research interests include social class and development in Hong Kong, China, and East Asia. His recent books include *East Asia and the World Economy* (coauthored with Stephen Chiu), *Asia's Environmental Movements* (coedited with Yok-Shiu Lee), *Hong Kong's Embattled Democracy*, and *China's Developmental Miracle* (editor).

**Utsumi Aiko** is professor of humanities at Keisen University in Tokyo. Her numerous books on Japanese colonialism, war, and war crimes include *Korean B and C Class War Criminals and Japanese Colonialism, The Thai–Burma Railroad and Japan's War Responsibility, War Crimes and Sexual Violence*, and *War Compensation for Asian Victims* (all in Japanese).

**Brian Daizen Victoria** is a senior lecturer in the Centre for Asian Studies at the University of Adelaide in South Australia. A fully ordained priest in the Sôto Zen sect, he received an M.A. in Buddhist studies from Sôto Zen sect–affiliated Komazawa University in Tokyo and a Ph.D. from Temple University. In addition to his recent *Zen War Stories*, his books include *Zen at War* and the coauthored *Zen Master Dôgen* (with Yokoi Yûhô).

**Lawrence S. Wittner** is professor of history at the State University of New York, Albany. A former president of the Peace History Society and of the Peace History Commission of the International Peace Research Association, he has written extensively on peace movements, foreign policy, and international history. His latest scholarly work is a three-volume history of the world nuclear disarmament movement, *The Struggle against the Bomb.*

**Marilyn B. Young** is professor of history and director of the International Center for Advanced Studies Project on the Cold War as Global Conflict. She is the author of *The Vietnam Wars, 1945–1990; Rhetoric of Empire: American China Policy, 1895–1901;* and *Transforming Russia and China: Revolutionary Struggle in the 20th Century* (with W. Rosenberg). She is a coeditor of *Vietnam and America: A Documented History* (with M. Gettleman, J. Franklin, and B. Franklin), *Human Rights and Revolutions* (with J. Wasserstrom and L. Hunt), and *The Vietnam War: A History in Documents* (with J. Fitzgerald and A. T. Grunfeld).